D1568967

The Illustrated Guide to
BIBLICAL HISTORY

KENDELL H. EASLEY

HOLMAN
REFERENCE

Nashville, Tennessee

The Illustrated Guide to Biblical History
© 2003 by Holman Bible Publishers
Nashville, Tennessee
All rights reserved

ISBN # 0-8054-2834-8

Maps © 2003 by Holman Bible Publishers
Nashville, Tennessee
All rights reserved

The Holman Editorial Staff gratefully acknowledges the contribution of Dr. James McLemore and the staff of *Biblical Illustrator* for consultation on *The Illustrated Guide to Biblical History*. The photos contained herein are from the archives of the *Biblical Illustrator*. For additional information about the *Biblical Illustrator* go to the following web address:
http://www.lifeway.com/shopping
Search on **Biblical Illustrator** in the box at the top of the left of the page.

Dewey Decimal Classification: 220.95
Subject Heading: Bible---History of Biblical Events

Printed in Italy
1 2 3 4 5 6 07 06 05 04 03
L

To my son Jordan,
whose life as a kingdom citizen encourages me every day.
May you always remember that
the Lord God through His Christ
is graciously building a kingdom of redeemed people
for their joy and for His own glory.

Table of Contents

(see p.40)

God Educates His Nation
Disobedient Israel Disciplined, 931-586 B.C. 72

(see p.79)

God Keeps a Faithful Remnant

Messiah's Space and Time Prepared,

(see p.126)

(see p.157)

God Purchases Redemption and Begins the Kingdom
Jesus the Messiah, 6 B.C.–A.D. 30

God Spreads the Kingdom through the Church
The Current Age, A.D. 30–?. 212

(see p.216)

(see p.260)

God Consummates His Eternal Kingdom
Redemption Completed 260

Epilogue
New Heaven and New Earth **283**

Features of *The Illustrated*

A. Striking, full color photographs show important places in biblical history.

B. Callout boxes provide historical and cultural information which enhances understanding of significant people, places, events, concepts, and Bible books.

A

The palace of Knosos on Crete.

Epistle to Titus

Paul sent this letter, written about A.D. 63, to his close friend Titus from an unknown location. Titus was on the island of Crete to consolidate the work of the Kingdom in a challenging situation. The key word for the book is "doctrine"; the key text is Titus 2:1. One-Sentence Summary: *Whatever challenges they face in life and ministry, Christian leaders are to maintain order in the congregation, but only according to sound doctrine.*

as his ambassador. The churches there needed guidance, particularly in returning to good order, and Titus was the right sort of leader to get the job done. Sometime later, Paul wrote a brief letter to Titus reminding him of his duties on Crete.

Another place to which Paul returned was Ephesus. This church that had been so successful had now experienced a number of difficulties that required immediate attention. Once again, false teachers were challenging the truth of the gospel. He left his closest friend Timothy there to meet the ongoing needs of the situation. Sometime later, Paul wrote a letter to Timothy reminding him of his personal responsibility to live a godly life as well as to fulfill his duties to the church in Ephesus.

Domitian Square at Ephesus.

ESTHER

The Book of **ESTHER** is the single biblical narr[...]
Three of the Kingdom Story that tells about J[...]
the land of Israel during the days of the Per[...]
occurred during the reign of Xerxes, call[...]
Hebrew, who ruled from 486 to 465.

Three events are dated within the book:

- 483 B.C.: Xerxes' fabulous banquet, the[...]
  Xerxes (Esth. 1:3)
- 479 B.C.: Esther's selection as queen, the[...]
  Xerxes (Esth. 2:16)
- 474 B.C.: Haman's plot against the Jews, t[...]
  Xerxes (Esth. 3:7)

The book is famous because it does not mention G[...]
God's providence in caring for His people, despite trem[...]
tion, cannot be missed. The events reported in the boo[...]
these events:

- Esther the Jew became Xerxes' queen as the winner o[...]
  pageant
- Haman, who hated Jews, plotted to have all Jews in P[...]
- Esther—who had hidden her Jewish identity—invite[...]
  Haman to a feast
- Esther exposed Haman's plot to the king, who ordered Haman's death
- The Jews were spared death and in triumph established the feast of Purim
- Esther's relative Mordecai became Xerxes' prime minister

Silver drinking bowl. The inscription in old Persian cuneiform tells that is was made for "Artaxerxes, the great king, king of kings...son of Xerxes, son of Darius the king, Achaemenian."

B

Book of Esther

This historical narrative is written in excellent Hebrew. It was perhaps composed by Mordecai shortly after the events it records, sometime after 474 B.C. It was prepared for Jews in Persia and became a treasured book of Scripture at least partly because of its explanation of the origin of Purim. The key word for the book is "providence"; the key text is Esther 4:14. One-Sentence Summary: *Esther, a Jewish beauty selected by Persian king Xerxes to become his new queen, saved the Jews from Haman's wicked plot, so her relative Mordecai established the yearly Jewish feast of Purim.*

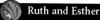

Ruth and Esther

The lives of these two remarkable women, the only women for whom Bible books were named, portray God's providential care of people committed to Him in the midst of overwhelming challenges to their faith. The characters Esther and Ruth, however, are a study in contrasts. One was a powerful and wealthy Jew who always lived outside the promised land and became the bride of a pagan king. The other was a humble and impoverished Gentile who moved to the promised land and became an ancestor of Israelite kings.

Guide to Biblical History

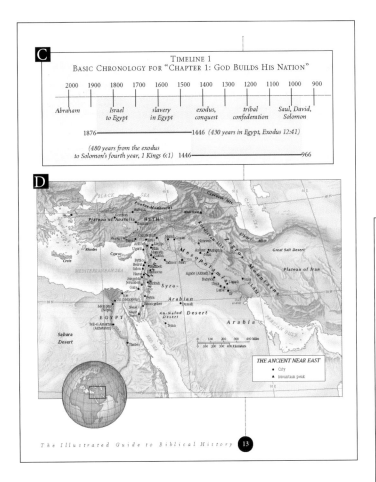

C. Timelines help to locate people and events in biblical history.

D. Full-color maps show the geographical context of events.

E. A topical index enables the reader to locate people, places, and concepts throughout the book.

F. A Scripture index allows the user to find where Scripture references are made.

Introduction

We humans sense the need to belong to a time and place. We perceive that we are part of something bigger than we are, that we are not isolated, random happenings, but that life has meaning and purpose. Religions, mythologies, larger-than-life stories of patriotism and national origin are some ways that we seek to satisfy this desire. For several decades, however, many observers of contemporary Western society have lamented that people in developed countries have gradually lost their sense of time and place. We don't seem to belong anymore. We don't know what "story" we are part of. In the language of specialists, there is no accepted metanarrative, no grand story to help us interpret time and space (generally) and our place in it (particularly).

Some recent thinkers have celebrated the loss of metanarrative. They have suggested that people only use such beliefs to marginalize others or to advance their own power agendas. But Christianity—at least historic Christianity—has always argued that there is a grand story. Christianity, in fact, can only be understood as part of God's story, or, as this book will call it, the Kingdom Story. Christians believe that the Bible wonderfully answers the questions, *What's life all about? What's the purpose of history? What story are we human beings involved in?*

The Bible is at its heart a story—a true story and the best story of all. Better than a book of theology, the Bible contains the one true grand narrative. It records more historical material than it does anything else (for example, laws, poems, prophecies, doctrinal explanations). If we are to understand the Bible, first of all we need to know its story, the Kingdom Story, from start to finish.

The Meaning of Space and Time

In Christian congregations, however, most people simply don't know the story anymore. In the twenty-first century people may be aware of individual biblical episodes (David and Goliath, the flood, Paul's shipwreck), but they don't know how to "connect the dots." They don't have an overall sense of the big picture of the story. The narrative, however, is not that complicated to grasp. A single Kingdom Story is consistently developed, from Genesis to Revelation and all books between. The entire biblical narrative is summed up in one sweeping statement:

The Lord God through His Christ
is graciously building a kingdom of redeemed people
for their joy and for His own glory.

Notice that there is one subject (*the Lord God*—it's His story) and one agent (*Christ*—the one actively bringing about God's story). There is one major activity (*building a kingdom*, the main theme of Scripture) and one object of that activity (*redeemed people*, the center of God's mighty acts in both Testaments). There are also specific goals for the Kingdom Story (*their joy*—the human goal; *His own glory*—the ultimate divine end for everything). When we keep this central truth before us, everything in Scripture falls into place as a development of this single concept.

It is helpful to think of the way the Kingdom Story advances by imagining it as something like a modern novel:

- There is a *prologue*, giving "deep background" information that helps make sense of the plot.

- Then the plot unfolds in a number of chapters. In the biblical narrative the story develops in *six chapters* that take into account everything from beginning to culmination.

- Then finally at the end is an *epilogue*, telling what happens after the main story has ended.

If you keep in mind the concept of *prologue … six chapters … epilogue* as you study this book, you will soon be able work your way through the entire Kingdom Story. More than that, you will grasp the Bible's overall message and understand your own place in God's story. In the chapters of this book that follow, Scripture references in **BOLD** type are the primary passages for the part of the Kingdom Story under discussion. This concise summary of biblical history is based on classroom presentations over the course of two decades. It is now expanded and offered in written form to serve a broader audience of God's people in the twenty-first century. As you read this Kingdom Story, remember that

The Lord God through His Christ
is graciously building a kingdom of redeemed people
for their joy and for His own glory.

Prologue

Egyptian King offering Ma'at to Amon Re in the inner hall.

The Need for Redemption (Genesis 1—11)

Genesis 1—11 introduces us to real human history, but the events are virtually impossible to date.[1] Theologians, archaeologists, and scientists have studied the evidence this passage gives to help date the creation of the universe and the creation of mankind. Genesis is claimed as evidence for both "old earth" and "young earth" theories. The riddle remains unsolved. The way around this impasse is found by recognizing that this part of the Kingdom Story answers the question *Why?* rather than the question *When?*

Eastern Wall of Doura Europa and the Euphrates River. The Euphrates River is one mentioned in connection with the garden of Eden.

Religions other than historic Christianity have always asserted that mankind can do enough good deeds or perform enough religious acts to earn acceptance with God and a place in heaven. The story of Genesis 1—11 leads to the opposite conclusion. The main thing to observe in these chapters—the Prologue to the Kingdom Story—is that they describe events involving the entire human race. They show that mankind has rebelled against God since the beginning. In three crucial events, the fall, the flood, and the tower of Babel, the whole race of humans demonstrated that we are a race of sinners in full revolt against God.

As the Introduction to this book has noted, the grand summary of the Bible is, *The Lord God through His Christ is graciously building a kingdom of redeemed people for their joy and for His own glory.* If this is true, then Genesis 1—11 demonstrates why God takes all the initiative in redeeming mankind in the rest of the Bible: All humans are sinners who cannot save themselves. He must save, and he does all the saving.

CREATION AND FALL

God created everything. **GENESIS 1—2** affirms that the universe, including the first man and woman, came about by the deliberate plan and power of God. God declared that His creation was good. This passage unquestionably describes that the first human couple was created in His image as a special divine act. He declared this to be very good.

Adam and Eve

The first human beings were created by the direct act of God. The name Adam comes from the Hebrew word for "red dirt," and it is used both as the personal name of the first man as well as a more general word for mankind. Eve means "life" or "living." The uniform teaching of the Bible is that (1) these two were created in the image of God; (2) these two chose to disobey God's word and so be-came subject to death; (3) all human beings on earth today are direct biological descendants of Adam and Eve. The image of God was marred but not lost when the first humans sinned, so every human being bears the divine image inherited from Adam and Eve.

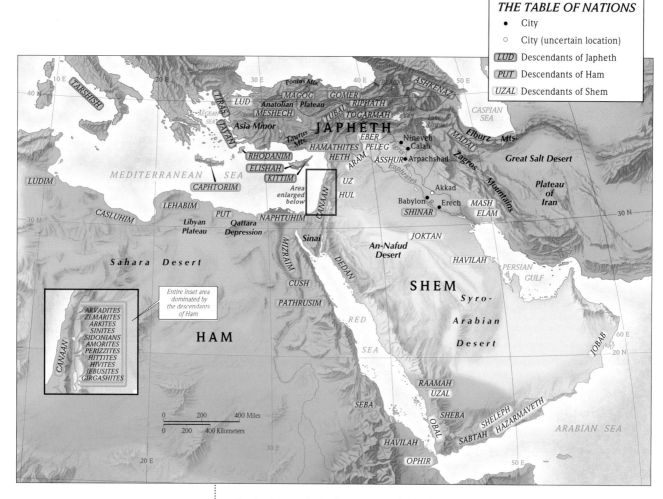

THE TABLE OF NATIONS
- • City
- ○ City (uncertain location)
- LUD Descendants of Japheth
- PUT Descendants of Ham
- UZAL Descendants of Shem

Stump-base juglet from Jericho.
Dates from 3200–2400 B.C.

Evolution—theistic or non-theistic—is not supported by this account. The later words both of Jesus and of Paul can be true only if all humanity has descended biologically from one man and one woman uniquely created by God (Mark 10:6-9; Rom. 5:12-14; 1 Cor. 15:45-46).

It doesn't matter *when* God created mankind as much as it does *that* He did so. If we miss the point that the first human pair was created and made accountable to their Creator, we will miss the meaning of the rest of the Kingdom Story, which tells how God has remedied human rebellion against Him. (A perfect garden with a mysterious tree of life, humanity's home during its time of innocence, will be reestablished in the final everlasting home of those God redeemed, Rev. 22:1-2.)

GENESIS 3 describes how Adam and Eve—the whole race—deliberately disobeyed God and fell under His curse. The story as told leaves many people frustrated by the questions it doesn't answer: How long did Adam and Eve live in innocence in the garden of Eden? Where did the serpent come from? How did evil enter the universe to begin with? The point of the narrative lies in another direction: all people have rebelled against their holy Creator. He does not tolerate such disobedience or affronts to

His holiness. The husband and his wife were both cursed by God. Moreover, they were expelled from their perfect environment and doomed to die. (Yet even at the moment of pronouncing His curse, God pledged that evil would one day be utterly defeated, Gen. 3:15.)

The events and genealogies of **Genesis 4—5** summarize all the centuries between Adam and Noah. They show humanity as a sinful, cursed race. With distressing regularity the words "and he died" occur, showing that the divine command for disobedience had full effect (Gen. 2:17). There is murder (Cain) and polygamy (Lamech). Despite great progress in agriculture, technology, and the arts, only three persons from many generations were commended later in Scripture as rightly related to God. As far as the biblical record shows, these alone came to God by faith rather than by works: Abel, Enoch, and Noah (Heb. 11:4-7).

FLOOD AND BABEL

What should a holy God do when the race He created in His image thought only of doing evil and offending Him (Gen. 6:5)? His justice required Him to judge mankind. He did this by sending a global flood. God could have destroyed the entire race, but He didn't. He extended grace to Noah, who in turn believed God and lived a righteous life that showed itself in obedience to God's word (Gen. 6:8-9; Heb. 11:7). The main point of the flood story, however, is not Noah's righteousness. The flood demonstrates both the sinfulness of sin and the holiness of God.

Mount Ararat (Western Slope). Region where the ark came to rest when the flood waters subsided.

Noah's Ark

As a wooden structure the ark was enormous. Its dimensions, about 450 feet long, 75 feet wide, and 45 feet high, make it comparable to a modern cargo ship. With three decks it housed hundreds of animals and the provisions they required in order to survive for more than a year on board. Nobody knows exactly the kind of wood that Noah used. Although recent explorers have claimed to discover evidence of the ark's ruins in the mountainous region east of Turkey, this has not been independently verified.

A covenant (*berith* in Old Testament Hebrew, *diatheke* in New Testament Greek) is basic to the message of the Bible. A covenant is a binding agreement between two parties, sometimes voluntary, sometimes imposed by a superior. God imposes the important biblical covenants on human beings as evidence of His grace. Sometimes God gave His covenant without conditions (as here, in the case of Noah); sometimes His covenant is conditional (as at Mount Sinai). The God-initiated covenants have God-initiated physical signs or seals, such as the rainbow.

Many archaeologists have dismissed the notion of a worldwide flood. There are two main reasons for believing that it literally happened. First, if the flood was only a regional event, then why did God ask Noah to preserve the animals in the ark? Why wouldn't Noah have simply moved the animals and his family to a safe location? Second, the way both Jesus and Peter spoke about the flood requires that it be taken as global rather than local (Luke 17:26-27; 1 Pet. 3:20). We are right to understand that **GENESIS 6—8** presents as historical fact that all humanity except for eight persons perished in a divinely-sent, worldwide flood. Thus, everyone alive today has descended biologically from Noah and his wife.

Just as the original fall of mankind in the garden contained a promise of future redemption, so did the flood. For the first time the Kingdom Story describes a covenant initiated by God and given to mankind. In **GENESIS 9** the rainbow became the God-ordained sign that no worldwide flood would ever come again (although the same chapter shows Noah and one of his sons engaged in grievous sin).

The events and genealogies of **GENESIS 10** summarize many centuries after Noah. The entire human race is described in three great family lines, the biological descendants of Noah's three sons. As in the post-Adam period, there was much human achievement, yet the culminating event shows, once again, that the entire race of human beings had rebelled against the Creator.

Ziggurat at Susa, Iran. Five floors. Top two destroyed. Many scholars believe the tower of Babel was a ziggurat.

The Kadesh Treaty between the Hittites and Egyptians is the earliest example of a written positical treaty in existence.

GENESIS 11 is the first biblical description of organized religion. (So far only *individuals* had offered sacrifices to God.) The tower of Babel, perhaps a model for surviving ruins of pyramid-shaped temples (ziggurats) in Mesopotamia, was built expressly for a religious reason. Arrogant people desired collectively to reach heaven by their own works, to build the "Gate of God" (the meaning of Babel). This was now the third event (first the fall and then the flood) in which the entire human race was guilty. The unity of the race is clearly indicated by the reference to everyone speaking the same language (Gen. 11:1).

Just as God cursed the whole race after the fall, so He cursed the whole human race at Babel by multiplying the languages and scattering all the people (Gen. 11:9). From that day until now, however, our race has kept on forgetting that God always rejects the arrogance of supposing that human-inspired religion can help people get to heaven.

From this point on in the Kingdom Story, the focus narrows to the smaller group of people whom God will graciously redeem. These are the kingdom people of the rest of Scripture. The genealogy at the end of Genesis 11 traces the lineage of humanity from Noah to Abraham. Beginning in Genesis 12, the narrative zooms in on one chosen man and the kingdom people.

The worldwide perspective will return only many centuries later. First, the commission the risen Jesus gave to spread the gospel is worldwide. Second, at the consummation of the ages, the returning Jesus will bring a global judgment not of water but of fire (Matt. 28:18-20; 2 Pet. 3:7-12). After that time God will undo the curse of Babel when redeemed people from all the languages and nations gather before His throne praising Him forever (Rev. 7:9-10).

Vista looking north from Haran.
(Gen. 11:27—12:4)

SUMMARY

The Prologue for the Kingdom Story, described in Genesis 1—11, has now been established. The following statements summarize what has happened. As noted earlier the dates for these events cannot now be determined.

- God made everything, culminating in creating humanity in His image.

- Our first parents sinned by disobeying God's word, and so they were cursed.

- Even at the fall God promised that evil would one day be defeated.

- The entire race that descended from Adam and Eve was so evil that God judged it by sending a worldwide flood.

- Only eight people, Noah and his family, survived the flood.

- God established a covenant with the human race never to send a global flood again.

- The entire race that descended from Noah became so evil that it tried to reach heaven unaided.

- God judged this sin by multiplying the languages and scattering all the people.

From this point on, the Kingdom Story focuses not on all people but on God's chosen people.

Genesis 1—11 clearly shows that mankind is in rebellion against God. We are sinners beyond the ability to redeem ourselves. If there is to be any salvation, it must come from God alone. That is the story that Chapter One of the Kingdom Story begins.

REFLECTIVE QUESTIONS

1. Why is it important for God's people today to affirm that God created everything? Is it harder or easier for those who deny God as Creator also to believe in God as Redeemer? Why do you say so?

2. In what ways has the curse that came on mankind at the fall impacted your own life?

3. How does the concept of "unconditional covenant" affect your relationship with God? your relationship to others?

4. Suppose archaeologists discovered ruins that were proven to be the remains of Noah's ark. Would that make people you know more likely to accept the Bible as trustworthy? Why or why not?

5. Compare Genesis 11 (the multiplication of languages as a curse) with Revelation 7 (the redeemed praising God in many languages). How are these accounts similar? Does Revelation show a reversal of Genesis 11? Why do you think so?

6 "All humanity is so sinful that it cannot save itself." What personal experiences have you had that confirm (or deny) this conclusion?

7. How is the glory of God seen in Genesis 1—11?

---

[1] No dates are assigned, therefore, to the events of the Prologue. Years and dates have been suggested beginning with Abraham. All biblical dates, however, are to be understood as approximate. For virtually every event recorded in the Bible, leeway of a year or two on either side is possible.

God Builds His Nation

The Jezreel Valley viewed from near Megiddo. The Valley was important both agriculturally and militarily.

Israel Chosen as the People of Promise,
2091–931 B.C.

The Prologue to the Kingdom Story told in Genesis 1—11 focused on the rebellion of the entire human race and God's three judgments on all mankind. First was the curse when Adam and Eve sinned in the garden; second was the flood during the time of Noah; and last was the confusion of languages at Babel. Beginning in Genesis 12, the thrust of the Kingdom Story changes from judgment to mercy. As we will see, God chose to call a single man and his descendants. The time from Abraham to Solomon was more than a thousand years. It was, however, only the first chapter in God's plan to build an everlasting kingdom. The goal was to build an earthly nation in a particular time and place.

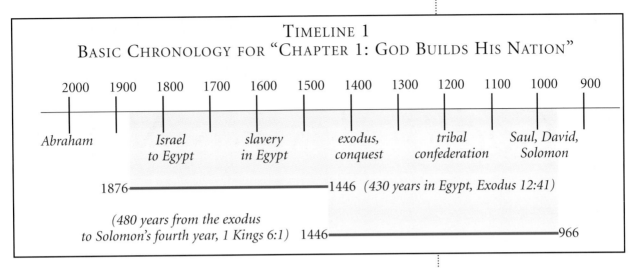

TIMELINE 1
BASIC CHRONOLOGY FOR "CHAPTER 1: GOD BUILDS HIS NATION"

2000	1900	1800	1700	1600	1500	1400	1300	1200	1100	1000	900

Abraham   *Israel to Egypt*   *slavery in Egypt*   *exodus, conquest*   *tribal confederation*   *Saul, David, Solomon*

1876 ————————— 1446 *(430 years in Egypt, Exodus 12:41)*

(480 years from the exodus to Solomon's fourth year, 1 Kings 6:1) 1446 ————————— 966

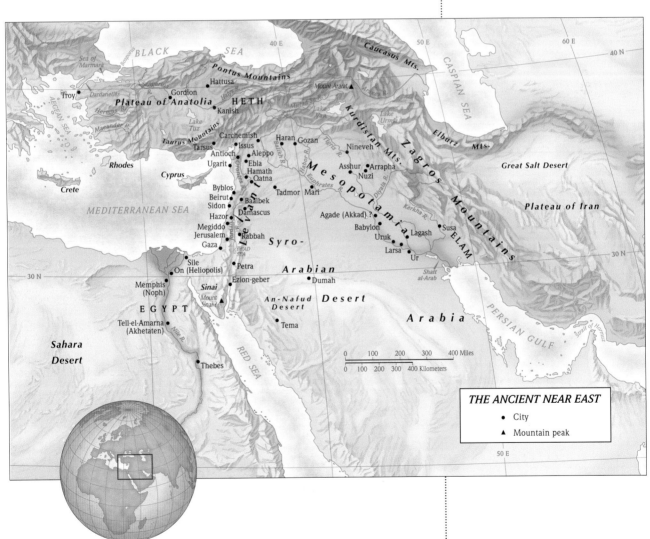

THE ANCIENT NEAR EAST
● City
▲ Mountain peak

As the Introduction noted, the grand summary of the Bible is, *The Lord God through His Christ is graciously building a kingdom of redeemed people for their joy and for His own glory.* If this is true, then Genesis 2 through 1 Kings 11 shows how God began to make eternal kingdom people. These passages can be compressed to a simple truth, *God builds His nation.* Chapter One of His plan involves a particular group in a particular place. God takes all the initiative in calling Abraham, redeeming Israel from slavery, making them a nation with a royal dynasty, and giving them a temple for worshipping Him properly. All of this displays His glory to His redeemed people. This chapter carries the plot from the original family with whom God made His covenant (Abraham and Sarah) to the full splendor of national Israel at its grandest expression (under David and Solomon).

THE FOUNDATION:
FROM ABRAHAM'S CALL TO JACOB'S MIGRATION TO EGYPT (2091–1876 B.C.)

Genesis 12—50 describes four generations of one remarkable family. People of these generations, often called the patriarchs, formed the foundation, the underlying structure, for what would become the nation of Israel. Based on His own purposes, God called Abraham, who then received God's unconditional promise to become the ancestor of a great nation and to be a worldwide blessing. This covenant promise extended to Abraham's son Isaac (but not to his son Ishmael). Then from Isaac the promise extended to Jacob (but not to Esau, the older twin). In turn the promise passed to Jacob's many sons. The events told in most detail surround Joseph, great-grandson of Abraham. Through Joseph God moved the covenant people into Egypt where they multiplied into numbers worthy of being called a nation.

Abraham and Sarah

The historical foundation of God's kingdom plan lay with one married couple. Their names, meaning "father of a multitude" and "princess," were changed by God (from Abram, "exalted father" and Sarai, "princess") as reminders of divine blessing. Their father was Terah, but they had different mothers. As Isaac's parents, Abraham and Sarah became the direct ancestors of the people of Israel and were the first people to be called "Hebrews." According to the New Testament, both Abraham and Sarah have become models of faith for all kingdom people who came after them (Heb. 11:8-12; 1 Pet. 3:6).

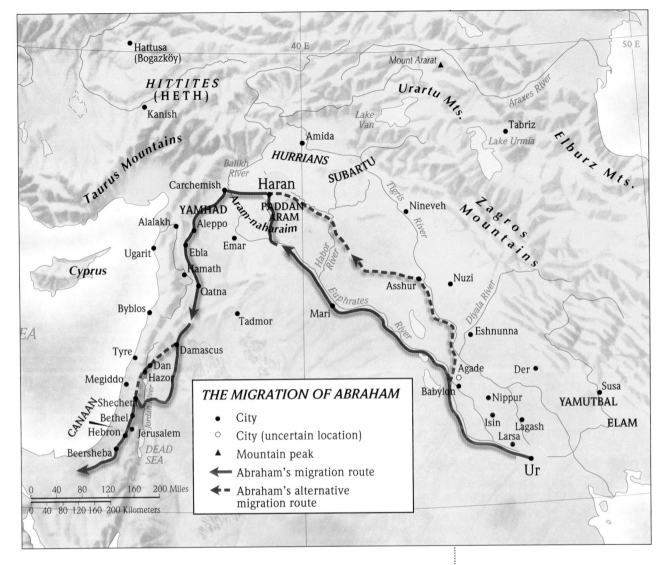

ABRAHAM'S YEARS

From a human perspective Abraham was just a migrating pagan who married his beautiful half-sister Sarah and had a number of exciting adventures. He had done nothing righteous for the seventy-five years he lived before God called him. From a divine perspective, however, Abraham was to become the spiritual forefather of all who are righteous by faith, both Jews and Gentiles. Although Abraham's place of origin was Ur (in Mesopotamia), he had moved to the city of Haran (north of Palestine) before God called him into a covenant relationship. The main description of Abraham's years is **GENESIS 12—25**.

Mud Houses (beehive houses) at Haran.

Abrahamic Covenant

God initiated this unconditional covenant to one who could do nothing to deserve it. The promises of the Abrahamic Covenant passed to Isaac (not Ishmael) and then to Jacob (not Esau). Paul interpreted this selection in terms of both God's sovereignty and His mercy in Romans 9. The Abrahamic Covenant forms the foundation for the Davidic covenant a thousand years later. These covenants (promises) find their great ongoing fulfillment in Abraham's seed, Jesus Christ (2 Cor. 1:20; Gal. 3:15-16). The divine sign of the Abrahamic covenant was circumcision.

Genesis 12:1-3 is the initial statement of God's covenant with Abraham. God gave His unilateral divine promise (1) to make Abraham's descendents into a great nation, (2) to bless Abraham and give him a great name, and (3) to use Abraham ultimately to bless all the earth's peoples. Genesis 15 and 17 expand on God's covenant-promise. Genesis 15:6 is remarkable for noting that Abraham believed a specific word from God (that he would have a biological son even though he was very old). His faith was credited to him as righteousness. Abraham is called the father of faith in the Kingdom Story (Rom. 4:3; Gal. 3:6; James 2:23). The covenant terms in Genesis 17 included both the promise about the land of Canaan to Abraham's descendants and the covenant sign of circumcision for all male descendants.

No doubt the greatest human event in the life of Abraham and Sarah was the birth of their son Isaac (to a 100-year-old father and a 90-year-old mother). What's more, Abraham enjoyed a number of fascinating adventures:

- Passing off his beautiful wife Sarah as his sister while staying in Egypt (Gen. 12)
- Fathering a son, Ishmael, by Hagar, the Egyptian slave of Sarah (Gen. 16)
- "Bargaining" with God concerning the destruction of Sodom (Gen. 18)
- Marrying Keturah and fathering other children after Sarah's death (Gen. 25)

Step Pyramid at Saqqara had likely been built by Abraham's time.

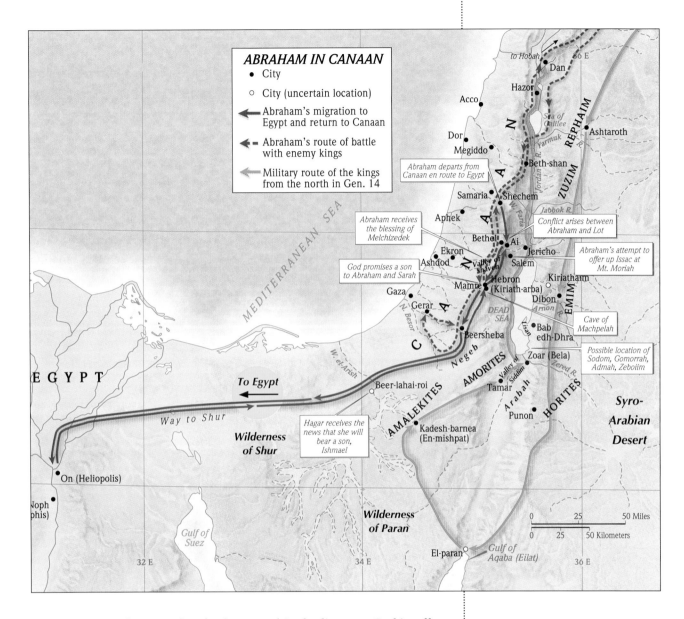

ABRAHAM IN CANAAN

- • City
- ○ City (uncertain location)
- ← Abraham's migration to Egypt and return to Canaan
- ◄- - Abraham's route of battle with enemy kings
- ← Military route of the kings from the north in Gen. 14

Abraham departs from Canaan en route to Egypt

Abraham receives the blessing of Melchizedek

Conflict arises between Abraham and Lot

Abraham's attempt to offer up Isaac at Mt. Moriah

God promises a son to Abraham and Sarah

Cave of Machpelah

Possible location of Sodom, Gomorrah, Admah, Zeboiim

Hagar receives the news that she will bear a son, Ishmael

To Egypt

Way to Shur

Wilderness of Shur

Wilderness of Paran

Syro-Arabian Desert

MEDITERRANEAN SEA

EGYPT

    The greatest adventure for Abraham was his obedience to God in offering Isaac as a sacrifice. God's purpose in doing this was to test Abraham. Other translations use the word *prove*.

    God commanded Abraham to take Isaac to Mount Moriah about fifty miles to the northeast and there offer him as a burnt offering. From this point forward, Mount Moriah figures prominently in Scripture. It became the location where Solomon built the temple in Jerusalem.

    According to Genesis 25:7 Abraham lived 175 years (about 2166–1991 B.C.).[1]

Bab Edh Dhra, believed by many archaeologists to be ancient Sodom and/or Gomorrah.

Book of Job

This book of Hebrew wisdom, with a historical introduction and conclusion, mainly contains poetry. Although Job lived during the time of the patriarchs, the book was not composed in its present form until the time of Solomon or later, when Hebrew wisdom literature flourished. The key word for the book is "suffering"; the key text is Job 1:21. **One-Sentence Summary:** *After the upright Job suddenly lost family, health, and possessions, he and his friends dialogued at length about the reasons for his sufferings, but God alone had the final word and ultimately restored Job's losses.*

SODOM AND GOMORRAH

Included in the story of Abraham is the tragic account of his nephew Lot in Genesis 19. He settled with his family in Sodom, a city near the Dead Sea. When the citizens of Sodom demonstrated their unspeakable moral perversion, God destroyed Sodom and its sister city Gomorrah so totally that archaeologists have never uncovered their remains. Perhaps the ruins lie at the bottom of the Dead Sea. A judgment of fire and burning sulfur became the standard way for later biblical writers to speak of the outpouring of God's wrath on sin.

MELCHIZEDEK AND JOB

The times of Abraham also included two independent characters—strange and unusual in that they were worshipers of the true God, yet evidently not part of the Abrahamic covenant family. They show God's freedom to work graciously in surprising ways. The first is Melchizedek, the king-priest of Salem (early Jerusalem) to whom Abraham gave a tithe (Gen. 14:18-20; Heb. 7:1-10). The second is Job, a righteous man from Uz, east of the Jordan River. His long life (Job 42:16), the measurement of wealth in livestock, and the fact that he acted as personal priest for his family suggests that he lived during the time of the patriarchs. His story, recorded in the book of **JOB**, became a test case for the question, Why do the righteous suffer? The man Job is best known for the following:

- Losing all his considerable fortune and children in one day (Job 1)

- Losing his health shortly thereafter to a loathsome skin disease (Job 2)

- Enduring the long-winded "comfort" of three friends (Eliphaz, Bildad, and Zophar) with erroneous views of God (Job 3—31)
- Hearing from a fourth friend, Elihu (Job 32—37)
- Hearing God speak to him out of a storm (Job 38—41)
- Being fully vindicated, with his fortune, family, and health restored (Job 42)

Isaac's Years

Less information is given about Isaac than any of the other patriarchs. His biography is found principally in **Genesis 21—28**. As the only child born to the aged Abraham and Sarah, he was reared with lavish care. The formative event for his life came when he was a young man. The famous story told in Genesis 22 of the sacrifice of Isaac at Mount Moriah (later the site of Solomon's temple) is usually given in terms of Abraham's obedience to God, yet surely this was just as much a test of Isaac's faith and obedience. Isaac as well as his father passed the test, yet for Isaac the experience was terrifying. From that time God was known by a new name, "The Fear of Isaac" (Gen. 31:42,53).

That the people in God's kingdom are to stand in fearful reverence of their holy God has been a biblical theme that began with the sacrifice of Isaac (Gen. 22:12). This event also stands as the first clear incident in which the shed blood of an animal substituted for the shed blood of a human being.

The other adventures of Isaac preserved in Genesis generally have to do with his wife Rebekah in one way or another:

- Rebekah, daughter of Abraham's nephew, is acquired for the forty-year-old Isaac after Sarah's death (Gen. 24)
- Rebekah gives birth to twins, Esau and Jacob, after twenty years of infertility (Gen. 25)
- Rebekah is passed off as Isaac's sister (Gen. 26)
- Rebekah helps Jacob, her favorite son, trick Isaac into blessing him instead of Esau (Gen. 27)
- Rebekah never saw Jacob again after the blessing was stolen, but Isaac would be reunited with Jacob many years later. According to Genesis 35:28, Isaac lived 180 years (2066–1886 B.C.).

Book of Genesis

This historical narrative, the first of Moses' five books (the Pentateuch), was written for the Israelites. It describes events from the creation of the world until the death of Joseph in Egypt around 1805 B.C. The key word for the book is "beginning"; the key texts are Genesis 1:1; 12:3. **One-Sentence Summary**: *The God who created mankind and punished disobedience with death began his great plan of redemption with his covenant to Abraham, whose descendants arrived in Egypt as God's cherished people.*

The beautiful octagonal Mosque of Omar, better known as the Dome of the Rock at Jerusalem, is supposedly the site of Mount Moriah.

The ruins of Bethel.

Jacob, the younger twin son of Isaac, was born when his father was sixty and his grandfather Abraham was one hundred sixty. His life was one of conniving and constant rivalry, first against his brother Esau, then between his principal wives (Leah and Rachel), and third against his father-in-law Laban. The greatest struggle came when Jacob wrestled with God Himself. **GENESIS 25—36** is the main account of Jacob's life.

Jacob stands as an example of a scoundrel who nevertheless received God's unmerited favor. When Jacob was running away from home to escape his brother's well-deserved anger, God revealed Himself in a wonderful dream. Jacob saw a ladder (or stairway) between heaven and earth, a renewal of the Abrahamic covenant (Gen. 28:12-19). He named the place where he had dreamed "Bethel," meaning "House of God." God planned for Jacob's children to be the founders of the famous "twelve tribes of Israel." The sons of Jacob (with their birth order in parentheses) are as follows:

- Sons of Leah: Reuben (1), Simeon (2), Levi (3), Judah (4), Issachar (9), Zebulun (10)

- Sons of Leah's servant Zilpah: Gad (7), Asher (8)

- Sons of Rachel: Joseph (11), Benjamin (12)

- Sons of Rachel's servant Bilhah: Dan (5), Naphtali (6)

Jacob (Israel)

God chose the scheming Jacob ("heel grasper" or "deceiver") to have the new name Israel ("he contends with God"), synonymous with the nation that descended from him. God confirmed the Abrahamic covenant to Jacob. His life span overlapped those of his grandfather Abraham, his father Isaac, and, of course, his twelve sons, so he knew all the other patriarchs. He was fifteen when Abraham died and he lived long enough to bless his grandsons Ephraim and Manasseh, the Egyptian-born children of Joseph.

When Jacob returned home to Isaac after twenty years, he came with wives, children, and great wealth. On this journey God revealed Himself again to Jacob, with whom He wrestled all night in the form of an angel (Gen. 32:24-30). Jacob named this place Peniel, "Face of God." God, in turn, gave Jacob the new name "Israel." This was, of course, the name by which Jacob's descendants (and the place they later settled) was known.

The Jabbok River between Jerash and Amman. Near this river Jacob wrestled with the angel.

After Jacob's return, he continued living in Canaan until he moved with all his family to Egypt to escape a severe famine. According to Genesis 47:28, Jacob lived the last 17 years in Egypt, a total of 147 years (2006 to 1859 B.C.).

JOSEPH'S YEARS

Joseph's story emphasizes God's grace and His sovereign plan to work out redemption according to His plan. The boy who rose from prisoner to prime minister of Egypt sets an important theme that the rest of the Kingdom Story tells. Joseph's story is the focus of **GENESIS 37—50.** *God's plans are so great and good that what evil-minded people do actually accomplishes His divine purposes* (Gen. 50:20; Rom. 8:28) The greatest and most wonderful example of this is, of course, the crucifixion of Jesus.

Joseph's exciting life story (1915–1805 B.C.) falls into three unequal parts:

- His childhood and youth as the spoiled son of Jacob, given the "coat of many colors" (17 years, Gen. 37:2)

- His slavery and imprisonment in Egypt, due to no fault of his own (13 years, Gen. 41:46)

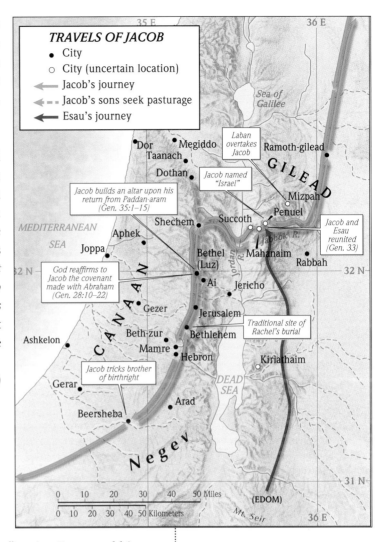

- His rise to power as Egypt's "prime minister," saving Egypt and his own family from starvation (80 years, Gen. 50:26)

Although in the beginning Joseph was spoiled and arrogant, from the time he was sold as a slave to Egypt he illustrates incredible faithfulness and obedience to God.

Joseph's role in the Kingdom Story was more immediately important than that of his brothers. Joseph's work preserved the chosen family, and all seventy members of the covenant family of Jacob entered Egypt. Jacob later adopted Joseph's sons, Manasseh and Ephraim, as his own. For this reason the descendants of Joseph's two sons were counted as separate tribes that later received land in Canaan. (This kept the total number of tribes at twelve, since the tribe of Levi later received the priesthood instead of land.) Ultimately Joseph's brother Judah (another immoral man undeserving of God's favor) was the most important brother. From Judah's line the Israelite royal dynasty was established, beginning with David and culminating with Jesus.

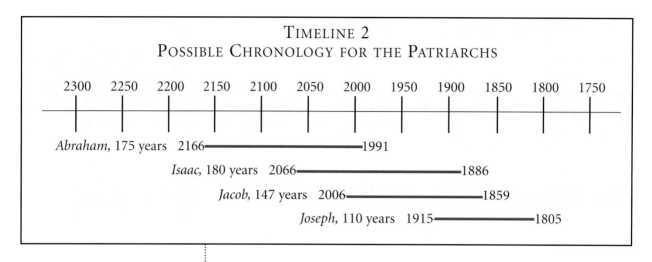

TIMELINE 2
POSSIBLE CHRONOLOGY FOR THE PATRIARCHS

| 2300 | 2250 | 2200 | 2150 | 2100 | 2050 | 2000 | 1950 | 1900 | 1850 | 1800 | 1750 |

Abraham, 175 years   2166————————————1991

Isaac, 180 years   2066————————————1886

Jacob, 147 years   2006————————————1859

Joseph, 110 years   1915————————————1805

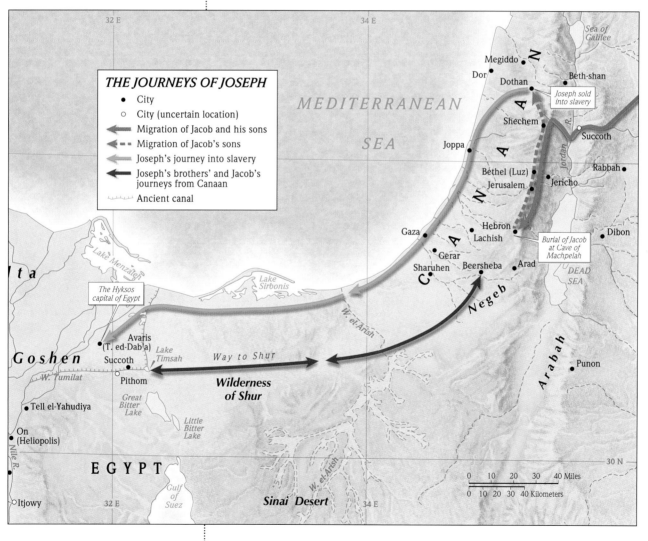

THE JOURNEYS OF JOSEPH
- ● City
- ○ City (uncertain location)
- ◄— Migration of Jacob and his sons
- ◄- - Migration of Jacob's sons
- ◄— Joseph's journey into slavery
- ◄— Joseph's brothers' and Jacob's journeys from Canaan
- ⌒⌒ Ancient canal

Joseph sold into slavery

Burial of Jacob at Cave of Machpelah

The Hyksos capital of Egypt

MEDITERRANEAN

SEA

Sea of Galilee

Megiddo
Dor
Dothan
Beth-shan
Shechem
Succoth
Joppa
Rabbah
Bethel (Luz)
Jerusalem
Jericho
Gaza
Hebron
Lachish
Dibon
Gerar
Sharuhen
Beersheba
Arad
DEAD SEA
Negeb
C A N A A N
Jordan R.

Lake Menzaleh
Lake Sirbonis
W. el-Arish

Avaris (T. ed-Dab'a)
Goshen
Succoth
Pithom
Way to Shur
Wilderness of Shur
Lake Timsah
W. Tumilat
Tell el-Yahudiya
On (Heliopolis)
Great Bitter Lake
Little Bitter Lake
Arabah
Punon

E G Y P T
Itjowy
Gulf of Suez
Sinai Desert
Nile R.

30 N

| 0 | 10 | 20 | 30 | 40 Miles |
| 0 | 10 | 20 | 30 | 40 Kilometers |

THE REDEMPTION:
FROM EGYPTIAN SLAVERY TO WILDERNESS FREEDOM
(1876–1446 B.C.)

Exodus 1—18 describes the next step in God's plan to build a nation. After His people multiplied from seventy to millions, God called a leader for the nation, Moses. Through Moses He sent ten plagues to redeem the Israelite nation from slavery in Egypt. He revealed the full significance of His glorious covenant name, "the LORD" (*YHWH* or *Yahweh* in Hebrew). Israel's exodus became the most powerful Old Testament portrayal of salvation. The period from Jacob's entry to Egypt until the exodus was 430 years (Exod. 12:40-41). Traditionally Bible scholars have dated the exodus around 1446 B.C.

SLAVERY

About 1876 B.C. the Egyptians had welcomed Jacob's family of seventy because Joseph had exhibited brilliant organizational leadership in preparing for seven years of famine. They settled in Goshen, a fertile section in the Nile Delta. Under these conditions God made His people flourish to such an extent that they threatened the security of the native Egyptians. **EXODUS 1** gives few details of how the Israelite people gradually came to be enslaved. The barbarity of their condition is highlighted by the pharaoh's decree that all male Israelite newborns must be drowned in the Nile River. According to archaeologists, the 350-year period between Israel's entry to Egypt and Moses' birth (1876–1526 B.C.) saw major political and social changes in Egypt. Israel's deliverance came during the time known as the New Kingdom.

Egypt

Egypt is well-known as one of the ancient cradles of human civilization. The lives of the patriarchs intersected with Egypt's "Middle Kingdom," the second great period of Egyptian culture. In the Bible Egypt is primarily mentioned as the place of slavery from which God redeemed His people through Moses, during the time of the "New Kingdom," the third age of Egyptian greatness. The encounters between Moses and the Egyptian king (the pharaoh) showed God's power over the powers of the Egyptians' gods. Egypt was the first oppressor kingdom bent on destroying the people of God.

Possible site of Goshen.

The Nile Valley from Maydum.

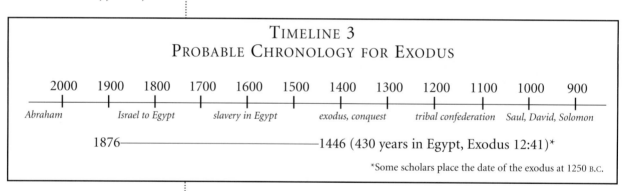

TIMELINE 3
PROBABLE CHRONOLOGY FOR EXODUS

2000	1900	1800	1700	1600	1500	1400	1300	1200	1100	1000	900

Abraham   *Israel to Egypt*   *slavery in Egypt*   *exodus, conquest*   *tribal confederation*   *Saul, David, Solomon*

1876————————————————————————1446 (430 years in Egypt, Exodus 12:41)*

*Some scholars place the date of the exodus at 1250 B.C.

MOSES' PREPARATION

Moses' first eighty years are told in **EXODUS 2—6.** The account of the infant Moses' rescue by a princess is well known. He was educated as Egyptian royalty, although he knew his Israelite identity (Acts 7:22; Heb. 11:24-25). At age forty, after killing an Egyptian on impulse, he escaped the pharaoh's anger[2] to relative obscurity in the Sinai Peninsula. There in the Sinai Peninsula Moses was taken in by Reuel, priest of Midian. Reuel gave his daughter Zipporah to be Moses' wife. Their first son was Gershom whose name means "stranger or sojourner in a foreign land." Moses served as a shepherd for his father-in-law for forty years and then came a life-changing event.

The crucial event came when Moses was eighty. God revealed Himself and His name, "I Am," at the burning bush on Mount Sinai. Despite his objections Moses was appointed and returned to Egypt to prove his authority to Israel's leaders and to pharaoh.

PLAGUES ON THE EGYPTIANS

The encounters between Moses and pharaoh were merely surface exhibitions. The true encounter was between "the LORD" and Egypt's idols (Exod. 12:12). The first nine plagues may have been divine intensification of natural phenomena, but no natural explanation accounts for the Israelites being spared the destruction sent to the Egyptians.

The order of the plagues, told in **EXODUS 7—11**, is as follows:

1. Water to blood
2. Frogs everywhere
3. Gnats
4. Flies
5. Livestock killed
6. Boils on people
7. Hailstorm
8. Locust swarm
9. Darkness
10. Firstborn killed

The parts in Chapter One of the Kingdom Story about the plagues demonstrate, once again, God's absolute sovereignty in bringing about His plan to redeem. For the last five plagues God is specifically stated to have hardened the pharaoh's heart in order to bring about the salvation of His people. (Yet for the earlier five plagues Scripture emphasizes that the pharaoh hardened his own heart. Divine sovereignty and human responsibility are never at odds with each other in the Kingdom Story.)

Sphinx at Giza with Pyramid of Khafre in the background.

God's Name (Yahweh)

The name that Israel's covenant making God chose to be called by His people was *Yahweh*, "The One Who Is," related to "I Am" of Exodus 3:14 (see also Exod. 6:3). In English Bibles "the LORD" in capital letters indicates this name. When "the Lord" appears in lowercase form, it is some other divine title, often *Adonai*, "Master." In later times the Jewish people refused to say the word Yahweh lest they misuse it. After Jesus' resurrection the early Christians self-consciously called Jesus "Lord," appropriating God's covenant name (Phil. 2:11). The book of Revelation expands this name to "the One who is, who was and who is coming" (Rev. 1:4).

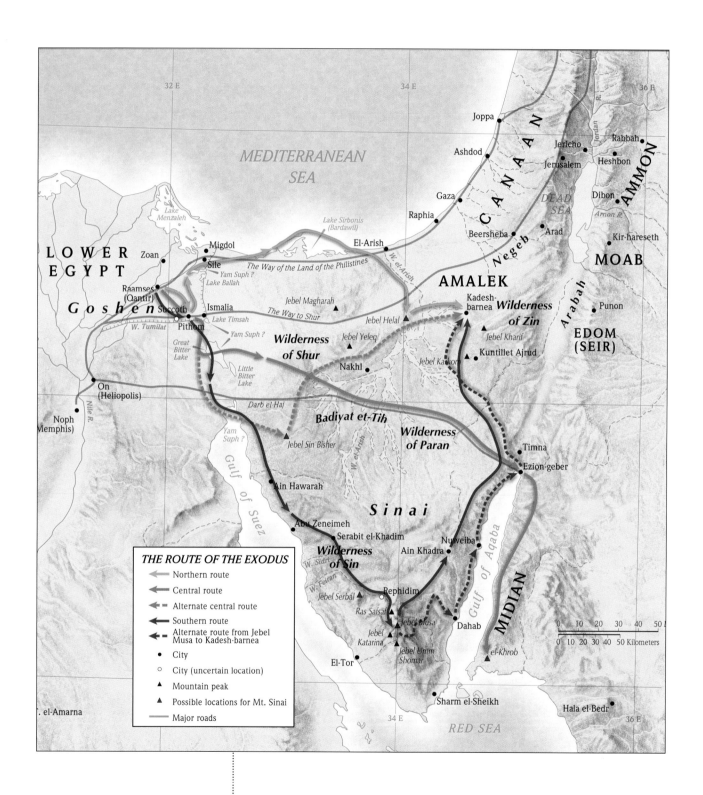

MEDITERRANEAN
SEA

Lake
Menzaleh

Lake Sirbonis
(Bardawil)

LOWER
EGYPT   Zoan   Migdol   El-Arish
                          Sile

                          Yam Suph ?
             Raamses   *Lake Ballah*
Goshen   (Qantir)   The Way of the Land of the Philistines
             Succoth
                 Ismalia   *Jebel Magharah*   AMALEK   Kadesh-
             Pithom   The Way to Shur   barnea   Wilderness
         W. Tumilat   Lake Timsah   *Jebel Helal*   of Zin
                       Yam Suph ?   *Jebel Yeleq*   Jebel Kharif
                  Great   Jebel Karkon   Kuntillet Ajrud
                  Bitter   Little   Wilderness   Jebel Karkon
                  Lake   Bitter   of Shur
On   Lake   Nakhl
(Heliopolis)
                       Darb el-Haj
Noph   Badiyat et-Tih
(Memphis)   *Yam Suph ?*   Wilderness
                              Jebel Sin Bisher   of Paran   Timna
                                                                               Ezion-geber
                    Gulf   S i n a i
                    of
                    Suez   Ain Hawarah
                                                                   Nuweiba
                           Abu Zeneimeh
                              Serabit el-Khadim   Ain Khadra
                           Wilderness   Gulf
                           of Sin   *W. Sidri*   of   MIDIAN
                              W. Feiran   Aqaba
                           Jebel Serbal   Rephidim
                           Ras Safsaf   Dahab
THE ROUTE OF THE EXODUS   *Jebel Musa*
⟵ Northern route   *Jebel Katarina*
⟵ Central route   *Jebel Umm*
⟵ - Alternate central route   *Shomar*
◀— Southern route   El-Tor   *el-Khrob*
◀ - Alternate route from Jebel
    Musa to Kadesh-barnea
 • City   Sharm el-Sheikh   Hala el-Bedr
 ○ City (uncertain location)
 ▲ Mountain peak   RED SEA
 ▲ Possible locations for Mt. Sinai
 — Major roads

Joppa
Ashdod   Jericho   Rabbah
         Jerusalem   Heshbon   AMMON
Gaza   Dibon
Raphia   DEAD
         Beersheba   Arad   SEA   Kir-hareseth
                                       MOAB
              Negeb
CANAAN   Punon
              Arabah   EDOM
                       (SEIR)

0 10 20 30 40 50
0 10 20 30 40 50 Kilometers

DEATH OF THE FIRSTBORN AND CROSSING THE SEA

In **EXODUS 12—18** the descendants of Jacob left Egypt after 430 years of waiting for God's mighty hand of deliverance (Exod. 12:40). Because this event marked the true beginning of Israel's national life, its religious calendar began each spring with the month in which the exodus occurred. In ancient times a new moon marked a new month. Thus, the moon was full the night Israel left Egypt (the fourteenth of the month, Exod. 12:6).

Sunrise over the Nile from Minia.

In preparation for this, God instructed the Israelites to sprinkle the blood of slaughtered lambs on their doors and to eat the lamb's meat. God said that in His search for the first born that He was going to kill, He would "pass over" the houses with blood on the doors. This was the origin of "the Passover," which became the most important yearly Israelite religious festival and was the season in which Jesus the Lamb of God was crucified. (Contemporary Jews, of course, still celebrate this festival annually.)

Feast of Passover

Israelite families celebrated God's redemption of their ancestors by an elaborate Passover meal every year on the fourteenth night of the first month of spring (*Nisan*). The menu included roasted lamb (to remember the original Passover lambs), bread made without yeast (to remember the haste of the original exodus), and bitter vegetables (to remember the bitterness of the slave years). Israelites celebrated the next seven days as the Feast of Unleavened Bread (Lev. 23:4-8). After the central place of worship was established, all able-bodied adult males were supposed to celebrate the Passover there (Deut. 16:16).

Passover prayers at the women's section of the Western (Wailing) Wall in Jerusalem.

The death of all Egypt's firstborn may seem to be unfair, but this is part of the biblical evidence that God will not allow people to reject Him with impunity. His justice must always be satisfied. Further, it made God's people keenly aware that the price for their redemption was extremely high. God orchestrated this event and the miraculous crossing of the sea in order to bring glory to His name, one of the great themes of the Bible (Exod. 14:4). It must not be forgotten that the reason God let His people go was so that they could worship (serve) Him (Exod. 5:1; 7:16; 8:1, 20-21). Assuming the 480 years mentioned in 1 Kings 6:1 are literal, then Israel left Egypt around the year 1446 B.C.

Moses not only led God's kingdom people out of Egypt, he brought them through the amazing miracle of crossing the sea on dry ground. In the Hebrew Scriptures this sea is called *Yam Suph*, which literally means "Sea of Reeds." Most English Bibles have translated it "Red Sea," following the lead of the ancient scholars who translated the Bible into Greek and Latin. The place where Israel crossed *Yam Suph* is not known and is highly disputed. Some believe the reference is to Lake Menzaleh, east of the Nile Delta and adjacent to the Mediterranean, or to the Bitter Lakes area somewhere along the present Suez Canal. Still others have argued for the northern end of the Gulf of Suez (one of the northern fingers of the "Red Sea" found on modern maps).

Suez Canal

Bitter Lake.

Jebel Musa, the traditional Mount Sinai .

The point of the miracle was not *where* it happened but *that* it happened to display God's great goodness and power for His people. (The victorious "Song of Moses" of Exodus 15 is also sung in Revelation 15 by those kingdom people finally and forever redeemed by the Lamb of God.) The days immediately following this deliverance demonstrate the pattern of obedience/victory and disobedience/punishment that characterized the rest of Chapter One of the Kingdom Story:

• Miraculous provision of heavenly bread (manna)

• Miraculous provision of heavenly meat (quail)

• Defeat of the Amalekites (as long as Moses held up his hands in prayer)

• Miraculous provision of water from a large rock

• Initial organization of the people into administrative units

• Encampment at Mount Sinai

The people arrived at Mount Sinai in the third month after they left Egypt (Exod. 19:1). Everything recorded in the Bible from Exodus 19:1 to Numbers 10:10 took place at this location. The people God had redeemed would now come to understand that they were also obligated to Him to be His holy people. Before they left Mount Sinai, they were bound together not only in leadership, but also in laws and in worship.

Book of Exodus

As the second of five books (Pentateuch) written by Moses for the Israelites, Exodus tells about events from the death of Joseph until the completion of the Israelite tabernacle (1805–1445 B.C.). The central section (chapters 19–31) contains laws for the Israelites, particularly the Ten Commandments and rules for the tabernacle and the priesthood. The key word for the book is "redeem"; the key text is Exodus 14:30-31. **One-Sentence Summary:** *When God redeemed His chosen people Israel though His servant Moses, He entered a covenant relationship with them and instituted His dwelling with them, the tabernacle.*

Rocky pathway down from Jebel Musa.

THE LAWS AND THE LAND:
FROM MOUNT SINAI TO THE CONQUEST OF CANAAN AND JOSHUA'S DEATH
(1446–1380 B.C.)

Throughout history, people with a true national identity have shared a land and laws. Usually the land identity comes first, and then the laws evolve over time (as in the Roman Empire, Japan, or the United States). God's plan to build His chosen nation included these as well, but in reverse order: laws first, then the promised land. Through Moses God gave the Israelites His laws: moral, ceremonial, and civil. The Israelite rebellion in the wilderness led to a forty-year delay in possessing the land. Under Joshua, a new leader for a new generation, the Israelites entered and began conquering their promised land around 1406 B.C.

COVENANT AT SINAI

Moses solemnly climbed the mountain to receive God's laws. **EXODUS 19—24** records in great detail the terms of the Sinaitic covenant that God made with the Israelites, more so than for either of His earlier covenants with Noah and with Abraham. Part of the reason is that the Sinaitic covenant functioned in the daily lives of Israelite people more directly than did the earlier ones. Another reason, as the New Testament makes clear, is that the earlier covenants were divine promises (unconditionally made by God), while the Sinaitic covenant had a built-in obsolescence (Heb. 8:13). Israel needed to know in detail the conditions of God's agreement with them. After centuries of Israel's violating the terms of the Sinaitic covenant, God declared it "null and void."

Many features of the covenant/treaty that God made with Israel at Sinai parallel ancient covenants/treaties discovered by archaeologists. The Sinaitic covenant began with a manifestation of God (Exod. 19) and ended with confirmation by blood (Exod. 24), with the "Book of the Covenant" stated in Exodus 20—23. Bible students have identified this as a "suzerain-vassal covenant" in which the master (suzerain) promised to protect and bless the subjects (vassals) as long as they obeyed and submitted to him.

The Ten Commandments are, of course, the most famous part of the Sinaitic covenant. As a succinct statement of Israel's obligations to God, they were given to a people already redeemed (Exod. 20:2). They were never intended to be a means of attaining salvation (as Paul later argued in Galatians 3). Further, just as God gave the two earlier covenants a special sign (the rainbow; circumcision), so he did with the Sinaitic covenant: Sabbath rest for the people on the seventh day of every week (Exod. 20:8; Deut. 5:15; Ezek. 20:12).

Sinaitic Covenant

Moses' name is forever linked with the (conditional) covenant initiated by God to the nation of Israel. The Sinaitic covenant promised blessings for obedience and curses for disobedience. This covenant, along with the books written by Moses, became the basis of Israel's Scriptures. Because Jesus brought the New Covenant (New Testament), Israel's Scripture is called the Old Testament. Christian interpreters frequently wrestle with how to understand the relationship between the Old Testament and the New Testament. The divine sign of the Sinaitic Covenant was the Sabbath.

The essence of the Ten Commandments is as follows:

Laws concerning loving the Lord with all one's being:	Laws concerning loving one's neighbor as oneself:
1. No other gods except Yahweh	5. Honor for parents
2. No images of Yahweh	6. Murder forbidden
3. Reverence for Yahweh's name	7. Adultery forbidden
4. The Sabbath as a holy day	8. Stealing forbidden
	9. False witness forbidden
	10. Coveting forbidden

RULES FOR THE PRIESTHOOD AND TABERNACLE

While Moses was still on Mount Sinai, God gave him rules for building the tabernacle (an elaborate tent for worship) and for establishing the priesthood (so that God could be served properly in the tabernacle). Moses' brother Aaron and his sons were designated as priests. **EXODUS 25—31** contains instructions for the following sacred artifacts:

- Ark of the covenant, table, lampstand (Exod. 25)
- Tabernacle, altar for burnt offerings (Exod. 26—27)
- Priestly garments (Exod. 28)
- Altar for incense, basin for washing (Exod. 30)

One extraordinary feature in these chapters is God's stated desire to live among the Israelites and be their God (Exod. 29:45-56). This was initially fulfilled when His glory filled the completed tabernacle. Centuries later the Prophet Jeremiah announced that this was to be fulfilled by the new covenant, and the book of Revelation shows the final fulfillment of God's intention in the heavenly eternal state of His redeemed people (Jer. 31:33; Rev. 21:3).

Tabernacle

The tent for worship was designed to be portable because it accompanied the Israelites throughout their travels until they had settled in Canaan. The elaborate descriptions of its furnishings and the rituals performed there showed the Israelites that God is to be worshiped only the in way that He prescribes. This tent (or its successors) was the central place of worship for the Israelites from the time it was constructed at Mount Sinai until the dedication of Solomon's temple (1445 to 959 B.C.).

A frieze of a Menorah with Shophar.

Ark of the Covenant

The most important and holy artifact in the history of Israel was its sacred ark of the covenant. This gold overlaid wooden box (about 4 feet long, 2 $^1/_2$ feet wide, and 2 $^1/_2$ feet tall) was covered by a solid gold lid on which two golden winged creatures were hammered out. God's visible presence was manifested between these creatures (cherubs). The ark contained the Ten Commandments and was kept in the holiest part of the tabernacle (and later Solomon's temple). It was evidently destroyed at the time the Babylonians demolished the temple in 586 B.C.

COVENANT VIOLATED AND RESTORED

EXODUS 32—40 includes both tragedy and triumph, and in both instances Moses' brother Aaron was central. First is the shameful incident in which Aaron led the Israelites to worship around a gold calf idol while Moses was still on the mountain. The result was that Moses physically broke the flat stones on which God had written the Ten Commandments, symbolizing that the covenant had been broken. The triumph—after Moses graciously received from God a second set of the Ten Commandments—was the successful construction of the tabernacle and its furnishings. This was followed by the consecration of the tabernacle. Exodus closes on a high note of worship: the glory of God filled the tabernacle in the center of the camp of God's redeemed people.

RULES FOR SACRIFICES

In **LEVITICUS 1—10** the laws for five different kinds of sacrifices at the tabernacle are given:

- Burnt sacrifice (a voluntary act of worship and commitment to God)
- Grain sacrifice (a voluntary non-animal offering)
- Peace or fellowship sacrifice (an offering that included eating some of the meat)
- Sin sacrifice (a mandatory offering for specific sins)
- Guilt sacrifice (a mandatory offering in which restitution was also made)

These chapters also describe the ordination of Aaron and his sons to serve as priests to offer acceptable sacrifices in the tabernacle.

RULES FOR UNCLEANNESS

LEVITICUS 11—16 introduces elaborate regulations concerning things that were unclean in themselves or could make someone unclean. These rules sometimes (incidentally) had to do with sanitation, but they should be understood mainly in terms of the overall theme of Leviticus: holiness (fitness for the Lord). Persons, places, animals, and things fell into one of three categories:

- Unclean: unfit for God's people, common
- Clean: fit for the life of God's people, suitable for worship

A frieze of a priest offering a sacrifice. Bells are around the bottom on the skirt.

Basalt altar for sacrifices.

- Banned: devoted to God and therefore to be totally destroyed for His sake

In these chapters the focus is on the unclean: certain animals, women who had just given birth, skin diseases ("leprosy"), molds and mildews, and bodily discharges. The solemn annual Day of Atonement (Leviticus 16) focused on removing uncleanness from the people.

IMPORTANCE OF HOLINESS

Holiness throughout Scripture, but especially in **LEVITICUS 17—27**, is first an attribute of God. It refers to His glorious moral perfections as the One who is the standard of ethical purity. Second, holiness was commanded by God to His redeemed people (Lev. 19:2). This holiness included both moral living (submitting gladly to God's laws) and being separated from common use (intentionally set apart to God and His service). Some of the rules for holiness among the ancient Israelites included the following:

- Not eating blood (Lev. 17)
- Having only certain sexual relationships (Lev. 18)
- Punishing sin (Lev. 19)
- Keeping God's festivals (weekly Sabbath and annual feasts, Lev. 23)
- Keeping the Sabbath Year (every seventh year) and the Jubilee Year (Lev. 25)

God meant for those He had redeemed to have a lifestyle characterized by obedience to His laws concerning holiness (Lev. 18:5). These laws, however, involved holy living in regard to one's fellow human beings, for within these chapters is the command to love one's neighbor, designated by Jesus as God's second most important command (Lev. 19:18; Mark 12:31).

A mikveh (Jewish ritual bath used for purification) at Masada.

Book of Leviticus

This is the third of the five books (Pentateuch) written by Moses for the Israelites. It mainly contains laws that God gave Israel during the time they camped at Mount Sinai. The key word for the book is "holiness"; the key text is Leviticus 11:45. **One-Sentence Summary:** *God forgives sin and makes people holy though blood sacrifice; further, He then expects His people to live in fellowship with Him though following His regulations concerning separated living.*

Eastern Sinai coming out of the Jebel Musa region.

Book of Numbers

As the fourth of the five books (Pentateuch) written by Moses for the Israelites, Numbers includes both narrative and laws. This book tells what happened to the Israelites during the thirty-eight years they traveled through the wilderness from Mount Sinai to the border of Canaan. The key word for the book is "wilderness"; the key text is Numbers 8:17. **One-Sentence Summary:** *God led Israel through Moses from Sinai to Kadesh, but even after they rejected Him there, resulting in the wilderness years, He remained faithful to them and led a new generation to the edge of the promised land.*

PREPARING TO LEAVE MOUNT SINAI

The Israelites arrived at Mount Sinai as a newly freed yet somewhat disorganized people. They left a year later highly organized, with God's laws and God's tabernacle fully functioning. **NUMBERS 1—9** describes how the Israelites prepared to move toward the promised land.

The first four chapters of Numbers describe the census of the adult men (those who could fight) and the organization of the camp around the tabernacle. Many scholars believe that the number of adult men is too high to be believable (more than 600,000 in Num. 2:32), for this suggests a total population of some two million that left Egypt. A variety of solutions have been proposed, including a different meaning than usual for the word usually meaning "thousand" or understanding the numbers as symbolic rather than literal. Yet Exodus 1:7-12 clearly indicates that, through God's providential blessing, the people of Israel multiplied greatly during their 430-year sojourn in Egypt.

JOURNEY TO KADESH AND WILDERNESS WANDERINGS

The nation Israel left Mount Sinai in high hopes that they would soon be living in the land God promised them. **NUMBERS 10—21** tells how the people's disobedience and lack of faith dashed those expectations. After

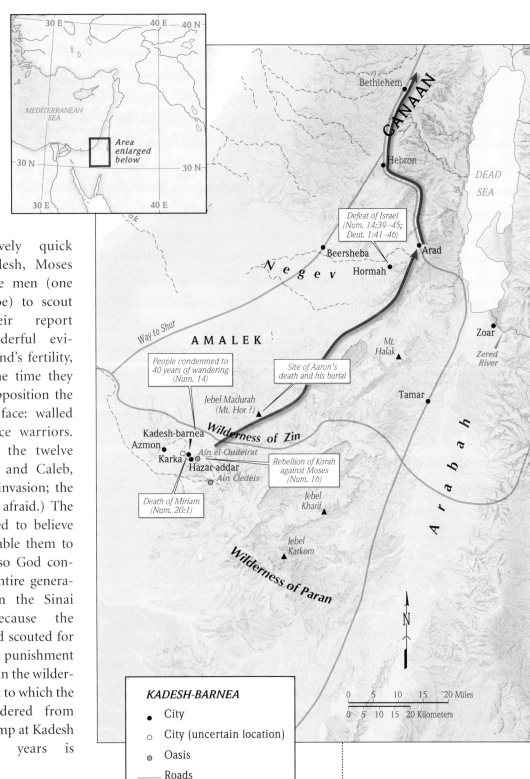

Israel's relatively quick march to Kadesh, Moses sent out twelve men (one from each tribe) to scout Canaan. Their report included wonderful evidence of the land's fertility, but at the same time they reported the opposition the people would face: walled cities and fierce warriors. (Only two of the twelve scouts, Joshua and Caleb, argued for an invasion; the other ten were afraid.) The Israelites refused to believe God would enable them to take the land, so God condemned that entire generation to die in the Sinai Peninsula. Because the twelve spies had scouted for forty days, the punishment was forty years in the wilderness. The extent to which the Israelites wandered from their central camp at Kadesh during these years is unknown.

MEDITERRANEAN SEA

Area enlarged below

CANAAN

Bethlehem

Hebron

DEAD SEA

Defeat of Israel (Num. 14:39–45; Deut. 1:41–46)

Beersheba

N e g e v

Arad

Hormah

Zoar

Way to Shur

AMALEK

Mt. Halak

Zered River

People condemned to 40 years of wandering (Num. 14)

Site of Aaron's death and his burial

Tamar

Jebel Madurah (Mt. Hor ?)

Wilderness of Zin

Kadesh-barnea

Azmon

Karka

Ain el-Qudeirat

Hazar-addar

Rebellion of Korah against Moses (Num. 16)

A r a b a h

Ain Qedeis

Jebel Kharif

Death of Miriam (Num. 20:1)

Jebel Karkom

Wilderness of Paran

N

0   5   10   15   20 Miles

0   5 10 15   20 Kilometers

KADESH-BARNEA

● City

○ City (uncertain location)

◉ Oasis

— Roads

← Invasion of Canaan

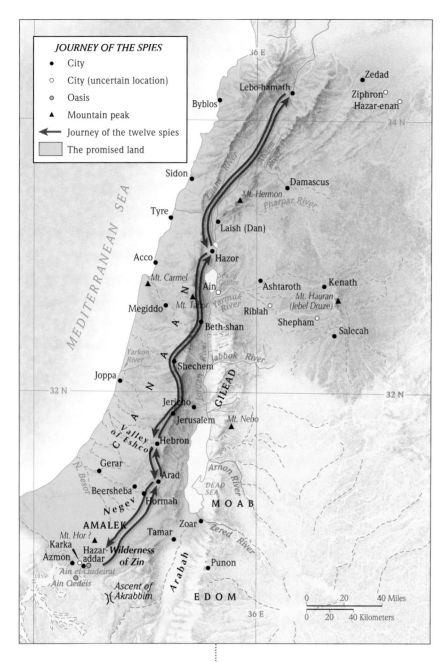

Three incidents are described in some detail. First, Korah, Dathan, and Abiram led a serious but unsuccessful rebellion (Num. 16). Second, Moses sinned when he struck a rock in providing water for the Israelites, and as a consequence he could not enter the promised land (Num. 20). Third, God punished the people who complained by sending poisonous snakes to bite many of them. Those who were bitten could spare their lives by gazing at the statue of a bronze snake that Moses erected (Num. 21). These chapters also include a number of supplementary laws.

JOURNEY FROM KADESH TO THE PLAINS OF MOAB

NUMBERS 22—36 describes the last stages of Israel's travels under Moses' leadership. At last the people made their encampment on the plains of Moab, east of the Jordan River. The most remarkable incident preserved in these chapters is the strange affair of the false prophet Balaam. He was hired by Moab's king to put a curse on Israel; instead he pronounced four poetic oracles of blessing (Num. 23—24). Forever after, however, the name "Balaam" was infamous, and even in the New Testament he was a byword for someone whose religion is utterly corrupt.

The last chapters moves the action to the anticipated conquest of Canaan:

- Joshua is installed as Moses' successor (Num. 27)

- The tribes of Reuben, Gad, and half of Manasseh decide to settle east of the Jordan River (Num. 32)

- National boundaries and designated "safe cities" are mandated (Num. 34—35)

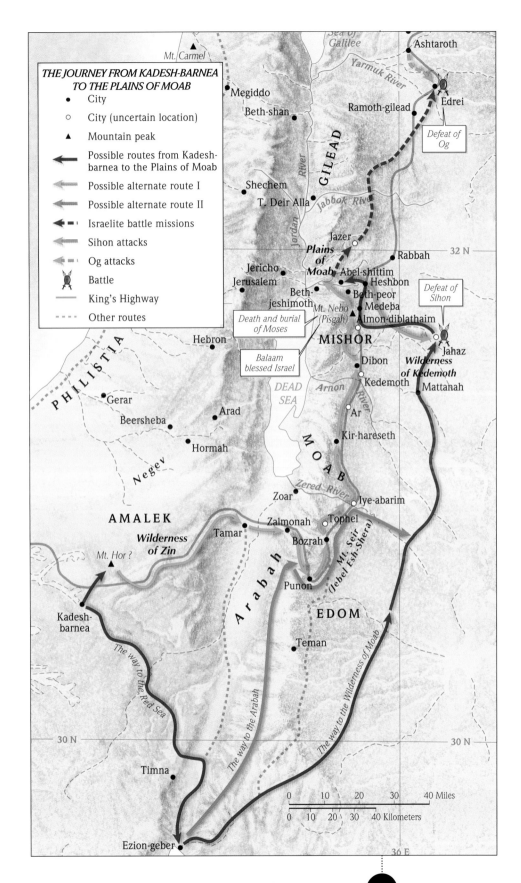

THE JOURNEY FROM KADESH-BARNEA
TO THE PLAINS OF MOAB

- • City
- ○ City (uncertain location)
- ▲ Mountain peak
- ← Possible routes from Kadesh-barnea to the Plains of Moab
- ← Possible alternate route I
- ← Possible alternate route II
- ← Israelite battle missions
- ← Sihon attacks
- ← Og attacks
- ⚔ Battle
- ― King's Highway
- ---- Other routes

Mt. Carmel

Sea of Galilee

Ashtaroth

Yarmuk River

Megiddo

Beth-shan

Ramoth-gilead

Edrei

Defeat of Og

GILEAD

Jordan River

Shechem

T. Deir Alla

Jabbok River

Jazer

32 N

Plains of Moab

Rabbah

Jericho

Jerusalem

Abel-shittim

Heshbon

Beth-peor

Beth-jeshimoth

Medeba

Death and burial of Moses

Mt. Nebo (Pisgah)

Almon-diblathaim

Defeat of Sihon

Balaam blessed Israel

MISHOR

Jahaz

Dibon

Wilderness of Kedemoth

Hebron

DEAD SEA

Kedemoth

Mattanah

Arnon River

Dibon

Ar

Gerar

Beersheba

Arad

Kir-hareseth

PHILISTIA

Hormah

M O A B

Negev

Zered River

Zoar

Iye-abarim

AMALEK

Tamar

Zalmonah

Tophel

Wilderness of Zin

Bozrah

Mt. Hor ?

Punon

Mt. Seir (Jebel Esh-Shera)

Kadesh-barnea

A r a b a h

EDOM

The way to the Red Sea

Teman

The way to the Arabah

The way to the Wilderness of Moab

30 N

30 N

0   10   20   30   40 Miles

0 10 20 30 40 Kilometers

Timna

Ezion-geber

36 E

Moses

More space is given to the life and teachings of Moses than any other Old Testament character. From a human point of view, in one way or another everything from Exodus 2 to the end of Deuteronomy—four Bible books—depended on Moses. From a chronological perspective his life may be organized into three equal portions: forty years as an Egyptian prince, forty years as a desert shepherd, and forty years as Israel's greatest leader. Assuming the traditional date of the exodus, Moses lived from 1526 to 1406 B.C.

These chapters tell about the Israelite census as they were about to enter Canaan (601,730 adult males, Num. 26:51). God had preserved the people remarkably despite their rebellion and despite the hardships of the wilderness. By this time almost everyone who had been an adult at the time of the exodus had died. A new generation would take the promised land.

South end of the Wilderness of Paran where Israel wandered (photo taken in sand storm).

Old Testament Dibon, the capital of Moab. Moses led Israel to the Plains of Moab, east of the Jordan River.

Last Speeches of Moses

At age 120 Moses was ready to "retire." His successor Joshua had been appointed. Yet before he left the scene, Moses gave the Israelites a series of passionate addresses. These reminded God's people of His mighty actions for them. His words also challenged Israel to hold fast to Him during the exciting days that lay ahead. They contain the famous *Shema*, "Hear, O Israel," with its ringing affirmation of God's unity as well as the Great Commandment to love God supremely (Deut. 6:4-5; see Jesus' affirmation of this in Matt. 22:37-38).

- Speech One: **DEUTERONOMY 1—4**. Moses reviews the history of the Israelites from the time they left Mount Sinai until they arrived on the plains of Moab.

- Speech Two: **DEUTERONOMY 5—28**. Moses repeats many of the laws that he first received on Mount Sinai. (For example, Deuteronomy 5 repeats the Ten Commandments.) He also gives a number of new regulations. This speech ends with a statement of the blessings that come on those who obey God and the curses that fall on those who do not.

- Speech Three: **DEUTERONOMY 29—30**. Moses proposes a renewal of the Sinaitic covenant for the new generation.

Book of Deuteronomy

As the last of the five books (Pentateuch) written by Moses for the Israelites, Deuteronomy records his farewell messages shortly before his death. The key word for the book is "commandments"; the key text is Deuteronomy 6:4-5. **One-Sentence Summary:** *Through Moses' great speeches near the end of his life, God reminded Israel on the verge of entering the promised land about His mighty acts, His covenant, and His many commands.*

The view of Canaan Moses had from Mount Nebo.

Mount Nebo and the Jordan Valley. Mount Nebo is where Moses was buried.

CONCLUSION OF MOSES' LEADERSHIP

Moses' leadership finally ended with the incidents described in **DEUTERONOMY 31—34**. He sang one last song (chap. 32); he gave the people his final blessing (chap. 33); he climbed Mount Nebo to look into the land he could not enter (chap. 34). Then he died and was mourned for thirty days. Until the coming of Jesus, he was the greatest leader and prophet of Israel (Deut. 34:10-12; Heb. 3:1-6).

 # Canaan (Palestine)

Canaan is one of the oldest names for the land Israel took. The term Canaanites refers to the pre-Israelite inhabitants. It was also called the promised land because of God's promise through the Abrahamic covenant (Gen. 17:7-8). After Joshua the land could be referred to generally as Israel, but often Israel refers to the northern section of the land with Judah referring to the southern section. The designation "holy land" occurs only rarely. The name Palestine, the name commonly used by the first century and until today, was adapted from the word Philistines.

MIRACULOUS ENTRANCE INTO THE LAND

By this point in the Kingdom Story, God had given His people almost everything needed to be constituted as a nation. The one missing ingredient was land, a place to live. God's promise to Abraham that Canaan would one day be the homeland of his descendants was about to be fulfilled after more than 600 years. **JOSHUA 1—5** begins this part of the story by telling how God supernaturally brought Israel into Canaan under Joshua's leadership.

Their entrance point was the Jordan River near Jericho, an ancient walled city. Just as God showed that Moses was His chosen leader at the miraculous crossing of the Red Sea, so He showed that Joshua was His chosen leader forty years later at the miraculous crossing of the Jordan River. God's people Israel always told the story that their redemption involved crossing a body of water as if it were dry land and that their gift of Canaan also involved crossing a body of water as if it were dry land.

Although the stories about the conquest of the land show that Joshua and his troops exercised considerable military strategy, the first battle was brought about entirely by the Lord. The battle of Jericho, with its seemingly absurd tactic of marching around the walls in silence, persuaded both Israel and its enemies that the battle—ultimately every battle—belonged to the Lord (see Ps. 44:6-7).

God commanded the Israelites to destroy completely every living thing in Jericho (except for Rahab, the prostitute who provided help for Joshua's scouts, and her family). This is the first of several instances in the book of Joshua in which the people were pronounced "banned" and therefore destroyed. (See the three categories of people and things in the earlier discussion of Leviticus 11—16, "Rules for Uncleanness.")

Book of Joshua

This historical narrative tells of events from Israel's entry into Canaan until Joshua's death (1406–1380 B.C.). Its author may have been Joshua or the Prophet Samuel. The key word for the book is "conquest"; the key text is 21:44–45. **One-Sentence Summary:** *God fulfilled His promises to Israel to give them a land through the conquest of Canaan and through the allocation of the land among the tribes, all under the leadership of Joshua.*

The oasis of Jericho taken from atop the Old Testament tel Jericho.

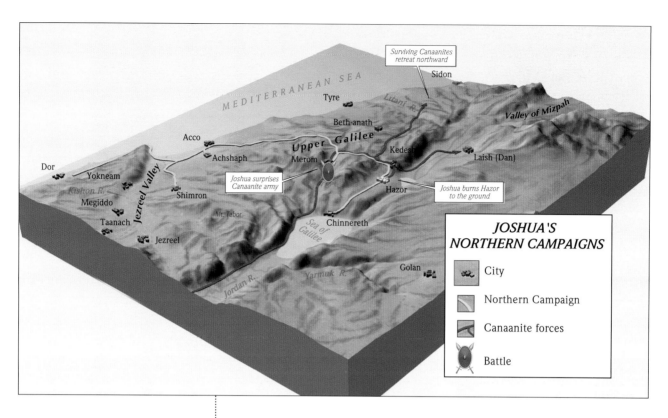

Surviving Canaanites
retreat northward

MEDITERRANEAN SEA

Sidon

Tyre

Beth-anath

Litani R.

Valley of Mizpah

Acco

Upper Galilee

Kedesh

Achshaph

Merom

Laish (Dan)

Dor

Yokneam

Joshua surprises
Canaanite army

Hazor

Joshua burns Hazor
to the ground

Jezreel Valley

Shimron

Kishon R.

Megiddo

Mt. Tabor

Chinnereth

Taanach

Sea of Galilee

Jezreel

Jordan R.

Yarmuk R.

Golan

JOSHUA'S NORTHERN CAMPAIGNS

City

Northern Campaign

Canaanite forces

Battle

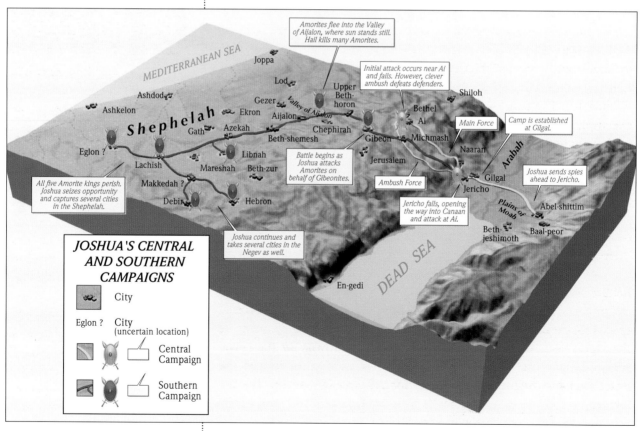

Amorites flee into the Valley
of Aijalon, where sun stands still.
Hail kills many Amorites.

Initial attack occurs near Ai
and fails. However, clever
ambush defeats defenders.

MEDITERRANEAN SEA

Joppa

Lod

Ashdod

Gezer

Upper Beth-horon

Shiloh

Ashkelon

Valley of Aijalon

Bethel

Ai

Main Force

Camp is established
at Gilgal.

Shephelah

Ekron

Aijalon

Gath

Azekah

Chephirah

Gibeon

Michmash

Naaran

Arabah

Beth-shemesh

Eglon ?

Lachish

Libnah

Mareshah

Beth-zur

Battle begins as
Joshua attacks
Amorites on
behalf of Gibeonites.

Jerusalem

Gilgal

Ambush Force

Jericho

Joshua sends spies
ahead to Jericho.

Makkedah ?

Debir

Hebron

Jericho falls, opening
the way into Canaan
and attack at Ai.

Plains of Moab

Abel-shittim

Baal-peor

All five Amorite kings perish.
Joshua seizes opportunity
and captures several cities
in the Shephelah.

Joshua continues and
takes several cities in the
Negev as well.

Beth-jeshimoth

DEAD SEA

En-gedi

JOSHUA'S CENTRAL AND SOUTHERN CAMPAIGNS

City

Eglon ? City
(uncertain location)

Central Campaign

Southern Campaign

Shechem. Here between Mount Gerazim and Mount Ebal, Joshua led Israel to renew their commitment to the law of Moses.

CONQUEST AND OCCUPATION OF THE LAND

The military victory at Jericho was followed by victory at the town of Ai. **JOSHUA 6—12** tells of one victory after another. Joshua's strategy was to "divide and conquer." His army launched an attack through central Canaan, culminating in the battle of the miraculously lengthened day (Joshua 10). The Israelite army crushed a coalition of five kings, which effectively broke the back of the opposition. Joshua then defeated cities in the southern part of Canaan (Joshua 10) and finally the northern cities (Joshua 11). Although there were still pockets of Canaanite population, the battle for control of Canaan apparently lasted no more than five years. (See Caleb's description in Josh. 14:7-10.)

JOSHUA 13—24 focuses on how the land was divided among the twelve tribes of Israel. Although the borders and towns for each tribe are listed in meticulous detail, much of this cannot be reconstructed today. Chapter 13 tells about the land east of the Jordan River, occupied by Reuben, Gad, and half of Manasseh. Chapters 14–19 describe the land assignments for the other 9 ¹/₂ tribes. Both Caleb and Joshua received special allocations of land in honor of their faithfulness to the Lord more than forty years earlier. Joshua 21 tells about the towns for the Levite tribe, who received no land allocation. They were given instead the priesthood and the privilege of caring for the place of worship. The last few verses of Joshua 21 triumphantly note that God kept every one of His promises to the Israelite people as they took possession of the land.

Holy War

As the holy and righteous Lord of His people, God has the right to declare that His people are to judge His (and their) enemies by destroying them, putting them under His ban. As long as God's people were a national entity, they could fight the Lord's military battles. Jesus, however, declared that His kingdom was not of this world, and therefore His followers would not use swords to fight God's cause (John 18:36). Thus, no holy war is now authorized for kingdom people. The fight is now spiritual (Eph. 6:11-17). Revelation describes the last holy war, in which Christ will judge God's enemies by destroying them.

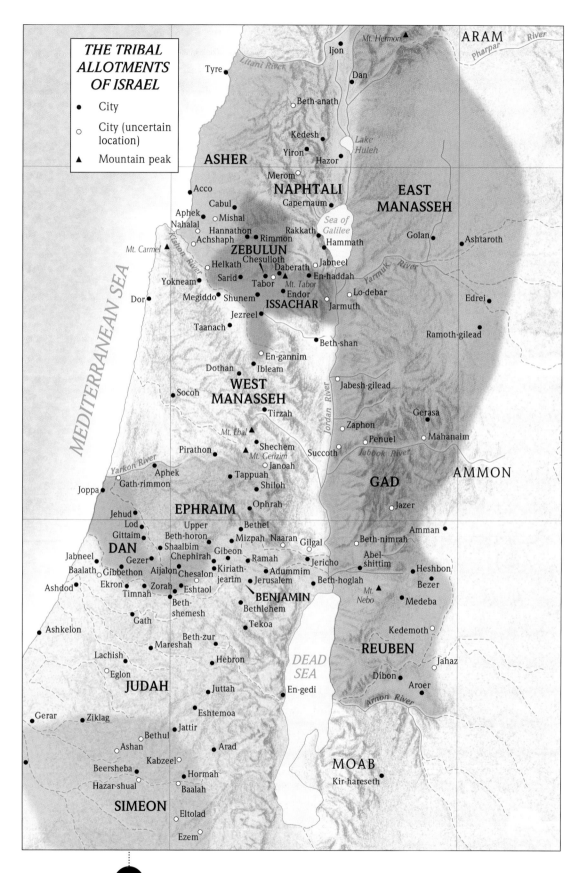

THE TRIBAL
ALLOTMENTS
OF ISRAEL

- City
○ City (uncertain location)
▲ Mountain peak

ARAM

Mt. Hermon ▲

Litani River

Pharpar River

Tyre

Ijon

Dan

Beth-anath

Kedesh

Lake Huleh

ASHER

Yiron

Hazor

Merom

Acco

Cabul

NAPHTALI

Capernaum

Sea of Galilee

EAST MANASSEH

Aphek

Mishal

Nahalal

Hannathon

Rakkath

Golan

Ashtaroth

Achshaph

Rimmon

Hammath

Mt. Carmel ▲

Kishon River

ZEBULUN

Chesulloth

Jabneel

Helkath

Daberath

En-haddah

Yokneam

Sarid

Tabor ▲ Mt. Tabor

Yarmuk River

Edrei

Dor

Megiddo

Shunem

Endor

Lo-debar

MEDITERRANEAN SEA

Taanach

ISSACHAR

Jezreel

Jarmuth

Ramoth-gilead

Beth-shan

En-gannim

Dothan

Ibleam

Jabesh-gilead

WEST MANASSEH

Socoh

Tirzah

Gerasa

Mt. Ebal ▲

Zaphon

Mahanaim

Pirathon

Shechem

Penuel

Mt. Gerizim ▲

Janoah

Succoth

Jabbok River

Yarkon River

Aphek

Tappuah

GAD

AMMON

Joppa

Gath-rimmon

Shiloh

Ophrah

Jazer

Jehud

Bethel

EPHRAIM

Lod

Upper

Gittaim

Beth-horon

Mizpah

Naaran

Gilgal

Amman

DAN

Shaalbim

Gibeon

Beth-nimrah

Jabneel

Chephirah

Ramah

Jericho

Abel-shittim

Baalath

Gezer

Aijalon

Kiriath-jearim

Heshbon

Gibbethon

Chesalon

Adummim

Beth-hoglah

Bezer

Ashdod

Ekron

Zorah

Eshtaol

Jerusalem

Mt. Nebo ▲

Timnah

Beth-shemesh

BENJAMIN

Medeba

Gath

Bethlehem

Ashkelon

Tekoa

Kedemoth

Beth-zur

REUBEN

Mareshah

Lachish

Hebron

Jahaz

Eglon

DEAD SEA

Dibon

JUDAH

Juttah

En-gedi

Aroer

Gerar

Ziklag

Eshtemoa

Arnon River

Bethul

Jattir

Ashan

Arad

Kabzeel

MOAB

Beersheba

Hormah

Kir-hareseth

Hazar-shual

Baalah

SIMEON

Eltolad

Ezem

Just as Moses said his formal farewell to Israel, so did his successor Joshua. His last speech to the leaders of Israel challenged them to obey everything that God had commanded (chap. 23). In Joshua 24 he summoned the leaders to a solemn assembly at Shechem in a covenant renewal ceremony. This was the occasion that he uttered his famous words that he and his household would serve the Lord (Josh. 24:15). Many families of God's people since then have been inspired to adopt Joshua's commitment as their own. The last event belonging to this part of the Kingdom Story is the death of Joshua, which effectively ended the entire period of the exodus, wilderness wanderings, and conquest.

The Monarchy and the Temple:
From Joshua's Death to Solomon's Death (1380–931 B.C.)

After Joshua's death the nation drifted through the dreadful period of the judges, which ended with the leadership of Samuel. The first king, Saul, failed. David, the next king, received God's unconditional covenant promise that his dynasty would endure forever. The promise included both an eternal kingdom and an eternal king. David wanted to honor the Lord by building a temple for His name in Jerusalem, but that privilege went to Solomon his son. The temple was dedicated in 959 B.C., and with that Israel reached its most glorious national expression.

Cycles of Defeat and Deliverance

Just as the glorious time of Joseph's popularity in Egypt gave way to a long dark age of defeat and despair, so the wonderful era of Joshua's victories gave way to a dark period of defeat and despair. Tragically, the Israelite people succumbed too easily to the disgusting pagan religions practiced by the people they had conquered. These cycles are the substance of **Judges 1—16**. The era of the judges with bitter regularity shows the following cycle:

- Turning away from God to idols
- Oppression by a neighboring country
- Repentance and asking for relief
- A divinely appointed judge who helps
- After a time of rest, a new time of turning away from God

A total of sixteen judges (local leaders) were involved in bringing temporary deliverance to Israel. (The number sixteen is arrived at by counting Deborah and Barak separately and by including Eli and Samuel, whose leadership is described in 1 Samuel, as the last two judges.) Although the years of oppression and the years individual judges led are often stated, some of the judges evidently overlapped, so it is impossible to develop a precise chronology for this period.

Book of Judges

This historical narrative describes events from Joshua's death until Samson's death, some three centuries (about 1380–1060 B.C.). Samuel may have been the author, showing how God delivered His people both *to* and *from* their oppressors. The key word for the book is "deliverance"; the key text is Judges 21:25. **One-Sentence Summary:** *Israel experienced the repeated cycle of apostasy, oppression, repentance, and restoration by divinely appointed judges throughout the long period following Joshua's death.*

FOUR NOTEWORTHY JUDGES

Four of the leaders God raised up are described in some detail. The story of each one highlighted a different oppressor nation. Each of these judges provides evidence of God's surprising grace in choosing to work through flawed human leaders. The twelve tribes of Israel were only loosely connected at this time, for after the death of Joshua, each tribe more or less "did its own thing."

DEBORAH was the only woman judge, and she was God's prophet as well. She led from a place in the tribal allotment of Ephraim (Judg. 4:4-5). The twenty-year oppression was caused by a Canaanite coalition—pockets of the pagan population not destroyed in Joshua's time—which gained new power within the northern part of the tribal allotment. Deborah's general, Barak, organized an army from the northern tribes to oppose a Canaanite army led by Sisera. Israel routed the Canaanite coalition at Mount Tabor (not far from the Sea of Galilee). Sisera was personally killed by the woman Jael. Judges 5 records the famous "Song of Deborah" that celebrated the victory. Because of Deborah's outstanding leadership, there was a forty-year period of peace (Judg. 5:31).

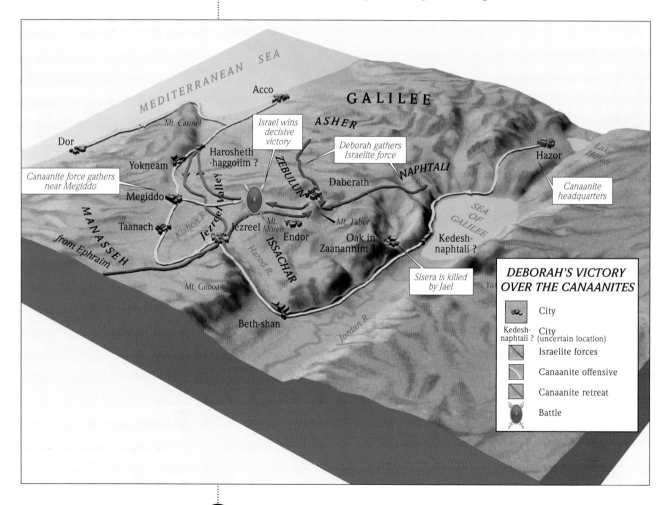

MEDITERRANEAN SEA

GALILEE

Acco

Mt. Carmel

Dor

ASHER

Israel wins decisive victory

ZEBULUN

Deborah gathers Israelite force

NAPHTALI

Hazor

Lake Huleh

Canaanite force gathers near Megiddo

Harosheth -haggoiim ?

Yokneam

Daberath

Canaanite headquarters

Megiddo

MANASSEH

Kishon R.

Jezreel Valley

Mt. Moreh

SEA OF GALILEE

Taanach

Jezreel

Endor

Mt. Tabor

from Ephraim

Haroд R.

ISSACHAR

Oak in Zaanannim ?

Kedesh-naphtali ?

Mt. Gilboa

Sisera is killed by Jael

Beth-shan

Jordan R.

Ya

DEBORAH'S VICTORY OVER THE CANAANITES

City

Kedesh-naphtali ? City (uncertain location)

Israelite forces

Canaanite offensive

Canaanite retreat

Battle

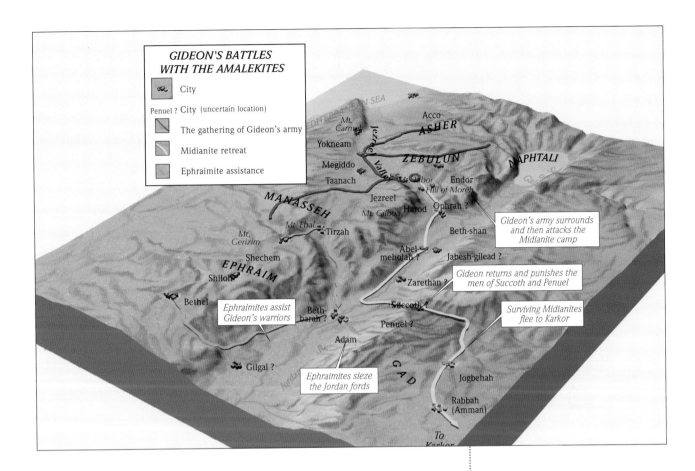

**GIDEON'S BATTLES
WITH THE AMALEKITES**

🐾 City

Penuel ? City (uncertain location)

◨ The gathering of Gideon's army

◩ Midianite retreat

▨ Ephraimite assistance

MEDITERRANEAN SEA

Mt. Carmel

Acco

ASHER

Yokneam

ZEBULUN

Jezreel Valley

Megiddo

Tabor

NAPHTALI

Taanach

Endor
Hill of Moreh

MANASSEH

Jezreel

Ophrah ?

Mt. Gilboa

Harod

Gideon's army surrounds
and then attacks the
Midianite camp

Mt. Ebal

Tirzah

Beth-shan

Mt. Gerizim

Abel-meholah ?

Jabesh-gilead ?

Shechem

Zarethan ?

Gideon returns and punishes the
men of Succoth and Penuel

Shiloh

EPHRAIM

Succoth ?

Surviving Midianites
flee to Karkor

Bethel

Ephraimites assist
Gideon's warriors

Beth-barah ?

Penuel ?

Adam

GAD

Gilgal ?

Ephraimites sieze
the Jordan fords

Jogbehah

Rabbah
(Amman)

To
Karkor

GIDEON was the reluctant judge who had to be persuaded by laying out a literal fleece before God (Judg. 6:37-40). He was from the tribe of Manasseh, which had fallen into the worship of Baal. The seven-year oppression Gideon broke was caused by an invasion of Midianites, nomads who usually stayed in the desert east of Moab and Ammon. When the Spirit of the Lord came on Gideon, he summoned an army from several northern tribes (Judg. 6:34-35). Gideon is best remembered for paring down his army of 32,000 to only 300, so that God would be credited with the victory (Judg. 7—8). During Gideon's forty-year leadership after the defeat of the Midianites, the land enjoyed peace despite Gideon's own lapse into idolatry (Judg. 8:27-28).

The Harod Spring at Ainharod at the foot of the Gilboa mountain range. This is where Gideon gathered his men before fighting the Midianites.

JEPHTHAH, the son of a prostitute, was from Gilead, the land east of the Jordan River. The Israelites this time had adopted the idolatrous religion of a variety of their pagan neighbors (Judg. 10:6). The eighteen-year opposition was caused by a resurgence of the Ammonites, a pagan nation east of the Jordan River that the Israelites had displaced but not totally destroyed. When the Spirit of the Lord came on Jephthah, he led an army from Gilead to defeat Ammon (Josh. 11:11,29,33). Jephthah is most remembered for making a reckless vow to the Lord that he would sacrifice the first thing he met at home if he won the battle. Tragically his only child, a daughter, was the one who paid for her father's vow by giving her life (Judg. 11:30-40). The period of peace after Jephthah's victory lasted six years (Judg. 12:7).

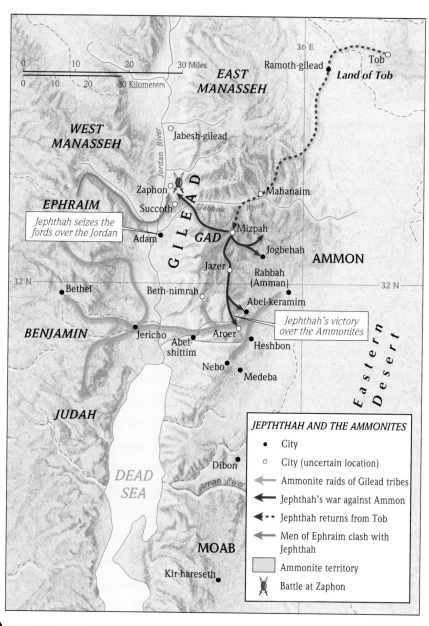

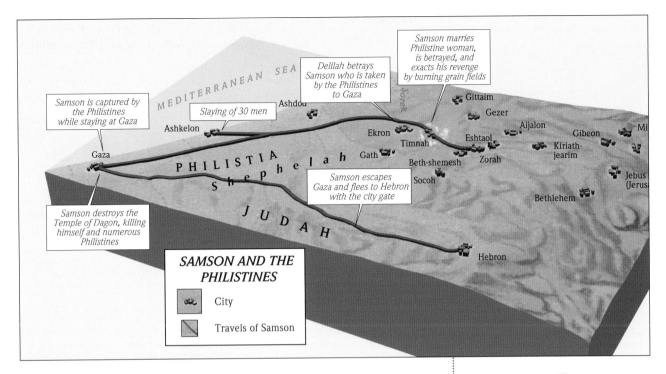

SAMSON AND THE PHILISTINES

Symbol	Legend
City	City
	Travels of Samson

Map labels:
- MEDITERRANEAN SEA
- Samson is captured by the Philistines while staying at Gaza
- Slaying of 30 men
- Ashdod
- Delilah betrays Samson who is taken by the Philistines to Gaza
- Samson marries Philistine woman, is betrayed, and exacts his revenge by burning grain fields
- Gittaim
- Gezer
- Aijalon
- Mi
- Gibeon
- Kiriath-jearim
- Ashkelon
- Ekron
- Eshtaol
- Gaza
- PHILISTIA
- Timnah
- Gath
- Beth-shemesh
- Zorah
- Jebus (Jerus...
- Shephelah
- Socoh
- Samson escapes Gaza and flees to Hebron with the city gate
- Samson destroys the Temple of Dagon, killing himself and numerous Philistines
- JUDAH
- Bethlehem
- Hebron
- Sorek

SAMSON, strong man of the Bible, receives more attention in the book of Judges than any other judge (Judg. 13—16). He seems to have lived just before the rise of the Israelite monarchy. God designated Samson before birth as the one who would begin to rescue Israel from the Philistines. He challenged the forty-year Philistine oppression single-handedly. Famous for his long hair, his strength came not by magic but from God's Spirit. (The Spirit is recorded as coming on Samson more than for any other judge, Judg. 13:25; 14:6,19; 15:14.) Although Samson failed miserably in his sexual morality, God nevertheless used him to show that Yahweh's power was greater than the power of Dagon, god of the Philistines. Samson's leadership—that of a local folk hero—lasted twenty years (Judg. 16:31).

The site of Old Testament Ashdod looking toward modern Ashdod.

Philistia

The Philistines, probably immigrants from the island of Crete, settled in the southern coastal plain of Canaan. They had five population centers: Ashdod, Gaza, Ashkelon, Gath, and Ekron. Their technology was more sophisticated than that of the Israelites (1 Sam. 13:19-22). Several of Israel's great leaders were involved in ongoing struggles against the Philistines: Samson, Saul, and David. Goliath of Gath was the most formidable of all the Philistine warriors. Our name "Palestine" is a variant of the word "Philistine," and even today the Gaza Strip is emphatically distinct from Israel.

Book of Ruth

This compact narrative, author unknown, shines as a beautiful jewel that tells of God's providence and the uncommon love between a husband and wife. The key word for the book is "redeemer" (or "kinsman"); the key text is Ruth 4:14. **One-Sentence Summary:** *Ruth, a Moabite widow, found love and fulfillment through Boaz, a rich Israelite bachelor who redeemed the land and the name of Ruth's deceased husband, thereby restoring Naomi, Ruth's mother-in-law, from emptiness to fullness.*

STORIES OF CORRUPTION AND HOPE

The 300-year-long agony of the judges' era is summarized by two examples of the religious and moral depravity in **JUDGES 17—21**. These stories are bracketed by the writer's note that because there was no king in Israel, everyone did as he pleased (Judg. 17:6; 21:25). The account of the idolatrous Micah, who hired his own personal priest, also explains how the tribe of Dan came to relocate entirely, moving from the coastal plain in southern Israel to the region north of the Sea of Galilee. The phrase "from Dan to Beersheba" came to mean "all Israel from north to south" (Judg. 20:1; 1 Sam. 3:20). The account of a savage sexual attack on an Israelite woman in the town of Gibeah in Benjamin, with the ensuing near-annihilation of the tribe of Benjamin by an army of Israelites, also explains why the tribe of Benjamin was so small in population.

Not everything was entirely dark, however. The story told in the book of **RUTH** shows that God was preparing the way for the dynasty of David, for Boaz and Ruth were David's great-grandparents. This elegant short story shows that at least a few in Israel, such as the devout Boaz, were living according to God's laws, particularly the law of the kinsman-redeemer. Of course, the inclusion of the (former) pagan Ruth as an ancestor of the royal family must be seen as nothing else than an example of God's undeserved mercy.

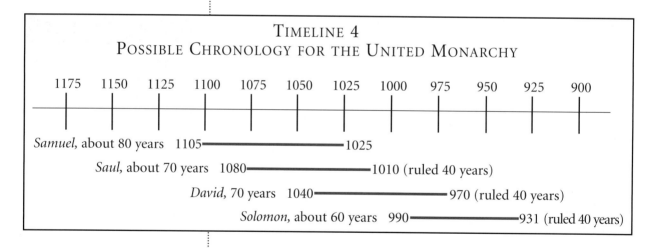

TIMELINE 4
POSSIBLE CHRONOLOGY FOR THE UNITED MONARCHY

1175 1150 1125 1100 1075 1050 1025 1000 975 950 925 900

Samuel, about 80 years 1105————————1025

Saul, about 70 years 1080————————1010 (ruled 40 years)

David, 70 years 1040————————970 (ruled 40 years)

Solomon, about 60 years 990————————931 (ruled 40 years)

SAMUEL'S YEARS

The opening sequence of God's plan to build his nation, told in Genesis 12—50, featured four remarkable men: Abraham, Isaac, Jacob, and Joseph. The closing sequence of Chapter One of the Kingdom Story features four equally noteworthy men: Samuel, Saul, David, and Solomon (1 Sam. 1—1 Kings 11). When the lives of these four had run their divinely appointed courses, God's earthly nation stood at its most shining moment.

Samuel is the key transition figure, the last of the judges and the first of the prophets (1 Sam. 3:20; 7:6). God used him to bring about the monarchy in Israel, first under Saul and then under David. Although an exact chronology for the life of Samuel is impossible, he may have lived around eighty years (about 1105–1025 B.C.). If so, he overlapped both Samson and David, but he did not live to see David established as king.

The life of Samuel is the focus of **1 SAMUEL 1—7**. The following are highlights of Samuel's life before he anointed Saul as king.

Samuel anoints Saul as king over Israel at Ramah

THE MINISTRY OF SAMUEL AND ANOINTMENT OF SAUL

City

Gilgal ? City (uncertain location)

Circuit where Samuel judged

- Born in answer to his mother Hannah's prayer (1 Sam. 1—2)

- Called by God to become a prophet (1 Sam. 3)

- Led the Israelite army to take back the ark of the covenant from the Philistines, captured twenty years earlier (1 Sam. 7)

- Led Israel as a "circuit judge," traveling between Ramah (his headquarters), Bethel, Gilgal, and Mizpah (1 Sam. 7)

Ramah, Samuel's birthplace, home, and burial place.

First Book of Samuel

This historical narrative describes the beginning of the monarchy in Israel, from the birth of Samuel to the death of Saul. An unknown author wrote it, possibly in the time of Solomon. The key word for the book is "monarchy"; the key text is 1 Samuel 18:7. **One-Sentence Summary:** *David became king after the people rejected Samuel's leadership and God rejected the unfaithful King Saul.*

SAUL'S YEARS

Saul's kingship over the united Israelite tribes began a new era for God's redeemed people. After centuries of defeat, they were about to move to a position of prominence in the ancient world. Although Saul ultimately must be judged a failure, his name was not considered utterly worthless—after all, he ruled Israel for forty years. (More than a thousand years later there was another famous Saul from the tribe of Benjamin, better known as Paul the apostle.) The main description of Saul is found in **1 SAMUEL 8—15**; he lived about seventy years (about 1080–1010 B.C.).

SAUL'S RISE

Saul did not initiate the idea of a unified Israelite monarchy. The Israelites had grown tired of the loose organization that existed under Samuel and were wary of the aptitude of Samuel's corrupt sons. They asked Samuel to give them a king like the surrounding nations had (1 Sam. 8:19-20). Saul was God's choice, which Samuel publicly affirmed by pouring oil on Saul's head. Like the judges before him, Saul was empowered by the Spirit to do God's work (1 Sam. 10:10). He secured his kingship by using great military skill in defeating an Ammonite army that threatened the Israelite town of Jabesh (1 Sam. 11). Saul's confirmation as king came through Samuel's farewell address to the people. Like Moses and Joshua before him, Samuel used his last speech to challenge Israel to stay faithful to the Lord and to His commands (1 Sam. 12).

Old Testament Gibeah. Gibeah was two miles north of what is now Jerusalem. Here Saul established his capital.

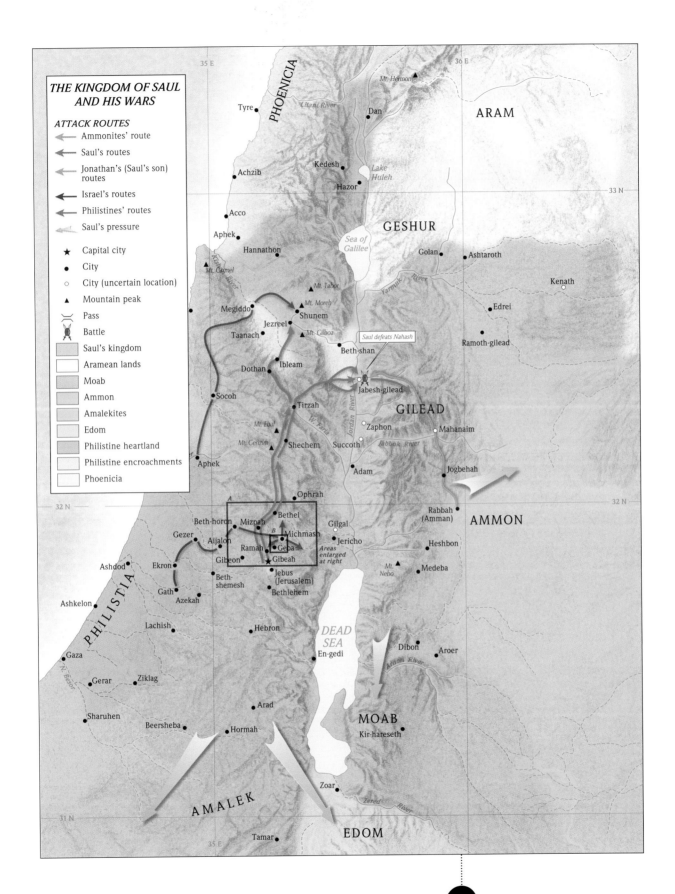

THE KINGDOM OF SAUL AND HIS WARS

ATTACK ROUTES

Ammonites' route
Saul's routes
Jonathan's (Saul's son) routes
Israel's routes
Philistines' routes
Saul's pressure

★ Capital city
● City
○ City (uncertain location)
▲ Mountain peak
⤭ Pass
Battle
Saul's kingdom
Aramean lands
Moab
Ammon
Amalekites
Edom
Philistine heartland
Philistine encroachments
Phoenicia

PHOENICIA
ARAM
GESHUR
GILEAD
AMMON
MOAB
EDOM
AMALEK
PHILISTIA

35 E
36 E
33 N
32 N
31 N
35 E

Mt. Hermon
Litani River
Tyre
Dan
Achzib
Kedesh
Lake Huleh
Hazor
Acco
Aphek
Hannathon
Sea of Galilee
Golan
Ashtaroth
Kenath
Mt. Carmel
Edrei
Mt. Tabor
Mt. Moreh
Megiddo
Shunem
Jezreel
Mt. Gilboa
Ramoth-gilead
Taanach
Beth-shan
Saul defeats Nahash
Dothan
Ibleam
Jabesh-gilead
Socoh
Tirzah
Zaphon
Mahanaim
Mt. Ebal
Jabbok River
Mt. Gerizim
Shechem
Succoth
Adam
Jogbehah
Aphek
Ophrah
Rabbah (Amman)
Beth-horon
Bethel
Mizpah
Gilgal
Gezer
Michmash
Heshbon
Aijalon
Geba
Jericho
Ramah
Gibeon
Gibeah
Areas enlarged at right
Ekron
Ashdod
Jebus (Jerusalem)
Mt. Nebo
Beth-shemesh
Bethlehem
Medeba
Gath
Azekah
Ashkelon
Lachish
Hebron
DEAD SEA
En-gedi
Dibon
Aroer
Amnon River
Gaza
Gerar
Ziklag
Arad
Sharuhen
Beersheba
Hormah
Kir-hareseth
N. Besor
Zoar
Zered River
Tamar
Kanah River
Wadi Farah
Jordan River
Yarmuk River

SAUL'S FALL

Saul soon disobeyed God so grievously that God refused to establish his dynasty. Through Samuel, God announced to Saul that he had been rejected. Several instances of his failures are noted:

- Directly sacrificing animals at Gilgal instead of waiting for Samuel (1 Sam. 13)

- Rashly requiring his army to fast before battle (1 Sam. 14)

- Refusing to put under the ban (destroy) all animals taken in battle (1 Sam. 15)

Saul's jealousy and frustrated attempts to kill David are recounted in the material about David. His final demise—consulting a "witch" at Endor and losing a major battle to the Philistines at Mount Gilboa—ended with his suicide (1 Sam. 28; 31).

DAVID'S YEARS

Many more Bible chapters are given to David than to any other Old Testament king: **1 SAMUEL 16—1 KINGS 2** and **1 CHRONICLES 11—29**. Like his greatest descendant Jesus, his story is told by more than one Bible author. The primary significance of David is that God made an unconditional covenant with him, just as He had with Abraham. The primary provision of the Davidic covenant was the Lord's promise of an everlasting dynasty of David's descendants to rule God's people.

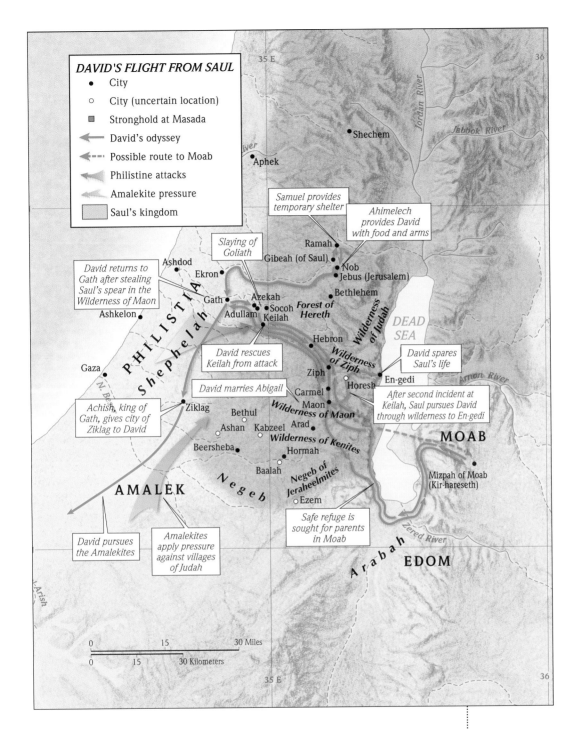

DAVID'S FLIGHT FROM SAUL

- • City
- ○ City (uncertain location)
- ▪ Stronghold at Masada
- ← David's odyssey
- ◄--- Possible route to Moab
- ◄ Philistine attacks
- ◄ Amalekite pressure
- ▭ Saul's kingdom

35 E   36

Jordan River

Jabbok River

Shechem•

River

•Aphek

Samuel provides temporary shelter

Ahimelech provides David with food and arms

Ramah•

Slaying of Goliath

Gibeah (of Saul)•   •Nob

Ashdod•   •Jebus (Jerusalem)

David returns to Gath after stealing Saul's spear in the Wilderness of Maon

Ekron•

•Bethlehem

Gath•   Azekah•

Ashkelon•   Adullam• •Socoh   *Forest of Hereth*

Keilah•

Wilderness of Judah

•Hebron

DEAD SEA

David rescues Keilah from attack

Wilderness of Ziph

Ziph○

David spares Saul's life

Horesh○   •En-gedi

Gaza•

David marries Abigail

Carmel•   *Arnon River*

Ziklag•   •Maon

Bethul○   *Wilderness of Maon*

After second incident at Keilah, Saul pursues David through wilderness to En-gedi

Achish, king of Gath, gives city of Ziklag to David

Ashan○   Kabzeel○   •Arad

Wilderness of Kenites

Beersheba•   •Hormah

MOAB

Baalah○

Negeb of Jeraheelmites

Mizpah of Moab (Kir-haraseth)•

Negeb

Ezem○

Safe refuge is sought for parents in Moab

Zered River

AMALEK

David pursues the Amalekites

Amalekites apply pressure against villages of Judah

Arabah   **EDOM**

el-Arish

PHILISTIA   Shephelah

0   15   30 Miles

0   15   30 Kilometers

35 E   36

Thus, after the Israelite kingdom later divided, that segment ruled by a Davidic king enjoyed at least the stability of an ongoing dynasty, while the others were faced constantly with the threat of one dynasty overthrowing another. (The eternal fulfillment of the Davidic covenant will be the visible and everlasting reign of Christ over all His redeemed people.) David ruled for forty years, living a total of seventy years (1040–970 B.C.).

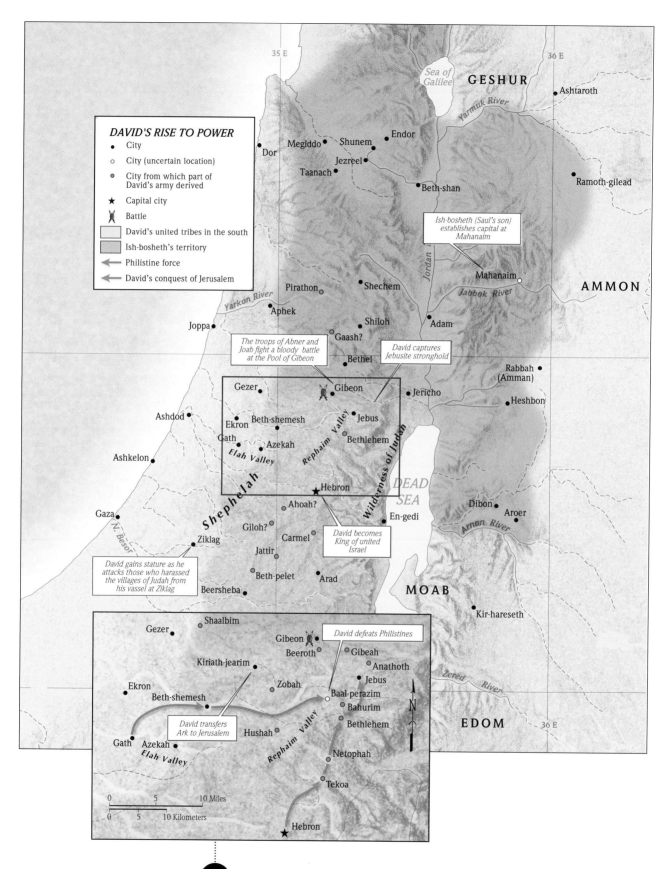

DAVID'S RISE TO POWER

- • City
- ○ City (uncertain location)
- ◉ City from which part of David's army derived
- ★ Capital city
- ⚔ Battle
- David's united tribes in the south
- Ish-bosheth's territory
- → Philistine force
- → David's conquest of Jerusalem

Ish-bosheth (Saul's son) establishes capital at Mahanaim

The troops of Abner and Joab fight a bloody battle at the Pool of Gibeon

David captures Jebusite stronghold

David becomes King of united Israel

David gains stature as he attacks those who harassed the villages of Judah from his vassal at Ziklag

David defeats Philistines

David transfers Ark to Jerusalem

GESHUR

AMMON

MOAB

EDOM

DEAD SEA

Sea of Galilee

Ashtaroth

Ramoth-gilead

Dor

Megiddo

Shunem

Endor

Jezreel

Taanach

Beth-shan

Mahanaim

Pirathon

Shechem

Aphek

Shiloh

Adam

Joppa

Gaash?

Bethel

Jericho

Rabbah (Amman)

Heshbon

Gezer

Gibeon

Jebus

Beth-shemesh

Ekron

Gath

Azekah

Bethlehem

Ashdod

Elah Valley

Rephaim Valley

Wilderness of Judah

Ashkelon

Hebron

Shephelah

Ahoah?

En-gedi

Dibon

Aroer

Gaza

Giloh?

Carmel

Ziklag

Jattir

Beth-pelet

Arad

Beersheba

Kir-hareseth

Jordan

Jabbok River

Yarmuk River

Yarkon River

N. Besor

Arnon River

Zered River

35 E

36 E

36 E

(Inset map)

Gezer

Shaalbim

Gibeon

Gibeah

Kiriath-jearim

Beeroth

Anathoth

Zobah

Jebus

Ekron

Baal-perazim

Beth-shemesh

Bahurim

Hushah

Bethlehem

Gath

Azekah

Netophah

Elah Valley

Rephaim Valley

Tekoa

Hebron

Rephaim Valley

N

0   5   10 Miles
0   5   10 Kilometers

DAVID'S RISE TO POWER

There was a long, difficult road between the time Samuel anointed a shepherd boy, David, as Saul's successor and the time he actually began his rule, perhaps about fifteen years (around 1025–1010 B.C.). **1 SAMUEL 16—31** tells a number of David's adventures during this time. He was probably about fifteen years old when Samuel anointed him as Saul's replacement. He enjoyed a number of successes:

- Anointed by Samuel and given the Spirit's power (1 Sam. 16)
- Killed the Philistine champion, Goliath, the giant warrior from Gath (1 Sam. 17)
- Married Saul's daughter Michal, for the price of 200 Philistines killed (1 Sam. 18)
- Escaped being speared by a jealous Saul (1 Sam. 19)
- Befriended by the heir apparent, Saul's son Jonathan (1 Sam. 20)
- Spared Saul's life in a cave when he could have killed him (1 Sam. 24)
- Married Abigail, the wise widow of the foolish Nabal (1 Sam. 25)
- Destroyed a raiding party of Amalekites (1 Sam. 29)

Brook Elah where David killed Goliath. View is looking eastward.

DAVID'S TRIUMPH

After the death of Saul, David became king over the southern tribe of Judah, ruling from Hebron. Saul's son Ishbosheth struggled for control of the entire nation, but he was finally murdered. After seven years of ruling only Judah, David was at last invited to be king over the entire nation. He captured the Jebusite stronghold Jerusalem and made it his capital city. The crowning event of his early years as king came when he brought the ark of the covenant into Jerusalem, thus effectively making the city both the political and the religious center of the nation. The Bible tells about many of David's victories as king in **2 Samuel 1—10** and **1 Chronicles 11—19**.

David built a cedar palace for himself in Jerusalem and began a process of expanding the extent of the city walls that continued throughout the time of the monarchy. By the days of Jesus, Jerusalem was many times larger than its original size in David's day. David was troubled, however, that while he had a permanent home, Israel's God (the ark of the covenant, thought of as God's presence) lived in a tent. David therefore conceived of a magnificent temple as a permanent home for the ark. In reply God promised by means of the Davidic covenant that David's "house" (dynasty) would rule His chosen people forever. The honor of building a temple would be deferred until the next generation (1 Sam. 7; 1 Chron. 17).

First Book of Chronicles

This historical narrative describes David's reign. Ezra may have written it after the Israelites returned from exile. It is famous for its extensive lists of names. The key word for the book is "dynasty"; the key text is 1 Chronicles 28:4. **One-Sentence Summary:** *After extensive introductory genealogies, the author tells how David ruled for forty years under the blessing of God, particularly as he lavished attention on Jerusalem, the priesthood, and preparation for building the temple.*

Jerusalem

From the time David made it his capital, Jerusalem has been Israel's royal city, the place where God was pleased to be worshiped. Two different Israelite temples were built there. All the kings of David's line ruled there. The city was gradually expanded in Old Testament times from the tiny "David's City" to the much larger city of Hezekiah's time. Jesus, his greatest descendant, died and was resurrected just outside Jerusalem. The city was so important that Revelation describes the final state of God's redeemed people as living in New Jerusalem.

Stairway from city of David up western hill.

David was commended not only for the covenant God made with him, but also for the way he later kept the covenant that Jonathan, Saul's son, had made with him. Although David could have completely destroyed all Saul's descendants, he showed great kindness to the crippled Mephibosheth, Jonathan's son (1 Sam. 20:16-17; 2 Sam. 9). The biblical writers also included the growth of David's royal harem as another indication of his success. Sadly, his successor and son Solomon inherited his father's fondness for a large harem, which proved to be his undoing. All David's wives and concubines are not named, but the following are identified with their children listed in parentheses:

- Michal, Saul's daughter
- Ahinoam of Jezreel (Amnon—David's oldest child)
- Abigail, Nabal's widow (Chileab/Daniel)
- Maacah, daugher of King Talmai of Geshur (Absalom)
- Haggith (Adonijah)
- Abital (Shephatiah)
- Eglah (Ithream)
- Bathsheba, widow of Uriah (unnamed infant, Solomon, Shammua, Shobab, Nathan)
- Unnamed (Tamar—David's only named daughter)

DAVID'S TROUBLES

The author of the books of Samuel (but not the author of Chronicles) described David's adultery with Bathsheba and the troubles that plagued the last part of his rule (**2 SAMUEL 11—20**). Nathan was David's court prophet during these troubles. David's difficulties may be outlined as follows:

- He committed adultery with Bathsheba (2 Sam. 11)
- He arranged for the murder of Uriah, Bathsheba's husband (2 Sam. 11)
- His and Bathsheba's son died in divine judgment (2 Sam. 12)
- His daughter Tamar was raped by the crown prince, his son Amnon (2 Sam. 13)
- His son Absalom murdered Amnon (2 Sam. 13)
- His son Absalom led a revolt against him, causing him to flee Jerusalem (2 Sam. 15)
- His son Absalom was killed by Joab, his leading military commander (2 Sam. 18)
- He endured a revolt led by Sheba (2 Sam. 20)

Davidic Covenant

God initiated this unconditional covenant to David, one who could not have deserved it. The promises of the Davidic covenant passed to Solomon and the royal line after him. Instead of David building a house (temple) for Yahweh, Yahweh promised to build a house (dynasty) for David. This forms the foundation for the New Covenant that Jesus established a thousand years later. The Davidic covenant finds its great ongoing fulfillment in Jesus Christ, the Son of David who will rule forever (Matt. 1:1; Rev. 11:15). The divine sign of the Davidic covenant was the presence of a Davidic king ruling over God's kingdom people.

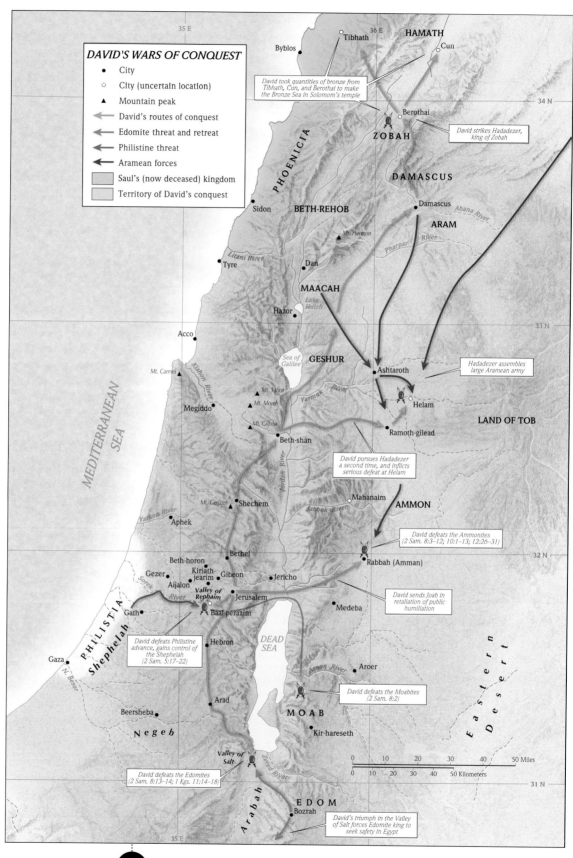

DAVID'S WARS OF CONQUEST

- ● City
- ⊙ City (uncertain location)
- ▲ Mountain peak
- → David's routes of conquest
- → Edomite threat and retreat
- → Philistine threat
- → Aramean forces
- ▬ Saul's (now deceased) kingdom
- ▬ Territory of David's conquest

Tibhath

Byblos

HAMATH

Cun

David took quantities of bronze from Tibhath, Cun, and Berothai to make the Bronze Sea in Solomom's temple

Berothai

ZOBAH

David strikes Hadadezer, king of Zobah

DAMASCUS

Damascus

Abana River

PHOENICIA

Sidon

BETH-REHOB

Mt. Hermon

ARAM

Pharbar River

Tyre

Litani River

Dan

MAACAH

Lake Huleh

Hazor

Acco

Sea of Galilee

GESHUR

Ashtaroth

Hadadezer assembles large Aramean army

Helam

Mt. Carmel

Kishon River

Mt. Tabor

Mt. Moreh

Yarmuk River

LAND OF TOB

Megiddo

Mt. Gilboa

Beth-shan

Ramoth-gilead

David pursues Hadadezer a second time, and inflicts serious defeat at Helam

MEDITERRANEAN SEA

Jordan River

Mt. Gerizim

Shechem

Mahanaim

Jabbok River

AMMON

Aphek

Yarkon River

Bethel

Beth-horon

Kiriath-jearim

Gibeon

Jericho

David defeats the Ammonites (2 Sam. 8:3–12; 10:1–13; 12:26–31)

Gezer

Aijalon

Sorek River

Valley of Rephaim

Jerusalem

Baal-perazim

Rabbah (Amman)

David sends Joab in retaliation of public humiliation

Gath

PHILISTIA

Shephelah

David defeats Philistine advance, gains control of the Shephelah (2 Sam. 5:17–22)

Hebron

DEAD SEA

Medeba

Gaza

N. Besor

Arnon River

Aroer

Eastern Desert

Arad

David defeats the Moabites (2 Sam. 8:2)

Beersheba

Negeb

MOAB

Kir-hareseth

Zered River

Valley of Salt

0 10 20 30 40 50 Miles
0 10 20 30 40 50 Kilometers

David defeats the Edomites (2 Sam. 8:13–14; 1 Kgs. 11:14–18)

Arabah

EDOM

Bozrah

David's triumph in the Valley of Salt forces Edomite king to seek safety in Egypt

35 E   36 E

34 N

33 N

32 N

31 N

Possibly David and his men took over the city through Warren's Shaft. Warren's shaft runs from the Gihon spring up to the old city of Jerusalem.

DAVID'S EFFECTIVENESS

There is a considerable amount of material showing that David was a capable king and leader. **2 SAMUEL 21—24** and **1 CHRONICLES 20—29** include both incidents and lists of men. Incidents include his census of the army and purchase of the property on which the temple was to be built (2 Sam. 24; 1 Chron. 21), battles against the Philistines (2 Sam. 21; 1 Chron. 20), and an elaborate collection of construction materials for the temple (1 Chron. 29). Lists include his mighty men (2 Sam. 23), the Levitical and priestly divisions (1 Chron. 23—24), the singers (1 Chron. 25), the gatekeepers (1 Chron. 26), and the military structure (1 Chron. 27).

A number of striking military figures swirled around David's career. Four of the most prominent were

- Asahel: a fast runner who was murdered by Abner

- Abner: Saul's general that later came to David's side but was murdered by Joab

- Joab: the commander who helped David take Jerusalem and who stayed loyal to David in the revolt of Absalom

- Amasa: captain of the rebel forces under Absalom but later made captain of David's army in place of Joab

Second Book of Samuel

This historical narrative, originally part of the same composition as 1 Samuel, describes events from Saul's death to David's last days (about 1110-970 B.C.). The key word for the book is "David"; the key text is 2 Samuel 7:16. **One-Sentence Summary:** *David's reign over Israel included times of elation, such as his conquest of Jerusalem and the Lord's promise of an everlasting dynasty, as well as times of failure, such as his adultery with Bathsheba and the treason of his son Absalom.*

David

More space is given to the adventures and rule of David than any other Israelite king. Raised by God from a shepherd to the founding king of an eternal dynasty, David was known as a man after God's heart. Not only did the biblical authors write about him, he also composed a number of psalms preserved in the Bible. From a chronological perspective, his life may be organized into two unequal portions: thirty years before he became king (probably anointed at age fifteen and in Saul's service for fifteen years) and forty years as Israel's greatest king. David lived about 1040–970 B.C.

Among the greatest of David's accomplishments were the gifted musical compositions that have been preserved in the Psalms. From his earliest days David was known as a skillful player of the harp, a hand-held stringed instrument (1 Sam. 16:23; 18:10). The relocation of the ark of the covenant was accompanied by David leading an entire orchestra (2 Sam. 6:5). One of David's psalms was preserved in 2 Samuel 22 (parallel to Psalm 18). Because of the great role that the book of Psalms has had in the worship life of God's people throughout the centuries, David's musical contribution as Israel's singer should be valued as much as his military and political successes (2 Sam. 23:1). For the rest of Scripture, the presence of music and singing by choirs is always connected with true worship.

Portion of a restored lyre: a stringed instrument plucked with the fingers. The tortoise shell served as a sound box. This was the type of instrument David played. Some translations call it a harp.

The Psalms

This compilation of religious poetry is timeless. The individual psalms were composed by a variety of poets, but David is credited with more than seventy of them. The collection grew over the years and was probably not edited into its present form until about 400 B.C. The key word for the book is "hallelujah" ("praise the LORD"); the key text is Psalm 150:6. **One-Sentence Summary:** *God, the true and glorious King, is worthy of all praise and prayer, thanksgiving and confidence—whatever the occasion in personal or community life.*

Like Samuel before him, David left the people of God with a final charge (2 Sam. 23). David's appointment of Solomon as his successor (after an abortive effort by Adonijah, David's oldest surviving son) and his death are recorded in 1 Kings 1—2 and 1 Chronicles 29.

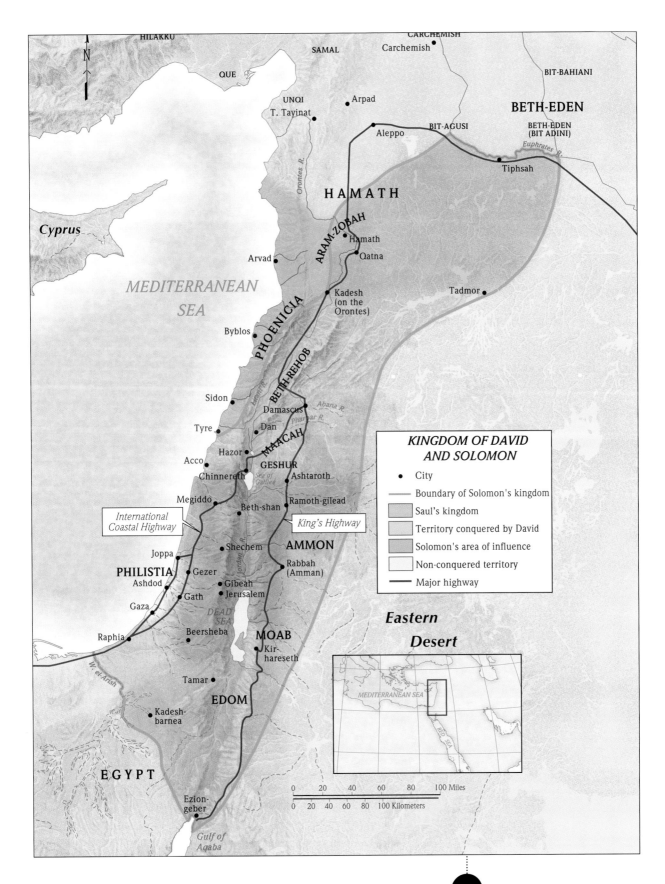

HILAKKU

CARCHEMISH
Carchemish

SAMAL

BIT-BAHIANI

QUE

UNQI
T. Tayinat

Arpad

BETH-EDEN

BIT-AGUSI

Aleppo

BETH-EDEN
(BIT ADINI)

Euphrates R.

Tiphsah

Orontes R.

HAMATH

Cyprus

ARAM-ZOBAH

Hamath

Qatna

Arvad

Tadmor

MEDITERRANEAN
SEA

Kadesh
(on the
Orontes)

PHOENICIA

Byblos

BETH-REHOB

Litani R.

Abana R.

Sidon

Damascus

Pharpar R.

Dan

Tyre

MAACAH

Acco

Hazor

GESHUR

Chinnereth

*Sea of
Galilee*

Ashtaroth

Megiddo

Beth-shan

Ramoth-gilead

**International
Coastal Highway**

Jordan R.

King's Highway

Shechem

AMMON

Joppa

Rabbah
(Amman)

PHILISTIA

Gezer

Ashdod

Gibeah

Gath

Jerusalem

Gaza

*DEAD
SEA*

Raphia

Beersheba

MOAB

Kir-
hareseth

W. et-Arish

Tamar

EDOM

Eastern

Desert

Kadesh-
barnea

EGYPT

Ezion-
geber

*Gulf of
Aqaba*

KINGDOM OF DAVID
AND SOLOMON

• City

— Boundary of Solomon's kingdom

Saul's kingdom

Territory conquered by David

Solomon's area of influence

Non-conquered territory

— Major highway

MEDITERRANEAN SEA

*RED
SEA*

| 0 | 20 | 40 | 60 | 80 | 100 Miles |

| 0 | 20 | 40 | 60 | 80 | 100 Kilometers |

Two views of the tripartite building at Megiddo, a building dating from the period of King Solomon, 970-930 B.C.

The Song of Solomon

In this romantic poem, an example of Hebrew wisdom literature, Solomon celebrated two lovers expressing their intimate feelings. The key word for the book is "beloved"; the key text is Song of Solomon 6:3. **One-Sentence Summary:** *A bride and groom (or wife and husband) celebrate with exuberant passion God's wonderful gift of the love they share by describing the intimate dimensions of their love—physical, emotional, and spiritual.*

SOLOMON'S YEARS

The era of Solomon must be regarded as the greatest flowering of Israelite civilization, told fairly briefly in **1 KINGS 1—11** and **2 CHRONICLES 1—9**. From a human point of view, the great wealth and considerable military influence that Solomon exercised in the Middle East of his day can be attributed to the weakness of surrounding civilizations. Neither the Egyptians to the south nor the Mesopotamians (Assyria and Babylon) were in a time of aggression or strength. From the perspective of the Kingdom Story, however, Solomon's forty-year rule was the time when, at last, what God had promised beginning with the call of Abraham (Genesis 12) was fulfilled. Chapter One of the Kingdom Story, "God Builds His Nation," reached its highest point. Solomon's life lasted some sixty years, about 990–930 B.C.

SOLOMON'S CHILDHOOD

Solomon was the "replacement baby" born to Bathsheba and David after the child born of their adultery died (2 Sam. 12:24-25). He was the divinely designated heir to the throne and recipient of the Davidic covenant. This shows, yet again, God's sovereign grace in dealing with individuals. The date of Solomon's birth is unknown, but he may have been about twenty when he came to the throne. He was surely aware of the circumstances surrounding his mother's marriage to his father and of the family turmoil that his older half brothers brought about. He clearly inherited his father's literary gift of writing, for he was credited with 3,000 proverbs and 1,005 songs (1 Kings 4:32). **THE SONG OF SOLOMON**, a long, passionate love poem, perhaps composed before Solomon ascended to the throne, is an early example of his skill.

SOLOMON'S SUCCESS AS KING

Because David established a firm foundation for the monarchy, Solomon enjoyed the greatest prestige and honor of any of the kings of Israel. When the Lord asked Solomon to name the blessing he desired, he chose wisdom to rule. God abundantly granted his request and promised riches and honor as well (1 Kings 3). Many of Solomon's insights are recorded in the **PROVERBS**, although other wise people also contributed to it.

From the perspective of Israel as a complete nation, Solomon is best known for building the magnificent temple to honor Yahweh's name. Construction began in the fourth year of his reign (about 966) and continued to its dedication seven years later (about 959), as recorded in 1 Kings 6. First Chronicles 3:1 notes that the temple site in Jerusalem was both "Mount Moriah"—thus connecting it to the Abrahamic covenant—and the threshing floor purchased by Solomon's father—thus connecting it to the Davidic covenant.

Book of Proverbs

Written entirely in Hebrew poetry, this book of wisdom literature was composed mainly by Solomon. It emphasizes short maxims that showed God's people how to live skillfully. The key word for the book is "wisdom"; the key text is Proverbs 3:5-6. **One-Sentence Summary:** *Those who follow God's wise design for living—particularly in areas of sexual purity and integrity of speech—avoid the perils that others fall into and enjoy life on earth as God meant it to be lived.*

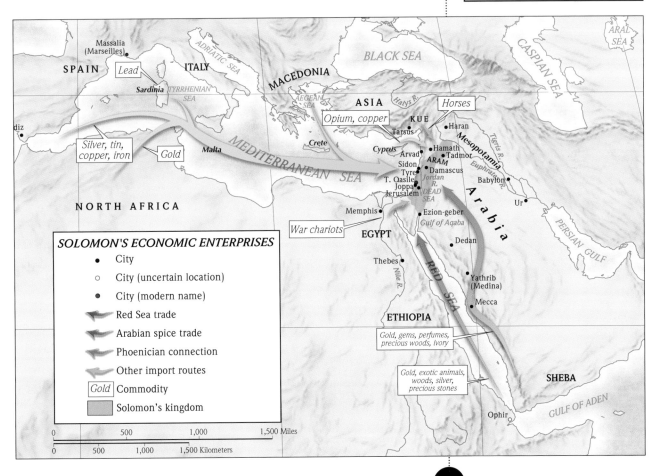

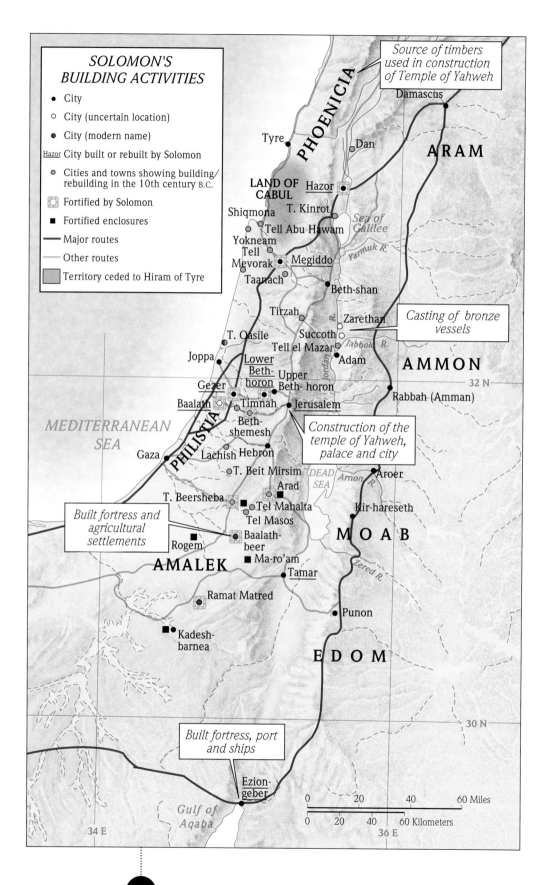

SOLOMON'S BUILDING ACTIVITIES

- • City
- ○ City (uncertain location)
- ● City (modern name)
- <u>Hazor</u> City built or rebuilt by Solomon
- ◉ Cities and towns showing building/ rebuilding in the 10th century B.C.
- ⊡ Fortified by Solomon
- ■ Fortified enclosures
- ▬ Major routes
- ▬ Other routes
- ▨ Territory ceded to Hiram of Tyre

Source of timbers used in construction of Temple of Yahweh

PHOENICIA

Damascus

ARAM

Tyre

Dan

LAND OF CABUL

Hazor

T. Kinrot

Sea of Galilee

Shiqmona

Tell Abu Hawam

Yokneam

Tell Mevorak

Megiddo

Yarmuk R.

Taanach

Beth-shan

Tirzah

Zarethan

Casting of bronze vessels

Succoth

Tell el Mazar

Jabbok R.

Adam

AMMON

Joppa

Lower Beth-horon

Upper Beth-horon

32 N

T. Qasile

Gezer

Jerusalem

Rabbah (Amman)

Baalath

Timnah

Beth-shemesh

Construction of the temple of Yahweh, palace and city

MEDITERRANEAN SEA

PHILISTIA

Gaza

Lachish

Hebron

T. Beit Mirsim

DEAD SEA

Arnon R.

Aroer

Arad

T. Beersheba

Tel Mahalta

Kir-hareseth

Tel Masos

Built fortress and agricultural settlements

Rogem

Baalath-beer

M O A B

AMALEK

Ma-ro'am

Tamar

Zered R.

Ramat Matred

Punon

Kadesh-barnea

E D O M

30 N

Built fortress, port and ships

Eziongeber

| 0 | 20 | 40 | 60 Miles |

| 0 | 20 | 40 | 60 Kilometers |

Gulf of Aqaba

34 E

36 E

With the completion of the temple, the ark of the covenant containing the Ten Commandments (connecting the temple to the Sinaitic covenant) was moved to its final home. It remained there until the Babylonians destroyed it when they burned the temple (586 B.C.). God's glory filled Solomon's temple at its dedication as He had earlier filled the wilderness tabernacle at its dedication (Exod. 40:34; 2 Chron. 7:1). The magnificent and extravagant consecration ceremony, with thousands of animals sacrificed, Solomon's dedication prayer, and God's response stand as a great reaffirmation of the eternal nature of the Davidic covenant (2 Chron. 6—7).

The success of Solomon in a variety of activities is told briefly:

- Stunning judicial wisdom (1 Kings 3)
- Lavish and extravagant food (1 Kings 4)
- A palatial dwelling larger than the temple (1 Kings 7)
- Fortifying such strategic cities as Hazor, Megiddo, and Gezer (1 Kings 9)
- Dazzling the fabled queen of Sheba (1 Kings 10; 2 Chron. 9)
- Success in international trade, as much as 25 tons of gold annually (1 Kings 10)
- Building a large standing military, including cavalry and chariots (2 Chron. 9)

Temple of Solomon

The temple was constructed of the costliest building materials available, including 600 talents (23 tons) of gold. By modern standards it was small, 60 cubits by 20 cubits by 30 cubits (90 feet by 30 feet by 45 feet). Everything about it was designed to show the magnificence of Yahweh, the God of Israel. It was the final element for consummating the earthly manifestation of God's kingdom. Solomon's temple went through several cycles of neglect and repair until the Babylonians destroyed it 373 years after its dedication. Solomon's temple stood from about 959 to 586 B.C.

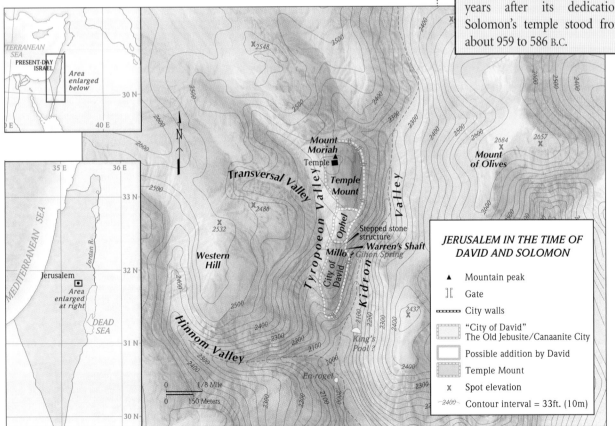

JERUSALEM IN THE TIME OF DAVID AND SOLOMON

▲   Mountain peak

⫩   Gate

┅┅┅   City walls

▢   "City of David" The Old Jebusite/Canaanite City

▢   Possible addition by David

▢   Temple Mount

x   Spot elevation

‑2400‑   Contour interval = 33ft. (10m)

Excavation trench through what has been identified as Solomon's Palace at Megiddo in Israel (962–922 B.C.)

For this brief period Jerusalem was truly crowned with glory and honor. The seed of Abraham occupied the land promised in the Abrahamic covenant; the laws of God and the worship of God were implemented at the temple in fulfillment of the Sinaitic covenant; and the son of David was ruling in fulfillment of the Davidic covenant. The queen of Sheba rightly understood all this as an expression of God's wonderful love for His covenant people (2 Chron. 9:8). The author of 1 Kings 10:23-25 summarized this as well.

Solomon inherited not only his father's love of composition, but also his father's love of many wives. His 700 royal wives and 300 concubines led him away from wholehearted devotion to God (1 Kings 11:4). He accommodated their religious wishes and allowed them to bring idol worship back into the land. Solomon himself was led astray, and God pronounced judgment that Solomon's successor would rule over a much smaller kingdom (Judah alone), while the rest of the tribes would follow a rival king.

Further, Solomon's use of forced labor and high taxes were deeply resented. God allowed a number of adversaries to come against Solomon, the most serious of whom was Jeroboam, who would later wrest the northern tribes from Solomon's son. During his last years Solomon reflected on everything he had achieved and wrote his thoughts in the Bible's most pessimistic book, ECCLESIASTES.

Solomon died after ruling forty years, but at a younger age than his predecessors. With his death the brief era of Israel's united monarchy came to an end.

CONCLUSION

In the space of something over a thousand years, God built His nation to its most perfect earthly expression.

1. Beginning with one family, He laid a foundation through the patriarchs, promising through the Abrahamic covenant that Abraham's many descendants would one day live in their land (2091–1805 B.C.).

2. After Abraham's descendants entered Egypt and grew to nation-size, God brought about the pivotal event, using Moses to set them free from bondage by His mighty hand (1876–1446 B.C.).

3. After salvation the Lord gave them His laws in the Sinaitic covenant by Moses, as well as a land to live in by Joshua (1446–1380 B.C.).

4. The final part of God's plan, after the seeming delay of the judges' era, was to establish a permanent dynasty through the Davidic covenant and to bring to the world a magnificent temple in which His redeemed people would worship Him (1380–931 B.C.).

The grand summary of the Bible is *The Lord God through His Christ is graciously building a kingdom of redeemed people for their joy and for His own glory.* We have seen now that God fully succeeded in building His nation. In the next chapter in the Kingdom Story, God will succeed in His purposes, but His plan involved demolishing the nation that He had taken centuries to build.

Ecclesiastes

This piece of "speculative wisdom" literature was composed in a mixture of prose and poetry and written in unusual Hebrew. The insights of Ecclesiastes come from late in Solomon's reign—after he had experienced everything life had to offer and was contemplating "what's it all about?" The key word for the book is "vanity" (or "absurdity"); the key text is Ecclesiastes 1:2–12:8. **One-Sentence Summary:** *Although human beings can accumulate many things, accomplish much, and achieve great wisdom, these are without profit and ultimately pointless unless one has lived in fear and obedience to God.*

REFLECTIVE QUESTIONS

1. How important is it to accept the logic that the Abrahamic covenant was completely unconditional on Abraham's part? Do you agree or disagree? Why?

2. Which secondary character from early in Chapter One is more interesting to you, Job or Melchizedek? Which would you rather meet? What do you find interesting?

3. Which family of the patriarchs do you most admire: Abraham and Sarah, Isaac and Rebekah, or Jacob and Rachel? What would you ask if you could interview them?

4. Was it wrong for Jacob and his family to leave the promised land and settle in Egypt? Why or why not?

5. About 3,500 years ago God revealed his name "the Lord" (Yahweh) to Moses. What implications should this name have for God's people today?

6. According to Exodus, God's judgment on the Egyptians means that thousands of Egyptian babies were killed. How do you reconcile this with the love of God? Does God have the right to do the same thing today?

7. In what sense are the Ten Commandments a valid expression of God's moral will today? Should the Ten Commandments be preached? Why, if Christians are not under the law?

8. How important is it to understand that the Sinaitic covenant was conditional and is now obsolete (Heb. 8:13)? What does this imply about Jews of today?

9. The elaborate requirements for the priests, the sacrifices, and the tabernacle suggest that God is concerned about forms of worship as well as motives for worship. How can God's people today be sure of the proper forms of worship?

10. What should "holiness" mean for God's people today? Do you think of yourself as holy? Why should holiness matter if salvation is by faith?

11. Was it fair for thousands of Israelites to wander (and die) in the wilderness for forty years just because of ten discouraged scouts? Explain your answer.

12. Why do you think the Old Testament gives more space to the life and teachings of Moses than to any other character?

13. Who was greater in the Kingdom Story, Abraham or Moses? Why do you say so?

14. Today the religion of Islam claims that "holy war" is a valid part of their religion. The book of Joshua shows that "holy war" was an important part of Israel's history. Are both right? Are both wrong? How should modern Christians understand "holy war"?

15. At the time of the judges, God delivered sinful Israelites to their enemies and then delivered them from their enemies. How can both be true? Why would God do this?

16. Which of the four greatest judges do you find the most intriguing, Deborah, Gideon, Jephthah, or Samson? Explain.

17. The four leading characters of Israel's early monarchy were Samuel, Saul, David, and Solomon. All of them had major family troubles. Which of these would you prefer to have as an earthly father? Why?

18. What impact should the Davidic covenant have on Christians today? What do you think the future holds for the Davidic covenant?

19. Why does the completion of Solomon's temple represent the climax of Chapter One of the Kingdom Story?

20. Which Bible book is more important to you, Psalms or Proverbs? Why?

21. How does God's redemption of His people work itself out in Chapter One of the Kingdom Story?

22. What evidences of God's glory are evident in Chapter One of the Kingdom Story?

23. What evidences of joy in the lives of God's redeemed people do you see in Chapter One of the Kingdom Story?

---

[1] Dates for events prior to David and Solomon are disputed. Furthermore, most events mentioned in the Bible can be dated only approximately (within a year or two). This book follows the traditional dating for an early (fifteenth-century B.C.) exodus, taking the statement in 1 Kings 6:1 (480 years between the exodus and Solomon's fourth year) as precisely literal, rather than figurative, as do those who argue for a late (thirteenth-century B.C.) exodus. See also Exodus 12:40 for the total time that the Israelites were in Egypt (430 years).

[2] This was probably Thutmose III of the Eighteenth Dynasty. If so, the pharaoh whom Moses challenged at the time of the plagues was Amenhotep II. According to scholars who hold to a "late exodus view," the pharaoh angry with Moses was Sethos I of the Nineteenth Dynasty and the pharaoh of the exodus was Rameses II.

God Educates His Nation

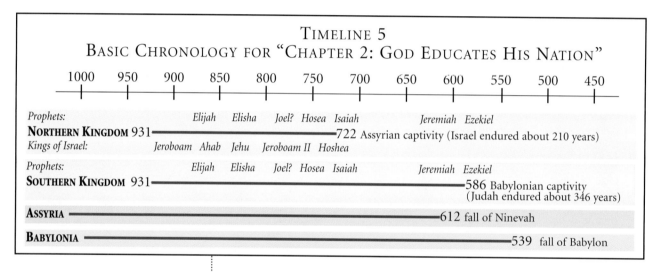

TIMELINE 5
BASIC CHRONOLOGY FOR "CHAPTER 2: GOD EDUCATES HIS NATION"

1000	950	900	850	800	750	700	650	600	550	500	450

Prophets: Elijah   Elisha   Joel?   Hosea   Isaiah   Jeremiah   Ezekiel

NORTHERN KINGDOM 931 ——————————————722 Assyrian captivity (Israel endured about 210 years)

Kings of Israel: Jeroboam   Ahab   Jehu   Jeroboam II   Hoshea

Prophets: Elijah   Elisha   Joel?   Hosea   Isaiah   Jeremiah   Ezekiel

SOUTHERN KINGDOM 931 ——————————————586 Babylonian captivity
(Judah endured about 346 years)

ASSYRIA ————————————612 fall of Ninevah

BABYLONIA ————————————539 fall of Babylon

Basal relief of Assyrian soldiers dating from the 7th century B.C. This was found at Tainat. The soldier is carrying a severed head and is walking among headless bodies. Isaiah (10:5-7) describes the brutality of the Assyrians and sees them as a club in God's hand.

Disobedient Israel Disciplined,
931–586 B.C.

For more than a thousand years, God had worked His plan to bring about His nation of redeemed people. After redeeming His people from Egyptian slavery, the culmination of Chapter One of His plan was to establish an everlasting covenant that pledged an ongoing dynasty of David. The magnificent temple that Solomon built stood in the fabulously wealthy city of Jerusalem. God's redeemed, covenant people had their place, their royal leader, and their laws.

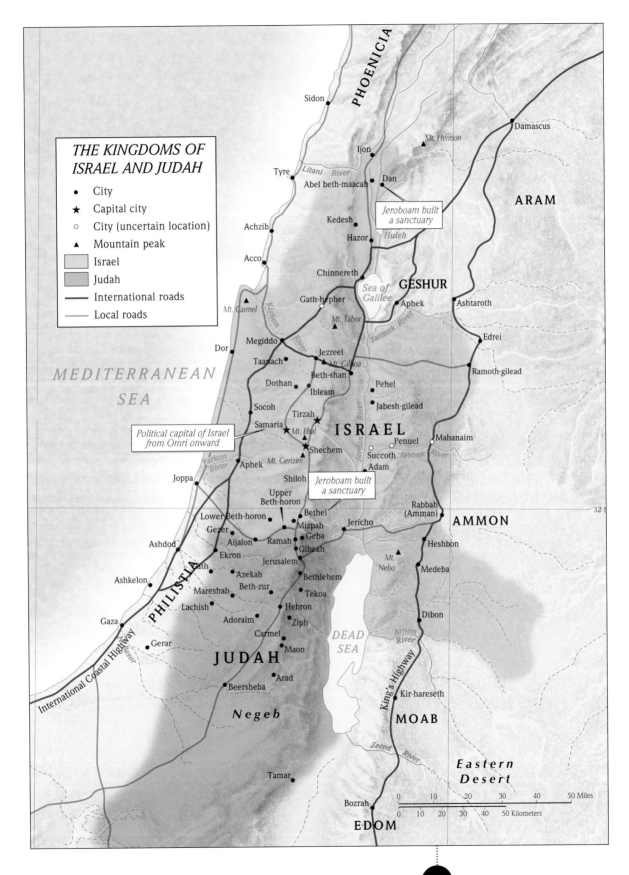

THE KINGDOMS OF
ISRAEL AND JUDAH

- • City
- ★ Capital city
- ○ City (uncertain location)
- ▲ Mountain peak
- Israel
- Judah
- ——— International roads
- ——— Local roads

PHOENICIA

Sidon

Damascus

▲ Mt. Hermon

Ijon

Tyre Litani River

Abel beth-maacah Dan

ARAM

Jeroboam built
a sanctuary

Achzib

Kedesh

Hazor Huleh

Acco

Chinnereth

GESHUR

Mt. Carmel

Gath-hepher

Sea of
Galilee

Aphek

Ashtaroth

Kishon River

▲ Mt. Tabor

Dor

Megiddo

Jezreel

Edrei

MEDITERRANEAN

SEA

Taanach

▲ Mt. Gilboa

Beth-shan

Ramoth-gilead

Dothan

Ibleam

Pehel

Socoh

Jabesh-gilead

Samaria

Tirzah

Jordan River

Political capital of Israel
from Omri onward

★ Mt. Ebal

ISRAEL

Mahanaim

Shechem

Penuel

Aphek

Mt. Gerizim

Succoth Jabbok River

Yarkon
River

Shiloh

Adam

Joppa

Upper
Beth-horon

Bethel

Jeroboam built
a sanctuary

Lower Beth-horon

Mizpah

Jericho

Rabbah
(Amman)

AMMON

Gezer

Ramah Geba

Heshbon

Ashdod

Aijalon

Gibeah

Ekron

Jerusalem

Gath

Azekah

Bethlehem

▲ Mt.
Nebo

Medeba

Ashkelon

Mareshah Beth-zur

Tekoa

Lachish

Hebron

DEAD
SEA

Dibon

Gaza

Adoraim

Ziph

Arnon River

PHILISTIA

Carmel

Gerar

Maon

King's Highway

Kir-hareseth

Besor

Arad

JUDAH

Beersheba

MOAB

International Coastal Highway

Negeb

Eastern
Desert

Tamar

Zered River

Bozrah

0 10 20 30 40 50 Miles

0 10 20 30 40 50 Kilometers

EDOM

32

A bronze bull found in Antioch of Pisidia (Antakya, Turkey). Dates possibly from the 9th–8th century B.C.

As the Introduction noted, the grand summary of the Bible is, *The Lord God through His Christ is graciously building a kingdom of redeemed people for their joy and for His own glory.* Chapter Two in God's plan was to educate His people about the consequences of sin. Throughout their long national history, Israel had violated the terms of the Lord's covenant with them. In particular they violated the first three of the Ten Commandments (no other gods, no idols, honoring the Lord's name; see Exod. 20:3-7). Over and over they had stumbled, beginning with the disastrous affair of Aaron and the golden calf idol, on through the cycle of idolatry during the period of the judges, and culminating in Solomon's defection.

In His great mercy God now intended to teach His people a lesson they would never forget. Chapter Two of the Kingdom Story about God redeeming an eternal kingdom people, told in 1 Kings 12 through 2 Kings 25, can be compressed to a simple truth, *God educates His nation.* Once they had completed their education in the Lord's schoolroom, the people He called by His name learned the lesson well. They knew that only those who have no other gods, keep no idols, and revere the Lord's name could be called kingdom people.

The children of Israel compromised by worshiping other gods during the entire time they lived in the promised land. God raised the prophets to be His special spokesmen to urge people to repent of idolatry and injustice, to warn of the coming "day of the LORD" in judgment. They also predicted the coming of Messiah more clearly than ever during the events of Chapter Two. Their predictions occupy a massive place in the overall Kingdom Story. In their own day, however, the prophets' message was largely ignored. This chapter carries the plot of the Kingdom Story from the division of the nation (because of sin) to its captivity (because of sin).

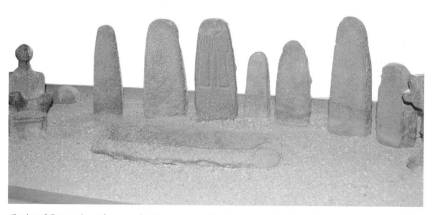

Copies of Canaanite stelae to gods. Note on one stele the upraised hands as though in prayer.

NATION DIVIDED:
NINETY YEARS OF FIGHTING BETWEEN ISRAEL AND JUDAH (931–841 B.C.)

The tomb of Cyrus the Great. It bore the following inscription: "Mortal! I am Cyrus, son of Cambyse, who founded the Persian Empire, and was Lord of Asia."

With the death of Solomon around 931 B.C., the nation of Israel began a sharp decline. The first step was God's division of the people into a Northern Kingdom (called Israel or Samaria, ruled by several dynasties of kings, all wicked) and a Southern Kingdom (called Judah, ruled by kings of the Davidic dynasty, some good and some wicked). For most of the ninety years they were at each other's throats, although they reached a truce by royal intermarriage by the end of this period. Periodically the two rival kingdoms warred against each other, draining their economic and human resources. At the same time the surrounding nations began picking off parts of these rival kingdoms.

The great Prophet Elijah became God's messenger to call the people back to true worship, ushering in a new breed of prophet, the "independent prophet." The only Davidic king to lead his people into a religious revival during this period was Asa, Solomon's great-grandson. The worst king of all was Ahab of Israel, whose evil wife Jezebel vigorously promoted idolatry.

REHOBOAM OF JUDAH AND HIS TWO SUCCESSORS

The compiler of the long account found in 1 and 2 Kings alternated between what happened to the Northern kings and what happened to the Southern kings. The compiler of 2 Chronicles focused only on the kings of the Davidic dynasty (the Southern kings). **1 KINGS 12—16** and **2 CHRONICLES 10—16** are the primary biblical passages that tell of the first three kings of Judah and the first five kings of Israel.

REHOBOAM

Solomon's son Rehoboam lost the Northern tribes to the rebel leader Jeroboam. From a human perspective this loss came because Rehoboam followed foolish political advice. From a divine perspective his loss fulfilled God's punishment of Solomon's sins (1 Kings 12). Rehoboam—whose mother was a pagan princess—turned the people away from the Lord and introduced idol worship. Five years into Rehoboam's reign God allowed a new, aggressive pharaoh (Shishak) to invade Judah and haul much of Solomon's fabulous wealth to Egypt (926 B.C.). Rehoboam was able to fortify a number of cities throughout Judah, but his rule of seventeen years was spent in constant petty warfare against Jeroboam's kingdom to the north (2 Chronicles 12).

Second Book of Chronicles

This historical narrative describes events from the beginning of Solomon's reign until the first year that Cyrus of Persia ruled (more than 430 years, about 970–538 B.C.). The book was possibly written by Ezra after the Israelites returned from exile. This book traces the history of the temple, from its dedication, through several repairs, and through its destruction. The key word for the book is "temple"; the key texts are 2 Chronicles 7:1 and 36:18. **One-Sentence Summary:** *After Solomon's glorious reign, which culminated in the dedication of the temple, kings of the Davidic dynasty—some righteous and some evil—continued ruling in Jerusalem, ending in the destruction of the temple and the Hebrews' exile to Babylon.*

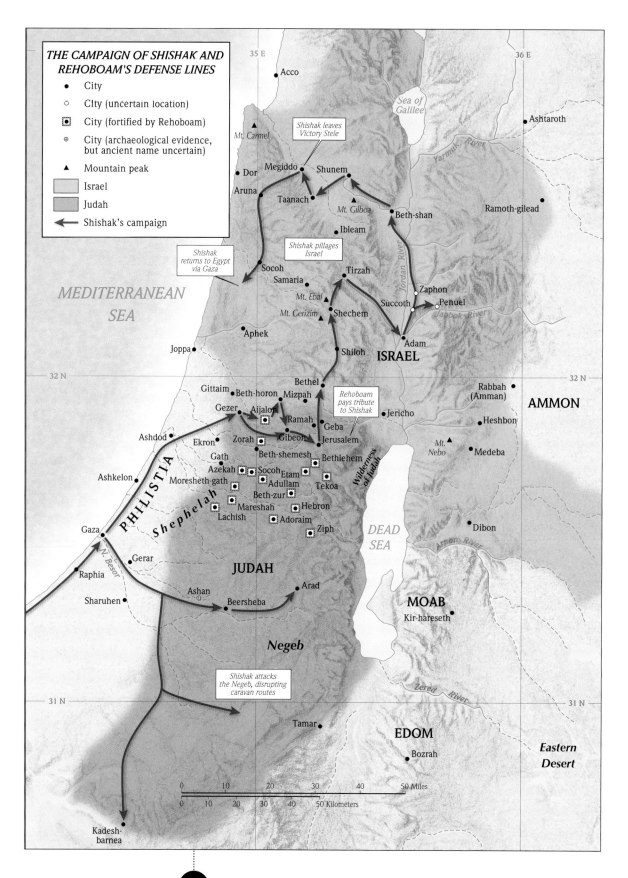

THE CAMPAIGN OF SHISHAK AND
REHOBOAM'S DEFENSE LINES

- ● City
- ↻ City (uncertain location)
- ◉ City (fortified by Rehoboam)
- ⊕ City (archaeological evidence,
  but ancient name uncertain)
- ▲ Mountain peak
- Israel
- Judah
- → Shishak's campaign

Shishak leaves
Victory Stele

Shishak pillages
Israel

Shishak
returns to Egypt
via Gaza

Rehoboam pays tribute
to Shishak

Shishak attacks
the Negeb, disrupting
caravan routes

35 E
36 E

Sea of
Galilee

Acco

Ashtaroth

Mt. Carmel

Megiddo
Shunem

Dor
Aruna
Taanach
Mt. Gilboa
Beth-shan
Ramoth-gilead

Ibleam

MEDITERRANEAN
SEA

Socoh
Tirzah
Samaria
Zaphon
Mt. Ebal
Succoth
Penuel
Mt. Gerizim
Shechem
Jabbok River

Aphek
Shiloh
Adam
ISRAEL

Joppa

32 N
32 N

Gittaim
Bethel
Rabbah
(Amman)
Beth-horon
Mizpah
AMMON
Gezer
Aijalon
Ramah
Jericho
Heshbon
Ashdod
Ekron
Zorah
Gibeon
Geba
Gath
Beth-shemesh
Jerusalem
Mt.
Nebo
Medeba
Azekah
Socoh
Etam
Bethlehem
Moresheth-gath
Adullam
Tekoa
Beth-zur
Wilderness
of Judah
Mareshah
Hebron
Lachish
Adoraim
Ziph
DEAD
SEA
Gaza
Dibon
Gerar
JUDAH
Raphia
N. Besor
Arad
Ashan
Sharuhen
Beersheba
MOAB
Kir-hareseth
Arnon River
Negeb
31 N
31 N

Tamar
EDOM
Bozrah
Eastern
Desert
Zered River

PHILISTIA
Shephelah

0   10   20   30   40   50 Miles
0   10 20 30 40 50 Kilometers

Kadesh-
barnea

Abijah

Rehoboam's son Abijah continued his father's policy of going to war against Jeroboam's kingdom. He gained one huge military victory against Jeroboam, but his reign lasted only three years (2 Chronicles 13).

Asa and His Temple Reform

Abijah's son Asa came to the throne exactly a century after his great-great-grandfather David began to rule. He was the fifth king of the Davidic dynasty to rule, beginning while he was young and reigning from Jerusalem for 41 years, longer than any king thus far. Some fifteen years into his rule (about 895, some 64 years after Solomon dedicated the temple in 959), Asa instigated a reform of the worship of Yahweh. The aging altar in front of the temple was repaired, and the king led the people of Judah to renew their covenant relationship with the Lord (2 Chron. 15:8-15). His ways were so righteous—including opposing his pagan grandmother—that the biblical writer compared him favorably to David (1 Kings 15:11-15).

Years later, however, when the current king of Israel (Baasha) built a fortress at Ramah near Jerusalem, Asa panicked. Instead of relying on God, he bribed Ben-hadad the king of Syria/Aram to attack Baasha. As divine punishment Asa's later years were characterized by warfare as well as by a terrible foot disease. His son Jehoshaphat co-ruled with him for three years before his death.

Interior of Bubastite portal with inscription of Shishak's campaign in Palestine (p. 75).

JEROBOAM OF ISRAEL AND FOUR SUCCESSORS

Jeroboam I

Palace coups and revolts led by a king's general are the familiar stuff of history. The story of the Northern Kingdom of Israel is full of such intrigue. Jeroboam, one of Solomon's officials in charge of forced labor, received word from God that he was to become ruler over the Northern tribes. He fled to the safety of Egypt until Solomon's death and then returned to challenge Rehoboam, capitalizing on the discontent of the Northern tribes under Solomon. He successfully led Israel (the Northern tribes) into revolt and established his own throne, first in the city of Shechem and finally in the city of Tirzah. He ruled a total of 22 years.

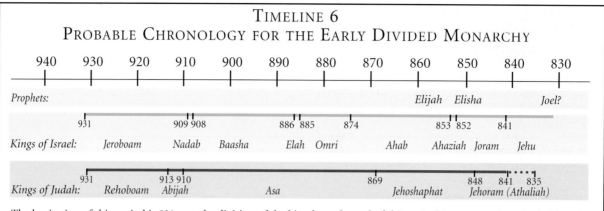

TIMELINE 6
PROBABLE CHRONOLOGY FOR THE EARLY DIVIDED MONARCHY

940	930	920	910	900	890	880	870	860	850	840	830

Prophets: Elijah   Elisha   Joel?

Kings of Israel: 931   909 908   886 885   874   853 852   841
Jeroboam   Nadab   Baasha   Elah   Omri   Ahab   Ahaziah   Joram   Jehu

Kings of Judah: 931   913 910   869   848 841 835
Rehoboam   Abijah   Asa   Jehoshaphat   Jehoram (Athaliah)

The beginning of this period is 931 B.C., the division of the kingdom; the end of this period is 841 B.C., the coup led by Jehu. (Kings ruling a year or less are not included; in cases of co-regency, date is for beginning of sole rule/death of predecessor.)

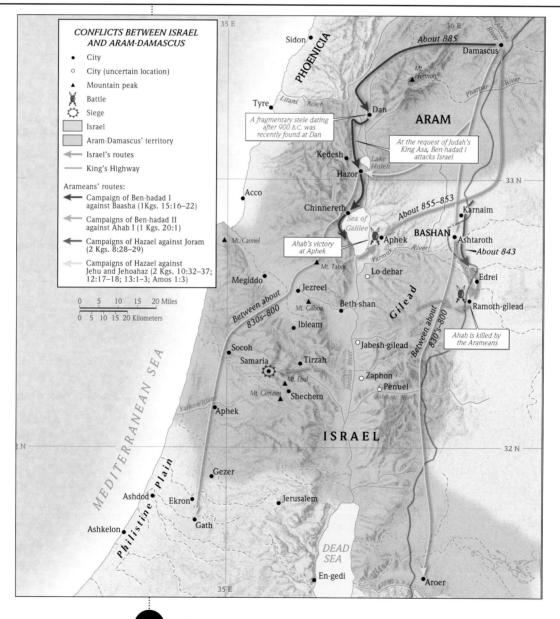

CONFLICTS BETWEEN ISRAEL AND ARAM-DAMASCUS

- • City
- ○ City (uncertain location)
- ▲ Mountain peak
- Battle
- Siege
- Israel
- Aram-Damascus' territory
- ← Israel's routes
- King's Highway

Arameans' routes:
- Campaign of Ben-hadad I against Baasha (1Kgs. 15:16–22)
- Campaigns of Ben-hadad II against Ahab I (1 Kgs. 20:1)
- Campaigns of Hazael against Joram (2 Kgs. 8:28–29)
- Campaigns of Hazael against Jehu and Jehoahaz (2 Kgs. 10:32–37; 12:17–18; 13:1–3; Amos 1:3)

0 5 10 15 20 Miles
0 5 10 15 20 Kilometers

A fragmentary stele dating after 900 B.C. was recently found at Dan

At the request of Judah's King Asa, Ben-hadad I attacks Israel

Ahab's victory at Aphek

Ahab is killed by the Arameans

About 885

About 855–853

About 843

Between about 830s–800

Between about 830s–800

The altar and worship area established by Jeroboam I at Dan.

In order to secure his rebel kingdom, Jeroboam chose a two-pronged approach: military and religious. Thus, he fortified cities on both sides of the Jordan River (Shechem and Peniel). The border between Judah and Israel, only a few miles north of Jerusalem, would be challenged many times during the next centuries.

Jeroboam's most brilliant (and wicked) policy was to revise the worship of the Northern tribes in a way directly forbidden by the Lord. Because he feared that the people of his kingdom would revert to the Davidic monarch if they returned to Jerusalem to worship, Jeroboam set up two shrines as alternate places to worship the Lord. In Bethel (in southern Israel near the border with Judah) and in Dan (in northern Israel near the border with Syria/Aram) he set up gold calf-idols. This was similar to what Moses' brother Aaron had done in the wilderness (compare Exod. 32:4 with 1 Kings 12:28). These were understood either as idolatrous representations of Yahweh or else as "pedestals" for His glory (as the ark of the covenant was a "pedestal" for His presence). Jeroboam also established alternate dates for the religious festivals commanded in the Law and established priests of his own choosing.

The people of the Northern Kingdom willingly followed their king and were led astray from the true worship of God. After his death the phrase "Jeroboam son of Nebat" was used in contempt by the composer of 1 and 2 Kings because he was the one who caused Israel to sin (for example, see 1 Kings 16:26; 21:22; 2 Kings 3:3; 10:29). God had promised Jeroboam (as He had promised Saul 120 years earlier)

First Book of Kings

This historical narrative describes events from David's death through Jehoshaphat's death (about 970–848 B.C.). Its author is not known but traditionally has been assigned to Jeremiah, about 560 B.C. The key word for the book is "division"; the key text is 1 Kings 11:35-36. **One-Sentence Summary:** *After Solomon's splendid rule, culminating in the dedication of the temple in Jerusalem, the kingdom divided, and God raised up prophets to confront idolatry, notably Elijah, who opposed the evil Ahab.*

The terraced hill in Israel of Samaria (N.T. Sebaste) and the surrounding hills and plain. This is the site of the ancient fortress-city of Omri.

an eternal dynasty if Saul remained faithful. He was, however, disobedient from the beginning. He set the tone for all the Northern kings that followed him, and they would all be more (or occasionally less) idolatrous than the founder of their independent nation.

NADAB

Jeroboam's son Nadab followed his father's sinful ways. He ruled Israel for only two years (early in Asa's long reign over Judah). During battle he was assassinated by Baasha, who was possibly an army officer (1 Kings 15:25-28). Thus the dynasty established by Jeroboam included only two kings and lasted only 24 years. (The term "dynasty" is used here to mean a father-son succession to a throne.)

BAASHA

The second Northern dynasty was established by Baasha. He secured his throne by wiping out Jeroboam's family, but he was not much different religiously from Jeroboam. He had to deal with a growing military threat from the north, the forces of Ben-Hadad king of Syria/Aram, who took over a number of Baasha's cities. He led Israel from Tirzah for twenty-four years (during the time of Asa's rule over Judah).

ELAH

Baasha's son Elah succeeded him, and he followed his father's ways. He ruled over Israel for only two years (during the latter part of Asa's reign). Zimri, a commander of the king's charioteers, assassinated Elah (1 Kings 16:9-11). Thus Baasha's dynasty included only two kings and lasted only 26 years.

ZIMRI

The Northern Kingdom had come to a crisis of political instability. Zimri was king for only a week when Elah's army general, Omri, took over. Omri led a palace coup, resulting in Zimri burning the palace down around him (1 Kings 16:16-18). For four years the forces of Omri and Tibni (another rival) fought each other until Tibni died and Omri became the sole survivor.

OMRI OF ISRAEL AND HIS DYNASTY

In **1 KINGS 16—2 KINGS 8** is the narrative of the reigns of Omri, his son Ahab, his grandson Ahaziah, and another grandson Joram. By far the greatest attention is given to Ahab. Ahab's great evil became the occasion for God to raise up the Prophet Elijah, the first of many who opposed wicked kings (rather than serving as court prophets as in the days of Saul, David, and Solomon).

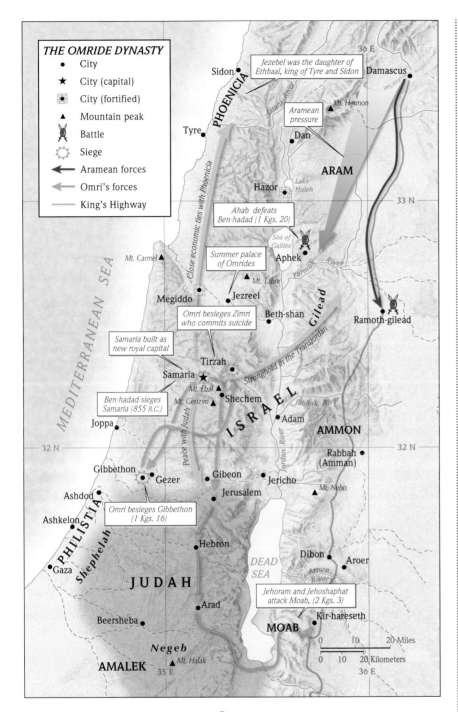

THE OMRIDE DYNASTY

- • City
- ★ City (capital)
- ▣ City (fortified)
- ▲ Mountain peak
- ⚔ Battle
- ⚙ Siege
- ← Aramean forces
- ← Omri's forces
- — King's Highway

Jezebel was the daughter of Ethbaal, king of Tyre and Sidon

Aramean pressure

Ahab defeats Ben-hadad (1 Kgs. 20)

Summer palace of Omrides

Omri besieges Zimri who commits suicide

Samaria built as new royal capital

Ben-hadad sieges Samaria (855 B.C.)

Omri besieges Gibbethon (1 Kgs. 16)

Jehoram and Jehoshaphat attack Moab, (2 Kgs. 3)

Close economic ties with Phoenicia

Stronghold in the Transjordan

peace with Judah

Sidon · Damascus · 36 E · Tyre · PHOENICIA · Litani River · Mt. Hermon · Dan · ARAM · Hazor · Lake Huleh · 33 N · Mt. Carmel ▲ · Sea of Galilee · Aphek · Yarmuk River · Mt. Tabor · Megiddo · Jezreel · Beth-shan · Gilead · Ramoth-gilead · Tirzah · Samaria ★ · Mt. Ebal ▲ · Mt. Gerizim ▲ · Shechem · Jabbok River · Adam · Joppa · AMMON · 32 N · Gibbethon · Gezer · Gibeon · Jericho · Rabbah (Amman) · Ashdod · Jerusalem · Mt. Nebo · Ashkelon · PHILISTIA · Shephelah · Hebron · Dibon · Aroer · Gaza · JUDAH · DEAD SEA · Arnon River · Jordan River · Arad · Kir-hareseth · MOAB · Beersheba · Negeb · AMALEK · Mt. Halak ▲ · 35 E · 36 E · MEDITERRANEAN SEA

0 10 20 Miles
0 10 20 Kilometers

OMRI

Although Omri's affairs are told in only thirteen verses (1 Kings 16:16-28), his rule began a change in the status of the Northern Kingdom. During the years of his dynasty (about 885–841 B.C.), Israel asserted itself as an international player in the world of its day and no longer warred openly against its sister kingdom, Judah. Omri's brilliance as a political-military leader rests on three achievements.

- He crushed the internal strife caused by Tibni. So clearly did Omri win that his twelve-year reign was reckoned from the death of Zimri.

- He moved the capital city from Tirzah to Samaria, which he built up as a fortress city to rival Jerusalem. Samaria remained the capital of Israel until the Assyrian captivity.

- He forged a political alliance with Phoenicia to the north, sealed by marrying his son Ahab to a princess of Tyre named Jezebel.

AHAB

Omri's son Ahab ruled for 22 years, overlapping with the last few years of Asa of Judah and the first years of Jehoshaphat. He was overshadowed by his wife Jezebel, who used every means at her disposal to make the religion of her homeland—the worship of Tyrian Baal—the religion of the Northern Kingdom. When Ahab had a temple to honor Baal built in his capital city of Samaria (1 Kings 16:32), he was deliberately competing with Jerusalem with its temple to Yahweh. Thus, Ahab's religious rebellion—pointing Israel to a different deity—was considered more evil than Jeroboam's rebellion, which "simply" perverted the worship of Yahweh.

Ahab's plan would have succeeded entirely—only seven thousand Israelites continued to worship the Lord (1 Kings 19:18)—if God had not raised up the thundering Elijah to turn the people back to Himself. No more dramatic moment in the history of the divided monarchy exists than Elijah's confrontation with the priests of Baal on Mount Carmel (1 Kings 18). This temporarily halted the Northern Kingdom's slide into utter rejection of the Lord.

The following are highlights of Ahab's reign from Samaria:

- Defeated an army from Syria/Aram that had laid siege to the city of Samaria (1 Kings 20)

- Defeated a large army from Syria/Aram again the following year (1 Kings 20)

- Stole a vineyard from the righteous Naboth of Jezreel and then had him murdered (1 Kings 21)

- Sealed an alliance with Jehoshaphat of Judah by marrying his daughter Athaliah to Jehoram, the crown prince of Judah (2 Chron. 18:1; 22:2)

- Led a coalition of troops from Israel and Judah to try to regain the city of Ramoth Gilead from the control of Syria/Aram (1 Kings 22)

A Phoenician wall at Herod's palace at Samaria. The wall dates from the 9th century B.C. which means it was built during the time of Omri or Ahab.

Ahab's palace in Samaria.

This last event proved to be a disaster, for it ended in Ahab's death according to the words of the prophet Micaiah. Jezebel continued to exert considerable evil influence as the queen mother while two of her sons successively served as kings in Samaria.

Ahab and Jezebel

This prince and princess became king and queen in Samaria and stand as the most evil couple described in the Old Testament. Jezebel was more aggressive than her husband, almost succeeding in turning Israel into a country of Baal worshipers. Both met with violent deaths, Ahab in a disastrous military campaign and Jezebel in a coup led by Jehu. Jezebel exerted strong influence on her sons, Ahaziah and Joram, who ruled successively after Ahab's death, and on her daughter, Athaliah, who become the tyrant queen of Judah. Strange as it seems, Ahab and Jezebel's great-grandson Joash was a king of the Davidic line, and therefore they are direct ancestors of Jesus.

Samaria

Omri of Israel named his capital city for "Shemer," the original owner of the hill. The city of Samaria rivaled Jerusalem as a military stronghold and as a political and religious center for the Northern Kingdom. In time "Samaria" was used to designate the entire Northern Kingdom. After the captivity of the Northern tribes, Samaria was resettled with non-Israelites. By the time of Jesus, Jews looked down on Samaritans as racially and religiously inferior.

AHAZIAH

Ahab's son Ahaziah ruled from Samaria only two years. He followed the evil practices of his parents and went so far as to worship a local Philistine god, Baal-zebub. (The name of this god eventually was used to refer to the devil.) He died of injuries caused by falling through an upstairs window, leaving no heir to the throne.

Baal

Meaning "lord" or "owner," there were as many Baals as there were locales in the land of Canaan. These local Baals were thought to be powerful only in their own region, but the Israelites continued to be seduced by Baal worship. Baal's female consort was Asherah, a mother goddess. The new and dangerous form of Baal worship introduced to Israel by Jezebel was that of Baal Marqart, a storm and fertility god revered in her native Tyre.

Statue of Baal, the Canaanite weather god from Minet-el-beida.

Syrian mother goddess dating from the middle to late Bronze Age.

Mount Carmel (vineyard of God) where Elijah held a contest with 450 prophets of Baal.

JORAM

Ahab's younger son Joram (sometimes spelled Jehoram) ruled from Samaria for twelve years. He was slightly better religiously than his parents were. His reign coincided with the last years of Jehoshaphat, his brother-in-law Jehoram, and his nephew Ahaziah, all Davidic kings in Jerusalem.

Early during Joram's rule, he lost control of Moab east of the Jordan, but he was able to retake it with the help of Jehoshaphat of Judah (2 Kings 3). Later on in his reign, God miraculously spared the city of Samaria from certain starvation. It had been besieged by an army of Syria/Aram led by Ben-hadad of Damascus (2 Kings 6). Joram was killed (along with his mother Jezebel and his nephew Ahaziah king of Judah) in the insurrection mounted by the general Jehu at the Lord's command (2 Kings 9).

ELIJAH, ELISHA, AND THE RISE OF INDEPENDENT PROPHETS

Elijah appears out of nowhere in the middle in the account of Ahab. Israel's king had abandoned Yahweh, and there was no legitimate priest left in the Northern Kingdom. God was still in the business of developing the Kingdom Story. He did not concede Israel to paganism but added a new tool to His educational arsenal. The Lord raised up a prophet, one who worked outside the institutional framework of officials in religion and government. (Sometimes God works to counter both "church" and "state.")

To be sure, there had been great prophets in Israel's past. Moses, Samuel, and Nathan were three of God's great spokesmen (Deut. 34:10; 1 Sam. 3:20; 2 Sam. 12:25). Such prophets, however, operated within official Israelite life and worked with the kings and priests, sometimes—as with Nathan—as court prophet even when they had to oppose something the king had done.

Elijah was the first of the independent prophets, those who worked primarily *against* the institutional kings and priests. These prophets continued their work throughout Chapter Two and Chapter Three of the Kingdom Story. Because the chosen people at last responded to the message of the independent prophets, they were spared from utter destruction.

Although Elijah wrote no Bible book, many of his successors did so. The writing prophets, authors of the Old Testament books Isaiah through Malachi, functioned in general as the Lord's spokesmen against institutionally sanctioned evil. God used them further to clarify the nature of the coming Messiah, who would one day reign over God's people in righteousness as a perfect King and Priest. So great was Elijah's role that God's entire Old Testament revelation—the Law and the Prophets—was later personified by Moses and Elijah's appearance with Jesus on the Mount of Transfiguration (Mark 9:2-4).

Elijah statue on Mount Carmel.

SURREXIT ELIAS
PROPHETA QUASI
IGNIS ET VERBUM
IPSIUS QUASI FACULA
ARDEBAT (ECCLI XLVIII,1)

Elijah

This ninth-century prophet's confrontational style, his bold "this-is-what-Yahweh-says" message, established for God's people, for all time, the idea of true prophetic ministry. Nothing is known about his background; even his hometown of Tishbe is unknown. Yet from a human point of view, Elijah was the one who single-handedly kept the Northern Kingdom from apostatizing to the worship of Baal. Strikingly, the last words of the Old Testament promised a return of Elijah, and the Gospel of Luke opens with the birth of John the Baptist, whose ministry was carried out with Elijah's spirit and power (Mal. 4:5; Luke 1:17). Elijah's age when he was called of earthly life, about 852 B.C., is not recorded.

ELIJAH'S MINISTRY

Most of **1 KINGS 17—2 KINGS 2** is about Elijah, halting what had been an uninterrupted account of the rival kings of Judah and Israel. In a sense the meaning of the name "Elijah"—Yahweh is my God—explains the essence both of his ministry and of all the later prophets. His life and ministry included the following:

- Announcing to Ahab a famine in Israel, which lasted three years (1 Kings 17)

- Being fed by ravens during the famine

- Raising to life the son of a (pagan) widow in Zarephath of Sidon

- Facing down Jezebel's priests of Baal at Mount Carmel (1 Kings 18)

- Hearing directly from God at Mount Sinai after a forty-day fast (1 Kings 19)

- Confronting Ahab about the murder of Naboth over a vineyard (1 Kings 21)

- Calling down fiery judgment on soldiers sent by Ahab's son, Ahaziah (2 Kings 1)

- Ending his earthly life by riding the whirlwind to meet his Maker (2 Kings 2)

Elijah's service was exclusively to the Northern Kingdom rather than to Judah. The exact time of his ministry is not certain, but the decade from 862 to 852 is likely.

Vistas from Mount Carmel.

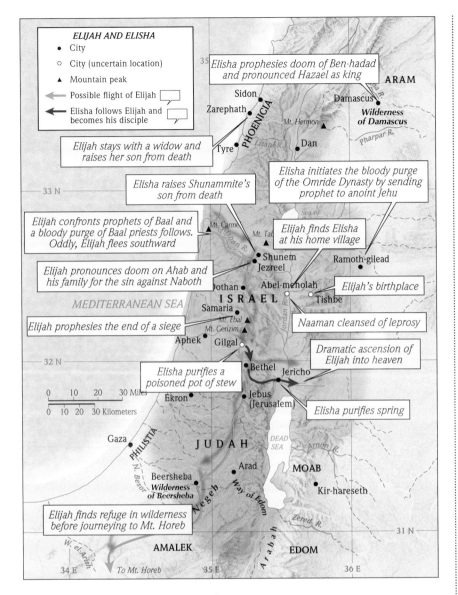

ELIJAH AND ELISHA
- City
- ○ City (uncertain location)
- ▲ Mountain peak
- ← Possible flight of Elijah
- ← Elisha follows Elijah and becomes his disciple

Elisha prophesies doom of Ben-hadad and pronounced Hazael as king

ARAM

Sidon

Damascus

Wilderness of Damascus

Zarephath

PHOENICIA

Mt. Hermon ▲

Pharpar R.

Elijah stays with a widow and raises her son from death

Tyre

Litani R.

Dan

Elisha raises Shunammite's son from death

Elisha initiates the bloody purge of the Omride Dynasty by sending prophet to anoint Jehu

Elijah confronts prophets of Baal and a bloody purge of Baal priests follows. Oddly, Elijah flees southward

Mt. Carmel ▲

Sea of

Mt. Tat ▲

Elijah finds Elisha at his home village

Shunem

Ramoth-gilead

Elijah pronounces doom on Ahab and his family for the sin against Naboth

Jezreel

Dothan

Abel-meholah

Elijah's birthplace

ISRAEL

Tishbe

MEDITERRANEAN SEA

Samaria

Mt. Ebal ▲
Mt. Gerizim ▲

Naaman cleansed of leprosy

Elijah prophesies the end of a siege

Aphek

Gilgal

Dramatic ascension of Elijah into heaven

Elisha purifies a poisoned pot of stew

Bethel

Jericho

Ekron

Jebus (Jerusalem)

Elisha purifies spring

Gaza

DEAD SEA

Arnon R.

JUDAH

PHILISTIA

N. Besor

Arad

MOAB

Beersheba

Wilderness of Beersheba

Kir-hareseth

Way of Edom

Negeb

Elijah finds refuge in wilderness before journeying to Mt. Horeb

Zered R.

31 N

W. el-Arish

AMALEK

Arabah

EDOM

To Mt. Horeb

34 E

35 E

36 E

0 10 20 30 Miles
0 10 20 30 Kilometers

32 N
33 N
35

ELISHA'S MINISTRY

Elijah's successor had a much longer ministry, all during the reigns of the Israelite kings Joram, Jehu, Jehoahaz, and Jehoash. Elisha's ministry lasted from about 852 (Elijah's ascent to heaven) until at least 798 (early in the reign of Jehoash, 2 Kings 13:10,14,20). Most of the events recorded about Elisha, told in 2 Kings 2—9, evidently come from Joram's reign. His life and ministry included the following highlights:

- Breaking decisively with his wealthy past when Elijah called him (1 Kings 19)
- Pronouncing a curse on the boys who mocked him (2 Kings 2)
- Multiplying a widow's oil so that she could pay debts (2 Kings 4)
- Raising to life the son of a (godly) woman in Shunem (2 Kings 4)

Second Book of Kings

This historical narrative describes events from Ahab's death until the thirty-seventh year of Jehoiachin's exile in Babylonia (about 853–561 B.C.). Its author is not known but traditionally has been assigned to Jeremiah (about 560 B.C.). The key word for the book is "dispersion"; the key text is 2 Kings 17:22-23. **One-Sentence Summary:** *Even after Elisha's ministry, Israel persisted in idolatry and so went into permanent captivity; yet, Judah, despite the prophets and a few righteous kings, continued to be so wicked that God sent the Babylonians to remove the people into exile.*

The Barada River in Damascus. In the Old Testament it was known as the Abana River, and it was there Naaman wanted to wash instead of washing in the Jordan as instructed by Elisha (2 Kings 5:12).

- Healing Naaman, a general from Syria/Aram, of leprosy (2 Kings 5)
- Trapping and blinding an army from Syria/Aram (2 Kings 6)
- Announcing to Hazael that he would become king of Syria/Aram (2 Kings 8)
- Having one of his fellow prophets anoint Jehu as king of Israel (2 Kings 9)

After these events there is silence concerning Elisha for more than forty years. Then his final ministry to King Jehoash is recorded in 2 Kings 13. Like his mentor Elijah, Elisha was called to restore worship of the Lord in the Northern Kingdom.

JOEL'S MINISTRY

Although he did not name the Davidic king of his time, Joel was possibly the earliest of the writing prophets. Elijah and Elisha had showed people in Israel that events affecting the agricultural cycle (such as rain) were under the Lord's control, not Baal's. Through Joel the Lord told the people of Judah that a locust plague was equally under His control and a sign of judgment yet to come—the day of the Lord.

Whether Joel's prophetic ministry was effectively received in his own lifetime is not recorded, but many later spokesmen for God developed Joel's theme of "the day of the LORD." The Book of **JOEL** introduced two long-lasting elements of biblical prophecy: "forthtelling" (a call to God's people to turn from their sins) and "foretelling" (predictions of remote events, such as the coming day of the Lord).

JEHOSHAPHAT OF JUDAH AND HIS TWO SUCCESSORS

In **2 CHRONICLES 17—22** (also 1 Kings 22:41-50; 2 Kings 8:16-29) the reigns of Jehoshaphat, Jehoram, and Ahaziah are described. This reflected a period in which Judah and Israel accepted each other as cooperating kingdoms rather than as rivals. Although Jehoshaphat was loyal to the Lord, his son and grandson abandoned the Lord in favor of Baal, leading to the first assassination of a ruling Davidic king.

JEHOSHAPHAT

Asa's son Jehoshaphat evidently shared the throne with his father for three years (because of Asa's diseased feet). He was then sole monarch for 22 years (compare 2 Kings 3:1; 8:16; 2 Chron. 20:31).

He followed the good religious example his father had set before him by following closely after the ways of the Lord. The author of 2 Chronicles 17 emphasized that because Jehoshaphat caused his people to be instructed in the law of the Lord, Judah was at peace with its enemies and enjoyed enormous prosperity (compare 2 Chron. 12:1; 17:9). According to 2 Chronicles 19, Jehoshaphat's major reform of Judah's judicial system emphasized justice and fair application of God's laws.

On the other hand Jehoshaphat made political decisions that had terrible religious consequences for the kingdom of Judah. Jehoshaphat's rule largely overlapped that of Ahab to the north. What could be more beneficial than to form an alliance between two royal houses? Thus, he arranged for his son, crown prince Jehoram, to marry Ahab's daughter Athaliah. Later on, Athaliah, in her fanatical devotion to Baal, destroyed every member of Jehoshaphat's family (except for the infant Joash).

Jehoshaphat's army joined with Ahab's army to take the city of Ramoth-gilead away from the control of Syria/Aram. This became the divinely appointed occasion for Ahab's death (2 Chron. 18). Sometime later the Lord brought an astonishing military victory to Jehoshaphat's army over an aggressive coalition from Moab and Ammon (2 Chron. 20). The noteworthiness of this victory rivaled Joshua's conquest of Jericho, and it equally brought the fear of the Lord to the surrounding nations. For the last four years of his reign, Jehoshaphat shared his rule with his son Jehoram.

Prophecy of Joel

Written entirely in Hebrew poetry, Joel is probably the earliest of the Old Testament prophetic books. Nothing is known of the author's personal life. The first hearers were people and priests living in Judah, perhaps about 800 B.C. (or as late as 500 B.C.). The key word for the book is "locusts"; the key text is Joel 1:4. **One-Sentence Summary:** *Joel proclaimed that the people of Judah should interpret a severe locust plague as a forerunner of the great and dreadful day of the Lord, which would consume the pagan nations, but also unfaithful Judah, unless the people repented.*

The hills of Gilead.

JEHORAM

Jehoshaphat's son Jehoram (sometimes spelled Joram) ruled from Jerusalem as sole king for only eight years. His brother-in-law with a similar name (Joram) was king in Samaria during the entire time he ruled. Through Jehoram and his wife Athaliah, worship of Tyrian Baal was introduced to the Southern Kingdom, one generation after it had been introduced to the Northern Kingdom by Ahab and Jezebel.

Jehoram ruled viciously, murdering his own brothers and other officials who perhaps objected to having a queen of Judah from the dynasty of Ahab. God punished Jehoram by allowing both Edom (east of the Jordan River) and Philistia (on the western coastal plain) to attack his kingdom. All his children were killed except for the youngest son, Ahaziah. God struck Jehoram with a terrible intestinal disease of which he died at age forty.

AHAZIAH

Jehoram's 22-year old son Ahaziah ruled only one year, around 841 B.C. (He should not be confused with his uncle of the same name, Ahab's son who ruled Israel about twelve years earlier.) He was firmly under the control of his mother, Athaliah, and continued to lead Judah toward Baal worship. When Ahaziah went to the city of Jezreel in Israel on a state visit to see his wounded uncle, Joram king of Israel, he was assassinated. This was part of the coup led by the general Jehu of Israel. In the dark days that followed Ahaziah's death, his infant son Joash was providentially taken away and hidden in the largely abandoned temple of Solomon. There his aunt Jehosheba secretly reared him for six years.

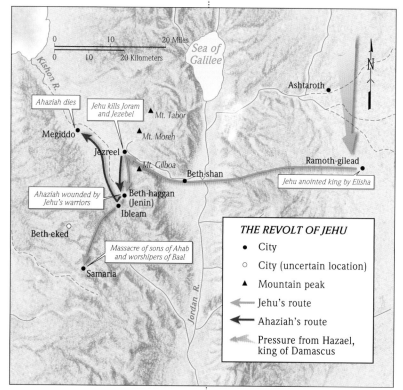

Ahaziah dies

Jehu kills Joram and Jezebel

Megiddo

Jezreel

Mt. Tabor

Mt. Moreh

Mt. Gilboa

Beth-shan

Ramoth-gilead

Jehu anointed king by Elisha

Ashtaroth

Sea of Galilee

Kishon R.

Jordan R.

Ahaziah wounded by Jehu's warriors

Beth-haggan (Jenin)

Ibleam

Beth-eked

Massacre of sons of Ahab and worshipers of Baal

Samaria

THE REVOLT OF JEHU
- ● City
- ○ City (uncertain location)
- ▲ Mountain peak
- → Jehu's route
- → Ahaziah's route
- → Pressure from Hazael, king of Damascus

SUMMARY OF "NATION DIVIDED"

In the ninety years that followed Solomon's death (931–841 B.C.), the people of God were divided into a Northern Kingdom and a Southern Kingdom that fought against each other and then finally made an alliance. In Israel to the north, three dynasties came and went, those of Jeroboam, Baasha, and Omri. Omri's daughter-in-law Jezebel led the nation to its lowest spiritual depth by popularizing Baal worship. The aggressive work of Elijah turned the tide, introducing a new independent prophetic role. The coup led by Jehu in 841 B.C. brought this major phase of Israelite history to a close.

In Judah to the south, the Davidic line of kings continued in unbroken succession. Only Asa and Jehoshaphat were loyal to the Lord, however. Jehoshaphat's alliance with Ahab, a brilliant political move, became a religious disaster. In 841 Jehu killed the Davidic king, allowing Athaliah to seize control of the throne of Judah. Jehu's deed thus also brought to an end a major phase in the history of Judah.

God's disciplinary lesson of dividing His people had fallen mainly on hard hearts. Those faithful to God—the true kingdom people—throughout this period were a small minority. His second lesson began by directing that the empire of the Assyrians rise to world prominence.

THE ASSYRIAN MENACE:
ONE HUNDRED TWENTY YEARS OF DECLINE AND DEFEAT (841–722 B.C.)

The second major lesson in God's discipline of His people was the captivity of the Northern Kingdom. Prophets such as Amos and Hosea warned Israelites in the Northern Kingdom of God's wrath against their sins. In Judah, Isaiah and Micah spoke equally powerfully. Finally the Lord sent the Assyrians, the world superpower of that era. Samaria fell and the Northern tribes were expelled from the land. They were absorbed into the places of their exile, losing their Israelite identity entirely. Israel fell to Assyria in 722 B.C.

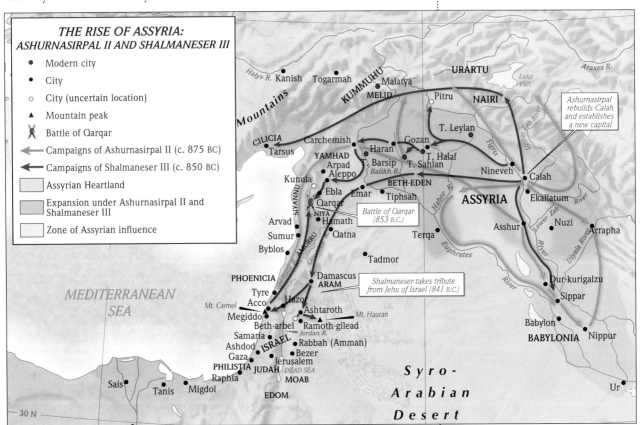

THE RISE OF ASSYRIA:
ASHURNASIRPAL II AND SHALMANESER III

- ● Modern city
- ● City
- ○ City (uncertain location)
- ▲ Mountain peak
- ⚔ Battle of Qarqar
- ← Campaigns of Ashurnasirpal II (c. 875 BC)
- ← Campaigns of Shalmaneser III (c. 850 BC)
- Assyrian Heartland
- Expansion under Ashurnasirpal II and Shalmaneser III
- Zone of Assyrian influence

Ashurnasirpal rebuilds Calah and establishes a new capital

Battle of Qarqar (853 B.C.)

Shalmaneser takes tribute from Jehu of Israel (841 B.C.)

Assyria

This ancient Mesopotamian civilization's center of strength was along the northern Tigris River (northern Iraq of today). By the time it rose to threaten Israel and Judah, the capital was Nineveh on the Tigris. Throughout the ninth to the seventh centuries, Assyria's aggressive tendencies ebbed and flowed, but Assyria finally became the world's superpower, noted for ruthlessness in battle. Assyria was conquered by the Babylonians, who became victorious over Nineveh in 612 B.C. Assyria was the second oppressor kingdom bent on destroying the people of God.

Replica of the black obelisk of Shalmaneser III, king of Assyria from 858–824 B.C. The obelisk was discovered at Nimrud.

JEHU OF ISRAEL AND HIS FIVE-GENERATION DYNASTY

The account contained in **2 KINGS 9—14** tells of the "Jehu Century," the nearly hundred-year period (841–753 B.C.) of the fourth and the longest ruling dynasty in the Northern Kingdom. Assyria was a military factor during the entire period of the Jehu dynasty, beginning with the Assyrian king Shalmaneser exacting tribute from Jehu.* On the other hand, Jeroboam II was able later to take advantage of a period of Assyrian weakness and expand the Northern Kingdom to another golden age.

JEHU

The Lord had told Elijah that the Israelite general Jehu was His choice to bring divine vengeance against the house of Ahab (1 Kings 19:16). Not until sometime later, however, was Jehu informed by one of Elisha's helpers that God had chosen him (2 Kings 9). Once anointed, however, Jehu lost no time in ridding the Northern Kingdom of Ahab's family and the worship of Baal. The revolt of Jehu included the following, all about 841 B.C.:

• Assassinated Ahab's son Joram, ruling king of Israel

• Assassinated Ahab's grandson Ahaziah, ruling king of Judah

• Assassinated Ahab's widow Jezebel, the queen mother of Israel

• Arranged for seventy of Ahab's descendants to be killed

• Arranged to kill all the Baal priests at the Baal temple in Samaria

• Tore down the Baal temple and turned it into a latrine

Because of Jehu's vigor in opposing Baal, God promised that four generations of kings would succeed him, yet Jehu continued to practice the perverted worship that Jeroboam had introduced to the Northern Kingdom a century earlier (the gold calf idols in Dan and Bethel). As punishment the Lord allowed Syria/Aram to take over part of Jehu's kingdom, particularly the land that lay east of the Jordan River. Jehu's rule coincided with the reign of Athaliah and the first part of Joash's rule in Jerusalem. He ruled a total of 28 years.

JEHOAHAZ

Jehu's son Jehoahaz continued the religious and political practices of his father. During his rule the kingdom was further reduced in size and humiliated by the aggressive forces of Syria/Aram to the north. Jehoahaz's army was reduced to ten chariots, fifty cavalry, and ten thousand infantry. He reigned for seventeen years, all during the time that Joash ruled Judah.

JEHOASH

Jehoahaz's son Jehoash (sometimes spelled Joash) ruled from Samaria for sixteen years. During his reign the aged Elisha finally died. Jehoash continued the religious and political policies of the Jehu dynasty. He was able to regain some of the northern Israelite cities previously taken by Syria/Aram, and he reintroduced warfare against the Southern Kingdom of Judah. During his last eleven years his son Jeroboam shared the throne with him.

JEROBOAM II

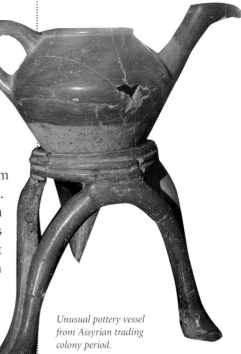

Unusual pottery vessel from Assyrian trading colony period.

Jehoash's son Jeroboam ruled for an amazing 41 years: 11 years as co-regent with his father and 30 years as sole king. During these thirty years Amaziah and then Uzziah ruled as kings of Judah. The nearby nations, particularly Assyria and Syria/Aram, were experiencing a period of weakness. Under Jeroboam, therefore, Israel enjoyed widely expanded borders and great prosperity, if only for a brief period. This golden age was the Northern Kingdom at its military and economic best. Jeroboam even took control of Damascus and ruled as far south as the Dead Sea.

AMOS'S MINISTRY

The prosperity of Jeroboam's day brought with it great economic and social oppression. God sent the rural Prophet Amos from Tekoa in Judah to warn the urban people of Samaria of coming judgment, recorded in the book of **AMOS**. His message reached the ears of Jeroboam, but the false priest Amaziah accused Amos of stirring up trouble, so he asked him to return home to Judah (Amos 7:10-16).

Prophecy of Amos

This book of prophecies and one short narrative is written mainly in Hebrew poetry. The first hearers were people living in the Northern Kingdom during Jeroboam's rule, perhaps around 760 B.C. The key word for the book is "injustice"; the key text is Amos 5:24. **One-Sentence Summary:** *Although Amos prophesied against the nations surrounding Israel including Judah, his main message was against Israel, who must repent of injustice and idolatry or else go into exile—but then be restored to divine favor.*

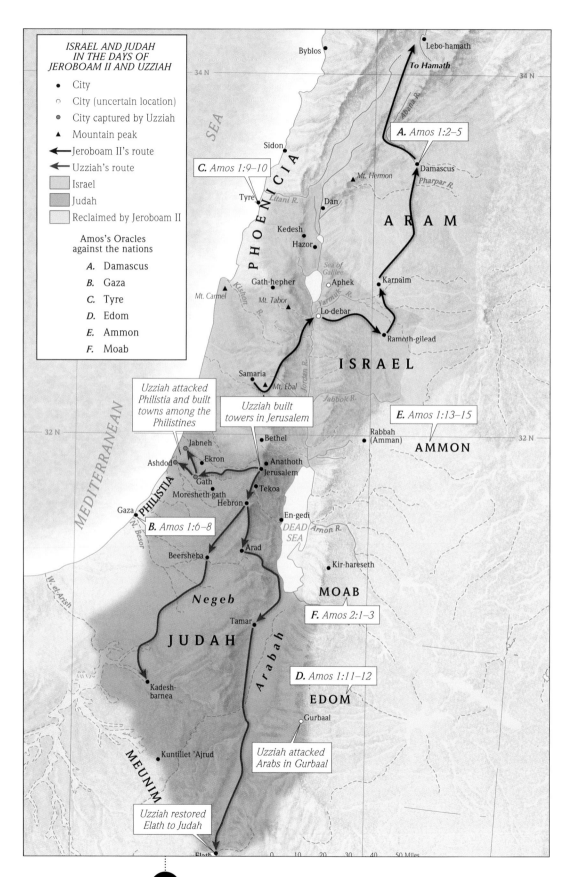

ISRAEL AND JUDAH
IN THE DAYS OF
JEROBOAM II AND UZZIAH

- • City
- ○ City (uncertain location)
- ● City captured by Uzziah
- ▲ Mountain peak
- ← Jeroboam II's route
- ← Uzziah's route
- Israel
- Judah
- Reclaimed by Jeroboam II

Amos's Oracles
against the nations

- A. Damascus
- B. Gaza
- C. Tyre
- D. Edom
- E. Ammon
- F. Moab

C. Amos 1:9–10

A. Amos 1:2–5

E. Amos 1:13–15

Uzziah attacked
Philistia and built
towns among the
Philistines

Uzziah built
towers in Jerusalem

B. Amos 1:6–8

F. Amos 2:1–3

D. Amos 1:11–12

Uzziah attacked
Arabs in Gurbaal

Uzziah restored
Elath to Judah

The Illustrated Guide to Biblical History

JONAH'S MINISTRY

One reason that Jeroboam's kingdom enjoyed a sense of security was that the Prophet Jonah had encouraged Jeroboam. He was doing the work of the Lord by expanding his border (2 Kings 14:25-27). Nevertheless, Assyria was still Israel's enemy, so it was with the greatest reluctance that Jonah discharged his God-given missionary responsibility. By way of travel in a fish's belly, Jonah preached in Assyria's capital city Ninevah, resulting in great repentance among the pagan inhabitants, as reported in the book of **JONAH**. (Two centuries later the Prophet Nahum preached God's message of final judgment against Assyria.)

ZECHARIAH

Jeroboam's evil son Zechariah ruled for only six months. Shallum assassinated him, thus ending the dynasty of Jehu. It would be only 31 years until the reawakened Assyrian Empire completely destroyed the Northern Kingdom.

JOASH OF JUDAH AND HIS TWO SUCCESSORS

The period of the Jehu dynasty to the north was paralleled in Judah by the restoration of the Davidic dynasty after Athaliah's reign of terror. Joash, Amaziah, and Uzziah had this in common: they began by following after the Lord, but they went astray in their later years. Together these three reigned about a century, from 835 to 740 B.C. Their story is told in **2 CHRONICLES 23—26**.

Prophecy of Jonah

Unlike the other Bible prophets, this book is essentially a narrative. The only prophecy is Jonah's message of repentance. The events evidently occurred sometime during Jeroboam's long rule. The key word for the book is "fish"; the key text is Jonah 4:11. **One-Sentence Summary:** *After Jonah's disobedience to God's command for him to preach in Nineveh resulted in his being swallowed by a fish, he then obeyed God and preached in Nineveh, with the result that the entire city repented and turned to God.*

An enormous public grain silo from the period of Jeroboam II (see p. 93).

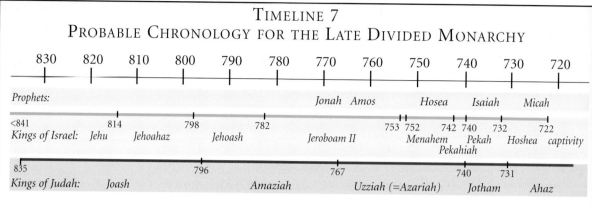

TIMELINE 7
PROBABLE CHRONOLOGY FOR THE LATE DIVIDED MONARCHY

830	820	810	800	790	780	770	760	750	740	730	720

Prophets: Jonah Amos Hosea Isaiah Micah

<841 814 798 782 753 752 742 740 732 722
Kings of Israel: Jehu Jehoahaz Jehoash Jeroboam II Menahem Pekah Hoshea captivity
Pekahiah

835 796 767 740 731
Kings of Judah: Joash Amaziah Uzziah (=Azariah) Jotham Ahaz

The beginning of this period is 841, the coup led by Jehu; the end of this period is 722, the Assyrian captivity of the Northern Kingdom. (Kings ruling a year or less are not included; in cases of co-regency, date is for beginning of sole rule/death of predecessor.)

ATHALIAH THE USURPER

Unfortunately for the people of Judah, Athaliah—daughter of Ahab and grandmother of Joash the true king—survived the violence of Jehu's rise to the throne of Israel. She went on a rampage and seized political control of Judah, assassinating all but one of the line of David. She ruled for more than six years. Athaliah promoted the worship of Baal, and during her rule (or perhaps during her husband's earlier reign) a temple to Baal was built in Jerusalem itself (2 Chron. 23:17).

The reign of Athaliah was the only breach in the rule of Davidic kings in Jerusalem from the time David made the city his capital until it was destroyed in 586 B.C. by the Babylonians. The covenant the Lord had made with David was challenged but not destroyed by the evil work of Athaliah.

JOASH AND HIS TEMPLE REFORM

Ahaziah's son Joash came to the throne when he was seven years old as a result of a conspiracy against Athaliah led by Jehoiada, a priest of the Lord. (He was husband of Jehosheba, Joash's aunt who had kept him hidden in the temple.) With Athaliah's murder and the subsequent destruction of the Baal temple, the people of Judah returned—at least temporarily—to the covenant of the Lord.

Under Jehoiada's tutelage Joash instigated a reform of the worship of Yahweh, asking for repairs to be made to the temple that had suffered from years of neglect and vandalism. The actual repairs occurred after Joash was an adult, having ruled for twenty-three years (2 Kings 12:6). This occurred about 812 B.C., so it had been 83 years since Asa's reform and Solomon's temple itself was by now 147 years old.

The revival proved to be temporary. After Jehoiada died, Joash abandoned the temple and even had Jehoiada's son killed. As a result God allowed the army of Syria/Aram to plunder Judah, and Joash himself was seriously wounded. He was murdered in a plot led by some of his own officials. Joash ruled for forty years.

AMAZIAH

Joash's son Amaziah ruled for twenty-nine years. His reign coincided with those of Jehoash and Jeroboam II of Israel (the grandson and great-grandson of Jehu). Amaziah began by putting to death the officers who had killed his father. He was a worshiper of Yahweh, but not exclusively.

After beginning to worship the foreign gods of Edom, Amaziah foolishly picked a fight with Jehoash of Israel, resulting in an embarrassing defeat for Judah. Amaziah was captured and taken hostage to Samaria. The army of Israel tore down a section of Jerusalem's wall and raided both the palace and the temple. It was perhaps in this context that his son Uzziah became co-regent with him for his last twenty-four years. Like his father before him, Amaziah was murdered in a plot led by his own officials.

UZZIAH

Amaziah's son Uzziah (also known as Azariah) was co-regent with his father for 24 years, ruled independently for 16 years, and then shared his throne with his son Jotham for 12 years. This led to an amazing total of 52 years, the longest for any king in the far north or south to this point.

The prosperity of Israel's golden age under Jeroboam II extended to Uzziah's kingdom as well. His military victories included Philistia to the west and Ammon to the east. He fortified Jerusalem and built up a considerable army, making a number of advances in military technology (2 Chron. 26:15).

Like his father and grandfather Uzziah began by following the Lord. Like them he also fell away. Uzziah's great sin was to intrude into the office of the priesthood, daring to offer incense at the temple. As divine punishment for his pride, he was stricken with a skin disease (leprosy) that made him unfit either to go to the temple or to continue ruling. As a result Jotham his son was co-regent for Uzziah's last twelve years.

The re-internment funerary inscription discovered in the 19th century of the Jewish King Uzziah. Its Aramaic writing translates: "Hither were brought the bones of Uzziah, King of Judah. Do not open." The inscription dates to the 1st century B.C. when Herod ordered all cemeteries to be moved outside the walls of Jerusalem, except for those of the Jewish kings. King Uzziah, who had been struck by God with leprosy (2 Chron. 26:16–21), was re-interred under Herod in the royal tombs, and this inscription was placed to mark the grave and act as a warning to looters.

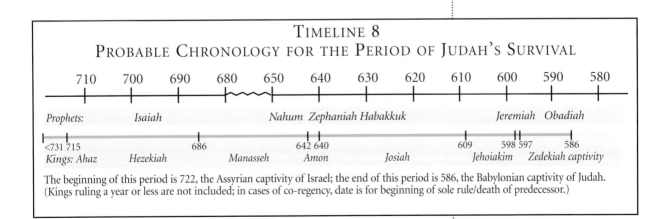

TIMELINE 8
PROBABLE CHRONOLOGY FOR THE PERIOD OF JUDAH'S SURVIVAL

710	700	690	680	650	640	630	620	610	600	590	580

Prophets: Isaiah   Nahum Zephaniah Habakkuk   Jeremiah Obadiah

<731 715   686   642 640   609   598 597   586
Kings: Ahaz   Hezekiah   Manasseh   Amon   Josiah   Jehoiakim Zedekiah captivity

The beginning of this period is 722, the Assyrian captivity of Israel; the end of this period is 586, the Babylonian captivity of Judah. (Kings ruling a year or less are not included; in cases of co-regency, date is for beginning of sole rule/death of predecessor.)

Recarved fragment of Assyrian soldiers shooting at a town.

THE LAST THREE DECADES OF THE NORTHERN KINGDOM

The Northern Kingdom completely fell apart only thirty years after the end of the Jehu dynasty. From a human perspective this was due to internal tensions and the growing menace of the Assyrians. Kings were either pro-Assyrian or anti-Assyrian and paid the consequences for their loyalties. Religiously, however, the people had become so apostate that sending them into captivity was the Lord's remedy. This difficult period, with the description of the Assyrian captivity of Israel, is told in **2 KINGS 15—17**.

SHALLUM

The man who assassinated Zechariah (last king of the Jehu dynasty) ruled in Samaria only one month. Then he was murdered by Menahem.

MENAHEM

The fifth and last dynasty of the Northern Kingdom consisted of Menahem and his son Pekahiah. After that no king of Israel was succeeded by his son. Religiously Menahem followed the policies of Jeroboam I; politically he faced the resurgence of the Assyrian Empire under Tiglath-pileser (called "Pul" by the Babylonians). Menahem was challenged throughout his entire reign by Pekah, an anti-Assyrian Israelite official. Pekah evidently set up a rival government east of the Jordan River.

Around 743 B.C. the Assyrian army invaded the Northern Kingdom. Menahem decided on a pro-Assyrian policy of appeasement, so his kingdom was spared for a time. After exacting an enormous tribute from Israel, raised by Menahem's heavy tax on the upper class, the Assyrians withdrew. Menahem reigned from Samaria for ten years.

PEKAHIAH

Menahem's son Pekahiah ruled for only two years. He was assassinated in Samaria by a military coup led by Pekah.

HOSEA'S MINISTRY

During this time of national turmoil, God's prophet Hosea was experiencing his own personal turmoil. His wife Gomer had abandoned him for a life of prostitution (and eventual slavery) from which he bought her back. The Lord inspired Hosea to show the people of Israel that their rejection of Him was just like Gomer's rejection of Hosea. God longed to take His people back, but they refused. Almost certainly Hosea lived to see his prophecy, written in the book of **HOSEA** about the coming captivity, fulfilled.

PEKAH

According to 2 Kings 15:27 Pekah ruled twenty years (about 752–732 B.C.). This probably includes the twelve years that he ruled as a rebel king from east of the Jordan and the eight years that he ruled from Samaria after assassinating Pekahiah.

Prophecy of Hosea

This book contains prophecies and a few historical narratives, written mainly in Hebrew poetry. The events of Hosea's personal family tragedy and his poignant cry to the people of the Northern Kingdom occurred sometime during the last thirty years of Israel's national life. The key word for the book is "unfaithfulness"; the key text is Hosea 1:10.

One-Sentence Summary: *Hosea's marriage to an adulterous wife and the children she bore graphically demonstrated God's "marriage" to His spiritually adulterous people Israel, who must respond to His covenant love and repent or face severe judgment.*

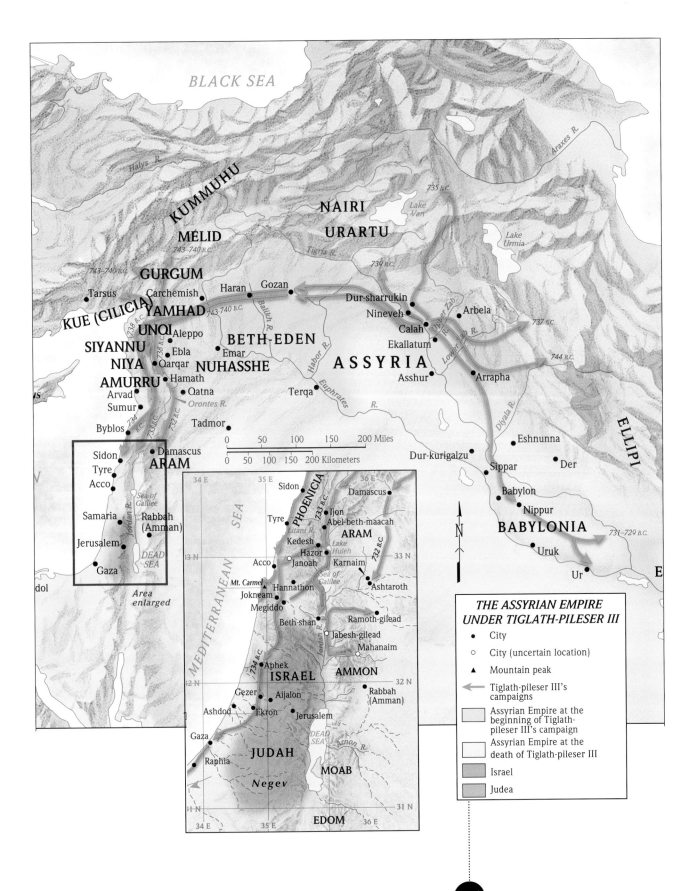

BLACK SEA

KUMMUHU

MELID
743–740 B.C.

NAIRI

URARTU

735 B.C.

Lake
Van

Lake
Urmia

Halys R.

Tigris R.

739 B.C.

Araxes R.

GURGUM

Tarsus   Carchemish   Haran   Gozan

KUE (CILICIA)   YAMHAD   *743–740 B.C.*

UNQI   Aleppo

SIYANNU   Ebla

NIYA   Qarqar   NUHASSHE

AMURRU   Hamath

Arvad   Qatna

Sumur   Orontes R.

Byblos

BETH-EDEN

Habor R.

Emar

Terqa

Dur-sharrukin

Nineveh

Calah

Ekallatum

ASSYRIA

Asshur

Arbela

Arrapha

Euphrates R.

Tadmor

737 B.C.

744 B.C.

Upper Zab R.

Lower Zab R.

Diyala R.

0   50   100   150   200 Miles

0   50 100 150 200 Kilometers

ELLIPI

Eshnunna

Der

Sidon   Damascus

Tyre   ARAM

Acco

Samaria   Rabbah
(Amman)

Jerusalem

Gaza

Sea of
Galilee

Jordan R.

DEAD
SEA

Area
enlarged

Dur-kurigalzu

Sippar

Babylon

Nippur

BABYLONIA

Uruk

Ur

731–729 B.C.

34 E   35 E   36 E

Sidon   Damascus

PHOENICIA   *1733 B.C.*

Tyre   Ijon   Abel-beth-maacah

Litani R.   ARAM

Kedesh   Lake
Huleh   *732 B.C.*

MEDITERRANEAN   Hazor   Karnaim

13 N   Acco   Janoah

SEA   Mt. Carmel   Hannathon   Sea of
Galilee   Ashtaroth   33 N

Jokneam   Karnaim

Megiddo   Ramoth-gilead

Beth-shan   Jordan R.

Jabesh-gilead

Mahanaim

12 N   ISRAEL   AMMON   32 N

Aphek   *734 B.C.*

Gezer   Aijalon   Rabbah
(Amman)

Ashdod   Ekron   Jerusalem

Gaza   DEAD
SEA

JUDAH   Arnon R.

Raphia   MOAB

Negev   31 N

N

EDOM

34 E   35 E   36 E

THE ASSYRIAN EMPIRE UNDER TIGLATH-PILESER III

- • City
- ○ City (uncertain location)
- ▲ Mountain peak
- → Tiglath-pileser III's campaigns
- Assyrian Empire at the beginning of Tiglath-pileser III's campaign
- Assyrian Empire at the death of Tiglath-pileser III
- Israel
- Judea

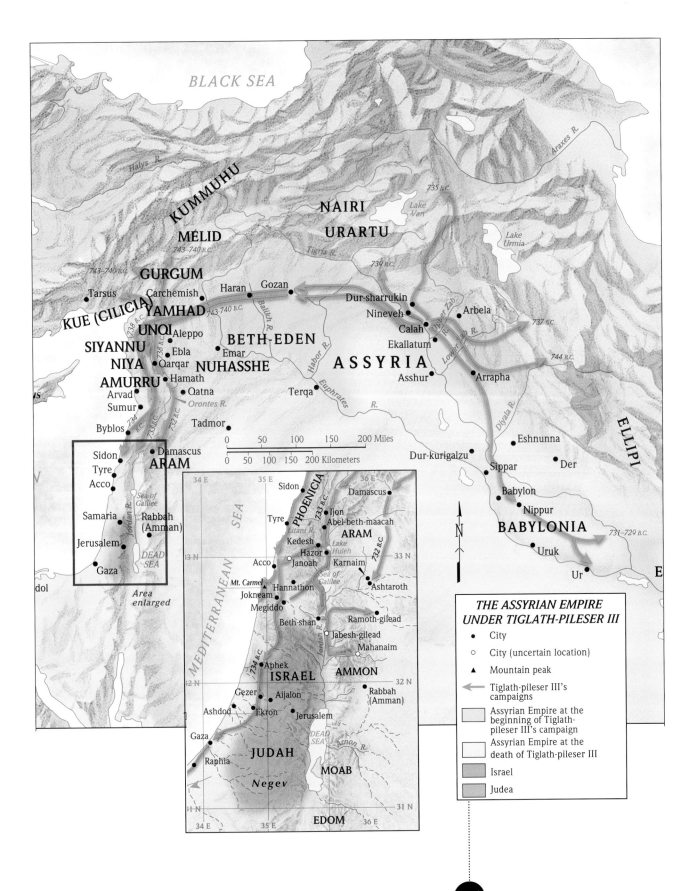

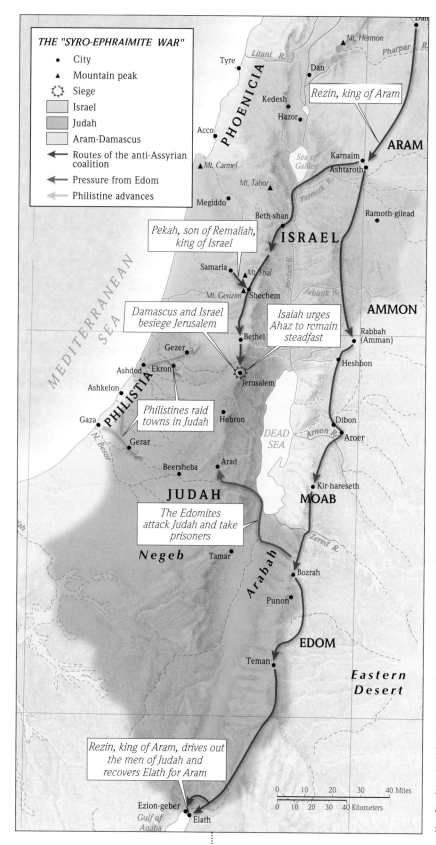

THE "SYRO-EPHRAIMITE WAR"

• City
▲ Mountain peak
☼ Siege
☐ Israel
☐ Judah
☐ Aram-Damascus
← Routes of the anti-Assyrian coalition
← Pressure from Edom
← Philistine advances

Rezin, king of Aram

Pekah, son of Remaliah, king of Israel

Damascus and Israel besiege Jerusalem

Isaiah urges Ahaz to remain steadfast

Philistines raid towns in Judah

The Edomites attack Judah and take prisoners

Rezin, king of Aram, drives out the men of Judah and recovers Elath for Aram

Pekah was less willing to submit to Assyria than his predecessors. He formed a coalition with Syria/Aram to oppose Assyria. About 735 the Syrian-Israelite coalition marched on Jerusalem to try to force the Davidic monarch (Ahaz) to join with them in opposing Assyria (see Isaiah 7). This endeavor ultimately failed, and Pekah soon faced a new invasion of the Assyrians under Tiglath-pileser. This time all Israel's territory east of the Jordan and most of the area around the Sea of Galilee was lost. Only Samaria and the nearby hill country was left under Pekah's control. At this time the Assyrians followed the brutal practice of sending many local inhabitants of conquered areas away into exile, although the majority of the people were left in the land.

Just as Pekah came to the throne by murder, so by murder he left the throne. He was assassinated by Hoshea about 732 B.C.

HOSHEA

The last king of Israel began by being pro-Assyrian and paying more tribute. Hoshea's nine-year reign took place while Ahaz was king in Jerusalem. After a new Assyrian king named Shalmaneser arose, Hoshea changed loyalties to Egypt. He appealed to the pharaoh for help and refused to send the tribute Assyria demanded. It is a matter of bitter irony that the people of Israel, having escaped Egyptian slavery under Moses around 1446, finally appealed to Egypt as a last-ditch effort to be spared from extinction some seven centuries later.

In 725 an infuriated Shalmaneser and his army arrived to lay siege to the city of Samaria. It is a credit to the strength of the city's fortifications that it endured the onslaught for three years. Shalmanezer was succeeded in 722 by Sargon, who evidently concluded the deportation of the Israelites. According to the annals of Sargon, 27,290 Israelites went into exile.

The fall of Samaria marked the end of the Northern Kingdom, which had endured as an independent country from 931 to 722 B.C., just over two centuries. This must have been a shock for the people of Judah, for they were next in line for the Assyrian wrath. The writer of 2 Kings 17:7-23 provided the divinely inspired commentary on why the Northern Kingdom was captured. In a single sentence: *Israel rejected its covenant with the Lord by worshiping other gods; therefore the Lord removed them from His presence.*

Sargon the King with visier and royal functionary from Sargon's palace.

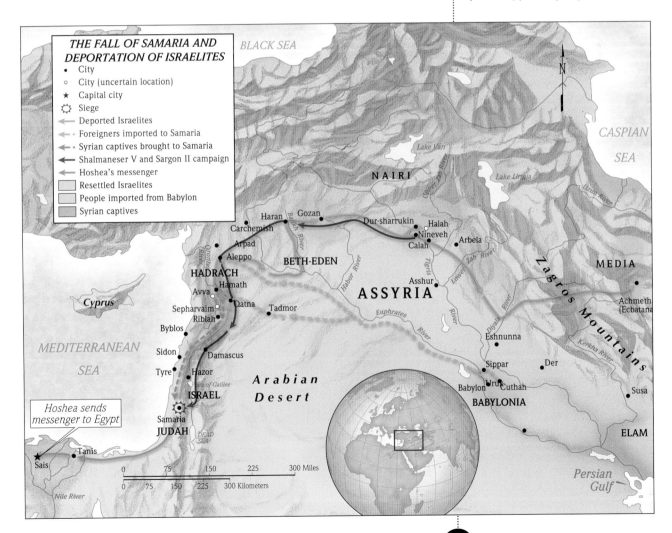

The Fall of Samaria and Deportation of Israelites

- • City
- ○ City (uncertain location)
- ★ Capital city
- ⬠ Siege
- ← Deported Israelites
- ← Foreigners imported to Samaria
- ← Syrian captives brought to Samaria
- ← Shalmaneser V and Sargon II campaign
- ← Hoshea's messenger
- ▢ Resettled Israelites
- ▢ People imported from Babylon
- ▢ Syrian captives

Hoshea sends messenger to Egypt

From the late Assyrian period an open-work plaque showing a human headed "winged-apron sphinx."

JOTHAM AND AHAZ OF JUDAH

Two kings of the Davidic dynasty ruled while the Northern Kingdom was attacked and dissolved by the Assyrians. Jotham and Ahaz were the son and the grandson of Uzziah (**2 CHRONICLES 27—28**). While Jotham was upright, Ahaz became entranced by the religion of Assyria and abandoned the Lord. He was even more evil than his ancestors Jehoram and Ahaziah, who had ruled more than a century before.

JOTHAM

Uzziah's son Jotham was co-regent after his father's leprosy made him unable to continue his royal duties. His official reign endured sixteen years (2 Chron. 27:1). This evidently includes twelve years of overlap with his father and four years of independent rule but not his overlap with his son Ahaz.

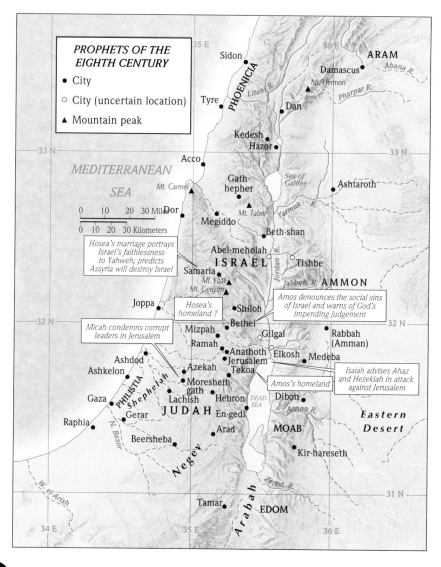

PROPHETS OF THE EIGHTH CENTURY

● City

○ City (uncertain location)

▲ Mountain peak

Hosea's marriage portrays Israel's faithlessness to Yahweh; predicts Assyria will destroy Israel

Hosea's homeland ?

Micah condemns corrupt leaders in Jerusalem

Amos denounces the social sins of Israel and warns of God's impending judgement

Amos's homeland

Isaiah advises Ahaz and Hezekiah in attack against Jerusalem

Basalt relief orthostats belonging to a doorway. They portray the classes of the Assyrian army. From the neo-Assyrian period during the reign of Tiglath-pileser (744–727 B.C.).

Jotham's rule was characterized by a continuation of the golden age of prosperity that the people of Judah had enjoyed under Uzziah. He was even able to bring the Ammonites (east of the Jordan River) under his control. Jotham avoided giving tribute to the Assyrians such as Menahem had agreed to. Toward the end of his reign (about 735), a Syrian-Israelite coalition marched against Jerusalem, but this was dealt with by his son Ahaz. By this time Ahaz was functioning as the king. Jotham died before the final Assyrian victory over King Hoshea of Israel and the city of Samaria.

ISAIAH'S MINISTRY

The greatest of the writing prophets was Isaiah, son of Amoz. According to Jewish tradition he was from a noble family of Jerusalem. He had a wife and at least two sons with symbolic names, "A Remnant Will Return" and "Speed the Spoil; Hasten the Plunder" (Shear-jashub and Maher-shalal-hash-baz, Is. 7:3; 8:3). Isaiah was possibly martyred by being sawed in half (see Heb. 11:37). The kings Isaiah mentioned ruled almost a century, from 792–686 B.C. He was called as a prophet at the beginning of Jotham's sole rule (the year of Uzziah's death); his heyday was about 740–700 B.C.

Isaiah's ministry intersected especially with the kings Ahaz and Hezekiah. As the Lord's spokesman he begged Ahaz not to fear the Syrian-Israelite army that came against him (Is. 7—8), and he urged Hezekiah not to fear the Assyrian invasion that had come against Jerusalem (Is. 36—37). Later on, he criticized Hezekiah for welcoming messengers sent to Jerusalem from Babylonia (Is. 39). In this way Isaiah functioned as the "bridge" prophet, speaking God's word about both the Assyrian menace (Is. 1—39) and the Babylonian menace (Is. 40—66).

For Christians Isaiah has been called "The Evangelist of the Old Covenant." The book of **ISAIAH** predicted the birth and ultimate eternal reign of David's greatest Son. He also, however, foresaw the death of the Messiah for the sins of His people in the great "Suffering Servant" passage (Is. 53).

Prophecy of Isaiah

This long book of prophecies and a few historical narratives is composed in excellent Hebrew poetry and prose. Isaiah's personal life and long ministry contributed to his book's impact. The first readers of the entire book were the people of Jerusalem, perhaps about 680 B.C. The key word for the book is "judgment"; the key text is Isaiah 1:19-20. **One-Sentence Summary:** *Isaiah prophesied that because of continued idolatry God would send Judah into Babylonian captivity, yet He would graciously restore them (through the work of His Servant, who would bear their sins by His death), so that His kingdom would be unending in the new heavens and the new earth.*

AHAZ

Jotham's son Ahaz was so thoroughly evil that the biblical writers had nothing positive to say about him. His official rule of sixteen years does not include the four previous years during which he was co-regent with his father.

Sometime around 735, an Syrian-Israelite army led by Rezin of Damascus and Pekah of Samaria marched on Jerusalem in order to force Judah to join an anti-Assyrian alliance. Judah suffered massive military losses, including the death of Ahaz's son (2 Chron. 28:6). Much of Judah's wealth was plundered.

Through the Prophet Isaiah, however, God promised Ahaz relief and told him to ask for a miraculous sign. When Ahaz refused—because he was not a follower of Yahweh—the Lord gave him a sign anyway, a child born to a virgin, one of the greatest and clearest promises of the coming Messiah (Is. 7:14).

Rather than trust God, Ahaz decided to align Judah with Assyria. He sent massive tribute to Tiglath-pileser and asked for his assistance. The Assyrians complied by attacking and conquering Damascus in 732. When Ahaz went to Damascus to congratulate the Assyrian king, he showed his submission and loyalty by arranging to have plans drawn up for a large Assyrian-style altar. This altar was built and placed before the temple in Jerusalem to replace the original one that Solomon had made, a striking example of religious syncretism.

Ahaz adopted many pagan religious practices. He was so spiritually and morally blind that he could not see that his unfaithfulness to the Lord was a major cause of Judah's ultimate collapse (2 Chron. 28:22-23). It is a testimony to God's grace that Judah was not taken by the Assyrians at the same time that Israel fell. By the time of his death, Ahaz's kingdom not only had endured the Syrian-Israelite invasion but also had witnessed close at hand the terrible might of the Assyrians. First, Damascus was taken (732) and then Samaria (722). Although Ahaz never learned to follow the Lord, his son Hezekiah—who evidently served as Ahaz's co-regent from 729 to 715—had taken notice. Reform and revival for Judah were just around the corner.

MICAH'S MINISTRY

Micah was Isaiah's less known contemporary. He was from the small town of Moresheth in southern Judah (Mic. 1:14). Micah's message to Judah included the same themes as the message Amos had delivered to the Northern Kingdom half a century earlier. He warned both Samaria and Jerusalem about their unjust ways, probably during the time of Ahaz. He saw the fulfillment of his predictions about the fall of Samaria to the Assyrians.

Micah also witnessed the great religious revival initiated by Hezekiah, which delayed by a century the fulfillment of his prophecies about the coming fall of Jerusalem. Thus, he was one of the few prophets whose

Prophecy of Micah

This book of prophecies was written entirely in Hebrew poetry. Almost nothing of Micah's personal life is known. He probably compiled his book around 700–690 B.C. during the last part of Hezekiah's rule. The key word for the book is "idolatry"; the key text is Micah 3:8. **One-Sentence Summary:** *Although Micah also prophesied against Israel, his main message was against Judah, who must repent of idolatry and injustice or else go into exile—but then be restored to divine blessing under the Ruler from Bethlehem.*

A Hellenistic site at Tell Sandahannah, Old Testament Moresheth-Gath, home of Micah the prophet.

warnings of judgment were at least partly heeded (Jer. 26:18). For Christians the book of **Micah** is most famous for foretelling the coming birth of the messianic King in Bethlehem, David's hometown (Mic. 5:2).

SUMMARY OF "THE ASSYRIAN MENACE"

In the 120-year period that followed Jehu's coup (841–722 B.C.), the people of God continued to be divided against each other, north against south. In Samaria, the five-generation Jehu dynasty brought an end to the threat of total capitulation to Baal worship, but the kings were not wholehearted servants of Yahweh either. After being brought low by Syria/Aram, Israel regained prominence, wealth, and power during the golden age of Jeroboam II. Sadly, economic corruption became the rule of the day, despite the warnings of Amos and Jonah.

About the same time as the Jehu dynasty, three kings of Judah—Joash, Amaziah, and Uzziah—ruled after the defeat of the wicked Athaliah. These three followed a similar pattern. They began their reigns by following the Lord but foolishly turned away from him later on. Uzziah's reign, however, was marked by a return to power and wealth for Judah parallel to the golden age in Samaria under Jeroboam II. Uzziah's son Jotham followed after the Lord, but his successor Ahaz most assuredly did not. Despite the warnings of Isaiah and Micah, Judah fell into a religious and moral slide. During Ahaz's rule in Jerusalem, the Northern Kingdom finally fell to Assyria.

The last thirty years of the Northern Kingdom was increasingly unstable. Kings came and went by violence. They were allied at one time with Assyria and another time with Syria/Aram. At last the Assyrian army under Sennacherib came and destroyed Samaria.

As during the period of the early divided kingdom, God's disciplinary lesson (sending the Assyrians) fell mainly on hard hearts. Those faithful to the Lord throughout this period continued to be a tiny minority. The final part of God's lesson began by directing that the empire of the Babylonians rise to world prominence again.

An overview of modern Damascus, capital of Syria/Aram.

THE BABYLONIAN MENACE:
JUDAH'S HUNDRED-THIRTY-YEAR PLUNGE TO DISASTER (722–586 B.C.)

The third step in God's discipline of His people was the captivity of Judah. After the fall of the Northern Kingdom, there were, in fact, two religious revivals in Judah, the first led by Hezekiah the king and then almost a century later one led by Josiah the king. The people, however, reverted to idolatry and injustice. The harsh rejection of the Prophet Jeremiah shows how low the people had fallen spiritually.

God called into being another world superpower, the Chaldeans or Babylonians. They invaded Judah three times, destroying Jerusalem, ending kingship in Judah (with Zedekiah as the last of the Davidic dynasty to rule in Jerusalem). The Babylonians destroyed the temple and forced thousands of people from Judah into exile in 586 B.C. With this, God's "educational program" of His people was complete. They learned their lesson well. Never again did the people of Israel worship idols.

HEZEKIAH AND MANASSEH

The father-and-son team of Hezekiah and Manasseh ruled Judah at the height of Assyrian power. Yet, in their day the Prophet Isaiah prophesied the people's return from Babylonian captivity two centuries later. It is hard to find two kings with such opposite religious affections. Hezekiah, son of the wicked Ahaz, sparked a revival of the worship of Yahweh that, in effect, delayed Judah's captivity for more than a century. (Hezekiah died exactly a hundred years before Jerusalem was destroyed.) On the other hand, Manasseh, long-ruling son of the righteous Hezekiah, reverted to the evil practices of his grandfather Ahaz. Because of Manasseh's sins, Judah's fate was sealed. Their story is told in **2 KINGS 18—21** and **2 CHRONICLES 29—33**.

The Gihon Spring in the Kidron Valley. King Hezekiah built a tunnel from the spring to the pool of Siloam which he also built to provide water for Jerusalem.

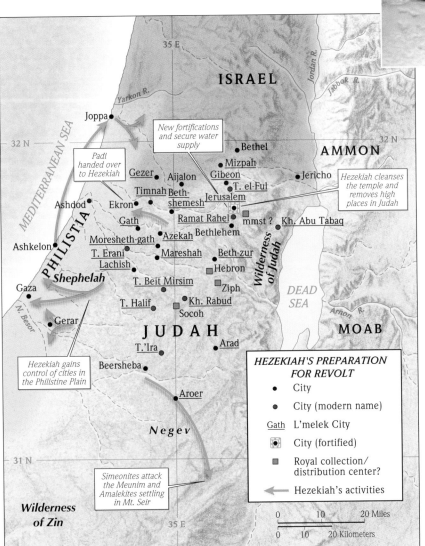

35 E

ISRAEL

Yarkon R.

Jordan R.

Jabbok R.

32 N

Joppa

Padi handed over to Hezekiah

New fortifications and secure water supply

Bethel

Mizpah

Gezer

Aijalon

Gibeon

AMMON

Jericho

32 N

Hezekiah cleanses the temple and removes high places in Judah

Timnah

Beth-shemesh

T. el-Ful

Jerusalem

Ashdod

Ekron

Gath

Ramat Rahel

mmst ?

Kh. Abu Tabaq

Ashkelon

Moresheth-gath

Azekah

Bethlehem

Wilderness of Judah

T. Erani

Lachish

Mareshah

Beth-zur

Hebron

DEAD SEA

Gaza

Shephelah

T. Beit Mirsim

Ziph

Kh. Rabud

Socoh

Arnon R.

MEDITERRANEAN SEA

PHILISTIA

N. Besor

Gerar

T. Halif

JUDAH

T.'Ira

Arad

MOAB

Hezekiah gains control of cities in the Philistine Plain

Beersheba

Aroer

31 N

Negev

Simeonites attack the Meunim and Amalekites settling in Mt. Seir

HEZEKIAH'S PREPARATION FOR REVOLT

- • City
- • City (modern name)
- Gath L'melek City
- ⊡ City (fortified)
- ▪ Royal collection/ distribution center?
- ← Hezekiah's activities

Wilderness of Zin

35 E

0   10   20 Miles

0   10   20 Kilometers

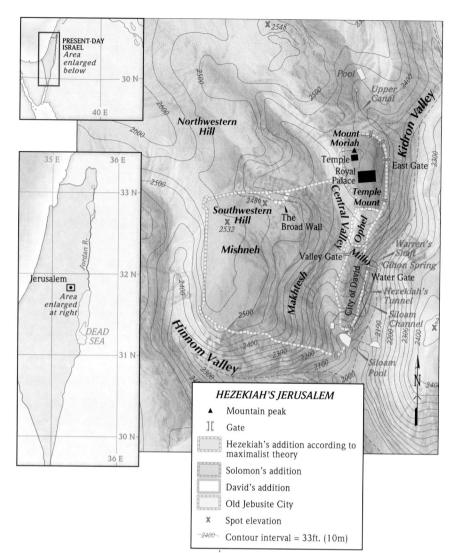

PRESENT-DAY ISRAEL
Area enlarged below

30 N

40 E

35 E 36 E

33 N

Jerusalem
Area enlarged at right

DEAD SEA

32 N

31 N

30 N

36 E

HEZEKIAH'S JERUSALEM

▲ Mountain peak

⫝ Gate

▢ Hezekiah's addition according to maximalist theory

▢ Solomon's addition

▢ David's addition

▢ Old Jebusite City

x Spot elevation

─2400─ Contour interval = 33ft. (10m)

(map labels:) 2548 • Pool • Upper Canal • Kidron Valley • Northwestern Hill • Mount Moriah • Temple • East Gate • Royal Palace • Temple Mount • 2486 x • Southwestern Hill • x 2532 • The Broad Wall • Ophel • Mishneh • Central Valley • Millo • Warren's Shaft • Valley Gate • Gihon Spring • Water Gate • Makhtesh • Hezekiah's Tunnel • City of David • Siloam Channel • Siloam Pool • Hinnom Valley • N

HEZEKIAH AND HIS TEMPLE REFORM

Ahaz's son Hezekiah became a kind of "second Solomon" in his attention to the Lord's temple. He ruled after his father's death for 29 years, including a fifteen-year extension granted by the Lord.

As co-regent with his father Ahaz, Hezekiah was unable to lead Judah to a renewal of its worship and covenant with the Lord. At age 25, however, in the very first month of his sole rule, he initiated a sweeping religious reform. This revival (about 715 B.C.) was 97 years since the reform by Joash, and Solomon's temple had been standing for 244 years. The list of Hezekiah's religious accomplishments is astounding:

- Completely purifying the temple of every unclean thing found there

- Restoring the proper furnishings of the temple (and removing Ahaz's altar)

- Consecrating the priests so that they could offer proper sacrifices

- Reestablishing worship, including both animal sacrifices and music

- Celebrating Passover (a month late) with a massive gathering in Jerusalem

- Destroying all the alternate places of worship throughout the land

- Destroying the bronze statue of a snake from Moses' day that had become an idol

- Reactivating the tithe from the Israelite people to support the priests and temple

Although the Northern Kingdom existed as a nation no more, many of the original Israelite population remained there. Thus, Hezekiah invited the people of "Ephraim and Manasseh" to come to Jerusalem for worship, and some indeed participated (2 Chron. 29:1,11,25).

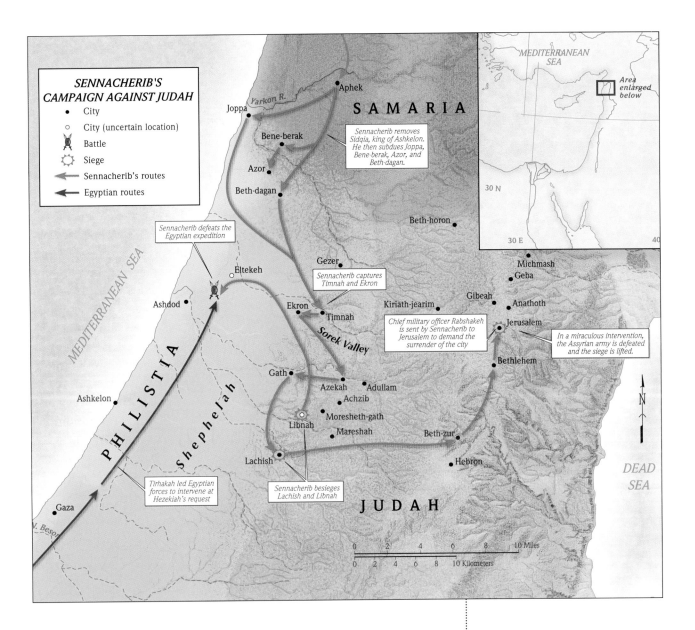

SENNACHERIB'S
CAMPAIGN AGAINST JUDAH

- • City
- ◦ City (uncertain location)
- ⚔ Battle
- ⬡ Siege
- → Sennacherib's routes
- → Egyptian routes

Sennacherib removes
Sidqia, king of Ashkelon.
He then subdues Joppa,
Bene-berak, Azor, and
Beth-dagan.

Sennacherib defeats the
Egyptian expedition

Sennacherib captures
Timnah and Ekron

Chief military officer Rabshakeh
is sent by Sennacherib to
Jerusalem to demand the
surrender of the city

In a miraculous intervention,
the Assyrian army is defeated
and the siege is lifted.

Tirhakah led Egyptian
forces to intervene at
Hezekiah's request

Sennacherib besieges
Lachish and Libnah

MEDITERRANEAN
SEA

Area
enlarged
below

30 N

30 E

SAMARIA

Aphek

Yarkon R.

Joppa

Bene-berak

Azor

Beth-dagan

Beth-horon

Eltekeh

Ashdod

Gezer

Michmash

Geba

Kiriath-jearim

Gibeah

Anathoth

Jerusalem

Ekron

Timnah

Sorek Valley

Bethlehem

MEDITERRANEAN SEA

PHILISTIA

Shephelah

Gath

Azekah

Adullam

Achzib

Moresheth-gath

Mareshah

Beth-zur

Ashkelon

Libnah

Lachish

Hebron

JUDAH

Gaza

N. Besor

DEAD
SEA

N

0   2   4   6   8   10 Miles
0 2 4 6 8 10 Kilometers

Fourteen years later (701 B.C.) Hezekiah faced the biggest military crisis
of his career. The Assryian army, this time led by Sennacherib, invaded
Judah as a part of a larger campaign. Most of the cities of Judah were captured, and Sennacherib established his military headquarters at Lachish
(a few miles southwest of Jerusalem). In order to spare Jerusalem,
Hezekiah tried a policy of appeasement, sending Sennacherib a massive
payment of gold and silver. Instead, however, Sennacherib sent officers to
demand that Hezekiah surrender himself and his city. Included in this
demand was language that deliberately insulted Yahweh as powerless to
protect His people, much as Goliath had insulted the God of David centuries before.

The pool of Siloam in Jerusalem. The pool was built in the 8th century B.C. by King Hezekiah to bring water from Gihon Spring into Jerusalem.

Hezekiah's response was to cry out to God at the temple in humble trust. This example of depending on the Lord in the face of overwhelming odds was so inspiring that the writers of Scripture recorded the episode in three separate places (2 Kings 18—19; 2 Chron. 32; Is. 36—37). Isaiah the prophet, rebuffed years earlier when he had asked Hezekiah's father Ahaz to trust the Lord, was now the Lord's messenger to promise Hezekiah a miraculous deliverance. The Lord showed His power by sending His angel to attack the Assyrian camp, and 185,000 soldiers died overnight. Sennacherib withdrew in disgrace, and he was murdered some years later in Nineveh by two of his own sons. Thus God showed His power to protect His covenant people and to honor His glory—just as He had done when the pharaoh of Moses' day had doubted God's power.

About the same time, Hezekiah fell gravely ill and would have died, except that he prayed earnestly. God healed him and gave him a fifteen-year extension of life, although his son Manasseh was his co-regent for his last eleven years. (Perhaps he was left debilitated after his recovery.) When ambassadors from Babylonia came to congratulate him on his recovery, Hezekiah learned from Isaiah that the Babylonians would one day destroy Jerusalem (2 Kings 20:12-19). Thus, beginning with the account of Hezekiah's reign, readers of Scripture are prepared for the Babylonian captivity of Judah.

MANASSEH

Hezekiah's son Manasseh had the longest reign of any king of Israel or Judah, 55 years. This evidently includes some 11 years of co-regency with his father beginning when he was 12 and 44 years as sole monarch. Why Manasseh rejected his father's religion and reverted to the ways of Ahaz is one of the sad unsolved mysteries of the Old Testament.

His rejection of Yahweh was so complete that he installed an idol in Solomon's temple. According to 2 Kings 21:10-15, the wickedness of Manasseh was so great that God's destruction of Jerusalem was the necessary consequence. According to Jewish tradition, Manasseh had Isaiah put to death by being sawed in half. An immediate consequence—described only sketchily in 2 Chronicles 33:10-13—was that the king of Assyria temporarily deposed Manasseh and made him spend time as a captive. The time of this incident is unknown, but after he returned to the throne he repented of his evil and reestablished the worship of the Lord. It was, however, too little too late.

AMON AND JOSIAH

The father-son team of Amon and Josiah witnessed the decline and fall of Assyria and the beginning of Babylonian prominence. Amon was evil like his father Manasseh. His rule was short. Josiah, by contrast, was a righteous king who initiated one last religious reform before the final slide into idolatry that concluded with the Babylonian captivity. Their reigns are reported in **2 KINGS 21—23** and **2 CHRONICLES 33—35**.

AMON

Manasseh's son Amon ruled for only two years. He was an idolater and was weak politically. At age 24 Amon was killed in a military conspiracy, leaving his 8-year-old son Josiah to become king.

NAHUM'S MINISTRY

God called the Prophet Nahum—of whom nothing personal is known—to warn the Assyrians of their arrogance and coming destruction. The Assyrians had captured Thebes in Egypt in 667, the most magnificent example of their world supremacy. Jonah had been a prophet of God's mercy to Assyria's capital, Nineveh, more than a century before; now Nahum was the prophet of Nineveh's doom and judgment. The predictions of the book of **NAHUM** were fulfilled in 612, an example that ultimately God will judge all His enemies and His kingdom will triumph.

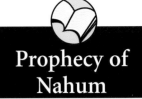

Prophecy of Nahum

This brief book is written entirely in Hebrew poetry. Nahum, a prophet of Judah, gave his message sometime after Assyria captured Thebes but before the Babylonians captured Nineveh (between 667 and 612 B.C.). The key word for the book is "Nineveh"; the key text is Nahum 1:2. **One-Sentence Summary:** *Nahum prophesied that God would destroy Nineveh because of its wickedness and violence, never to rise again.*

Lachish was the last fortress to fall before Jerusalem fell to the Babylonians. The small mound to the right was the siege ramp.

Zephaniah wrote his prophecies entirely in Hebrew poetry. Zephaniah's astute criticism of the sins of his day support the idea that he was familiar with—and perhaps part of—upper class Jerusalem society, probably around 625 B.C. The key term for the book is "day of the LORD"; the key text is Zephaniah 3:17. **One-Sentence Summary:** *Although Zephaniah prophesied coming judgment against the nations, his main message was against Judah, whose sins were so serious that they would go into exile on "the day of the LORD," but later they would be restored to righteousness.*

ZEPHANIAH'S MINISTRY

Zephaniah identified himself by a more complete genealogy than any other prophet (Zeph. 1:1) and ministered during the reign of Josiah. He was the great-great-grandson of a certain Hezekiah, probably the famous king. If so, Zephaniah belonged to the royal family. (King Josiah was Hezekiah's great-grandson.) Zephaniah's attacks on the sins of the elite—princes, priests, judges, and false prophets—suggest that he was acquainted with the powerful and that he had true boldness (Zeph. 3:3-5). The evils that he described match the religious corruption rooted out by Josiah's reform. If, as appears likely, Zephaniah preached shortly before 622, he contributed greatly to the reforms of Josiah's rule.

Zephaniah warned darkly of the coming day of the Lord when God's people would be judged. Yet the book of **ZEPHANIAH** looked forward to the day of restoration. God's plans to be the King in the midst of His people is a magnificent prophecy that will ultimately be fulfilled in the final expression of God's kingdom.

JOSIAH AND HIS TEMPLE REFORM

Josiah, the 8-year-old son of Amon, came to the throne after his father was assassinated. The 31-year rule of this righteous king was Judah's last gasp at independence. After Josiah's untimely (and unnecessary) death, Jerusalem was taken by the Babylonians within 25 years.

Josiah's religious reform (after having an evil father and grandfather) is as hard to understand as is Manasseh's evil. Ultimately it must be understood as divinely ordered. From a human perspective, righteous advisors such as Hilkiah the priest guided the young king. According to 2 Chronicles 34, the revival under Josiah occurred in three phases.

- In Josiah's eighth year (when he was about 16), he began personally following the Lord.

- In Josiah's twelfth year (when he was about 20), he directed that the idols throughout the entire land be destroyed.

- In Josiah's eighteenth year (when he was about 26), he directed that the temple be refurbished. This was the fourth and final restoration of Solomon's temple. It had been 93 years since Hezekiah's reform, and the temple structure was now 337 years old. It would stand for only 36 more years.

This final temple renovation was remarkable for four reasons. First, the long-abandoned "book of the law of the LORD" was discovered in the temple. Many Bible students believe that this was either Deuteronomy or else all five of Moses' books. Second, the king humbled himself before God at the realization of how sinful the people had been. Third, Josiah led the people in a great covenant renewal ceremony. Fourth, the Passover was celebrated by a large gathering in Jerusalem, including people from both Judah and Israel. According to 2 Chronicles 35:18, this was the

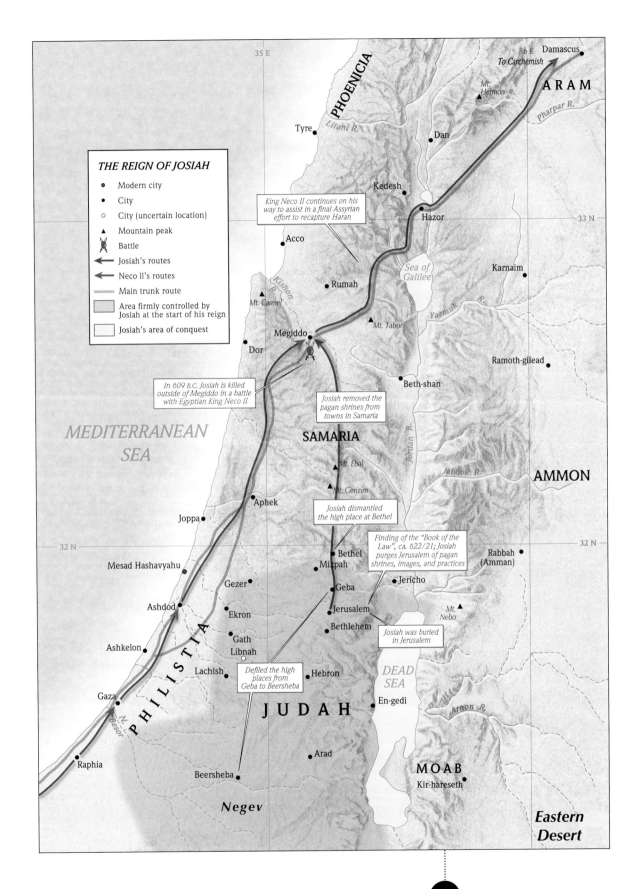

THE REIGN OF JOSIAH

- • Modern city
- • City
- ○ City (uncertain location)
- ▲ Mountain peak
- ⚔ Battle
- ← Josiah's routes
- ← Neco ll's routes
- ┊┊┊ Main trunk route
- ▨ Area firmly controlled by Josiah at the start of his reign
- ▢ Josiah's area of conquest

To Carchemish
Damascus

ARAM

Mt. Hermon

PHOENICIA

Tyre

Litani R.

Dan

Kedesh

Pharpar R.

Hazor

33 N

Karnaim

Sea of Galilee

Acco

Yarmuk R.

Kishon R.

Rumah

King Neco II continues on his way to assist in a final Assyrian effort to recapture Haran

Mt. Carmel

Mt. Tabor

Ramoth-gilead

Megiddo

Dor

Beth-shan

Jordan R.

In 609 B.C. Josiah is killed outside of Megiddo in a battle with Egyptian King Neco II

Josiah removed the pagan shrines from towns in Samaria

SAMARIA

MEDITERRANEAN SEA

Mt. Ebal

Jabbok R.

AMMON

Mt. Gerizim

Aphek

Josiah dismantled the high place at Bethel

Joppa

Bethel

Finding of the "Book of the Law", ca. 622/21; Josiah purges Jerusalem of pagan shrines, images, and practices

32 N

Rabbah (Amman)

32 N

Mizpah

Mesad Hashavyahu

Jericho

Gezer

Geba

Mt. Nebo

Ashdod

Ekron

Jerusalem

Bethlehem

Josiah was buried in Jerusalem

Gath

Ashkelon

Libnah

DEAD SEA

Defiled the high places from Geba to Beersheba

Lachish

Hebron

Gaza

N. Besor

En-gedi

Arnon R.

JUDAH

Arad

Raphia

MOAB

Beersheba

Kir-hareseth

Negev

Eastern Desert

Megiddo, a Canaanite stronghold that guarded the main pass through the Carmel Mountains.

greatest single Passover celebration in the entire history of the Israelite monarchy. For one last time, a Davidic king was ruling the people of God according to the law of the Lord. By this time, however, God had pronounced sentence on Judah that he would not revoke.

In 609 B.C. at age 39, Josiah made a foolish military decision that cost him his life. An Egyptian army under Pharaoh Neco had marched north up the coastal plain of Palestine in order to join forces with the remnant of the Assyrian army to form a coalition against the Babylonians. (The Babylonians had conquered Nineveh a few years earlier.) Josiah decided to challenge Neco's right to pass through Judah, so his army advanced against Neco. At the battle of Megiddo, Josiah was killed.

So tragic was this loss that the Prophet Jeremiah composed a special funeral lament for the death of Josiah (2 Chron. 35:25). One of his sons (Jehoahaz) later died as a prisoner in Egypt; two more sons (Jehoiakim and Zedekiah) died as prisoners in Babylonia. Josiah's grandson Jehoiachin survived in Babylonia, keeping the hopes of a restored Davidic dynasty alive.

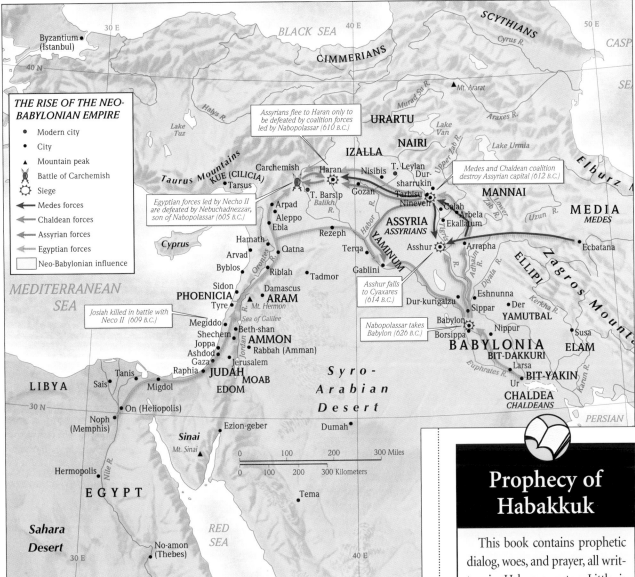

THE RISE OF THE NEO-BABYLONIAN EMPIRE

- ● Modern city
- ● City
- ▲ Mountain peak
- ⊗ Battle of Carchemish
- ✻ Siege
- ← Medes forces
- ← Chaldean forces
- ← Assyrian forces
- ← Egyptian forces
- ☐ Neo-Babylonian influence

Assyrians flee to Haran only to be defeated by coalition forces led by Nabopolassar (610 B.C.)

Medes and Chaldean coalition destroy Assyrian capital (612 B.C.)

Egyptian forces led by Necho II are defeated by Nebuchadnezzar, son of Nabopolassar (605 B.C.)

Asshur falls to Cyaxares (614 B.C.)

Nabopolassar takes Babylon (626 B.C.)

Josiah killed in battle with Neco II (609 B.C.)

HABAKKUK'S MINISTRY

The Prophet Habakkuk left no traces of himself in Scripture beyond his book. Because of his references to the international situation of his times, however, he almost certainly ministered near the end of the seventh century, sometime after Nineveh fell to the Babylonians but before Josiah's death. Habakkuk is known as a prophet especially burdened for the honor of God's name, and the book of **HABAKKUK** is written in a question-and-answer format in which the prophet questions God and God responds. For Christians the best known teaching of Habakkuk is that the just will live by faith (Hab. 2:4).

Prophecy of Habakkuk

This book contains prophetic dialog, woes, and prayer, all written in Hebrew poetry. Little is known of the author's personal life except that he ministered in Judah at the end of the seventh century. The key word for the book is "dialogue"; the key text is Habakkuk 2:4. **One-Sentence Summary:** *When Habakkuk asked God questions about the nature of evil and its punishment, God answered by revealing His righteousness and sovereignty, and the prophet then responded with worship and faith.*

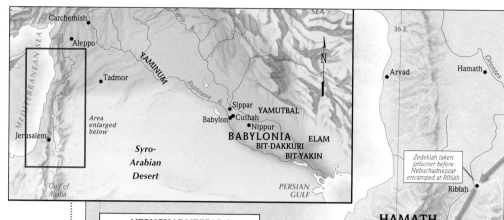

NEBUCHADNEZZAR'S CAMPAIGNS AGAINST JUDAH

- • City
- ▲ Mountain peak
- ✧ Siege
- → Nebuchadnezzar's first campaign (604)
- → Nebuchadnezzar's second campaign (598–597)
- → Nebuchadnezzar's third campaign (587–586)
- → Egyptian campaign of 604–601
- → Zedekiah's escape route
- → Edomite's attack on Jerusalem
- Area of Babylonian dominance

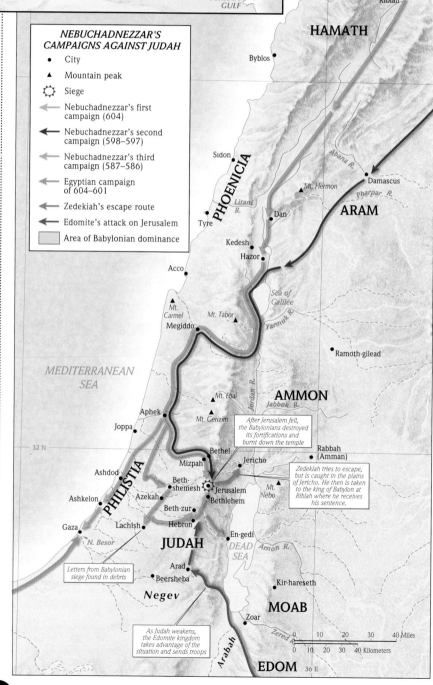

Zedekiah taken prisoner before Nebuchadnezzar encamped at Riblah

After Jerusalem fell, the Babylonians destroyed its fortifications and burnt down the temple

Zedekiah tries to escape, but is caught in the plains of Jericho. He then is taken to the king of Babylon at Riblah where he receives his sentence.

Letters from Babylonian siege found in debris

As Judah weakens, the Edomite kingdom takes advantage of the situation and sends troops

Nebuchadnezzar

This king of Babylon is mentioned by name nearly ninety times in the Bible, in nine different books (2 Kings, 1 and 2 Chronicles, Ezra, Nehemiah, Esther, Jeremiah, Ezekiel, and Daniel). As the greatest king of the neo-Babylonian Empire, he ruled from 605 until his death in 562. His father Nabopolassar led the Babylonians into an aggressive period of military advance. His death put Nebuchadnezzar—a brilliant military strategist—on the throne at the right time to push his empire into a brief but shining period of world dominion. His period of insanity described by the Book of Daniel is not reported in any official Babylonian records.

Babylonia

The southern Euphrates River (southern Iraq of today) was the location of Babylon, capital city of one of the world's ancient superpowers. Although the Babylonians had a long history, they rose to superpower status, often called the neo-Babylonians or Chaldeans, after taking Nineveh in 612 and defeating the Egyptians at Carchemish in 605. The city of Babylon fell to the Persians in 539 B.C. The early Christians used the code name "Babylon" to refer to Rome, the anti-God superpower of the first century. Babylonia was the third oppressor kingdom bent on destroying the people of God.

JUDAH'S LAST FOUR KINGS

All of the last four kings of Judah were vassals of a greater empire, either of Egypt or of Babylonia. Three were Josiah's sons; one was his grandson. None followed the way of the Lord, and Jeremiah was brutalized during this time. This last period, lasting less than twenty-five years, is told in **2 KINGS 23—25** and **2 CHRONICLES 36**. Supplementary details are included in the book of **JEREMIAH**.

JEHOAHAZ

Josiah's son Jehoahaz (also called Shallum) was not the oldest, but the people of Judah chose him to become king after Josiah was killed in battle. He was king for only three months when he was taken as Pharaoh Neco's prisoner. Neco levied a huge tribute from Judah and installed Jehoahaz's older brother Jehoiakim as his vassal in Jerusalem, believing that Jehoiakim would be more compliant.

JEHOIAKIM

This son of Josiah had the birth name Eliakim, but Neco forced him to take the name Jehoiakim, showing that he was subject to Neco's will. He was in fact two years older than his brother Jehoahaz and may have been bypassed at first because of his pro-Egyptian sympathies. He ruled for eleven years and was known for his vicious persecution of Jeremiah.

After the Babylonian army defeated the Egyptian army in 605, it attacked Jerusalem (Dan. 1:1-2). Jehoiakim shifted his loyalty to Babylon, and a number of the upper-class members of Jerusalem nobility, along with a number of articles from Solomon's temple, were taken to Babylon. This was the occasion that Daniel was deported as an exile, and Daniel's interpretation of Nebuchadnezzar's dream took place the following year (Dan. 2:1). In the meantime, however, Jehoiakim, was allowed to continue reigning as Nebuchadnezzar's vassal, even though at one point he had been arrested by Nebuchadnezzar (2 Chron. 36:6).

After three years Jehoiakim foolishly tried to shake off the Babylonian yoke (2 Kings 24:1), believing that re-alliance with Egypt would provide a better opportunity for Judah to maintain independence. Nebuchadnezzar retaliated by sending the Babylonian army against Jerusalem again. Jehoiakim died at age thirty-six of unstated causes before the invasion force arrived. His eighteen-year-old son Jehoiachin was left to deal with the Babylonian crisis.

JEREMIAH'S MINISTRY

More is known about Jeremiah than any of the other writing prophets. He was a member of a priestly family from Anathoth, a short distance from Jerusalem. God called him to ministry during the rule of Josiah, and he was required to remain single and childless as a symbol of the desperate times he lived through. He faced grave personal calamity during the reigns of Jehoiakim and Zedekiah. Because he exposed his inner feelings in his writings, Jeremiah is called "the Weeping Prophet."

During Jehoiakim's reign Jeremiah was almost put to death because of his prophecy that Judah would be destroyed (Jer. 26). In Jehoiakim's fourth year (605 B.C.) Jeremiah wrote a "first draft" of his book with the help of his scribe Baruch (Jer. 36). The king contemptuously burned the scroll, a few columns at a time.

During Zedekiah's reign, Jeremiah prophesied further that Jerusalem would be destroyed. He was therefore considered a traitor, resulting in imprisonment, beating, and finally being thrown into a muddy pit (Jer. 37—38). He is famous because of his prediction of seventy years of captivity for the Israelites. This may be reckoned two ways: (1) the years between the time the first captives went to Babylon and the time the first exiles returned (605–536 B.C.) or (2) the time between the destruction of Solomon's temple and the dedication of the second temple (586–516 B.C.); see Jer. 25:11–12; 29:10.

After the Babylonians destroyed Jerusalem, Jeremiah stayed behind to support Gedaliah, the Babylonian-appointed governor. After the governor was murdered, Jeremiah was forcibly taken to Egypt where he presumably died.

The book of **JEREMIAH** is of special interest to Christians because—recognizing that Israel had abandoned the old (Sinaitic) covenant—it prophesied the coming of God's new covenant that would surpass the old. Jesus established the new covenant with His death, establishing the Lord's Supper as its special sign (Jer. 31:31-33; Luke 22:20; Heb. 9:15). The new covenant prophecy of Jeremiah is thus a special link showing that God's plan to build an everlasting kingdom of redeemed people has been a coherent, unified plan from the beginning.

JEHOIACHIN

Jehoiakim's son Jehoiachin was also known as Coniah or Jeconiah. He ruled in Jerusalem for a hundred days while he was eighteen years old,

Prophecy of Jeremiah

This book of prophecies and historical narratives, written in a mixture of Hebrew poetry and prose, is the longest book of the Bible (by word count). Jeremiah had a long ministry during the days of Judah's last five kings (late seventh century and early sixth century), extending on into the period of the exile. The key word for the book is "curse"; the key texts are Jeremiah 30:15; 31:31. **One-Sentence Summary:** *Anguished by the burden of his prophetic call and the rejection of his message, Jeremiah witnessed what he warned about, the Babylonian captivity, yet he prophesied God's gracious restoration through the new covenant.*

Modern Anathoth which is a few miles east of Jerusalem. Anathoth was the home of Jeremiah the prophet.

from December 598 until March 597 when he surrendered to Nebuchadnezzar. Jerusalem had been besieged once more; this time Nebuchadnezzar took the king, the queen mother, and 10,000 people (including the Prophet Ezekiel) away as captives.

The temple was stripped of anything of value (2 Kings 24:12-24). Nebuchadnezzar installed the king's uncle, Zedekiah, as his vassal in Jerusalem. Zedekiah no doubt promised that he would keep Jerusalem properly submissive. The people of Judah always considered Jehoiachin to be their true king as long as he lived, carefully dating events by referring to him (2 Kings 25:26; Jer. 52:31; Ezek. 1:2; Matt. 1:12).

OBADIAH'S MINISTRY

Obadiah may have ministered at the time of the Babylonian invasions of Judah. Others believe that he lived as early as the time of Elisha. In any event, the book of **OBADIAH** was against the land of Edom, south of the Dead Sea, where the descendants of Esau lived. These people—distant relatives of the people of Judah—were gloating over Judah's invasion by foreign powers. Obadiah said that as a result, God would judge them, while ultimately rescuing His own people and making them prosper.

Prophecy of Obadiah

This brief book—the shortest in the Old Testament—is written entirely in Hebrew poetry. This prophet, unknown outside his book, brought God's word of judgment concerning the coming fall of Edom. The key word for the book is "Edom"; the key text is Obadiah verse 15. **One-Sentence Summary:** *Obadiah prophesied that God would destroy the nation of Edom because of its pride and violence, particularly in looking down on Judah's misfortune, and ultimately the kingdom will be the Lord's.*

Vistas of Edomite territory (p.119).

ZEDEKIAH

Josiah's third son to be king had the birth name Mattaniah, but Nebuchadnezzar forced him to take the name Zedekiah, showing that he was subject to Nebuchadnezzar's will. Just as Jehoiakim had rebelled against the king that put him in power, so did Zedekiah. Both experienced invasions of the Babylonian army. Zedekiah ruled from Jerusalem eleven years, from 597 to 586.

For at least four years Zedekiah submitted to the Babylonians, even visiting the city of Babylon (Jer. 51:59). Later, however, he rebelled, evidently seeking help from the Egyptians (Jer. 37:5). In retaliation Nebuchadnezzar came against Jerusalem for the third time, arriving with his army in Zedekiah's ninth year (January 588 B.C.). The city was besieged and held out for two years until Zedekiah's eleventh year (August 586 B.C.).

This time the Babylonians took no chances that Jerusalem would ever be a problem again. The temple, the palace, and all important buildings were torched, and the walls of the city were pulled down. Everything valuable was carted away as the spoils of war. An even larger number of citizens was taken away into captivity. Zedekiah was captured; his children brought before him and killed; he was blinded and then carried away to Babylon. Judah was no more. The Babylonian captivity had at last begun.

SUMMARY OF "THE BABYLONIAN MENACE"

During the 130-year period between the Assyrian destruction of Israel and the Babylonian destruction of Judah, there were only two bright spots. Early in the period Hezekiah led a religious revival that was brought to an end by his long-ruling son Manasseh. A century later Josiah led a revival that, again, was rejected by his sons. The sins of Manasseh in turning to idolatry were so grievous that the wrath of the Lord was determined to express itself.

Prophets of God such as Zephaniah, Jeremiah, and Habakkuk had only limited influence with the people of God. Nahum and Obadiah were God's messengers to other nations. By the time of Josiah's untimely death, the balance of power had shifted in favor of the Babylonians. Josiah's successors refused to follow the Lord or hear the voice of His prophets. In three attacks on Jerusalem (605, 598–597, 588–586), the Babylonians finally crushed Judah. There was no longer a descendant of David ruling from Jerusalem. The Sinaitic covenant between God and Israel was no more. All hope lay in the establishment of a new covenant—and in the coming of David's greatest Son, who would be born of the line of Jehoiachin, the last true Davidic monarch.

CONCLUSION

In the space of about three and a half centuries, God educated the nation He had built concerning the sin of idolatry.

1. Beginning by dividing the kingdom after Solomon's death, He sent the Northern Kingdom and the Southern Kingdom in separate directions. The Northern Kingdom's defection to the worship of Baal propagated by Ahab was stopped by the prophetic ministry of Elijah and the divinely ordained revolt led by Jehu (931–841 B.C.).

2. Next God brought the Assyrians into world prominence. There was a brief time of Israelite power and prestige under Jeroboam II (in Israel) and Uzziah (in Judah). Prophets such as Amos, Hosea, Micah, and Isaiah had little spiritual impact. The Northern Kingdom, therefore, was judged by God through the fall of Samaria and the Assyrian captivity (841–722 B.C.).

3. Judah survived alone for another 130 years. Despite two periods of revival, the people continued mainly following other gods. Zephaniah, Habakkuk, and Jeremiah warned God's people of the coming Babylonian disaster. The Southern Kingdom was judged by God through the fall of Jerusalem and the Babylonian captivity (722–586 B.C.).

The grand summary of the Bible is *The Lord God through His Christ is graciously building a kingdom of redeemed people for their joy and for His own glory.* We have seen how God succeeded in educating His nation. In the next chapter in the Kingdom Story, God will succeed in His purposes, but His plan will involve quietly preserving the remnant of His nation in preparation for establishing the new covenant.

REFLECTIVE QUESTIONS

1. Contrast Rehoboam of Judah and Jeroboam of Israel. What were their respective strengths and weaknesses?

2. Why did the biblical writers keep attacking the sin of Jeroboam? What was so terrible about what he did?

3. Do you agree with the assessment that Ahab and Jezebel were the most evil husband-and-wife team in the Scriptures? Why? How did they gain such a powerful influence?

4. Compare the ministries of Elijah and Elisha. Which one would you prefer to be like? Why?

5. What was so special about Elijah that he was one of the two Old Testament persons that appeared with Jesus on the Mount of Transfiguration?

6. How important is it for God's people today for there to be independent "prophets" that can criticize both kings ("state") and priests ("church")? Are there such individuals today? How would you recognize them?

7. Why do you suppose the Israelites fell into idol worship so readily for hundreds of years, even though they had repeated warnings? What does this imply for today?

8. Assess Jehoshaphat of Judah. Was he evil, righteous, or a mixed character? What evidence can you find to support your view?

9. Assess Jehu of Israel. Was he evil, righteous, or a mixed character? What evidence can you find to support your view?

10. Why did God allow an idolatrous king such as Jeroboam II to experience such economic and political success? To what extent should political and economic success be seen as an indication of God's blessing on someone?

11. The Prophets Amos and Jonah lived about the same time. How were their messages alike? How were they different?

12. The two boy kings of Judah were Joash and Josiah. Both instituted religious reforms. Which one was more important? Why?

13. The Assyrians utterly destroyed the Northern Kingdom of Israel. Which statement do you prefer: "God *planned* for Assyria to destroy Israel" or "God *permitted* Assyria to destroy Israel"? What is the difference? Does God still plan events that result in the deaths of many people?

14. Two men with similar names lived during the last days of the Northern Kingdom, Hoshea the king and Hosea the prophet. How were they alike? How were they different?

15. What made Isaiah the prophet so important? What made him the greatest of all the writing prophets?

16. The Lord's victory over Sennacherib during the rule of Hezekiah is the only Old Testament event narrated three times (2 Kings 18–19; 2 Chron. 32; Is. 36–37). What made this event so memorable?

17. What was the importance of the "book of the law of the LORD" that Josiah recovered? What is the relationship between the Word of God and renewal of God's people?

18. Why does Nebuchadnezzar's name appear so often in the Bible? How was he God's servant, or was he?

19. Compare the initial Babylonian conquest of Jerusalem (605 B.C.) with the final conquest (586 B.C.).

20. What makes the book of Jeremiah memorable to you? How important should his prophecy of the new covenant be for God's people today?

21. Why was it important for the biblical writer to report the survival of Jehoiachin the king in Babylon?

22. How does God's redemption of His people work itself out in Chapter Two of the Kingdom Story?

23. What evidences of God's glory are evident in Chapter Two of the Kingdom Story?

24. What evidences of joy in the lives of God's redeemed people do you see in Chapter Two of the Kingdom Story?

God Keeps a Faithful Remnant

A white marble statue of Alexander the Great (p.144).

Messiah's Space and Time Prepared,

586–6 B.C.

From the call of Abraham to the full establishment of the Israelite nation, God had worked His magnificent thousand-year plan to build His nation. The nation of Egypt had enslaved His people, but He gloriously redeemed them. The nation had been fully complete with land and law and temple under Solomon's great reign.

After Solomon's death a variety of dynasties ruled the Northern Kingdom of Israel. None of the kings was faithful to the Lord. After little more than two centuries, God raised up the nation of the Assyrians to take the people away in slavery. In Jerusalem kings of the Davidic dynasty ruled the people of God from Jerusalem for more than three centuries. Despite occasional revivals the people of Judah were no more faithful than their northern counterparts. God raised up the Babylonians to take the people out of the land He had given them. The temple was no more.

The message of God's prophets had seemingly fallen on deaf ears. Yet some had listened. The prophetic writings were preserved. God graciously sent more prophets after the captivity. After seventy bitter years He brought the people back to their land. At last they had learned to follow Him faithfully. Their first concern was to rebuild the temple so that He could be properly worshiped.

As the Introduction noted, the grand summary of the Bible is *The Lord God through His Christ is graciously building a kingdom of redeemed people for their joy and for His own glory.* Chapter Three in the Kingdom Story is the quiet chapter. Outwardly it appeared that God was doing nothing for more than five centuries. For those who read the story carefully, however, He was doing two extraordinary things. On one hand, God was keeping a minority of His people—now called the Jews— together as a nation. They had their own land, laws, and temple, even though kingship and national independence had disappeared. God was preparing to send His Son "in the fullness of time."

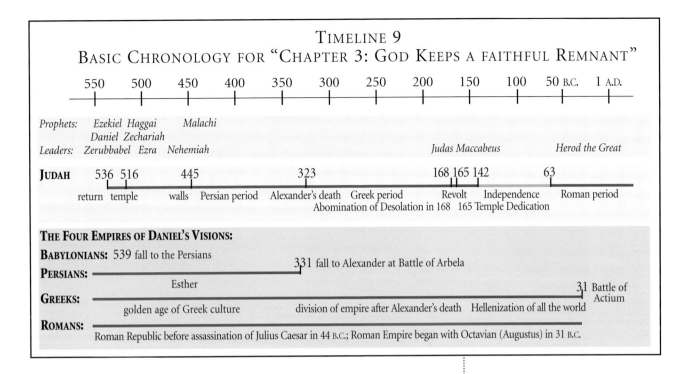

TIMELINE 9
BASIC CHRONOLOGY FOR "CHAPTER 3: GOD KEEPS A FAITHFUL REMNANT"

550	500	450	400	350	300	250	200	150	100	50 B.C.	1 A.D.

Prophets: Ezekiel Haggai   Malachi
           Daniel Zechariah
Leaders: Zerubbabel Ezra Nehemiah   Judas Maccabeus   Herod the Great

JUDAH 536 516   445   323   168 165 142   63
           return temple   walls Persian period Alexander's death Greek period Revolt Independence Roman period
                                        Abomination of Desolation in 168 165 Temple Dedication

THE FOUR EMPIRES OF DANIEL'S VISIONS:

BABYLONIANS: 539 fall to the Persians

PERSIANS: ————————————————————— 331 fall to Alexander at Battle of Arbela

                        Esther

GREEKS: ——— 31 Battle of
                                                                            Actium
              golden age of Greek culture   division of empire after Alexander's death   Hellenization of all the world

ROMANS: ——
              Roman Republic before assassination of Julius Caesar in 44 B.C.; Roman Empire began with Octavian (Augustus) in 31 B.C.

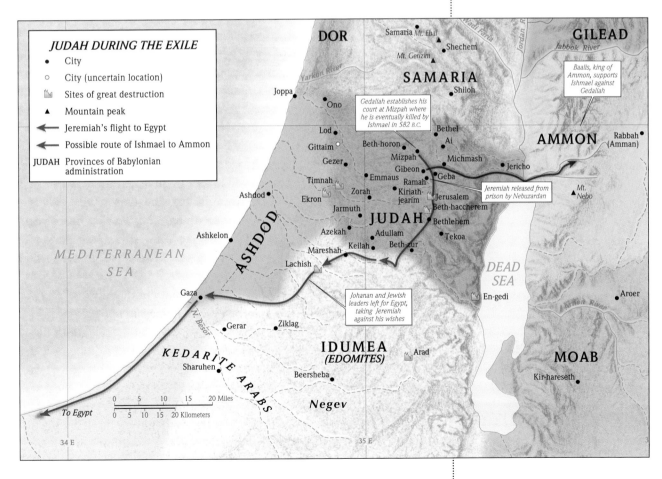

JUDAH DURING THE EXILE

- City
- ○ City (uncertain location)
- ♛ Sites of great destruction
- ▲ Mountain peak
- ← Jeremiah's flight to Egypt
- ← Possible route of Ishmael to Ammon
- JUDAH Provinces of Babylonian administration

DOR
SAMARIA
GILEAD
Samaria Mt. Ebal
Shechem
Mt. Gerizim
Shiloh

Baalis, king of Ammon, supports Ishmael against Gedaliah

Joppa
Ono

Gedaliah establishes his court at Mizpah where he is eventually killed by Ishmael in 582 B.C.

Lod
Bethel
Ai
AMMON
Rabbah (Amman)
Beth-horon
Mizpah
Gittaim
Michmash
Gezer
Gibeon
Jericho
Timnah
Emmaus Ramah Geba
Ashdod
Ekron Zorah Kiriath-jearim
Jerusalem
Beth-haccherem

Jeremiah released from prison by Nebuzardan

Mt. Nebo
Jarmuth
JUDAH
Bethlehem
ASHDOD
Azekah Adullam Beth-zur
Keilah
Tekoa
Ashkelon
Mareshah
Lachish

MEDITERRANEAN SEA
DEAD SEA
En-gedi
Aroer

Gaza
W. Besor

Johanan and Jewish leaders left for Egypt, taking Jeremiah against his wishes

Gerar Ziklag
IDUMEA (EDOMITES)
Arad
MOAB
KEDARITE ARABS
Sharuhen
Beersheba
Kir-hareseth

| 0 | 5 | 10 | 15 | 20 Miles |
| 0 | 5 | 10 | 15 | 20 Kilometers |

To Egypt
Negev

34 E
35 E

Synagogue at Sardis dating from the late 1st century A.D. to the 2nd century.

On the other hand, God scattered most Jews throughout the nations to be testimonies to His name. By building synagogues to preserve their religious identity, Jews were often the starting point for proclaiming the message that the promised Messiah had come. The biblical key for understanding this chapter in the Kingdom Story is Daniel's interpretation of the four-metal image (Dan. 2) and the corresponding interpretation of the four beasts (Dan. 7). Four world superpowers rose during this time: Babylon, Persia, Greece, and Rome. Chapter Three carries the plot of the Kingdom Story from the Babylonian captivity until the birth of the Messiah.

BABYLONIAN DOMINATION:
THE "HEAD OF GOLD"—ISRAELITES BECOME JEWS
(605–539 B.C.)

Only a few incidents from the time the Israelites were in captivity to Babylon survived in the biblical narrative. We are essentially limited to **2 KINGS 25, 2 CHRONICLES 36, JEREMIAH 40—44,** and parts of **DANIEL** and **EZEKIEL.** The earliest exiles of Jerusalem had been sent to Babylon during the rule of Jehoiakim of Judah in 605 (including Daniel). The second group had gone to Babylon at the time Jehoiachin of Judah was exiled in 597 (including Ezekiel). The final and largest group had gone into captivity after Jerusalem was destroyed in 586. At this time Jeremiah chose to stay in Judah but was later forced to go to Egypt. (For a fuller description of the three Babylonian invasions of Judah, see the last part of the previous chapter.)

The Babylonian monarchs mentioned in the Bible are as follows:

- Nebuchadnezzar (605–562), the general who attacked Jerusalem three times
- Evil-Merodach (562–560), who released Jehoiachin from prison (Jer. 52:31)
- Belshazzar (552–539), co-regent with his father Nabonidus (Dan. 5)

The empire that Nebuchadnezzar built was destroyed only twenty-three years after his death.

Tile (glazed brickwork) relief from early 6th century Babylon. Tile reliefs including this one repeated at regular intervals along the Ishtar Gate and its walls which adjoined Procession Street, the main highway to the city. The Ishtar Gate was one of Nebuchadnezzar's most impressive architectural achievements.

JEWISH LIFE IN CAPTIVITY

The Babylonians had learned from the Assyrians that massive relocation of rebellious people was an effective way to curb future rebellions. The thousands of people of Judah taken away to cities in Babylon were no exception. Most managed to survive, work, marry, and have children. They forgot their native Hebrew and adopted Aramaic, the international trade language of their day. The situation was radically different, of course, than when they had lived in their own land. If they completely adopted Babylonian culture, language, and religion, they disappeared into the surrounding society. Most followed that path and became lost tribes.

Others, however, learned the lesson that the prophets had been hammering. They managed to live as obediently to the Lord as they could, although without a temple and without sacrifices, they had to make adjustments. Those who did so remembered (and evidently told people around them) that they had been exiled from the land of Judah. Thus, during their captivity, they came to accept the designation "Jew," which has remained until the present day.

Jews

The name "Jew" is found only in the following late Old Testament books: Ezra, Nehemiah, Esther, Jeremiah, Daniel, and Zechariah. Originally it meant those Israelites who had lived in the land of Judah, that is, members of the tribe of Judah. After the return from exile, it came to mean anyone who was a biological descendant of Jacob (whom God named Israel). By the time of the first century, the term could also be used for non-biological Jews who accepted the Jewish religion. Today "Jew" has both ethnic and religious implications.

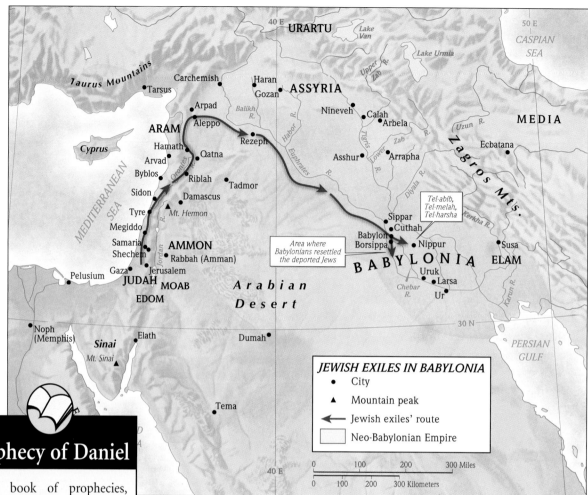

Map labels:

URARTU · Lake Van · 40 E · 50 E · CASPIAN SEA
Taurus Mountains · Tarsus · Carchemish · Haran · Gozan · ASSYRIA · Upper Zab R. · Lake Urmia
Arpad · Balikh R. · Nineveh · Calah · Arbela · Uzun R. · MEDIA · Ecbatana
ARAM · Aleppo · Rezeph · Habor R. · Tigris R. · Asshur · Arrapha · Lower Zab R. · Zagros Mts.
Cyprus · Hamath · Qatna · Euphrates R. · Diyala R. · Kerkha R.
Arvad · Byblos · Orontes R. · Riblah · Tadmor
Sidon · Damascus
Tyre · Mt. Hermon · Sippar · Cuthah · Tel-abib, Tel-melah, Tel-harsha
Megiddo · Jordan R. · Babylon · Borsippa · Nippur · Susa
Samaria · AMMON · Area where Babylonians resettled the deported Jews · B A B Y L O N I A · ELAM
Shechem · Rabbah (Amman) · Uruk · Larsa
Pelusium · Gaza · Jerusalem · JUDAH · MOAB · A r a b i a n · Chebar R. · Ur
EDOM · D e s e r t · 30 N
Noph (Memphis) · Elath · Dumah · PERSIAN GULF
Sinai · Mt. Sinai · Tema

JEWISH EXILES IN BABYLONIA
• City
▲ Mountain peak
← Jewish exiles' route
▢ Neo-Babylonian Empire

0 100 200 300 Miles
0 100 200 300 Kilometers
40 E

Prophecy of Daniel

This book of prophecies, including visions and interpretations, is written partly in Hebrew and partly Aramaic. Many details of the author's life are included. Daniel, a Jewish captive, lived in Babylonia the entire time of the Jews' captivity. The first readers were Jews living in Babylon, perhaps around 530 B.C. The key word for the book is "kingdoms"; the key text is Daniel 4:3. **One-Sentence Summary:** *Daniel demonstrated remarkable trust in God and revealed God's plans for the future, not only for his own day but also for the Maccabean period and on through the time that God's kingdom is established by the Son of Man.*

DANIEL'S MINISTRY

Daniel was a young man of the Jerusalem nobility taken to Babylonia in the first deportation (605 B.C.). His success as court advisor to Nebuchadnezzar shows that many of the captives from Judah managed to adapt and survive quite well. His long ministry as a prophet and royal counselor endured until the early Persian period. The colorful events of his life include the following:

- Being promoted to a prominent government position (with his friends Shadrach, Meschach, and Abednego) after choosing to eat only food allowed in God's law

- Interpreting Nebuchadnezzar's dream of a giant four-metal image

- Leading Nebuchadnezzar to worship Daniel's God after his insanity

- Explaining the meaning of the writing on the wall (as an old man, in 539 B.C.)

- Escaping from being eaten by hungry lions (as an old man, under the Persians)

- Writing down prophecies that would be fulfilled at the time of the Maccabean revolt

What is particularly helpful about the book of **Daniel** is the way it paves the way for understanding the overall picture for Chapter Three of the Kingdom Story. Daniel 2 gives the meaning of the four-metal image of Nebuchadnezzar's dream; Daniel 7 describes a vision of four beasts; Daniel 8 describes a vision of a ram and a goat. When Daniel 2, 7, and 8 are compared, the following plot emerges.

1. **Head of gold (2:36-38); lion (7:4).** The Babylonians were the first superpower that God caused to triumph during the period when He was holding a remnant of His faithful people. The Babylonians were fabulously powerful but endured for less than a century, from their conquest over Nineveh in 612 to their defeat by the Persians in 539.

2. **Chest and arms of silver (2:39); bear (7:5); ram (8:3-4).** The Persians (in alliance with the weaker Medes) were the second superpower God brought to world prominence during Chapter Three. Persia endured for just over two centuries, from the conquest of Babylon in 539 until their defeat by the army of Alexander the Great in 331.

3. **Belly of bronze (2:39); four-headed leopard (7:6); goat (8:5-14).** The Greeks were the third world superpower that God called into preeminence. The Greeks, including the fourfold division of their empire after Alexander's death, endured for exactly three centuries, from the Battle of Arbela (331) to the Battle of Actium (31 B.C.).

4. **Legs of iron (2:40-43); monstrous beast with iron teeth (7:7).** The Romans were the fourth world superpower, the world's greatest military machine until the Industrial Revolution. In the days of the Romans, God's everlasting kingdom was to be established (2:44-45) and the Son of Man would begin to be acknowledged by people everywhere (7:13-14). God's kingdom would finally be revealed in all its splendor.

This understanding of Chapter Three is developed in the pages that follow. When this perspective is kept in view, God's long-term plan of waiting for fullness of time in order to send His Son can be better appreciated (Gal. 4:4).

A mold of a pilgrim's flask showing a depiction of Daniel holding two lions. The mold is Byzantine and dates from the 4th–5th centuries A.D.

This Torah scroll dates from the 16th century A.D. It was used in the Spanish Jewish synagogue in the city of Zafed. Part of the scroll was damaged in the earthquake in 1837. The scroll was then placed in a genizah, a repository for old, damaged, worn, or defective scrolls. The scroll is written in a beautiful Sephardic hand. The wooden rollers, while not originally belonging to this scroll, are of approximately the same age, as is the Torah scroll cover.

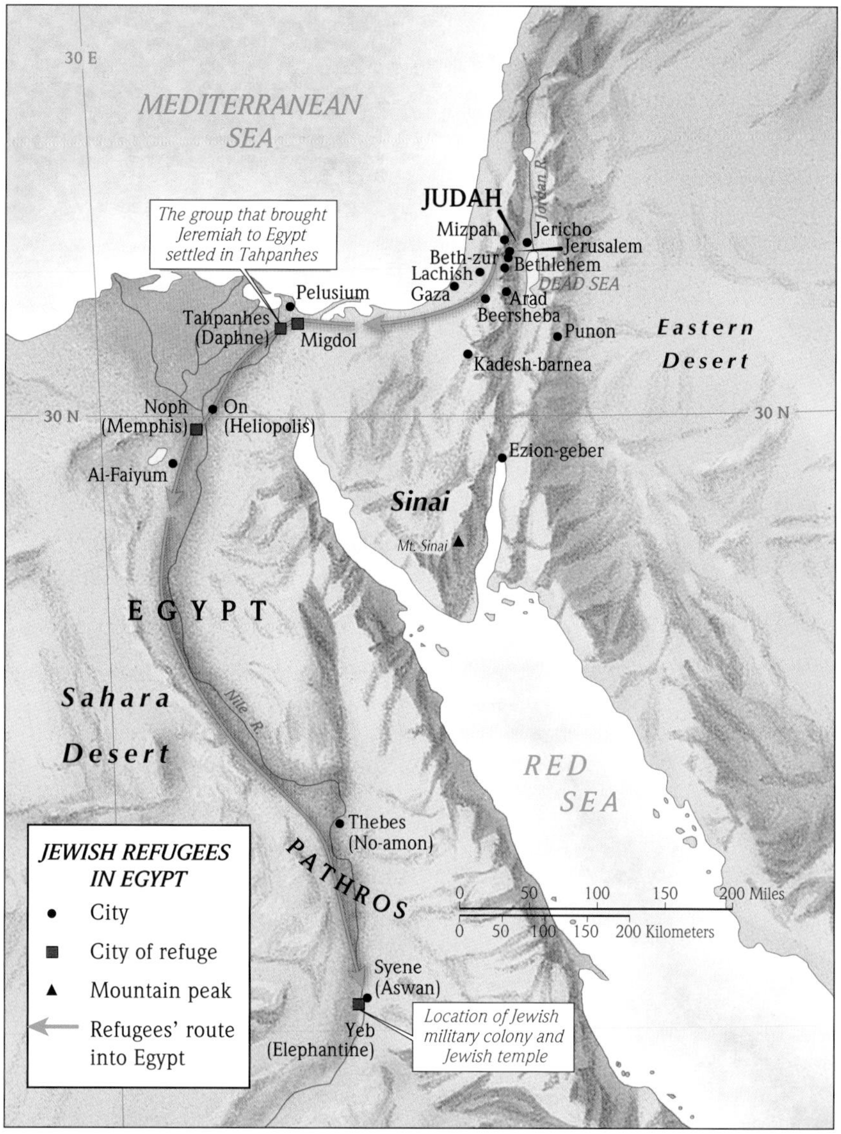

The group that brought Jeremiah to Egypt settled in Tahpanhes

Location of Jewish military colony and Jewish temple

JEWISH REFUGEES IN EGYPT
● City
■ City of refuge
▲ Mountain peak
← Refugees' route into Egypt

EZEKIEL'S MINISTRY

Ezekiel had a different kind of ministry than Daniel did. He spoke and wrote for the Jewish captives among whom he lived. From a priestly family Ezekiel was taken to Babylonia in the second deportation (597), when Jehoiachin and 10,000 others were also led away as prisoners. He lived with the Jewish exiles by the Chebar (Kebar) Canal that connected the Euphrates and the Tigris Rivers.

Ezekiel foresaw the fall of Jerusalem, emphasizing its sins. His wife's death when the siege of Jerusalem began broke his heart, but he was not allowed to mourn. The book of **EZEKIEL** includes a number of highly unusual symbolic actions. After Jerusalem's fall Ezekiel prophesied the restoration and glorious future for God's people. God used Ezekiel as a major factor to encourage the exiles to stay true to the "faith of their fathers."

Prophecy of Ezekiel

This book of prophecies, including visions and symbolic actions, is written mainly in Hebrew prose but with some poetry. Some details of the author's life are included. Ezekiel, a Jewish captive, lived in Babylonia. His ministry can be precisely dated from 593 to 571 B.C. The key word for the book is "visions"; the key text is Ezekiel 38:23. **One-Sentence Summary:** *From exile in Babylon, Ezekiel's stunning visions and startling symbolic acts were prophecies for the Israelites to teach God's sovereign plan over them in the history of His kingdom, so that "they shall know that I am the LORD."*

JUDAH IMMEDIATELY AFTER JERUSALEM'S FALL

Although Daniel and Ezekiel were serving the Lord in Babylonia, Jerusalem still stood for a few years. When the city finally fell in August of 586, Nebuchadnezzar's army utterly demolished everything of value but carried away tons of bronze. They had already carted off the gold and silver. The book of **LAMENTATIONS** memorialized this tragedy.

Nebuchadnezzar appointed Gedaliah as governor of the remaining people, and Jeremiah stayed to support him. Gedaliah ruled from the town of Mizpah, but he was soon murdered in a conspiracy. Out of fear of further retaliation by the Babylonians, a group of survivors determined to flee to Egypt. Although Jeremiah gave them God's promise that they would survive peacefully if they stayed in Judah, they decided to go to Egypt anyway. Thus Jeremiah ended his prophetic ministry in Egypt against his own wishes (Jer. 43:6–7).

RESTORATION FROM CAPTIVITY:
LAND, TEMPLE, AND GOD'S LAW UNDER EZRA AND NEHEMIAH

The Babylonians fell to the Persians in 539 B.C. Under the Persians' enlightened policies, exiles were allowed to return to their homeland. King Cyrus of Persia became God's agent, and under Sheshbazzar's leadership thousands of Jews migrated back to Jerusalem, arriving sometime around 536 B.C. This was about seventy years after the first deportation of Jews from Jerusalem, the one in which Daniel and many others were first taken to Babylon in 605 B.C. Their first order of business was to restore the temple. God later blessed them with two remarkable leaders: Ezra, who taught God's law for a new day, and Nehemiah, who led the people to rebuild Jerusalem. The books of **EZRA** and **NEHEMIAH** describe these events.

Book of Lamentations

This book of Hebrew poetry expresses the bitter grief the author felt after Jerusalem was destroyed by the Babylonians. According to Jewish tradition it was written by Jeremiah. It was probably composed within a year of the city's fall in 586 B.C. The key word for the book is "lament"; the key text is Lamentations 1:1. **One-Sentence Summary:** *A skillful and emotional poet described the devastation of the city of Jerusalem—brought by the Babylonians but ultimately caused by the Lord's anger against His people—and poured out His own personal expressions of sorrow.*

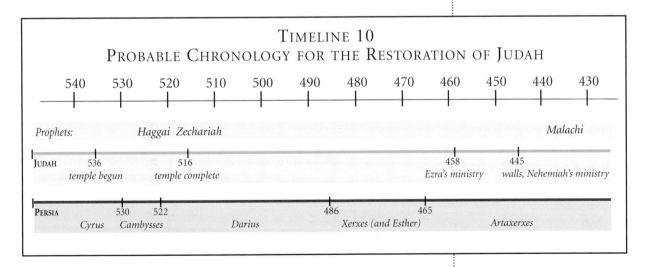

TIMELINE 10
PROBABLE CHRONOLOGY FOR THE RESTORATION OF JUDAH

540 530 520 510 500 490 480 470 460 450 440 430

Prophets: Haggai Zechariah   Malachi

JUDAH 536   516   458   445
       temple begun   temple complete   Ezra's ministry   walls, Nehemiah's ministry

PERSIA 530 522   486   465
        Cyrus Cambysses   Darius   Xerxes (and Esther)   Artaxerxes

SECOND TEMPLE BUILT

The Jews who returned from exile were truly committed to the Lord, yet there was some delay in rebuilding the temple. God raised up the Prophet Haggai to kindle their commitment to complete the temple. The Jewish governor that led the people in this project was Zerubbabel. This temple was dedicated in 516 B.C., exactly seventy years after Solomon's temple was destroyed. Much later it was expanded and made more splendid during the time of Herod. This second temple endured until the Romans destroyed it in A.D. 70.

RETURN UNDER SHESHBAZZAR

Cyrus the Great, ruler of the Persians from 559 until his death in 530, reversed the policy of the Babylonians. He encouraged conquered people to return to their homeland and to build temples to their own gods. Cyrus's decree authorizing the Jews to return—and to take with them the furnishings from Solomon's temple—is reported in Ezra 1:2-4.

Column with inscription in Old Persian script ascribed to Cyrus.

This decree came in 538, a year after the fall of Babylon, and it took the Jews some time to organize the large party of nearly 50,000 who were willing to relocate from Babylon (Ezra 2:64). Their journey took at least four months, and the leader to whom the temple furnishings were entrusted was Sheshbazzar, a Jewish "prince." Sheshbazzar was the original governor for the returning exiles, and he was also involved in helping lay the foundation for the second temple.

One of the first orders of business was to build an altar on the site of the temple so that animal sacrifices could begin again. The leadership for achieving this was Zerubbabel (possibly another name for Sheshbazzar) and Joshua the priest. Immediately after this, the temple reconstruction was begun. The second temple was built on the site of Solomon's temple, but it was a much simpler structure since the people had no access to the vast material resources such as David had made available for the first temple. The Gentile inhabitants of the region opposed the rebuilding project, so it was stopped for about twenty years.

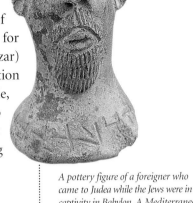

A pottery figure of a foreigner who came to Judea while the Jews were in captivity in Babylon. A Mediterranean background is suggested by the Aramaic writing on the base of the figure.

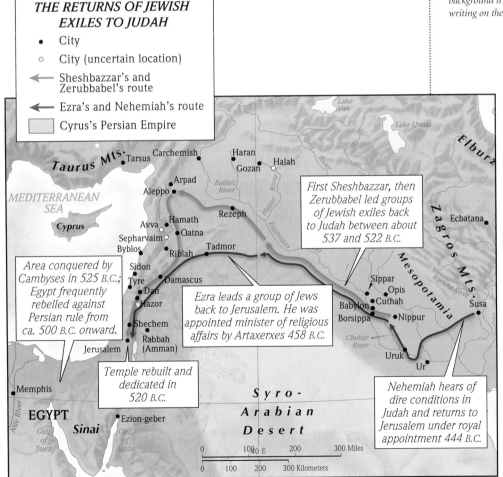

THE RETURNS OF JEWISH EXILES TO JUDAH

- • City
- ○ City (uncertain location)
- ← Sheshbazzar's and Zerubbabel's route
- ← Ezra's and Nehemiah's route
- ▭ Cyrus's Persian Empire

First Sheshbazzar, then Zerubbabel led groups of Jewish exiles back to Judah between about 537 and 522 B.C.

Area conquered by Cambyses in 525 B.C.; Egypt frequently rebelled against Persian rule from ca. 500 B.C. onward.

Ezra leads a group of Jews back to Jerusalem. He was appointed minister of religious affairs by Artaxerxes 458 B.C.

Temple rebuilt and dedicated in 520 B.C.

Nehemiah hears of dire conditions in Judah and returns to Jerusalem under royal appointment 444 B.C.

Prophecy of Haggai

This book of prophetic sermons is written in Hebrew prose. Nothing is known of the author's background except that he was a Jewish exile who had returned to Jerusalem. His ministry can be precisely dated to 520 B.C. The key word for the book is "rebuilding"; the key text is Haggai 1:8. **One-Sentence Summary:** *When Haggai proclaimed God's command to rebuild the temple, giving God's promises that the glory of the second temple would exceed that of the first temple, the people obeyed with a willing heart.*

Prophecy of Zechariah

This book of prophecies, including visions and words from God, is written mainly in Hebrew prose but with some poetry. Zechariah traced his lineage briefly. His ministry can be dated to 520–518 B.C. The key word for the book is "Jerusalem"; the key text is Zechariah 8:3. **One-Sentence Summary:** *Through night visions and prophetic oracles Zechariah predicted the welfare of Jerusalem as God's beloved holy city, into which the King would enter riding a donkey, the one also called God's Servant and Branch.*

HAGGAI'S MINISTRY

In 522 B.C. the Persian army general Darius seized the throne, ruling until 486. In Darius's second year God spoke to one of the exiles who had returned by the name of Haggai. Haggai brought a prophetic word to Zerubbabel and Joshua the priest that the Lord's temple was to be finished. The book of **HAGGAI** promised that the glory of the second temple would surpass the one that Solomon built. (This was fulfilled when the Messiah Himself personally came to the second temple.) There was an immediate response to Haggai's message, however, and the work of rebuilding was resumed. According to Ezra 6:14 Haggai saw the successful conclusion of his ministry in the completion of the temple.

ZECHARIAH'S MINISTRY

Zechariah was a contemporary of Haggai. The only thing known about him is that he was the son of Berechiah and grandson of Iddo (Zech. 1:1). Presumably he too was one of the exiles that returned to Judah. He dated two of his visions, which enables scholars to integrate his ministry with that of Haggai. He prophesied for at least two years and wrote the book of **ZECHARIAH**, a considerably longer book than Haggai. Zechariah focused on the city of Jerusalem, which still lay in ruins. Both the near-term rebuilding of the city and the ultimate, everlasting destiny of Jerusalem as the city in which God delights were part of his burden. He probably did not live to see Jerusalem's walls complete, more than sixty years after his initial ministry.

DEDICATION OF THE SECOND TEMPLE

The rebuilding of the temple, encouraged by the ministry of Haggai, took four years to finish. Part of this had to do with receiving official government permission from the Persian king, Darius, who was by then ruling. The completed temple was dedicated with much rejoicing in March 516, seventy years after it had been destroyed in August 586. Both Haggai and Zechariah were present for the reestablishment of the temple services (Ezra 6:14).

Some temple furnishings that Nebuchadnezzar had taken to Babylon were restored to their proper use. There is no further record, however, of the ark of the covenant that contained the Ten Commandments, which was apparently destroyed in 586 (see Jer. 3:16). The second temple endured until at last the Romans destroyed it in A.D. 70.

The great audience hall begun by Darius and completed by Xerxes.

LAW AND LAND REESTABLISHED

There is almost a sixty-year break between the dedication of the second temple and the ministry of Ezra. The events of the book of **ESTHER** happened in far-off Persia. Then God called Ezra to teach a new generation of Jews how to live according to God's law. The land itself was then made more secure by building Jerusalem's walls, led by Nehemiah. With the dedication of the city walls in 445 B.C., everything—people, temple, law, and land—was in place for the coming of the Messiah. Although there were some developments such as the rise of the Pharisees and Sadducees, there was a fundamental continuity in Judea and in Judaism during the centuries between Nehemiah and Jesus.

RETURN UNDER EZRA

Ezra had mastered the Scriptures of his day—the books of Moses—in the land of captivity. With great skill as an interpreter of the old law for a new day, Ezra persuaded a large group of Babylonian Jews to relocate to Jerusalem. With the approval of Artaxerxes, king of Persia, Ezra led a group of fewer than 2000 men, plus women and children, on the difficult journey back to Judah. They arrived in 458 B.C., Artaxerxes' seventh year (Ezra 7:8).

Ezra

"Ezra the scribe" was the most important character of the post-exile period. Reared in Babylon, he returned to Judah in 458 and led a reform of Jewish marriage. God used this priest to interpret the meaning of His word for a new day. After Nehemiah rebuilt Jerusalem, Ezra led in further reforms. According to Jewish tradition, he wrote the book of Ezra and 1 and 2 Chronicles. Some scholars believe that he also wrote the book of Nehemiah. His influence greatly shaped Jewish life and thought, and in a sense all later interpreters of Scripture owe a debt to Ezra as their prototype (Ezra 7:10; Neh. 8:8).

Book of Ezra

This book contains Persian court documents, lists, and narratives written in Hebrew, with some Aramaic sections. Ezra traced his priestly lineage extensively. His return to Jerusalem and his ministry there in the mid 400s B.C. is found both in this book and in Nehemiah. The key word for the book is "restoration"; the key text is Ezra 6:16. **One-Sentence Summary:** *The first group of returning exiles restored worship of the Lord, culminating in a rebuilt temple, but Ezra, who led the second group, reestablished Israelite community under Mosaic law, culminating in putting away mixed marriages.*

Obverse of a Samaritan coin that mentions Sanballat.

EZRA'S REFORM OF MARRIAGE

Moses' law had expressly forbidden God's covenant people to marry pagans (Deut. 7:3). Disregard for this laid a foundation for apostasy, as in the case of Solomon (1 Kings 11:1-8). Ezra discovered that many of the returning exiles had married those who were not followers of the Lord. His prayer of grief is one of the truly heartbreaking prayers in the Bible (Ezra 9). In response the guilty parties decided to end these unlawful marriages. Out of concern for God's law, a divorce court was set up that dissolved these marriages (Ezra 10:16-17).

RETURN UNDER NEHEMIAH

The book of **NEHEMIAH** describes the ministry of another important Jewish leader. Nehemiah had become a valuable, trusted attendant for Artaxerxes, the king of Persia. Thirteen years after Ezra's return to Judah (in Artaxerxes' twentieth year, 445 b.c., Neh. 2:1), Nehemiah received a discouraging report about the exiles in Jerusalem. He was able to get a leave of absence from the king to travel to Jerusalem with an official Persian military escort (Neh. 2:9).

Book of Nehemiah

This book contains mainly Nehemiah's first-person memoirs and official lists, written in Hebrew. Because Ezra-Nehemiah was originally one book, the setting and authorship is the same as for Ezra. Nehemiah's return to Jerusalem and ministry there occurred in the mid 400s B.C. The key word for the book is "walls"; the key text is Nehemiah 6:15. **One-Sentence Summary:** *Through Nehemiah's leadership God enabled the Israelites to rebuild and dedicate Jerusalem's walls as well as to renew their commitment to God as His covenant people.*

REBUILDING THE WALLS

After he arrived, Nehemiah was able to coordinate a massive project to reconstruct the walls of Jerusalem. Nehemiah stands as one of the great organizers of the Bible, keeping elaborate records of the way the work was divided, section by section. This project was strategic because having a strong wall completely surrounding a city was an important point of civic pride in the ancient world. A city without walls was brushed off as insignificant.

Just as there had been opposition to rebuilding the temple, so there was opposition to the wall project. Sanballat (the Persian-appointed governor of Samaria to the north) and Tobiah (evidently the Persian-appointed governor of the land east of the Jordan River) became Nehemiah's great enemies during this period. They accused Nehemiah of wanting to set up Jerusalem as a rebel city.

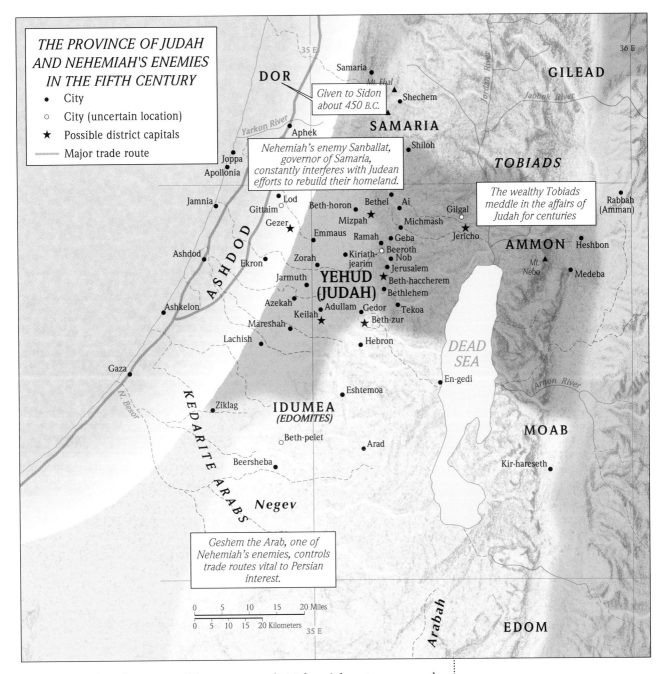

THE PROVINCE OF JUDAH
AND NEHEMIAH'S ENEMIES
IN THE FIFTH CENTURY

- • City
- ○ City (uncertain location)
- ★ Possible district capitals
- ═══ Major trade route

Given to Sidon about 450 B.C.

Nehemiah's enemy Sanballat, governor of Samaria, constantly interferes with Judean efforts to rebuild their homeland.

The wealthy Tobiads meddle in the affairs of Judah for centuries

Geshem the Arab, one of Nehemiah's enemies, controls trade routes vital to Persian interest.

DOR
GILEAD
SAMARIA
TOBIADS
AMMON
ASHDOD
YEHUD (JUDAH)
MOAB
IDUMEA (EDOMITES)
KEDARITE ARABS
Negev
DEAD SEA
EDOM
Arabah

Samaria · Mt. Ebal · Shechem · Shiloh · Aphek · Joppa · Apollonia · Jamnia · Lod · Gittaim · Gezer · Beth-horon · Bethel · Ai · Gilgal · Mizpah · Michmash · Emmaus · Ramah · Geba · Jericho · Ashdod · Ekron · Zorah · Kiriath-jearim · Beeroth · Nob · Jerusalem · Jarmuth · Beth-haccherem · Bethlehem · Azekah · Adullam · Gedor · Tekoa · Keilah · Beth-zur · Mareshah · Hebron · Lachish · Eshtemoa · En-gedi · Gaza · Ziklag · Beth-pelet · Arad · Beersheba · Kir-hareseth · Rabbah (Amman) · Heshbon · Mt. Nebo · Medeba

Jordan River · Jabbok River · Yarkon River · N. Besor · Arnon River

35 E · 36 E

0   5   10   15   20 Miles
0   5   10   15   20 Kilometers

   This hostility, however, did not succeed. Nehemiah set up armed guards to protect the builders, and the entire project was completed in only 52 days (Neh. 6:15). (Archaeological evidence indicates that Nehemiah's Jerusalem was not as extensive as it had been before the Babylonian captivity.)

   The dedication festivities for the wall were full of joy and music, including two great choirs that proceeded around the city and then converged at the temple (Neh. 12). After an interval of more than 140 years (August 586–October 445 B.C.), Jerusalem stood as a complete city once more.

Sabbath

"Sabbath" (rest) included not only the seventh-day rest but also the seventh-year rest for the people of Israel. Remembering the seventh-day Sabbath was God's gracious provision for people and animals, but it was also a legal requirement built into the Ten Commandments. As such, it was the appointed sign of the Sinaitic covenant between God and Israel (Ezek. 20:12). After the return from exile, the Jews increasingly took the Sabbath seriously. By the time of the first century, the Sabbath had also become a day for Jews to gather for worship in their synagogues, a custom not found in the Old Testament. According to Paul, the Sabbath was a shadow fulfilled by Christ's coming (Col. 2:16).

Ezra led the people to further reforms as recorded in **NEHEMIAH 8—9**. This appears to have occurred immediately after the completion of the walls. Ezra led in the following:

- Thoroughly explaining the meaning of God's word to a great assembly of people
- Honoring the Feast of Tabernacles in the finest celebration of this festival ever
- Leading the people to a solemn renewal of their covenant with the Lord
- Agreeing to live as a community under covenant laws, especially the Sabbath
- Excluding all foreigners from the assembly of God's people

The revival under Ezra was comparable to the earlier restoration and covenant renewal under Josiah, with a similar emphasis on the law of the Lord. In both instances there was a clear sense of an official body of Scripture for the people of God, a concept which became increasingly important for the Jews.

MALACHI'S MINISTRY

Nehemiah served as governor in Jerusalem for twelve years (445–433), after which he returned to the king's service (Neh. 5:14; 13:6). He was away for an unknown length of time during which the people of Jerusalem became lethargic about their worship of the Lord. God called one final prophet to address the situation. Sins that the book of **MALACHI** condemned match those that Nehemiah attacked. The priests were corrupt (Mal. 1:6—2:9; Neh. 13:7-8); the tithe was neglected (Mal. 3:8-10; Neh. 10:37-39); Jewish men had married pagan wives (Mal. 2:11-15; Neh. 10:30; 13:23-27).

Prophecy of Malachi

This book contains disputations and prophecies written in Hebrew prose. The prophet did not name his parents or the rulers of his day, which makes precise dating of his life impossible. Almost nothing is known about him. He was probably born in the land of Judah after the exiles began returning from Babylon in the 530s and ministered in the mid 400s. The key word for the book is "messenger"; the key text is Malachi 1:11. **One-Sentence Summary:** *Malachi rebuked God's people for specific violations of the covenant, such as laws concerning sacrifices, divorce, and tithes, but he also prophesied the coming of the Messenger who would set all things right.*

Malachi's ministry may have preceded Nehemiah's original arrival in Judah. He has usually been understood as the last prophet, however, so more likely he challenged people that had reverted to their old ways after Nehemiah's first time as governor. According to Nehemiah 13:6-31, Nehemiah returned to Jerusalem once more, addressing some of the same issues as in his previous administration. Malachi's ministry may have aided him.

SUMMARY OF "RESTORATION FROM CAPTIVITY"

Two historical books (Ezra and Nehemiah) and three prophetic books (Haggai, Zechariah, and Malachi) form the biblical record of the Jewish remnant's return to their own homeland. After the Babylonians destroyed Jerusalem, the people of God were never prone to the idolatry of their forefathers. The work of the last three prophets, however, shows that many people settled for a nominal approach to the Lord.

Through the ministry of the prophets and the great Bible expositor Ezra, the people were renewed to a right relationship to God. Through the organizational abilities of Zerubbabel (for the temple) and Nehemiah (for Jerusalem's walls), the people of God were worshiping Him according to His covenant requirements. They lived in the "holy city" (Neh. 11:1) and foreigners were excluded. Everything was in order for the coming of the Messiah, but the fullness of time had not yet come.

This is the place where the Old Testament narrative stops, at least as far as God's people in their land is concerned. It is not an accident that the New Testament ends with a parallel portrait: the people of God worship Him forever in the everlasting holy city (New Jerusalem). The unclean are excluded. But because the Messiah has come, no temple is needed, and they will be with Him forever (Rev. 21—22). This is the great eternal goal of the Kingdom Story. The Old Testament ends with a pale portrait of this, a kind of anticipation of what will one day last forever.

PERSIAN DOMINATION:
THE "CHEST AND ARMS OF SILVER"—
JEWS REMAIN LARGELY SCATTERED (539–331 B.C.)

God's activity in the world was never limited to the land of Israel. The visions of Daniel showed that He is sovereign over every earthly kingdom. If He humbled the proud Nebuchadnezzar (the head of gold), He could equally show His power in the days that the "chest and arms of silver," the Persians, ruled the world. The beautiful story of Esther shows God's providential work outside the land of Israel during Chapter Three of the Kingdom Story. It is the only biblical narrative that shows God's hand at work among the (pagan) people of the world during the centuries He was preparing for Messiah's coming.

Persia

The area east of the Persian Gulf (Iran of today) was the center of Persian power. The Persians rose to superpower status after they overthrew the Medes to their north, around 550. Their greatest monarch was Cyrus the Great. The city of Babylon fell to the Persians in 539 B.C. The empire at its greatest extended to India in the east, Egypt in the south, and west as far as Asia Minor. Ultimately the Persians fell to the forces of Alexander the Great in 331. Persia was the fourth oppressor kingdom that tried to destroy the people of God (after Egypt, Assyria, and Babylonia), but as the Book of Esther shows, the plan failed.

THE RISE OF THE PERSIANS

The biblical description of Persia's conquest of Babylon is found in **DANIEL 5**, the famous account of the handwriting on the wall. The blasphemous feast of Belshazzar (co-regent of Nabonidus, the last Babylonian emperor) became the occasion for God to pronounce judgment on Babylon. The Persians were able to sneak into the city by redirecting the Euphrates River and then entering the city of Babylon by using the dry riverbed to tunnel under the city wall.

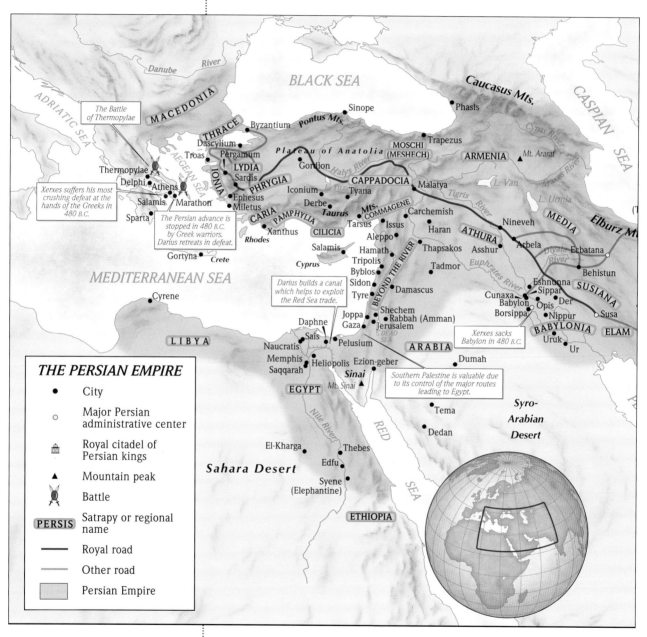

THE PERSIAN EMPIRE

- ● City
- ○ Major Persian administrative center
- 🏛 Royal citadel of Persian kings
- ▲ Mountain peak
- ⚔ Battle
- PERSIS Satrapy or regional name
- ▬▬ Royal road
- ── Other road
- ▨ Persian Empire

The Battle of Thermopylae

Xerxes suffers his most crushing defeat at the hands of the Greeks in 480 B.C.

The Persian advance is stopped in 480 B.C. by Greek warriors. Darius retreats in defeat.

Darius builds a canal which helps to exploit the Red Sea trade.

Xerxes sacks Babylon in 480 B.C.

Southern Palestine is valuable due to its control of the major routes leading to Egypt.

According to Daniel 5:31, the first Persian ruler over the city of Babylon was Darius the Mede. This person is not mentioned outside the book of **Daniel**, so this may be an alternate name for Cyrus the Persian military genius, or it may refer to Gubaru, the man noted in other ancient records as ruling Babylon for the Persians.

When the Persians fully developed their imperial organization, they divided the empire into administrative districts. They often allowed local kings to rule under them, but the emperor was the "king of kings" (Ezra 7:12). There were four official capitals: Babylon, Ecbatana (Ezra 6:2), Susa (Neh. 1:1; Esth. 1:2), and Persepolis (the greatest Persian city, east of the Persian Gulf in the Persian homeland). The Persian kings mentioned in the Bible are these:

- Cyrus (559–530), the great empire builder, called the Lord's shepherd (Is. 44:28)

- Darius (522–486), who reauthorized the building of the Jewish temple (Ezra 6:12)

- Xerxes (486–465), also called Ahasuerus, husband of Esther (Esth. 1:1)

- Artaxerxes (464–424), who supported Ezra and Nehemiah (Ezra 7:12; Neh. 2:1)

A Persian horse and rider from the late Persian period, the time of Nehemiah.

The second tomb from the left was the tomb of Artaxerexes I. He died in 424 B.C. of natural causes. His wife was said to have died the same day.

Silver drinking bowl. The inscription in old Persian cuneiform tells that is was made for "Artaxerxes, the great king, king of kings…son of Xerxes, son of Darius the king, Achaemenian."

ESTHER

The book of **ESTHER** is the single biblical narrative for Chapter Three of the Kingdom Story that tells about Jewish life outside the land of Israel during the days of the Persians. The events occurred during the reign of Xerxes, called Ahasuerus in Hebrew, who ruled from 486 to 465.

Three events are dated within the book:

- 483 B.C.: Xerxes' fabulous banquet, the third year of Xerxes (Esth. 1:3)
- 479 B.C.: Esther's selection as queen, the seventh year of Xerxes (Esth. 2:16)
- 474 B.C.: Haman's plot against the Jews, the twelfth year of Xerxes (Esth. 3:7)

The book is famous because it does not mention God by name, yet God's providence in caring for His people, despite tremendous opposition, cannot be missed. The events reported in the book center around these events:

- Esther the Jew became Xerxes' queen as the winner of a royal beauty pageant
- Haman, who hated Jews, plotted to have all Jews in Persia destroyed
- Esther—who had hidden her Jewish identity—invited Xerxes and Haman to a feast
- Esther exposed Haman's plot to the king, who ordered Haman's death
- The Jews were spared death and in triumph established the feast of Purim
- Esther's relative Mordecai became Xerxes' prime minister

Book of Esther

This historical narrative is written in excellent Hebrew. It was perhaps composed by Mordecai shortly after the events it records, sometime after 474 B.C. It was prepared for Jews in Persia and became a treasured book of Scripture at least partly because of its explanation of the origin of Purim. The key word for the book is "providence"; the key text is Esther 4:14. **One-Sentence Summary:** *Esther, a Jewish beauty selected by Persian king Xerxes to become his new queen, saved the Jews from Haman's wicked plot, so her relative Mordecai established the yearly Jewish feast of Purim.*

Ruth and Esther

The lives of these two remarkable women, the only women for whom Bible books were named, portray God's providential care of people committed to Him in the midst of overwhelming challenges to their faith. The characters Esther and Ruth, however, are a study in contrasts. One was a powerful and wealthy Jew who always lived outside the promised land and became the bride of a pagan king. The other was a humble and impoverished Gentile who moved to the promised land and became an ancestor of Israelite kings.

A building at Shiloh believed to be the oldest remains of an ancient synagogue in all of Israel.

RISE OF THE SYNAGOGUES

The vast majority of Jews that had been scattered throughout the Babylonian Empire never returned to Israel. Ultimately they came to be referred to as the Jews of the dispersion, or Diaspora. The synagogue was the institution that enabled the Jews to maintain a distinct identity. Not specifically mentioned in the Old Testament, synagogues are assumed to be everywhere in the New Testament.

Nobody knows exactly when the first synagogue—meaning "gathering place" in Greek—came into being, but it may have been as early as the Babylonian period. As with Christian churches, at first the synagogues probably met in homes, but later on buildings constructed for the purpose. Synagogues were certainly functioning by the Persian period, for the united Jewish community action implied in Esther 9 implies an effective Jewish organization in each urban area.

As far as the Jews of the dispersion were concerned, the synagogue served three major purposes: to educate Jews in the law of God; to provide worship on the Sabbath; and to regulate Jewish life to the extent allowed by the secular government. In God's overall kingdom purposes, synagogues played a major function early in Chapter Five of the Kingdom Story. As witnesses to belief in one God and to the hope of a coming Messiah, the synagogues were often the starting place for early Christian preachers, as the book of Acts clearly shows.

Synagogue

The Jews' gathering place in cities and communities originated after the Babylonian exile and until this day continues as the main way Jewish religion and culture is preserved. Synagogues were constituted only in cities where there were enough adult Jewish men to provide adequate leadership. The chief officer was called the ruler of the synagogue, who was assisted by elders, responsible for maintaining order and discipline. The synagogue worship services each Sabbath included prayers, Scripture reading, and, whenever possible, an interpreter to explain the meaning of the Scriptures to the people.

GREEK DOMINATION:
THE "BELLY OF BRONZE"—JEWISH INDEPENDENCE FOR LESS THAN A CENTURY (331–63 B.C.)

The equivalent of the belly of bronze in Nebuchadnezzar's dream was a four-headed leopard and then a goat in Daniel's visions (Dan. 2:39; 7:6; 8:5-14). The goat from the west (Greece) trampled down the ram (Persia). Then the goat's prominent horn was broken off and in its place grew four more horns. This vivid picture perfectly summarizes the swift rise of Alexander the Great (356–323 B.C.) as a world leader, his destruction of the Persian Empire, and the division of his own kingdom into four parts after his death at a young age.

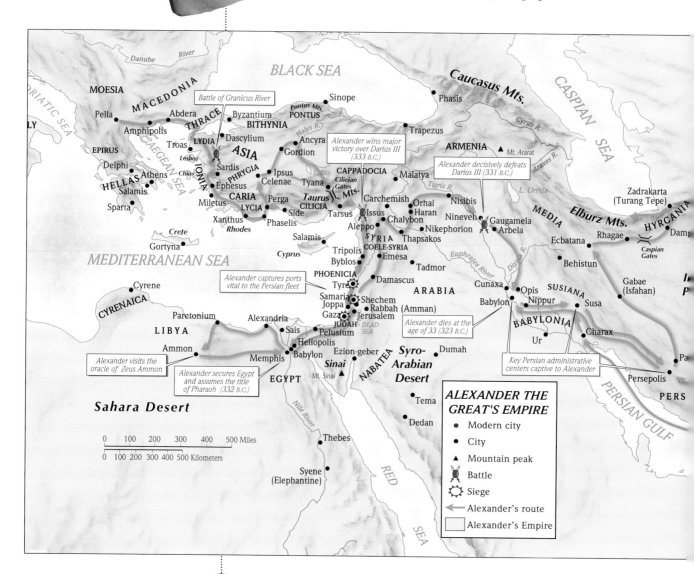

Head of Alexander the Great, son of Philip II of Macedon.

Battle of Granicus River

Alexander wins major victory over Darius III (333 B.C.)

Alexander decisively defeats Darius III (331 B.C.)

Alexander captures ports vital to the Persian fleet

Alexander dies at the age of 33 (323 B.C.)

Alexander visits the oracle of Zeus Ammon

Key Persian administrative centers captive to Alexander

Alexander secures Egypt and assumes the title of Pharaoh (332 B.C.)

ALEXANDER THE GREAT'S EMPIRE
- ● Modern city
- ● City
- ▲ Mountain peak
- ⚔ Battle
- ✣ Siege
- → Alexander's route
- ▭ Alexander's Empire

ALEXANDER THE GREAT

Greek civilization was ancient by Alexander's time. Their golden age of literature and the arts had already peaked, but politically the Greeks had never exerted much power. Alexander's father, Philip, king of Macedonia, left his son a great foundation for expanding the Greek Empire by uniting the Hellenic League. Philip died when Alexander was only twenty (336 B.C.), giving Alexander's military genius full opportunity to express itself. Alexander's army quickly conquered the Persians in Asia Minor, swept south down the coast of Palestine and took Phoenicia and then Egypt, founding the city of Alexandria. Then he moved into Mesopotamia, putting a final end to the Persian Empire at the Battle of Arbela in 331. He conquered all four Persian capitals. In a matter of only five years he moved from being the inexperienced king of Macedonia to being emperor of the entire world. He died of a fever only a few years later in Babylon at age 33.

Coin bearing the image of Philip of Macedon.

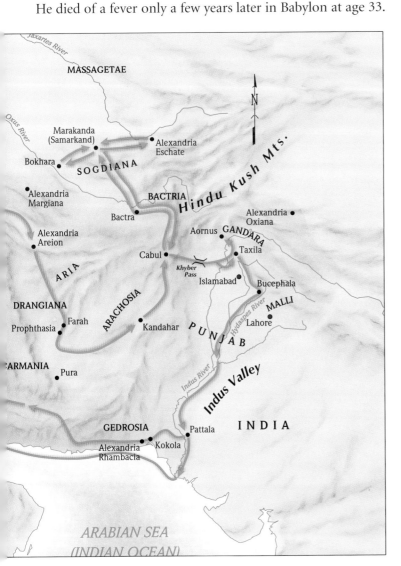

Hellenization

The Greek name for Greece was *Hellas*. The worldwide spread of the Greek language and culture initiated by Alexander is therefore called Hellenization. The form of the language that was spread was the Koine (common) Greek of ordinary people rather than the Attic (Athenian or classical) Greek of the scholars. Many Jews adopted the Greek language while maintaining their own religion and looked to Alexandria, Egypt, as a cultural center. They produced a translation of Scripture into Greek called the Septuagint. Because Greek was the accepted trade language of the world by the time of Christ, the early Christian preachers had an easier time spreading the message of God's kingdom.

Greece

The Greek peninsula included a number of districts, such as Macedonia and Thrace. Athens, the literary and artistic center, was an independent city-state without political ambition. The Greeks rose to superpower status after Alexander overthrew the Persians in 331. Alexander's empire was divided into four parts, beginning three centuries of the Hellenistic era. The last Greek monarch was Cleopatra of Egypt, who died in 30 B.C. as the last ruler of the Ptolemy dynasty. Greece—in the person of Antiochus Epiphanes of the Seleucid Empire—was the fifth oppressor kingdom bent on destroying the people of God (after Egypt, Assyria, Babylonia, and Persia). This period is predicted in Daniel 11.

Although he did not live long enough to fully consolidate his empire, Alexander carried with him a passionate love of the Greek culture and language. The language in which the New Testament would be written was popularized worldwide by the troops of Alexander. His personal tutor Aristotle taught him well. For the first time in world history, a civilization with a European focus—rather than African or Asian—was dominant in spreading its ideas. Greek-style theaters, stadiums, and marketplaces became common. Greek language, literature, religion, and philosophy spread and were widely accepted.

THE PTOLOMIES AND THE SELEUCIDS

Just as Daniel had envisioned Greece as a four-headed leopard (Dan. 7:6), so the empire of Alexander was divided into four parts by competing generals after several years of internal struggle. These were as follows:

- Cassander took Macedonia and Greece
- Lysimachus took Thrace and Asia Minor
- Seleucus took Syria and the East
- Ptolomy took Palestine and Egypt

Only two of these are important for understanding the Kingdom Story. Seleucus founded Antioch as his capital city, which became a major population center by the first century (and the beginning point for Paul's missionary travels). Ptolomy ruled from Alexandria. Daniel 11 predicts the intrigues between Ptolomy (and his successors) and Seleucus (and his successors), calling them "the king of the South" and "the king of the North" respectively. (These directions are understood as north and south from Judah.) The Ptolomies allowed Judaism to flourish in their realm, enabling the Jews in Alexandria to become a vibrant subculture and permitting the Jews in Judah freedom of religion.

Judah, however, lay precisely between Antioch and Alexandria, and therefore it bore the brunt of an ongoing tug of war between the bitter rivals, the Ptolomies and the Seleucids. In 198 B.C. the Seleucid army, led by their general and king Antiochus III (called "the Great"), defeated the Egyptian army at Panium in northern Palestine (later called Caesaria Philippi). At this time Judah fell under the control of the Seleucids. They were aggressive Hellenizers, much less willing than the Ptolomies to allow local people to express their local religion. As one example the Seleucids had a Greek-style gymnasium built in Jerusalem where they expected Jewish men to exercise without any clothes—the Hellenistic fashion but an abomination to the modest Jews.

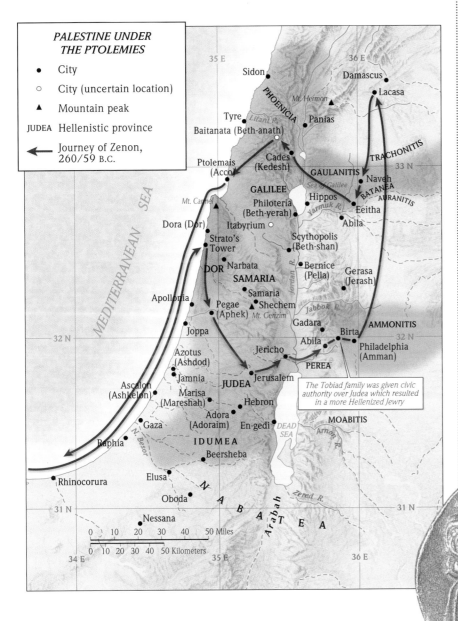

PALESTINE UNDER THE PTOLEMIES

- ● City
- ○ City (uncertain location)
- ▲ Mountain peak
- JUDEA Hellenistic province
- ← Journey of Zenon, 260/59 B.C.

35 E

36 E

Sidon

Damascus

Lacasa

Mt. Hermon ▲

PHOENICIA

Tyre · Litani R.

Panias

Baitanata (Beth-anath) ○

TRACHONITIS

33 N

Ptolemais (Acco)

Cades (Kedesh)

GAULANITIS

Naveh

Sea of Galilee

BATANEA

Mt. Carmel ▲

GALILEE

Philoteria (Beth-yerah)

Hippos

Eeitha

AURANITIS

Dora (Dor)

Itabyrium ○

Yarmuk R.

Abila

Strato's Tower

Scythopolis (Beth-shan)

Narbata

Bernice (Pella)

Gerasa (Jerash)

DOR

SAMARIA

Samaria

Apollonia

Pegae (Aphek)

Shechem ▲

Mt. Gerizim

Jabbok R.

Joppa

Gadara

Birta

AMMONITIS

32 N

Abila

Azotus (Ashdod)

Jericho

Philadelphia (Amman)

32 N

Jamnia

PEREA

Ascalon (Ashkelon)

Marisa (Mareshah)

JUDEA

Jerusalem

The Tobiad family was given civic authority over Judea which resulted in a more Hellenized Jewry

MEDITERRANEAN SEA

Gaza

Adora (Adoraim)

Hebron

En-gedi

DEAD SEA

MOABITIS

Raphia

IDUMEA

Beersheba

Arnon R.

Rhinocorura

Elusa

N A B A T E A

Zered R.

31 N

Oboda

Arabah

31 N

Nessana

0 10 20 30 40 50 Miles

0 10 20 30 40 50 Kilometers

34 E

35 E

36 E

Tetradrachm of Antiochus IV Epiphanes.

ANTIOCHUS EPIPHANES AND THE ABOMINATION OF DESOLATION

The Seleucid king Antiochus IV took the name *Epiphanes* ("the Manifest [God]") and ruled from 175 to 163. His evil reign is described beginning in Daniel 11:21. He believed that the key to unifying his people lay in having them all united in the same religion, and he went to great pains to try to eradicate the worship of the Lord from Judah. Antiochus was supported by a renegade Jewish priest that rallied many Jews to abandon the Lord.

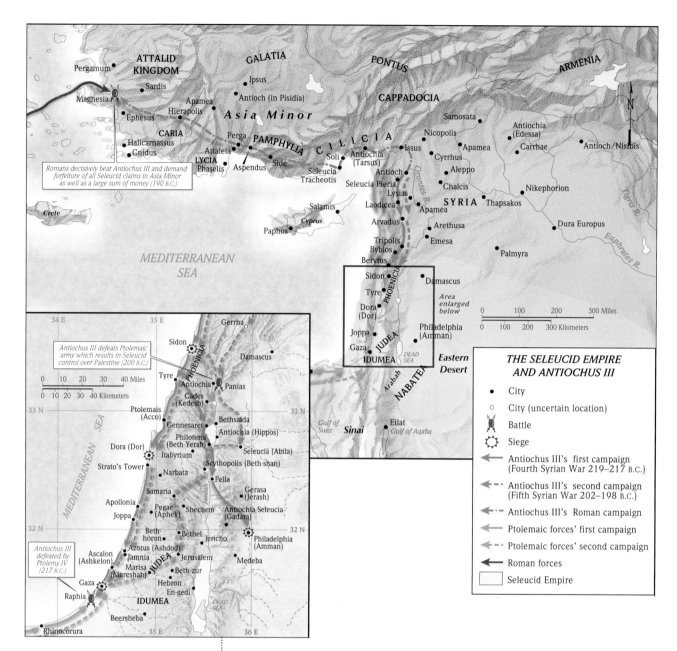

THE SELEUCID EMPIRE AND ANTIOCHUS III

- • City
- ○ City (uncertain location)
- ⚔ Battle
- ✻ Siege
- → Antiochus III's first campaign (Fourth Syrian War 219–217 B.C.)
- ⇢ Antiochus III's second campaign (Fifth Syrian War 202–198 B.C.)
- ⇢ Antiochus III's Roman campaign
- → Ptolemaic forces' first campaign
- ⇢ Ptolemaic forces' second campaign
- → Roman forces
- ▭ Seleucid Empire

In 168 B.C. things reached rock bottom for the Jews. The Lord was now forcibly identified as the Greek Zeus, and the temple in Jerusalem was dedicated to Zeus, with his statue to be revered. Circumcision and recognition of the Sabbath were forbidden. Pigs were offered daily on the temple altar (the abomination of desolation of Dan. 11:31), and Seleucid soldiers used the temple as a brothel. Antiochus's excesses had gone too far, as he would soon discover.

THE MACCABEAN REVOLT

The people of Judah in 600 B.C. had been eager to worship idols (during the reign of Jehoiakim). The descendants of these people four centuries later had become eager to preserve worship of the Lord in His temple according to His law. The revolt of the Jews against the Seleucids began in 167. It was sparked by an elderly Jewish priest named Mattathias, who refused to sacrifice on a pagan altar at his small village of Modein. He then killed the Jew who was willing to make the sacrifice. Mattathias and his five sons soon organized a guerilla-like insurrection, destroying pagan altars and raiding Seleucid camps. The great military organizer was Mattathias's son Judas (the Greek spelling of "Judah"). He gained the nickname Maccabeus ("the Hammer") because of the hammer-like blows his troops inflicted on the Seleucids. The movement came to be called the Maccabean Revolt.

Exactly three years after the original abomination of desolation, on the twenty-fifth day of Kislev (December 15, 165 B.C.), the Maccabean forces gained sufficient control of Jerusalem to clear the temple of all pagan symbols. The resulting celebration lasted for eight days, and according to Jewish tradition, God miraculously supplied oil for the temple lamps

St. Catherine's from above on Jebel Musa, traditional site of Sinai and the place where Codex Sinaiticus was found (see p.152).

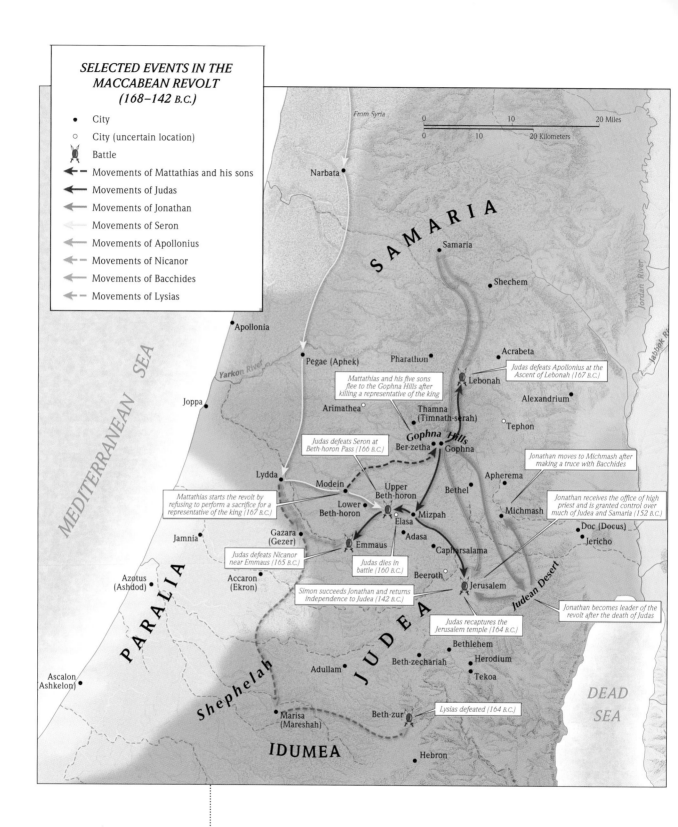

SELECTED EVENTS IN THE MACCABEAN REVOLT (168–142 B.C.)

- ● City
- ○ City (uncertain location)
- ⚔ Battle
- Movements of Mattathias and his sons
- Movements of Judas
- Movements of Jonathan
- Movements of Seron
- Movements of Apollonius
- Movements of Nicanor
- Movements of Bacchides
- Movements of Lysias

From Syria

0   10   20 Miles
0   10   20 Kilometers

Narbata

SAMARIA

Samaria

Shechem

Apollonia

Jordan River

Jabbok Rv.

Pegae (Aphek)

Pharathon

Acrabeta

Judas defeats Apollonius at the Ascent of Lebonah (167 B.C.)

Lebonah

Alexandrium

MEDITERRANEAN SEA

Yarkon River

Joppa

Arimathea

Thamna (Timnath-serah)

Tephon

Mattathias and his five sons flee to the Gophna Hills after killing a representative of the king

Gophna Hills

Ber-zetha   Gophna

Apherema

Jonathan moves to Michmash after making a truce with Bacchides

Judas defeats Seron at Beth-horon Pass (166 B.C.)

Lydda

Modein

Upper Beth-horon

Bethel

Michmash

Jonathan receives the office of high priest and is granted control over much of Judea and Samaria (152 B.C.)

Mattathias starts the revolt by refusing to perform a sacrifice for a representative of the king (167 B.C.)

Lower Beth-horon

Mizpah

Elasa

Doc (Docus)

Jericho

Gazara (Gezer)

Jamnia

Emmaus

Adasa

Capharsalama

Judas defeats Nicanor near Emmaus (165 B.C.)

Judas dies in battle (160 B.C.)

Accaron (Ekron)

Azotus (Ashdod)

Beeroth

Jerusalem

PARALIA

Simon succeeds Jonathan and returns independence to Judea (142 B.C.)

Judas recaptures the Jerusalem temple (164 B.C.)

Judean Desert

Jonathan becomes leader of the revolt after the death of Judas

Ascalon (Ashkelon)

Bethlehem

Herodium

JUDEA

Beth-zechariah

Adullam

Tekoa

DEAD SEA

Shephelah

Beth-zur

Lysias defeated (164 B.C.)

Marisa (Mareshah)

IDUMEA

Hebron

when there was only a one-day supply on hand. Thus, the time came to be called Hanukkah (the Feast of Lights or the Feast of Dedication). This has become an important annual event in the Jewish calendar.

The battle for Jewish control of the land was not over, however. After Judas was killed in battle, his youngest brother Jonathan assumed leadership. Warfare continued intermittently against the Seleucids for another twenty years. In 142 B.C. Jonathan was murdered and leadership fell to the aged Simon, another brother. The Jews finally won independence for their land later that year.

The Jewish people were so grateful for Simon's leadership that they chose him to be both high priest and king. This move was highly unorthodox in light of the history of Israel. First, Simon was from a priestly family, but not the *high* priestly line. Second, until this point, there had always been a strict separation between the priests and the kings. (King Uzziah had been struck with leprosy for intruding into the priesthood.)

The success of the Maccabean Revolt brought about a number of important developments. The most important are as follows:

- *The rise of the Hasidim or "Pious Ones."* These Jews were passionately committed to keeping the law of Moses and the Jewish traditions. These probably evolved into the Pharisees of the first century.

Acropolis in Athens epitomizes Greek civilization. A process of hellenization was a part of Alexander the Great's military mission around and beyond the Mediterranean world. The Maccabean revolt sought to reverse this process in Israel.

- *Jewish independence.* For a brief time (142–63 B.C.), the Jews were independent of a foreign power, ruled by a Jewish but non-Davidic king, for the first time since 586 b.c.

- *Slowdown of Hellenization.* The rebuff of the Seleucids meant that the Jews could determine their own way of life again, even if they reinterpreted God's law in certain ways, such as allowing one man to be both priest and king.

- *Increased literary production.* A number of works composed in Greek were included with the Greek translation of the Scriptures, such as 1 and 2 Maccabees. (These became known as the apocryphal books.) Others emphasized the coming end of the world, using symbolism and other bizarre features. (These are known as apocalyptic books.)

THE HASMONEAN DYNASTY

Beginning in 142 B.C. with Simon's leadership as priest and king, the independent Jewish state—now known by its Greek name Judea rather than by its old name Judah—was ruled by successive generations of Mattathias's descendants. These went by Hasmon, the family name, so this period is referred to as the Hasmonean dynasty. These rulers continued to combine the office of high priest and king. Some turned out to be corrupt, easily persuaded by the lure of power and wealth. This dynasty endured only eighty years and was ended by the Romans in 63 B.C.

Cave and temple at Banias showing god niches. "Banias" is a derivation from the word "Pan," the Greek god of woods and fields, sheep and shepherds. Pan, whose name means "all," came to represent all the gods of paganism. Here in this place of pagan gods, Jesus asked his disciples, "who do you say that I am?" (Matt. 16:15)

JEWISH EXPANSION UNDER
THE HASMONEAN DYNASTY

- ● City
- ○ City (uncertain location)
- ▲ Mountain peak
- Judea before the Maccabean revolt
- Conquests of Jonathan
- Conquests of Simon
- Conquests of Hyrcanus I
- Conquests of Aristobulus I
- Conquests of Alexander Jannaeus

Sidon

Damascus

Abana

COELE-SY

ITUREA

Mt. Hermon ▲

Panias

Pharpar R.

Tyre

PHOENICIA

Litani R.

Cadasa
(Kedesh)

*Aristobulus completes the conquest of Upper
Galilee by defeating the Itureans (104 B.C.)*

Gischala
(Gush Halav)

Asor
(Hazor)

Seleucia

Ptolemais (Acco)

Jotapata
Asochis
(Hannathon)

Taricheae
(Magdala)

Gennesaret

Bethsaida

Dathema

Sea of
Galilee

Gamala

Cana

Arbela

Sepphoris

GALILEE

Hippos

Geba

Mt. Carmel ▲

Mt. Tabor ▲

Philoteria
(Beth-Yerah)

Gadara

Abila

Yarmuk R.

MEDITERRANEAN
SEA

Dora

Legio
(Megiddo)

Strato's Tower

Scythopolis
(Beth-shan)

Pella

Narbata

SAMARIA

Dion

*Jannaeus subdues the attack of
Demetrius III and executes 800
Pharisees in reprisal (88 B.C.)*

Gerasa
(Jerash)

Samaria

Mt. Ebal ▲

Amathus

Jordan R.

Jabbok R.

*Hyrcanus I destroys
Samaritan temple (128 B.C.)*

Shechem

Gilead

Apollonia

Pegae
(Aphek)

Mt. Gerizim ▲

Acrabeta

Coreae

Pharathon

Alexandrium

Lebonah

Yarkon R.

Joppa

Arimathea

Zeredah

Gophna

*Simon is murdered in a
palace coup (135 B.C.)*

Gedor (Gadara)

Jazer

Adida

Apherema

PEREA

Tyrus

Philadelphia (Amman)

Lydda

Modein

Ber-
zetha

Bethel

Doc

Abila

Gazara
(Gezer)

Beth-horon

Mizpah

Jericho

Esbus
(Heshbon)

Jamina

Adasa

Michmash

Beth-ramatha

Samaga

Kidron

Emmaus

JUDEA

Jerusalem

Mt. Nebo ▲

Azotus
(Ashdod)

Beth-haccherem

Hyrcania

Medeba

Accaron
(Ekron)

Bethlehem

Herodium

*John Hyrcanus attacks
and conquers Medeba
in 129 B.C.*

Ascalon
(Ashkelon)

Adullam

Beth-basi

Tekoa

Marisa
(Mareshah)

Keilah

Nezib

Beth-zur

Asphar

Lemba

Lachish

Adora
(Adoraim)

Hebron

Machaerus

Anthedon

PHILISTIA

DEAD
SEA

Gaza

En-gedi

Gerar

IDUMEA

Orda

Masada

Eglaim

Raphia

N. Besor

Beersheba

Malatha

Kir-Moab

N A B A T E A

nocorura

Arish

Elusa

Oronaim
(Horonaim)

Gabalis

Zoar

Zered R.

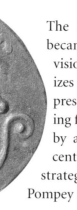

Denarius struck in Sicily bearing the image of Pompey the Great.

ROMAN DOMINATION:
THE "LEGS OF IRON"—
JEWS BECOME SUBSERVIENT AGAIN
(63 B.C.–A.D. 70)

The legs of iron in Nebuchadnezzar's dream became an iron-toothed monster in Daniel's vision (Dan. 2:33; 7:8). This certainly characterizes the military might of the growing Roman presence. Roman civilization had been expanding for centuries. A republican government ruled by a Senate provided stable leadership. In the century before Christ, two brilliant military strategists greatly expanded Rome's borders: Pompey and Julius Caesar.

POMPEY AND THE ROMANS

Pompey played a decisive role in ending the Hasmonean dynasty. The last of the Seleucids surrendered to Pompey and the Roman power, and he was present in Damascus in 63 B.C. Two Hasmonean brothers (Aristobulus and Hyrcanus) were fighting for control of the Hasmonean throne. Both went to Damascus seeking Pompey's support for their respective claims. Pompey replied by marching with his army on Jerusalem. Aristobulus was taken captive. Pompey entered the city and ultimately—after a three-month siege—the temple itself. He found to his surprise that the inner shrine (the holy of holies) was empty.

This sacrilege outraged the Jews, an unfortunate beginning for the Roman rule of Judea. Pompey's troops did not, however, destroy the city. Instead, he allowed Hyrcanus, the weaker brother, to function as high priest in return for his promise of submission to Rome. Hyrcanus was not allowed to become king, thus ending the Hasmonean dynasty in Judea. The Romans exerted their rule through the presence of a governor. The Jews were once again subject to foreign overlords.

THE RISE OF HEROD

The ruler of Idumea (formerly called Edom) at this time was Antipater, whose mother was a Jew. He became an influential advisor for the Hasmonean high priest, Hyrcanus. Antipater was even appointed in 47 B.C. by Julius Caesar as governor of Judea. This enabled him to promote the political careers of his two ambitious sons, particularly Herod. In 40 B.C. (during the Roman civil war following the murder of Julius Caesar in 44 B.C.) the Roman Senate declared Herod "king of the Jews." By this time Herod had gained the support of Mark Antony and Octavian (later known as Augustus Caesar) by promising to regain Judea for the Romans, who were occupied with their own civil war.

Statue of Augustus, Roman emperor from 27 B.C. to A.D. 14.

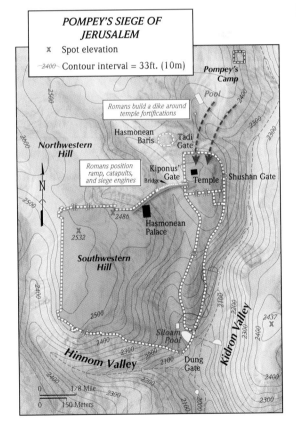

POMPEY'S CAMPAIGN AGAINST JERUSALEM AND THE RESULTING ROMAN SETTLEMENT 63 B.C.

- • City
- ○ City (uncertain location)
- ▲ Mountain peak
- ☼ Siege of Jerusalem
- ← Pompey's campaign
- ◄- - The Romans break through the walls into Jerusalem
- ← Aristobulus's route
- ▨ Jewish state after Pompey's settlement
- ▨ Jewish territories ceded to Iturea and Ptolemais
- ▨ Samaritan state
- •○ Cities of the Decapolis

POMPEY'S SIEGE OF JERUSALEM

- ✗ Spot elevation
- ─2400─ Contour interval = 33ft. (10m)

Pompey's Camp

Pool

Romans build a dike around temple fortifications

Northwestern Hill

Hasmonean Baris

Tadi Gate

2600

Romans position ramp, catapults, and siege engines

Kiponus' Gate
Bridge

Temple

Shushan Gate

✗ 2486

Hasmonean Palace

✗ 2532

Southwestern Hill

2500

Siloam Pool

✗ 2437

Hinnom Valley

Dung Gate

Kidron Valley

0   1/8 Mile
0   150 Meters

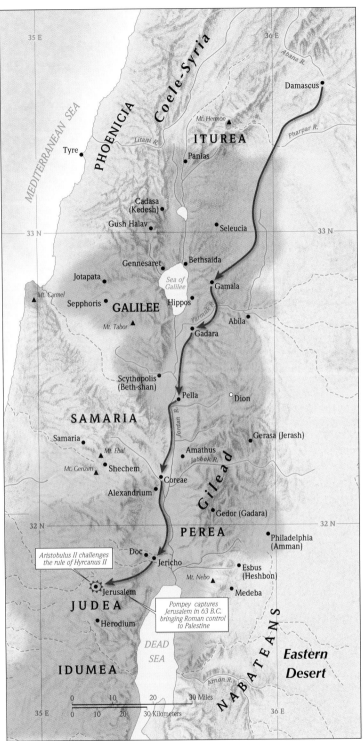

MEDITERRANEAN SEA

PHOENICIA

Coele-Syria

Abana R.

Damascus

Mt. Hermon

ITUREA

Litani R.

Pharpar R.

Tyre

Panias

Cadasa (Kedesh)

Gush Halav

Seleucia

33 N

Gennesaret

Bethsaida

Jotapata

Sea of Galilee

Gamala

Mt. Carmel

Sepphoris

GALILEE

Hippos

Abila

Mt. Tabor

Yarmuk R.

Gadara

Scythopolis (Beth-shan)

Pella

Dion

SAMARIA

Jordan R.

Gerasa (Jerash)

Samaria

Mt. Ebal

Amathus

Jabbok R.

Gilead

Mt. Gerizim

Shechem

Coreae

Alexandrium

Gedor (Gadara)

32 N

PEREA

Philadelphia (Amman)

Aristobulus II challenges the rule of Hyrcanus II

Doc

Jericho

Esbus (Heshbon)

Mt. Nebo

Medeba

Jerusalem

JUDEA

Pompey captures Jerusalem in 63 B.C. bringing Roman control to Palestine

Herodium

DEAD SEA

NABATEANS

Eastern Desert

IDUMEA

Arnon R.

0   10   20   30 Miles
0   10   20   30 Kilometers

35 E   36 E

The adjacent mountain to Lebonah from which Judas Maccabeus stormed down on the Assyrians (p.149).

The anti-Roman forces threatening Palestine were outside invaders rather than the Jews. It took Herod three years, but by 37 B.C. he had secured control of Judea for the Romans. They allowed him to stay on as king until his death in 4 B.C. (two years after Jesus' birth).

The Jews despised Herod, for he was not a Jew, and he ruled as a vicious tyrant. He tried to appease them by taking the granddaughter of Hyrcanus as one of his wives but to no avail. Further, in 20 B.C. he began a lavish expenditure on the temple site in order to win the Jews' favor. The main temple building became an extravagant marble and gold structure the height of a fifteen-story building. The site was vastly expanded and continuously improved until A.D. 64. This was the temple that the Romans destroyed in A.D. 70.

The Jews continued to be subservient to Herod, his successors, and a variety of Roman governors until the Jewish revolt of A.D. 66. That story does not belong here, but rather to Chapter Five of the Kingdom Story.

JUDEA IN THE DAYS OF HEROD

By the end of Herod's reign, the temple and the high priesthood were firmly under the control of the Sadducees. These aristocrats were few in numbers and gave their support to the Romans. Many Jews became so fed up with the system that they withdrew to the desert and tried to live according to God's law in their own little communes. These are now known as Essenes. One of their communities produced the famous Dead Sea Scrolls, discovered only in 1947.

The most powerful religious group with the ordinary Jews was the Pharisees. They worked hard at making the law of Moses understandable for a new day. They later clashed with Jesus because they had made the law a matter of external observance, but Jesus and the Pharisees never disagreed about the importance of the law.

The time was now ripe for God to send His Son. Those living in the last days of Herod's rule, however, had no expectation that the most important birth in history was about to occur.

CONCLUSION

For the space of about six centuries, God kept a faithful remnant of Jewish people in the land and sent the majority of the Jews throughout the world as witnesses to the one true God.

1. During the Babylonian captivity, the Israelites finally learned to stay true to the Lord. They became identified as Jews, and perhaps as early as the captivity they began worshiping in synagogues. Daniel and Ezekiel were God's great prophets during this time (605–539 B.C.).

2. As soon as the Persians came into world dominance, they allowed the Jews to return home from captivity. The first group to return was especially concerned about the restoration of the temple. This was completed in 516 under Zerubbabel's leadership, aided by the Prophets Haggai and Zechariah. Through Esther's courage the Jews were spared extinction. The law was renewed under the ministry of Ezra; the walls of Jerusalem were rebuilt through Nehemiah's leadership. The last prophet of the Old Testament period was Malachi (539–331 B.C.).

A model of the temple at Jerusalem at the Holyland Hotel in Jerusalem.

Area around Qumran.
Inset: Cave Four at Qumran
(p.156).

3. The next world superpower to rise up was the Greeks. Alexander was responsible for the remarkable phenomenon of Hellenization. Judea was caught between two rival Hellenistic powers, the Ptolemies and the Seleucids. When the Seleucids pushed the Jews too hard, they fought back with the leadership of the Maccabees. This gained them a brief period of independence during the Hasmonean dynasty (331–63 B.C.).

4. Rome's power became effective in Judea in 63 B.C. through the presence of Pompey and the establishment of Roman governors. Herod came to power as king of the Jews, arousing bitter resentment by the people of Judea. Herod and the succeeding Roman rulers became so oppressive that the Jews finally revolted again. The second temple would be destroyed A.D. 70 by the Roman iron-toothed beast. Yet before that happened the Messiah would come and establish the kingdom of God on earth.

The grand summary of the Bible is *The Lord God through His Christ is graciously building a kingdom of redeemed people for their joy and for His own glory.* We have seen in Chapter Three how God graciously kept His redeemed people as a faithful remnant. In Chapter Four of the Kingdom Story, God will purchase redemption for sinners through the death of the Messiah.

REFLECTIVE QUESTIONS

1. The intense sorrow caused by Jerusalem's fall is described in the book of Lamentations. Why is expression of grief important to God's people? How do you express sorrow?

2. What made the Babylonian captivity a time both of tragedy and of hope for God's people?

3. Two great prophets during the Babylonian captivity were Daniel and Ezekiel. Which one would you most like to spend an evening with? Why?

4. Were the Jews who returned to Judah right to emphasize worship (rebuilding the temple) over security (rebuilding the walls)? Why?

5. The Bible teacher Ezra and the wall builder Nehemiah had different tasks in the Kingdom Story. What persons do you know that are "Ezras" and "Nehemiahs" today?

6. The renewal of the Sinaitic covenant under Ezra included a renewed emphasis on resting on the Sabbath as the sign of the covenant. Do you consider the Sabbath important for your life today? Why or why not?

7. Are there any circumstances today (as in Ezra's day) in which divorce is the will of God?

8. How do you recognize God's activity in the book of Esther even though He is not directly mentioned in the book?

9. Two Bible books are named for great women, Ruth and Esther. Which one is a better example for your life? Why?

10. Synagogues arose as a meeting place for God's people during the Babylonian captivity. What is the difference between a synagogue and a church?

11. In what ways was the powerful worldwide cultural movement called Hellenization a way that God was working out the Kingdom Story?

12. Why did God's kingdom plan call for the abomination of desolation (a direct insult to Him)? How did the abomination of desolation serve God's kingdom plan?

13. How did the Roman presence change life for Jews in Palestine? Do you think they were better off under the Greeks or under the Romans? Why?

14. How does God's redemption of His people work itself out in Chapter Three of the Kingdom Story?

15. What evidences of God's glory are evident in Chapter Three of the Kingdom Story?

16. What evidences of joy in the lives of God's redeemed people do you see in Chapter Three of the Kingdom Story?

God Purchases Redemption and Begins the Kingdom

View overlooking Bethlehem, birth place of King David and Jesus, Son of David.

Jesus the Messiah,

6 B.C.–A.D. 30

An "objective" Greek or Roman historian living just before Jesus' birth would not have found much to write about concerning the Kingdom Story for the last four centuries. Such an observer might have recognized Israel's glorious past, particularly the wonderful growth of the monarchy in Jerusalem under David and Solomon a millennium earlier. The same observer would know of the collapse of Israel, ending in the Babylonian captivity in 586 B.C.

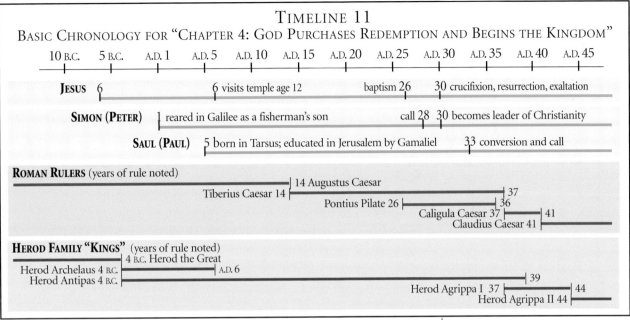

TIMELINE 11
BASIC CHRONOLOGY FOR "CHAPTER 4: GOD PURCHASES REDEMPTION AND BEGINS THE KINGDOM"

10 B.C.　5 B.C.　A.D. 1　A.D. 5　A.D. 10　A.D. 15　A.D. 20　A.D. 25　A.D. 30　A.D. 35　A.D. 40　A.D. 45

JESUS 6   6 visits temple age 12   baptism 26   30 crucifixion, resurrection, exaltation

SIMON (PETER) 1 reared in Galilee as a fisherman's son   call 28   30 becomes leader of Christianity

SAUL (PAUL) 5 born in Tarsus; educated in Jerusalem by Gamaliel   33 conversion and call

ROMAN RULERS (years of rule noted)
14 Augustus Caesar
Tiberius Caesar 14 — 37
Pontius Pilate 26 — 36
Caligula Caesar 37 — 41
Claudius Caesar 41

HEROD FAMILY "KINGS" (years of rule noted)
4 B.C. Herod the Great
Herod Archelaus 4 B.C. — A.D. 6
Herod Antipas 4 B.C.
Herod Agrippa I 37 — 39
Herod Agrippa II 44 — 44

PALESTINE IN THE TIME OF JESUS

- • City
- ○ City (uncertain location)
- ◉ Decapolis city
- ○ Decapolis city (uncertain location)
- ★ Administrative capital
- ▲ Mountain peak
- — Major roads
- — Other roads
- First procuratorship
- Territory of Antipas
- Territory of Philip
- Syrian territory

Coponius was named the first prefect and established the administrative capital at Caesarea Maritima

35 E   36 E

ABILENE
Sidon
ITUREA
Damascus
Abana R.
PHOENICIA (TYRE)
Litani R.
Mt. Hermon ▲
Caesarea-Philippi (Panias)
Tyre
GAULANITIS
Pharpar R.
King's Highway
Raphana
Cadasa (Kedesh)
Gischala (Gush Halav)
L. Huleh
TRACHONITIS
BATANEA
Ptolemais (Acco)
Capernaum
Bethsaida
GALILEE
Jotapata
Sea of Galilee
Gergesa (Kursi)
Gamala
Canatha
Sepphoris
Geba
Mt. Carmel ▲
Nazareth
Tiberias
Hippos
Abila
Adraa (Edrei)
Xaloth (Chesulloth)
Gadara
AURANITIS
Bostra
Dora
Legio (Megiddo)
Esdraelon Valley
Mt. Tabor ▲
Kishon R.
Yarmuk R.
Caesarea Maritima (Strato's Tower) ★
Scythopolis (Beth-shan)
Dion
Ginae (Jenin)
Pella
Aenon
Salim
Gerasa (Jerash)
DECAPOLIS
SAMARIA
Jordan R.
Amathus
Sebaste (Samaria)
Mt. Ebal ▲
Neapolis (Shechem)
Mt. Gerizim ▲
Coreae
Apollonia
Antipatris (Aphek)
Yarkon R.
Joppa
Alexandrium
Ephraim (Ophrah)
Gedor (Gadara)
Jabbok R.
PEREA
32 N
Lydda
Archelais
Philadelphia (Amman)
MEDITERRANEAN SEA
JUDEA
Jericho
Jamnia
Emmaus (Nicopolis)
Cyprus
Esbus (Heshbon)
Azotus (Ashdod)
Jerusalem
Bethany
Mt. Nebo ▲
Medeba
Ascalon (Ashkelon)
Hyrcania
Mesad Hasidim (Qumran)
Eastern Desert

Since 586, however, the Jews had been an insignificant factor in the Near East. Most remained scattered, maintaining a separate religious and cultural existence by means of synagogues. To be sure, a minority of Jews had returned to their historic land and rebuilt their temple (especially under Ezra and Nehemiah). Under the Maccabees, they had defeated a vicious attempt at forced Hellenization. They had even maintained an independent kingdom ruled by the Hasmoneans, but that had fallen apart in less than a century.

Now, however, they were ruled by a client king for the Romans, Herod, the king of the Jews who was not even a Jew. Some Jews, such as the Sadducees, were content with the status quo. Others expressed longings for a return to the old days, when a direct descendant of David ruled in Jerusalem. About the only thing that they all agreed on was that Yahweh, the Lord of Israel, was the one true God to be worshiped. They also all accepted at least the five books of Moses as God's word.

Such an imaginative secular historian could not have known that Chapter Four in God's plan to build an everlasting kingdom was about to unfold. This chapter would be the most important one of all but would take in the shortest span of history of all the "chapters of redemption." This is the story told by the four Gospels. It shows how God's unconditional covenant promises—first to Abraham, later to David—were fulfilled by the new covenant Jesus established. This chapter carries the plot of the Kingdom Story from the birth of the Messiah to His resurrection and exaltation.

As the Introduction noted, the grand summary of the Bible is, *The Lord God through His Christ is graciously building a kingdom of redeemed people for their joy and for His own glory.* Chapter Four in the Kingdom Story is the climax. In the fullness of time, God sent His Son to secure everlasting redemption for His people and to establish His everlasting kingdom.

A view of the three towers Herod built to guard his palace, Hippicus, Phasael, and Mariamne. These towers are on the western wall of Jerusalem.

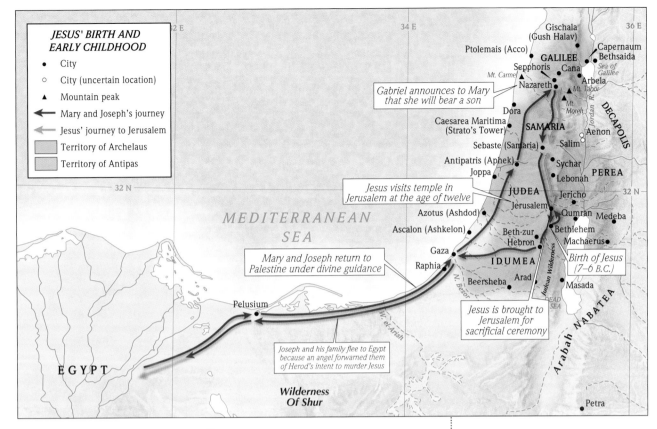

Gabriel announces to Mary that she will bear a son

Jesus visits temple in Jerusalem at the age of twelve

Mary and Joseph return to Palestine under divine guidance

Birth of Jesus (7–6 B.C.)

Jesus is brought to Jerusalem for sacrificial ceremony

Joseph and his family flee to Egypt because an angel forewarned them of Herod's intent to murder Jesus

"IMMANUEL," GOD WITH US:
THE VIRGIN BIRTH AND GROWTH OF JESUS
(6 B.C.–A.D. 26)

"Immanuel," God with us, may be the best title of Jesus to summarize His coming to planet earth. This title had been prophesied in Isaiah 7:14, and Matthew 1:23 reports its fulfillment. When Jesus came, God wonderfully entered the world in a fresh way.

The event that split human history—the change from B.C. (before Christ) to A.D. (*anno domini*, in the year of our Lord) has been called the greatest of all God's miracles. That God became human, that the Word became flesh, is the miracle that made redemption possible. Yet this miracle is recounted directly in only five Bible chapters: **MATTHEW 1—2**, **LUKE 1—2**, and **JOHN 1**. The Fourth Gospel emphasizes that God became incarnate as a human being, Jesus Christ. Matthew and Luke describe the coming of Jesus into human history in terms of His virgin birth to Mary. Wherever the Christian message has gone, three beliefs have gone hand in hand. Together they stand; together they fall: the doctrine of the incarnation; the doctrine of the virgin birth; and the doctrine of the deity of Christ (that He is fully God).

Even so, nobody is exactly sure in which calendar year Jesus was born. It was not later than 4 B.C. (the death of Herod the Great) and was perhaps two or three years earlier. A good estimate is that Jesus was born about 6 B.C.[1]

Mary

The New Testament name "Mary" is the same as Miriam, Moses' sister. The virgin Mary was probably only fourteen or fifteen, the marriageable age for girls, when Jesus was conceived. Her assent to become the mother of Jesus, willingly accepting the challenge of being the human mother of God's Son, stands as a primary biblical example of costly obedience to the will of God. Although God especially blessed Mary, she is to be respected rather than worshiped.

THE VIRGIN BIRTH

Was Jesus born to a young woman who had never had intimate relations with a man? There can be no question that this is the plain meaning of the Gospels. Both Matthew and Luke use the Greek term *parthenos* ("virgin," a sexually pure, unmarried woman) to describe Mary. Both Gospels also include other language that can only mean Jesus was conceived and born without a human father (Matt. 1:18,25; Luke 1:34-35). The Holy Spirit brought about Mary's supernatural conception, so that it may be more technically correct to speak of the "virgin conception" of Jesus. The Gospels do, however, affirm that Mary did not experience the normal intimacy of a wife to her husband until after Jesus was born.

Mary and Joseph were from Nazareth, an out-of-the-way village in the region of Galilee. Jesus would have been born there except that a Roman census required them to travel to Bethlehem, the hometown of their ancestor David, to be registered. Of course it was important—and a fulfillment of messianic prophecy, Micah 5:2—for the Messiah to be born in David's town. And it was to shepherds, with the same profession that David had before he was king, that the news of Jesus' birth was first announced.

Shepherds' fields at Bethlehem.

Both Matthew and Luke provide extensive genealogical material for Jesus' ancestry. Luke shows Jesus' identification with all humanity by tracing His lineage all the way back to Adam. Matthew emphasizes Jesus as both a descendant of Abraham (with the right to the promises of the Abrahamic Covenant) and as a descendant of David through the royal line of the Davidic dynasty (with the right to the promises of the Davidic covenant).

Luke, the only Gentile writer of a Gospel, unexpectedly emphasized the *Jewish* customs completed after Jesus was born. He was circumcised and named "Jesus" in Bethlehem when He was eight days old. When He was forty days old, He was taken to the temple in Jerusalem for Mary's ritual purification. Mary and Joseph's offering of two doves—the least expensive permitted by the Law—shows their poverty. Evidently Joseph set up his carpentry trade in Bethlehem, believing that it was fitting for the Messiah to be reared in David's town.

THE MAGI

Matthew, the Gospel writer with the most interest in showing how Jesus fulfilled Scripture, emphasized the *Gentiles* that came to Jesus after He was born. Apparently after Jesus had become a toddler, magi came from the East to pay Him their respects. These were probably members of a Persian religion who had observed a mysterious but meaningful star in the heavens. They used the rules of their own religion to determine that the star meant that a Jewish king had been born—and that He deserved gifts and recognition.

Nobody knows how many magi came. Nobody knows what they rode. They must have been impressive to stir up Jerusalem. They surely did not intend to insult Herod the Great when they asked about finding one *born* king of the Jews. After following the star from Jerusalem to Bethlehem, they found Jesus "at home" and offered their worship and their gifts. The gold soon proved to be needed for the family's escape to Egypt.

The slaughter of the Bethlehem babies that Herod the Great ordered is unknown in secular history. It fits perfectly, however, with what is known of the aging tyrant-king. This event helps fix the date of Jesus' birth, at least approximately. (Herod died in 4 B.C.; the babies two years old or less were killed, suggesting Jesus' birth in 6 B.C. or earlier, Matt. 2:16.)

Nobody knows where Jesus, Mary, and Joseph lived in Egypt. Nobody knows how long they lived there. Many Jews lived in Alexandria, and Jesus was safe from Herod's grasp anywhere in Egypt. It is surely an irony that Egypt was a better place of safety for the Messiah than Judea. Joseph's carpentry skills were portable, which he no doubt used in Egypt. While they were there, the family no doubt spoke Aramaic (the native tongue of Judea) at home but used Greek (the trade language used throughout the Roman Empire) in public.

Gospel According to Luke

This Gospel presents Jesus' life from the angel's announcement of His birth to His ascent to heaven. From the earliest days Luke, the Gentile physician and friend of Paul, has been recognized as its author. Luke wrote more self-consciously as a historian than the other evangelists did. The first reader was Theophilus, an otherwise unknown friend of Luke, probably in the late A.D. 50s. The key word for the book is "Savior"; the key text is Luke 19:10. **One-Sentence Summary:** *Jesus not only lived and ministered as the perfect human, but He also died and rose to new life as the Savior for sinners.*

Harbor at Alexandria. Joseph, Mary, and Jesus may have lived in Alexandria among a Jewish community until Herod the Great died.

After Herod the Great died, Joseph believed it was safe to return to Palestine. He did not, however, return to Bethlehem. It was too close to Jerusalem, where Herod's evil son Archelaus ruled. Instead, the family moved back to Nazareth where Mary and Joseph had lived before Jesus was conceived. It was better for Jesus to be reared safely in Nazareth than in Bethlehem, where they had tried to kill Him, even if the people of Nazareth looked down on Mary and Joseph as morally suspect because of Jesus' "untimely" birth. Sadly, the day came when the people of Nazareth also wanted to kill Jesus.

THE HIDDEN YEARS

Almost nothing is known of the "hidden years" of Jesus. He probably received a basic education—reading, writing, and numbers—at the synagogue school of Nazareth. He certainly learned the Scriptures well—as His later teaching demonstrated. He no doubt learned carpentry skills from Joseph, who may have died before Jesus' baptism. Perhaps He assisted Mary with care for a growing number of brothers and sisters (Matt. 13:55-56).

As far as first-century Jewish tradition is now understood, in Jesus' day a boy went to Jerusalem for the Passover only when he came of age as a responsible adult. (Jews call this a bar mitzvah; many Christians also have recognized a similar age for confirmation or age of moral accountability.) Thus, when Jesus was twelve, Mary and Joseph took Him to the temple for His first Passover there. As the only specific incident from Jesus' childhood that has been preserved, this event shows that Jesus already had a specific consciousness of His special relationship to God. For Him to refer to the temple as "my Father's house" (Luke 2:49) was a remarkable claim, yet this account also shows Him as obedient to Mary and Joseph.

Bible students have lamented that so little is known about these hidden years. What should be emphasized is that they were not wasted years. Preparation for ministry is invaluable. One of the secrets of Jesus' fabulous teaching ministry was some thirty years of being rooted in the down-to-earth-ness of life. How much did Jesus know about His messianic identity and mission? We don't know. We do know that He grew in wisdom (Luke 2:52). No doubt He learned from Mary about the amazing events surrounding His birth. He also mastered Scripture. For years He waited for the time to begin His ministry.

An overview of modern Nazareth from the southwest.

Son of Man

According to the Gospels, Jesus did not call Himself by the title Messiah, Christ, Son of David, Son of God, or Savior. He called Himself Son of Man, yet nobody else ever addressed Him by that title! Earlier generations of Bible students have thought the term emphasized Jesus' humanity. More recent study, however, has indicated that Jesus took certain Old Testament texts (Ps. 8:4; 80:17; Dan. 7:13; 10:16,18) which spoke obscurely of a mysterious Son of Man. Jesus poured into it His own meaning. The Son of Man is the Messiah whose first coming was characterized by suffering, but who would return in great glory. Jesus perhaps called Himself Son of Man to avoid the military or political assumptions first-century Jews attached to the title Messiah.

THE SON OF MAN:
MINISTRY, TEACHINGS, AND MIGHTY WORKS OF JESUS (A.D. 26–30)

The title by which Jesus called Himself during His public ministry was "Son of Man." This title had been prophesied in Daniel 7:13, and Jesus claimed it for Himself. It summarizes all that He said and did during His ministry. All four Gospels tell about Jesus' extensive public ministry: MATTHEW 3—20; MARK 1—10; LUKE 3—19, and JOHN 2—11. They all report Jesus' central message: the good news of the kingdom of God. They show that His miracles were signs (like a highway sign indicating a city ahead) that God's kingdom had arrived in His person.

The beginning of Jesus' ministry is reckoned from His baptism, possibly late in the summer of A.D. 26. He ministered for more than three years, until the spring of A.D. 30. Although the four Gospels do not focus on chronology, it appears likely that Jesus organized His ministry into five distinct phases or stages:[2]

1. Early ministry in Judea (autumn A.D. 26 to spring A.D. 27)

2. The ministry in Galilee (summer A.D. 27 to spring A.D. 29)

3. The ministry of discipling and traveling (summer and early autumn A.D. 29)

4. Later ministry in Judea (late autumn and early winter A.D. 29)

5. The ministry in Perea (late winter and early spring A.D. 30)

PREPARATION FOR JESUS' MINISTRY (LATE SUMMER A.D. 26)

All four Gospels describe John the Baptist as the one who prepared people for Jesus' ministry. The Fourth Gospel did not tell about Jesus' baptism and temptation in the wilderness, but the others did so. The Son of Man emerged from these experiences as the Spirit-empowered Messiah who had passed the test of being victorious over Satan.

JOHN THE BAPTIST'S MINISTRY

As a distant cousin of Jesus, John fulfilled the Scriptural prophecies about an Elijah-like figure who would prepare the Lord's "road" (Mal. 4:5-6; Luke 1:17,76). He chose to begin his ministry, probably in the spring of A.D. 26, in a dramatic way beside the Jordan River (which had connections with Elijah) as it flowed through the wilderness of Judea. Even in his clothing, John deliberately paralleled the appearance of Elijah (2 Kings 1:8; Mark 1:6).

Like Elijah, John called God's people to repent, to turn from their sins. He preached about a coming One, whose identity he did not know. This roused hopes of many Jews in Judea that at long last God's silence of many centuries was about to be broken. Indeed, John was the first true prophetic voice since Malachi preached in the days of Nehemiah.

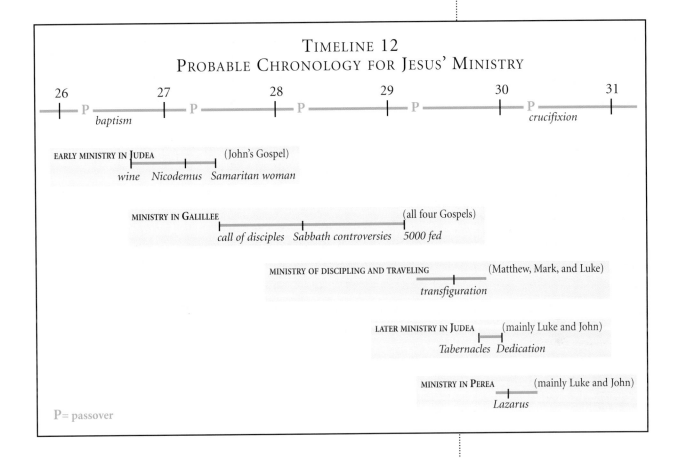

TIMELINE 12
PROBABLE CHRONOLOGY FOR JESUS' MINISTRY

26   27   28   29   30   31

P   P   P   P   P

baptism   crucifixion

EARLY MINISTRY IN JUDEA   (John's Gospel)

wine   Nicodemus   Samaritan woman

MINISTRY IN GALILLEE   (all four Gospels)

call of disciples   Sabbath controversies   5000 fed

MINISTRY OF DISCIPLING AND TRAVELING   (Matthew, Mark, and Luke)

transfiguration

LATER MINISTRY IN JUDEA   (mainly Luke and John)

Tabernacles Dedication

MINISTRY IN PEREA   (mainly Luke and John)

Lazarus

P= passover

Not only did John create a stir with his message of repentance, he insisted that the people who responded must be baptized in water (dipped in the Jordan River) as a sign of their repentance. They came, evidently by the hundreds, if not by the thousands. This was all preparation, however, for the work of the coming One. He would perform a baptism in the Holy Spirit that would cleanse from the inside out (Matt. 3:11).

JESUS' BAPTISM

Jesus traveled from Nazareth south to the Jordan Valley to be baptized by John presumably some months after John had established his ministry. John initially refused to baptize Jesus, perhaps because he had learned from his own mother of the amazing events surrounding Jesus' birth. He did not yet know Jesus was the coming One.

Why was Jesus baptized if He had nothing of which to repent? Jesus explained it was necessary to fulfill all righteousness (Matt. 3:15), another way of saying, "This is the right thing to do." Certainly Jesus was identifying publicly with John's ministry; perhaps He was also showing His willingness to associate with the sinful people that came to John for baptism.

John the Baptist

Luke alone reported the unexpected birth of John to the aged Elizabeth and Zechariah. His traditional title "the Baptist" could be more accurately translated "the Baptizer." His blunt manner and message were appropriate for the one who fulfilled the prophecies of an Elijah-like figure. He was the first to announce that God's kingdom was about to come. John's call to repentance reached not only the people but also the ruler of Galilee and Perea, Herod Antipas, son of Herod the Great. Antipas's adultery with his married niece Herodias provoked John's wrath. Months after John was arrested, Herodias found an evil way to have John beheaded.

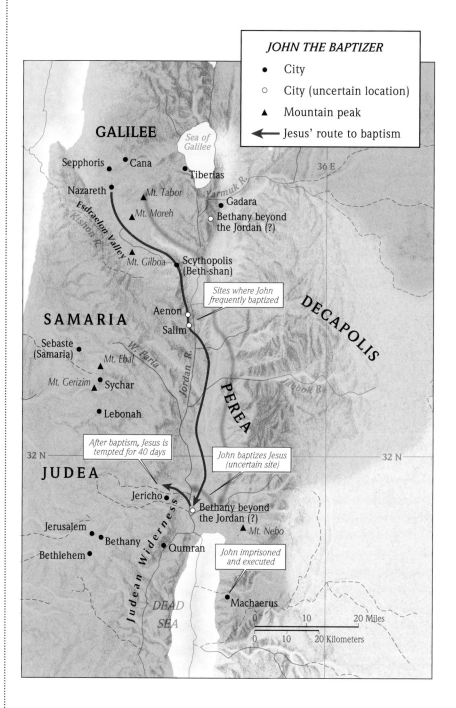

JOHN THE BAPTIZER
- • City
- ○ City (uncertain location)
- ▲ Mountain peak
- ← Jesus' route to baptism

GALILEE

Sea of Galilee

Sepphoris • Cana
Tiberias
36 E

Nazareth
▲ Mt. Tabor
Gadara
▲ Mt. Moreh
Bethany beyond the Jordan (?)

Esdraelon Valley
Kishon R.
Yarmuk R.

▲ Mt. Gilboa
Scythopolis (Beth-shan)

DECAPOLIS

Sites where John frequently baptized

Aenon
Salim

SAMARIA

Sebaste (Samaria) •
▲ Mt. Ebal
W. Fariʿa
Jordan R.
Jabbok R.

Mt. Gerizim ▲ • Sychar

PEREA

• Lebonah

After baptism, Jesus is tempted for 40 days

John baptizes Jesus (uncertain site)

32 N
32 N

JUDEA

Jericho •
Bethany beyond the Jordan (?)

Jerusalem •
▲ Mt. Nebo
• Bethany
Bethlehem •
• Qumran

Judean Wilderness

John imprisoned and executed

DEAD SEA
• Machaerus
0   10   20 Miles
0   10   20 Kilometers

The Jordan River where tradition says Jesus was baptized.

The descent of the Spirit on Jesus in a dove-like form was a powerful visual sign that Jesus was indeed the Anointed One, the Messiah. This was explained by God's voice from heaven. The words about Jesus being the Father's beloved Son were in fact a quotation of Psalm 2:7 about the messianic King. The other words of the heavenly voice about God being pleased with Jesus' obedience seem also to be a quotation. They come from Isaiah 42:1, a "Suffering Servant" passage. The Spirit's coming on Jesus, therefore, was the time when He was

• anointed by the Spirit—declared to be the messianic King

• empowered by the Spirit—enabled to do the work of the Servant of the Lord

Until this time Jesus had proclaimed nothing about the coming kingdom of God, nor had He done any mighty work. Afterward He preached the message of the kingdom (because He was the King), and He did miracles (by the Spirit's power) that the Father told Him to do (Matt. 12:28; John 5:19).

Telephoto close-up of the rugged wilderness terrain on the east face of the Mount of Temptation.

Satan

Satan is a Hebrew word meaning adversary. He is a personal being created by God who stands against both God and mankind. In the Old Testament little is revealed about his origin or identity. In the New Testament this same being is called the devil, a Greek word meaning accuser. He is revealed as the evil leader of a kingdom opposed to God with evil spirits and evil humans obeying him. His hatred of God and God's righteous kingdom drives him to try (unsuccessfully) to thwart God's purposes. He was defeated by Christ's death, and according to Scripture his destiny is everlasting punishment.

JESUS' TEMPTATION

Jesus was driven immediately from being empowered to being tested. As the "final lawgiver" and the "final prophet" He experienced a forty-day fast just as Moses and Elijah did (Exod. 34:28; 1 Kings 19:8). At the end of this experience, the devil came and tempted Him. Bible students have wrestled with the question "Why was Jesus tempted?" just as they have with the question "Why was Jesus baptized?" At the very least this event showed His full humanity. It further is an instance of Jesus as an example—showing kingdom people how to succeed against temptation. Jesus was more concerned with obeying God than He was with anything else, including the promise of a highly successful ministry. Jesus prevailed against the devil by relying on the same two resources available to all kingdom people: the word of God and the Spirit of God.

As Jesus' earliest ministry shows, John the Baptist successfully prepared people for the Messiah because he entrusted his own disciples to Jesus (John 1). Jesus was proclaimed to be the Anointed One and the Servant of the Lord in the events surrounding His baptism. In His victory over the devil's temptations, He showed His dependence on the Spirit and the word, hallmarks of His entire ministry to come. Once Jesus entered the sphere of public activity, He gave vigorous attention to fulfilling His mission, one stage at a time.

EARLY MINISTRY IN JUDEA
(AUTUMN A.D. 26 TO SUMMER A.D. 27)

John's Gospel alone describes Jesus' ministry in Judea before He began a traveling ministry throughout Galilee. He carried out a baptizing ministry, parallel to that of John the Baptist, and began attracting followers. Although no healing miracles from this period are mentioned, He turned water to wine and cleared the temple of animals as evidence of His messianic authority. Jesus concluded this period of His ministry when John the Baptist was put in prison.

Judea

Judea was the Greek equivalent of the Hebrew name Judah when applied to a geographical or political region. Jerusalem was its religious center, with the magnificent temple—lavishly rebuilt by Herod the Great beginning in 20 B.C.—as the centerpiece. The Romans conquered Judea in 63 B.C., and Rome determined the form under which Judea was ruled. By the time of Jesus' ministry, a Roman governor ruled Judea from the Roman capital of Caesarea on the Mediterranean coast. A religious council (the Sanhedrin) regulated Jewish affairs. Its membership was divided between Pharisees and Sadducees.

Sunset over Judean hills taken from the fortress Machaerus in Jordan. The Dead Sea is in the background.

Gospel According to John

This Gospel presents Jesus' life from a unique perspective, often telling of incidents omitted by the other three evangelists. A good example is the description of Jesus' ministry in Judea and Jerusalem, both before and after His Galilean ministry. From the earliest days it was known, John the apostle has been recognized as its author. John wrote more self-consciously as a reflective theologian than the other evangelists did. The first readers were probably Christians living in the Roman province of Asia in the A.D. 80s. The key word for the book is "Lord"; the key text is John 3:16. **One-Sentence Summary:** *Jesus is the sign-working Son of God who gives eternal life on the basis of His death and resurrection to all who believe in Him.*

EARLY DISCIPLES

John 1:28-51 describes the earliest encounter Jesus had with those who would later become full-time apostles. After Jesus' triumph over the devil in the wilderness, He returned to the site of His baptism. John the Baptist now realized that Jesus was the Lamb of God who would take away sin. He therefore pointed his own followers to Jesus: Andrew and an unnamed person, almost certainly John (who later became an apostle). In turn Simon (who became Peter), Philip, and Nathaniel were introduced to Jesus.

These all appear to have learned from Jesus for a brief period of time before they returned to their routine way of living. Some months later Jesus invited Peter, Andrew, James, and John to leave their fishing business and begin following Him full time.

EARLY MIGHTY WORKS

Jesus did two noteworthy deeds during this period to demonstrate His power. Both are described only in John 2. As His first miracle He turned water to wine at a wedding in Cana. People began to believe in Him from this time forward (John 2:11).

At the Passover of A.D. 27, Jesus cleared the temple courts of animals and money changers—an event He repeated three years later, a few days before His crucifixion. While this was not a miracle in the formal sense,

Khirbet Cana in the Asochis Valley. Cana was where Jesus performed His first sign (miracle).

it was an extraordinary show of Jesus' authority and the beginning of His challenge to the Jewish religious establishment. He used this as an opportunity to give them a riddle about His coming death and resurrection, something they (inaccurately) remembered and threw back at Him when He was finally brought to trial (John 2:19; Mark 14:58).

JESUS AND THE KINGDOM OF GOD

Aside from His teaching about the meaning of His coming death (see the later section on "Jesus' Mission"), no topic was more important to Jesus than "the kingdom of God." This phrase or the equivalent "kingdom of heaven" occurs about eighty times in the Gospels. The first time Jesus is known to have mentioned the kingdom was in His encounter with Nicodemus, a rabbi who understood the kingdom of God as an important biblical theme (John 3:3,5).

Because the central claim of the present work is that the entire Bible is best understood as the Kingdom Story, it is important to consider the meaning of the "kingdom of God" as Jesus proclaimed it. First, it should be noted that the standard English translation is not particularly good. The kingdom (*basileia*) is not a place but rather a condition, a state of affairs. The kingdom is the rule of God through His messianic King. John the Baptist had earlier announced that the kingdom was near, meaning that the promised Messiah was about to arrive. Later, Jesus proclaimed that the kingdom had already arrived (Matt. 12:28). He brought the kingdom because He was the King of the kingdom. It arrived in His person.

Jesus proclaimed the kingdom in a way that diverged sharply from what we know of the typical first-century Jewish expectation. The Jews were generally looking for a military-political leader that would destroy the Roman yoke. His coming ("the day of the LORD") would be sudden, irresistible, and visible to everyone. At the risk of oversimplifying, we may suggest that a timeline for the Jewish understanding looked like this:

The model of the colonnaded court area of the temple. This is part of a model of Jerusalem at the Holyland Hotel, Jerusalem.

JEWISH VIEW OF THE KINGDOM OF GOD

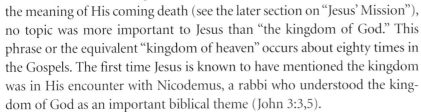

"This Age"   "Age to Come" = Kingdom of God

Messiah/Day of the Lord

This view of the kingdom was certainly a reasonable interpretation of the Old Testament, particularly Daniel 2, in which the stone mountain (God's kingdom) suddenly, irresistibly, and visibly destroyed the four-metal image of Nebuchadnezzar's vision. If Rome was the fourth world empire (legs and feet of iron), then it was not unreasonable to believe that God's irresistible kingdom was imminent.

Jesus' view was shaped by His understanding that, as the Messiah, He was to have two comings, not just one. Thus, in His first coming (during the days of the fourth world empire of Daniel 2), He truly brought the kingdom. Yet He brought it in a form that was gradual, resistible, and largely invisible. Only in His glorious second coming would the kingdom of God come with irresistible might. (Many of Jesus' parables of the kingdom were directed to help His disciples understand this view of the kingdom.)

Jesus' understanding concerning the kingdom of God looked like this:

JESUS' VIEW OF THE KINGDOM OF GOD

With Jesus' first coming He really brought the "age to come." Yet He did not do away with "this age," which will occur only at His second coming. Thus, followers of Jesus today experience the tension of being partakers of the kingdom—submitting to the King as Lord—yet still living in this age, which does not acknowledge the King. Later on, Jesus explained to His followers that they were in the world but not of the world (John 17:13-14). In summary, Jesus inaugurated the kingdom of God in His first coming, but in His second coming He will consummate the kingdom.

EARLY EVANGELISM

John 3:22-36 describes the early baptizing and preaching ministry of Jesus. He soon eclipsed John the Baptist in popularity, and John graciously conceded his place to Jesus. This period is described only generally.

Jesus' evangelistic encounters with two individuals show the incredible variety of those He came to save. Nicodemus was a leader of the Pharisees in Jerusalem, who sought out Jesus at the time that Jesus cleared the temple (John 3). The unnamed woman at the well was an immoral member of the Samaritans, a religiously suspect ethnic group (John 4). Both of these needed eternal life through Jesus, and Jesus used

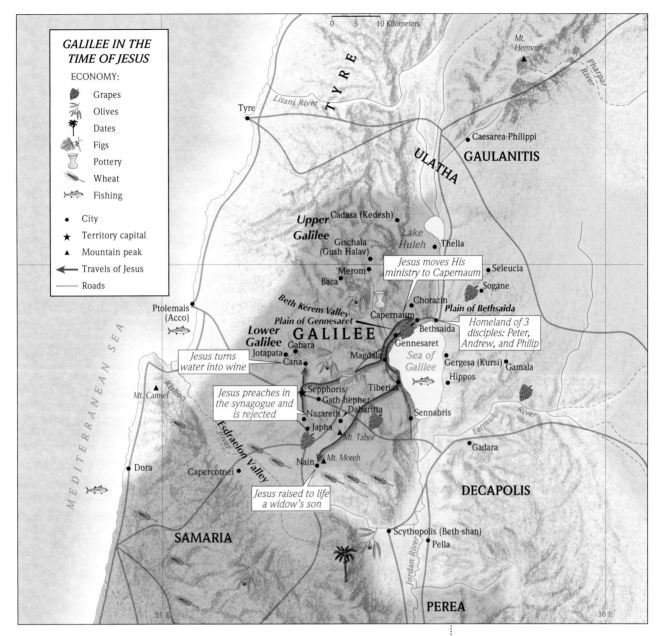

GALILEE IN THE TIME OF JESUS

ECONOMY:

- Grapes
- Olives
- Dates
- Figs
- Pottery
- Wheat
- Fishing

- • City
- ★ Territory capital
- ▲ Mountain peak
- ← Travels of Jesus
- Roads

0   5   10 Kilometers

Mt. Hermon

Litani River

TYRE

Tyre

ULATHA

GAULANITIS

Caesarea-Philippi

Pharpar River

Upper Galilee

Cadasa (Kedesh)

Lake Huleh

Thella

Gischala (Gush Halav)

Merom

Baca

Seleucia

Sogane

Chorazin

Jesus moves His ministry to Capernaum

Capernaum

Plain of Bethsaida

Bethsaida

Homeland of 3 disciples: Peter, Andrew, and Philip

Beth Kerem Valley

Plain of Gennesaret

Lower Galilee

GALILEE

Gabara

Jotapata

Cana

Jesus turns water into wine

Ptolemais (Acco)

Gennesaret

Magdala

Sea of Galilee

Gergesa (Kursi)

Gamala

Hippos

MEDITERRANEAN SEA

Mt. Carmel

Kishon

Jesus preaches in the synagogue and is rejected

Sepphoris

Gath-hepher

Nazareth

Dabaritta

Tiberias

Sennabris

Yarmuk River

Japha

Mt. Tabor

Nain

Mt. Moreh

Jesus raised to life a widow's son

Esdraelon Valley

Dora

Capercotnei

Gadara

DECAPOLIS

SAMARIA

Scythopolis (Beth-shan)

Pella

Jordan River

PEREA

35 E

36 E

different techniques for reaching out to each one. To Nicodemus He spoke about the possibility of being born again; to the woman He spoke of life-giving water.

According to Mark 1:14, Jesus arrived in Galilee to begin His extensive traveling ministry after John was imprisoned. Galilee, ruled by King Herod Antipas, was in fact a different country than Judea, ruled by a Roman governor, Pontius Pilate. Jesus no longer used John's method (baptizing) or location (the Jordan Valley). Instead, He established a traveling ministry in Galilee where He taught in the synagogues and engaged in an extensive healing ministry. (He encountered the Samaritan woman during His journey from the Jordan Valley north to Galilee.)

This shortest Gospel is believed by many Bible students to be the earliest. It emphasizes the activities of Jesus more than His teachings. From the earliest days John Mark, a character in the Book of Acts, been recognized as its author. According to Christian tradition he wrote his Gospel based on the eyewitness memories of Simon Peter. The first readers were probably Christians living in the city of Rome in the A.D. 50s. The key word for the book is "Servant"; the key text is Mark 10:45. **One-Sentence Summary:** *In His life, death, and resurrection, Jesus did the deeds of the (suffering) Servant of the Lord, notably through His death as a "ransom for many."*

THE MINISTRY IN GALILEE
(AUTUMN A.D. 27 TO SPRING A.D. 29)

All four Gospels describe Jesus' ministry in Galilee, with Mark giving proportionately more attention (Mark 1—6) and John proportionately the least (John 4—6). Perhaps the most beloved stories of Jesus' healings and teachings come from this phase of His ministry. This was the time of His greatest popularity with the masses, but it was also the time that He selected twelve apostles to become His official representatives. As with the other stages of Jesus' ministry, this one is impossible to date precisely. For perhaps a year and a half Jesus was on the move throughout Galilee. If Jesus began this stage of His ministry after John the Baptist was imprisoned, He ended it shortly after John was beheaded (Matt. 4:12; 14:12; 15:21). The miraculous feeding of 5,000—the only mighty work Jesus did which all four Gospels record—represents the climax and conclusion to this stage of Jesus' ministry.

PREACHING AND HEALING TOUR IN GALILEE

When Jesus returned to Galilee after several months' absence, He was a man with a mission rather than the quiet, hometown carpenter from Nazareth He had been. He had acquired a certain reputation because of His ministry in Judea, and certainly there was a great deal of curiosity about Him. When He began a remarkable ministry of healing the sick, excitement about Him raised to fever pitch, with accompanying resentment by the religious establishment.

Forum columns from Sebaste, formerly Samaria. Herod the Great renamed the city when he gained control of it (p.176).

A 4th century A.D. *synagogue built on the foundation of a 1st century* A.D. *synagogue.*

After Jesus preached in His hometown synagogue, the people of Nazareth refused to accept His claim that He fulfilled Isaiah's prophecy (Is. 61:1-2; Luke 4:14-30). Thus He selected Capernaum, a fishing town on the Sea of Galilee, to be the place He was "at home" when He was not traveling. At the lakeside He called two pairs of brothers—Simon and Andrew, James and John—to begin following Him full time. This marked the second stage of their encounter with Jesus. The crowd of followers was soon staggering.

Mark 1:21-38 records events from a single 24-hour period in Jesus' Galilean ministry. It shows what a typical busy day in Jesus' ministry looked like.

- Extraordinary teaching on the Sabbath in the Capernaum synagogue

- Driving out an evil spirit from a man present in the synagogue

- Healing the mother-in-law of Simon (Peter) from a fever

- Healing all the sick that came after sundown (when the Sabbath ended)

- Praying alone before daybreak

- Beginning a preaching and healing tour throughout Galilee

Jesus' travel throughout the region included a number of remarkable encounters. He completely healed a man with leprosy (an incurable skin disease). The amazement this caused was something like what would happen today if someone dying of AIDS was suddenly restored to full health. He healed a paralyzed man who was dropped down on a mat through the roof. He called Levi, a social outcast because he was a tax gatherer, to follow Him.

Galilee

"Galilee" was the name, even in Old Testament times, for a geographical region in the northern part of Israel. The most prominent feature is the small but beautiful "Sea of Galilee," renamed "Sea of Tiberias" or "Sea of Gennesaret" in the first century. Because Galilee had been part of the Northern Kingdom of Israel, it had always had a separate identity from Judah/Judea. In the first century Galilee had a racially mixed population. Jews of Judea looked down on Jews of Galilee. By the time of Jesus' ministry Galilee was ruled by a "king," Herod Antipas (ruled 4 B.C.–A.D. 39). Herod's capital city, Tiberias, lay on the Sea of Galilee, but Jews apparently avoided it.

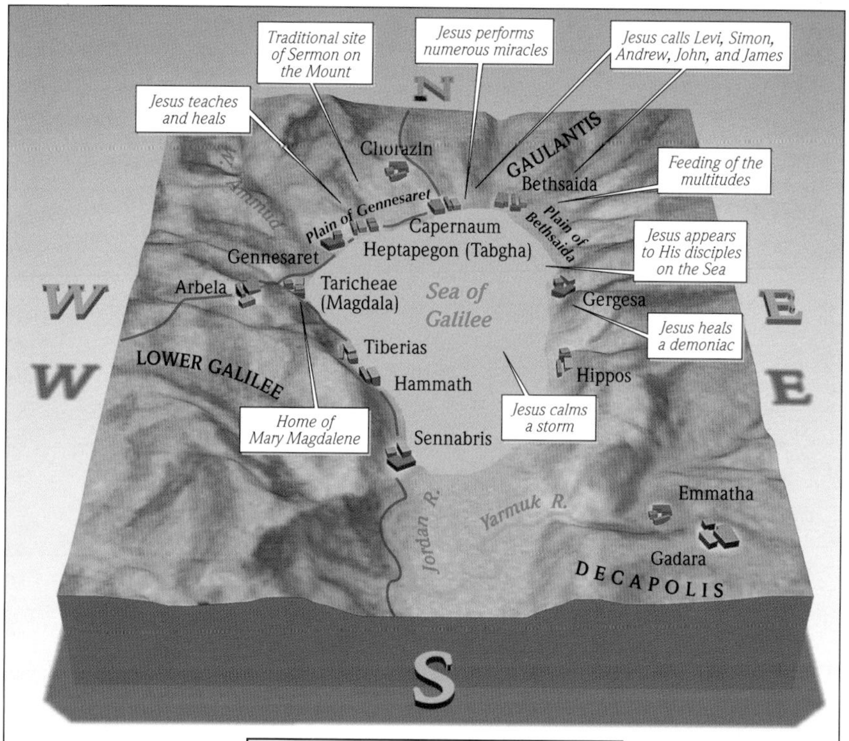
Traditional site of Sermon on the Mount
Jesus performs numerous miracles
Jesus calls Levi, Simon, Andrew, John, and James
Jesus teaches and heals
N
Chorazin
GAULANTIS
Bethsaida
Feeding of the multitudes
Plain of Gennesaret
Capernaum
Plain of Bethsaida
Jesus appears to His disciples on the Sea
Gennesaret
Heptapegon (Tabgha)
Arbela
Taricheae (Magdala)
Sea of Galilee
Gergesa
W
E
Jesus heals a demoniac
Tiberias
LOWER GALILEE
Hammath
Hippos
Home of Mary Magdalene
Jesus calms a storm
Sennabris
Emmatha
Jordan R.
Yarmuk R.
Gadara
DECAPOLIS
S

THE MINISTRY OF JESUS AROUND THE SEA OF GALILEE

City

Road

Miracles

There is no single word for "miracle" in the New Testament; instead, words translated "sign," "deed of power," "wonder," or "work" are used. In a formal sense a miracle is an event in which a supernatural being intervenes in the created order (rather than an unusual or awe-inspiring event). Thus, Jesus' healings, exorcisms, and nature miracles may be thought of as His interference with nature—in an entirely wholesome way. Although it has been fashionable for critics to explain away or deny that Jesus worked miracles, many of His teachings make sense only if His miracle-working power is granted. In the first century even Jesus' opponents recognized Him as doing miraculous works.

Jesus' Miracles

The Galilean phase of Jesus' ministry was noteworthy as the time He performed so many miracles, especially healings. Several passages record that He healed all who came (Matt. 8:16; 12:15; Mark 6:56; Luke 4:40; 6:19). Jesus' miracles pointed to His true identity because the Messiah was expected to do these things (Matt. 11:2-6). Jesus wanted people to recognize that His miracles were signs that the kingdom of God had come, but He also knew that a faith based on miracles was inadequate (Matt. 12:28; John 6:26-29). When faith is mentioned in reference to Jesus' miracles, it usually precedes. The order is "If I believe in Jesus, then I will see a miracle" rather than "If I see a miracle, then I will believe in Jesus."

In fact, there are relatively few specific miracles described—less than forty. Most are physical healings of human bodies. What stands out is the variety of patients Jesus cured: bleeding, paralysis, leprosy, blindness, deafness, and so on. Sometimes He healed at a distance, and three times the patient had already died (a widow's son, Jairus's daughter, and Lazarus).

Gergesa and the Sea of Galilee. Gergesa is the place there Jesus cast the demons into the pigs who then ran into the Sea of Galilee. The view is looking toward Tiberias from the eastern side of the Sea of Galilee.

A second category is the exorcisms, most puzzling for people today but readily accepted in the first century. Jesus successfully cast out demons or unclean spirits. These usually manifested themselves by their victim's bizarre behavior. In such cases the exorcism proved that Jesus' will was stronger than the will of the unclean spirit. In no case was the faith of the victim mentioned, contrary to His usual habit with physical healings. He cast out demons by a word of command.

The third category is Jesus' "nature miracles," that is, everything except healings and exorcisms. Only nine are recorded, and these are possibly all that Jesus performed:

1. Miraculous provision of food and drink:

- Turning water to wine
- A miraculous catch of fish
- Feeding the 5000
- Feeding the 4000
- Post-resurrection catch of 153 fish

2. Control over the ordinary laws of nature:

- Stilling a storm on the Sea of Galilee
- Walking on water (and enabling Peter to do so, after which the wind stopped)
- Telling Peter where to find tax money (in a fish's mouth)
- Cursing a fig tree (the only negative miracle)

Demons

Demons are also called evil spirits or unclean spirits. They are also referred to as fallen angels. In the New Testament they are supernatural beings that are the opposite of the holy angels. They exhibit traits of personality such as intellect and will. The Scriptures assume that demons are able to gain control of the will of a human being, resulting in behavioral (or sometimes physical) abnormality. Jesus' successful exorcism of all those who were "demon possessed" was evidence of the presence of God's kingdom. The demons will share the same destiny (the lake of fire) as their leader, Satan.

Sunrise on the Sea of Galilee at Tiberias.

JESUS' APOSTLES AND HIS "INAUGURAL ADDRESS"

Several months into His Galilean ministry, perhaps in the spring or summer of A.D. 28, Jesus designated twelve of the disciples (learners) that had been following Him to become His apostles (commissioned representatives). They were the ones who knew Him best and therefore were authorized to continue His ministry. They also taught, healed, and exorcised as Jesus did (Mark 3:14-15; Luke 9:2). The success of the Kingdom Story from this point forward depended on the faithfulness of the apostles to fulfill their responsibilities. Jesus and the Twelve formed the framework for the new covenant community just as Jacob and his twelve sons were the framework for the old covenant community.

Details are known about only a few of the Twelve; in fact several are mentioned only in the four biblical lists (Matt. 10:2-4; Mark 3:16-18; Luke 6:14-16; Acts 1:13).

1. Simon Peter: first in every list and the chief spokesman; later wrote two epistles and was probably the direct source for the Gospel according to Mark

2. James: first apostle to die as a martyr (Acts 12); brother of John ("James" is actually "Jacob" in Greek)

3. John: probably the youngest; called himself the disciple whom Jesus loved; later wrote one Gospel, three epistles, and Revelation

4. Andrew: Peter's brother who seems to have lived in his brother's shadow

5. Philip: little is known about him; not the same as Philip in the Book of Acts

6. Bartholomew: possibly the same as the one named Nathaniel in John's Gospel

7. Matthew: a tax gatherer whose birth name was Levi; later wrote a Gospel

8. Thomas: also called Didymus ("Twin"); famous for his post-resurrection confession of Jesus as Lord and God

Sea of Galilee from the Church of the Beatitudes.

9. James: son of Alphaeus; called "the less" to distinguish him from the other James

10. Thaddeus: also known as Judas, but for obvious reasons later dropped this name

11. Simon: called "the Zealot" perhaps because of his earlier political involvement

12. Judas Iscariot: evidently the only non-Galilean, the treasurer and the traitor

Like a king who had chosen his beloved courtiers, Jesus came down from the mountainside with His apostles. They came to a level place among the hills where a tremendous crowd was waiting (Matt. 5:1; Luke 6:17). Jesus delivered to them the most famous and most important sermon ever heard, "The Sermon on the Mount." The primary audience was the newly minted apostles, but the crowds were straining to hear.

This teaching may be called more descriptively "Life in the Kingdom of God." It is a comprehensive presentation of the moral guidelines relevant for those who have already made a commitment to the King. They are therefore already citizens of the kingdom of God.

Two different summaries of this sermon have evidently been preserved: Matthew 5—7 and Luke 6:20-49. Virtually everything in Luke's abridgment is found in Matthew's longer version. Jesus masterfully addressed the following topics:

- Character traits for kingdom people (including the "Beatitudes"), Matt. 5:3-16

- Kingdom people and the law of Moses, Matt. 5:17-47

- Kingdom people and religious practices, Matt. 6:1-18

- Kingdom people and choosing the right alternatives, Matt. 6:19-34

- Kingdom people and their personal conduct, Matt. 7:1-27

SABBATH CONTROVERSIES

Jesus' authoritative, powerful preaching about the kingdom of God delighted the ordinary people of Galilee. Jesus was a master of Scripture and always taught with the highest regard for God's law (Matt. 5:18). When it came to tradition, however, Jesus had no patience for customs that sabotaged the true intention of the law. Of all the Jewish sects, the one with the greatest concern for keeping the law—but only as their traditions understood it—was the Pharisees. Thus, it is no surprise that Jesus and the Pharisees clashed.

Jesus challenged the Pharisees particularly concerning the right way to keep the Sabbath holy. Three incidents show how bitterly the Pharisees resented—and rejected—Jesus' interpretation.

In Jerusalem, probably when He went to celebrate the Passover of A.D. 28, Jesus healed a paralyzed man on the Sabbath (John 5:1-14). This was so disturbing that His opponents wanted to kill Him then and there (John 5:18).

In Galilee, probably shortly after the Passover when the grain fields were ripe, Jesus' disciples picked grain and ate it as they walked along (Mark 2:23-27). His claim to be Lord of the Sabbath was especially annoying to the Pharisees.

In Galilee He healed a man with a disabled hand one Sabbath day, a deliberate act of defiance. This too became an occasion for the Pharisees to make a plot to get rid of Jesus (Mark 3:1-6).

JESUS' PARABLES

Sometime later during Jesus' Galilean ministry, His confrontation with the Pharisees reached a point of no return. They accused Him of casting out evil spirits by the power of Satan. In turn He proclaimed that they were so spiritually bankrupt that they could not tell the power of the devil from the power of the Holy Spirit. Such persons had so blasphemed against the Holy Spirit that forgiveness was impossible (Mark 3:22-29). From this time on, there is no record that Jesus ever tried to conciliate the Pharisees. They were set on a hostile path that inevitably led to the crucifixion.

In the context of the Pharisees' outright rejection, Jesus began using a new teaching form, the parable. This approach had the advantage of being less direct. The meaning of parables could be hidden from outsiders but revealed to insiders (Mark 4:10-12). Although contemporary readers of the Gospels may be surprised to find that Jesus often intentionally obscured the truth, in a sense this was true of all of Jesus' ministry and teaching. Throughout the ages people have heard the word of God and never understood or responded to its message.

On the other hand, parables are the teaching form at which Jesus was the master. Literary experts who are not themselves Christians acknowledge that nobody has ever told parables better than Jesus has. Their vividness made them memorable, and Jesus used them to invite a response. The way persons responded to the parables was essentially their response to the King and to the kingdom of God.

About forty of Jesus' parables are recorded. (The exact number depends on whether certain short sayings are counted as parables.) Luke records more than any other Gospel, including the two that are the most widely remembered and loved: "The Good Samaritan" (Luke 10:25-37) and "The Prodigal Son" (Luke 15:11-32). The parables of Matthew 13 are organized around the "mysteries" or secrets of the kingdom (Matt. 13:11). In particular these parables explain Jesus' understanding of the kingdom of God as opposed to the Jewish expectations (see the earlier discussion of "Jesus and the Kingdom of God"). For example, "The Sower and the Soils" teaches that the kingdom of God can in fact be resisted in this age (Matt. 13:1-9,18-23). In addition "The Yeast" teaches that the kingdom works invisibly rather than visibly (Matt. 13:33).

CLIMAX TO THE GALILEAN MINISTRY

Jesus continued a marvelous healing ministry even as He turned to the use of parables. A number of memorable events evidently belong to the last part of His Galilean ministry:

- The healing of a Roman centurion's servant
- Stilling a storm on the Sea of Galilee
- Healing demon-possessed men near Gadara
- Healing a woman with a flow of blood
- Raising Jairus's daughter from the dead
- Allowing a sinful woman to anoint Him during dinner
- Preaching (yet again) in the Nazareth synagogue

After the Twelve had plenty of time and teaching from Jesus, He sent them out two by two throughout Galilee to teach and heal as His ambassadors (Mark 6:7-12). They reported back to Him the wonderful success of their ministries. They had also learned of the unjust murder of John the Baptist because of the evil scheme of Herod Antipas's mistress. When

Parables

The word parable means literally "something thrown beside," that is, a comparison. It is related to the term metaphor or simile. Parables have been defined in a variety of ways. They are "a thought-provoking, realistic, fictional incident illustrating a spiritual point" or "an earthly story with a heavenly meaning." Jesus' parables are reported only in Matthew, Mark, and Luke, and they are to be distinguished from allegories (stories with multiple points of spiritual identification). Bible students generally agree that parables have one central truth. Jesus' parables have His person, His mission, or His kingdom as their central concern.

Main fortress of Machaerus built by Herod the Great. Here John the Baptist was killed.

Jesus was informed that He also had come under Herod's scrutiny (Mark 6:14), He made plans to change His ministry pattern—but not until the great climactic event of His Galilean ministry.

Just before the Passover of A.D. 29 (a year before His crucifixion), Jesus faced a huge, hungry crowd in a deserted area near Bethsaida. With the resources of only five loaves of barley bread and two small fish, He multiplied the available food so that it fed not only the 5,000 adult men, but also the women and children. This miracle is the only one told by all four Gospels (Matt. 14; Mark 6; Luke 9; John 6), so it must be considered highly significant. In John's account the people interpreted Jesus' miracle as a Moses-like provision of food in a deserted place, so Jesus must be "the" Prophet whom Moses had predicted (John 6:14; Deut. 18:15,18). Jesus recognized that they meant to force Him to act as a military/political king, a notion that He refused all along. When He turned down the popular expectation, the crowds diminished significantly (John 6:66).

The night after He fed the multitude, Jesus walked on the water—and Peter walked out to meet Him. The Twelve confessed Him as the Son of God (Matt. 14:33); now, however, He would have to explain to them that His mission as God's Son included suffering and death.

The Ministry of Discipling and Traveling (Summer and Early Autumn a.d. 29)

The death of John the Baptist and the loss of public following may have been negative factors pushing Jesus to a new phase of ministry. A positive factor was His desire to give the apostles more in-depth teaching. Thus Jesus withdrew to the region north of Galilee, out of Herod Antipas's reach, yet still accessible to the crowds.

Evidence that Jesus was losing in popular support was that "only" 4,000 were fed at Jesus' next miraculous feeding (Mark 8:1-13). Particularly moving was Jesus' encounter with a Gentile woman from Syrian Phoenicia. Jesus praised her great faith, a startling contrast to the apostles, whom He had recently criticized for little faith (Matt. 14:31; 15:28).

The religious hostility against Jesus did not let up. The Pharisees had been dead set against Him for some time. Now, however, they found new allies, the Sadducees, whom they normally despised (Matt. 16:1). Jesus knew that it was useless to reach out to these people, whom He called representatives of an evil and adulterous generation.

The road from Jerusalem to Jericho, part of the precipitous drop from the east side of the Mount of Olives down to the Jordan Valley (p.185).

Sea of Galilee at Nof Ginnosar looking across the Sea to the Mount of Beatitudes.

Peter

His birth name (Simeon) was usually shortened to Simon. Jesus gave him the nickname or title "Peter" (in Greek; the Aramaic equivalent is "Cephas," translated Rock or Rocky or Rock Man). The son of Jonah and brother of Andrew, this Galilean fisherman became the chief spokesman for the apostles and the early leader of Christianity. He fulfilled his responsibility as the "key man" in the Book of Acts, and there is no indication that he transferred this authority to any successor. Paul called him "the apostle to the Jews." According to unbroken Christian tradition, Simon Peter was crucified in the city of Rome during the reign of Nero Caesar. He lived from about A.D. 1 to A.D. 65.

APOSTOLIC RECOGNITION

One of the places Jesus traveled with the Twelve during this time was the region near Caesarea Philippi, a pagan city north of the Sea of Galilee. In discipling the Twelve, He not only gave them didactic material (such as "The Sermon on the Mount") and stories (the parables), He used questions to help them learn. It was now time for them to become fully persuaded about who He was.

After hearing from the Twelve "what people are saying," He asked for their view of who He was. As the spokesman for the group, Simon Peter made the important confession that Jesus was both Christ (Messiah) and Son of God (Matt. 16:16). As far as the record shows, this was the first time that the apostles really grasped that the Messiah was also fully divine. (Biblical prophecies about the Messiah had not been interpreted along these lines.) This confession was especially important because it demonstrated that the apostles accepted Jesus as the Messiah, even though He had done things contrary to expectations (such as reject the "crown" that was offered at the feeding of the 5,000).

Jesus praised Peter, not for his ability to arrive at this conclusion deductively, but because he had received it by divine revelation. Not only that, Jesus began immediately to speak about an ongoing assembly of people (*ekklesia* or church) that He would be building. This assembly could not be destroyed even when the powers of Hades attacked it. (This was evidently Jesus' first teaching about an ongoing assembly—one that He would continue to build even though He was facing death.)

In this context Jesus promised Peter the "keys of the kingdom" (Matt. 16:19), a personal responsibility to open up the kingdom of God for people. (The Book of Acts records how Peter discharged this duty, first on the Day of Pentecost for Jews, then to the Samaritans, and finally to Gentiles at the house of Cornelius, Acts 2,8,10.) This was a great step forward in the Kingdom Story.

PASSION PREDICTION

It was now the summer or autumn before the crucifixion. Jesus was ready to prepare the apostles—insofar as it was possible—for what lay ahead in Jerusalem. Up to this time He had spoken of His death only in figurative language, such as His promise to rebuild the temple in three days or that the Prophet Jonah's experience was a sign that He would fulfill (John 2:19; Matt. 12:39-40). Now that the apostles knew that He was both Messiah and God's Son, He could teach them plainly about His crucifixion and resurrection.

Thus Jesus immediately began to explain that in Jerusalem He would be betrayed, killed, and rise again on the third day (Mark 8:31). This was the first of three times He predicted this, always connecting His death with a third-day resurrection (Mark 9:31; 10:33-34). These three prophecies are often referred to as the passion predictions, and they certainly show that Jesus had a clear understanding of the difficult days that lay ahead for Him. At the same time Jesus taught that this suffering was not to be limited just to Himself. Following Him always means self-denial and taking up the cross (Mark 8:34). For both Jesus and those committed to Him, the pattern was that suffering (and perhaps a martyr's death) was the normal pathway that led to glory.

Floor mosaic from the church at Tabgha in Galilee showing the bread and fish (p.186).

Harbor at Tyre showing ancient Phoenician harbor (facing northwest) (p.187).

Jesus' Mission

Some recent critics of the life of Jesus have judged Him to be a failure. After a brilliant career as a traveling teacher of righteousness, they say that He was needlessly sacrificed based on a misjudgment by the religious authorities. Every attempt, however, to evaluate the success of Jesus' mission should begin with an understanding of what Jesus believed about His mission. Certainly Jesus knew He would die. But why?

Jesus' death must be understood as the central event of the Kingdom Story. During His ministry He spoke many times of the purpose of His death. The following are representative claims He made, with one taken from each of the Gospels:

- As the Good Shepherd He would die so that His people would live (John 10:11).

- He called sinners to repentance and forgiveness (Luke 5:31-32)

- He came to give His life as a ransom for (in the place of) many (Mark 10:45).

- His death was a sacrificial offering to God, for His words instituting the Lord's Supper make no sense without this understanding (Matt. 26:26-28)

Jesus plainly thought of His mission primarily in terms of dying as a sacrifice for sins, substituting His death for sinners, so that they could have eternal life. In the Fourth Gospel He spoke of this "time" or "hour" that was ahead for Him (John 2:4; 7:6) and then of its arrival (John 12:23; 13:1; 17:1). Since this was Jesus' understanding of His mission, any fair evaluation must conclude that He was a complete success.

DIVINE GLORY

Jesus' teaching about His coming death and resurrection was a frightening riddle for the disciples. They were about to see the King killed, and this would be the darkest time of their life. A week after the apostles confessed Him as Messiah and He began teaching them about His death, He led Peter, James, and John up a mountain. (This was probably Mount Hermon, a snow-capped mountain not too far from Caesarea Philippi.) While they were there, Jesus gave them a "sight and sound experience" to assure them of who He was.

Mount Hermon.

Jesus' appearance was transformed to glistening white. Moses (the law-giver) and Elijah (the prophet) appeared with Him. The heavenly Father spoke audibly that this was indeed His Son, to whom people must listen. This event, called the transfiguration, showed representative apostles the unveiled glory of Jesus—despite what He was about to endure in Jerusalem. This event surely serves as the spiritual high mark of Jesus' days of ministry. (The feeding of the 5,000 had been the popular high mark of His ministry.)

After this, Jesus returned to "normal," teaching and ministering as He had been doing. Luke 9:51, however, notes that shortly after the transfiguration He set out steadfastly for Jerusalem to fulfill His destiny. Although He actually entered the city twice more before His final royal entry, from this moment everything was tinged by the candor of the passion predictions and their looming fulfillment.

LATER MINISTRY IN JUDEA
(LATE AUTUMN AND EARLY WINTER A.D. 29)

Luke and John are the two Gospels that provide the best information about the next stage of Jesus' ministry. The sense of urgent movement toward the Passover at which He must be offered as a sacrifice looms large. So does the current of mounting hostility.

AT THE FEAST OF TABERNACLES

John 7 describes Jesus' participation in the annual Feast of Tabernacles, a celebration of the completed harvest. Occurring in October, it was also a time when the Jews remembered the forty years they had spent in the wilderness by living in tents ("tabernacles") during the time of the festival. Jesus took this occasion to provoke further debate by claiming to be "I am" (John 8:58), a prerogative so infuriating to the religious establishment that they tried to stone Him. On this same occasion Jesus healed on the Sabbath a man born blind, further aggravating the situation.

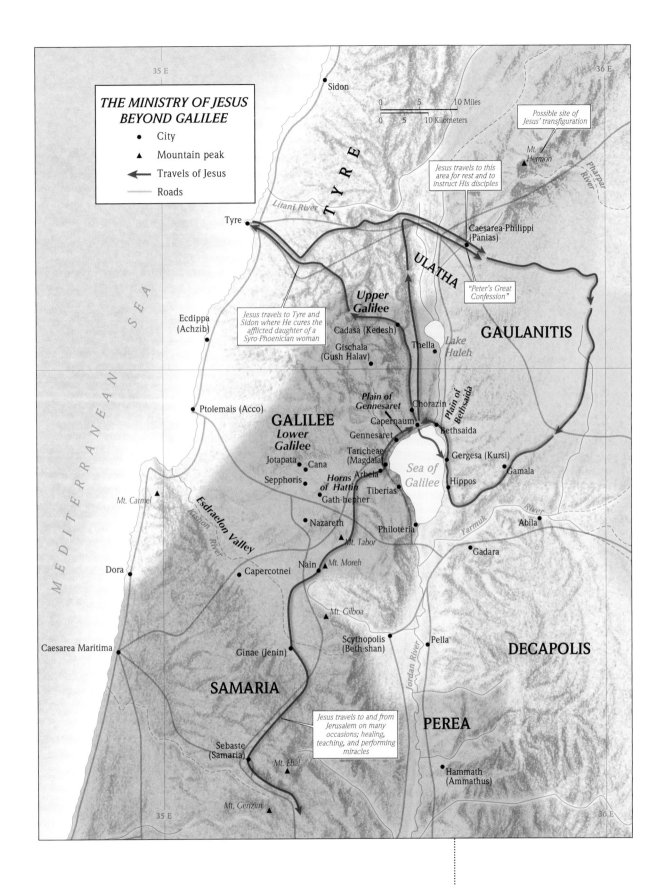

THE MINISTRY OF JESUS BEYOND GALILEE

- • City
- ▲ Mountain peak
- ← Travels of Jesus
- Roads

Sidon

TYRE

Litani River

Possible site of Jesus' transfiguration

Mt. Hermon

Pharpar River

Jesus travels to this area for rest and to instruct His disciples

Tyre

Caesarea-Philippi (Panias)

ULATHA

"Peter's Great Confession"

GAULANITIS

MEDITERRANEAN SEA

Ecdippa (Achzib)

Jesus travels to Tyre and Sidon where He cures the afflicted daughter of a Syro-Phoenician woman

Upper Galilee

Cadasa (Kedesh)

Gischala (Gush Halav)

Thella

Lake Huleh

Ptolemais (Acco)

GALILEE

Lower Galilee

Plain of Gennesaret

Chorazin

Capernaum

Gennesaret

Plain of Bethsaida

Bethsaida

Jotapata

Cana

Taricheae (Magdala)

Sepphoris

Horns of Hattin

Arbela

Gergesa (Kursi)

Gamala

Gath-hepher

Tiberias

Sea of Galilee

Hippos

Mt. Carmel

Esdraelon Valley

Kishon River

Nazareth

Philoteria

Yarmuk River

Abila

Mt. Tabor

Dora

Capercotnei

Nain

Mt. Moreh

Gadara

Mt. Gilboa

Caesarea Maritima

Ginae (Jenin)

Scythopolis (Beth-shan)

Pella

DECAPOLIS

SAMARIA

Jordan River

PEREA

Jesus travels to and from Jerusalem on many occasions; healing, teaching, and performing miracles

Sebaste (Samaria)

Mt. Ebal

Hammath (Ammathus)

Mt. Gerizim

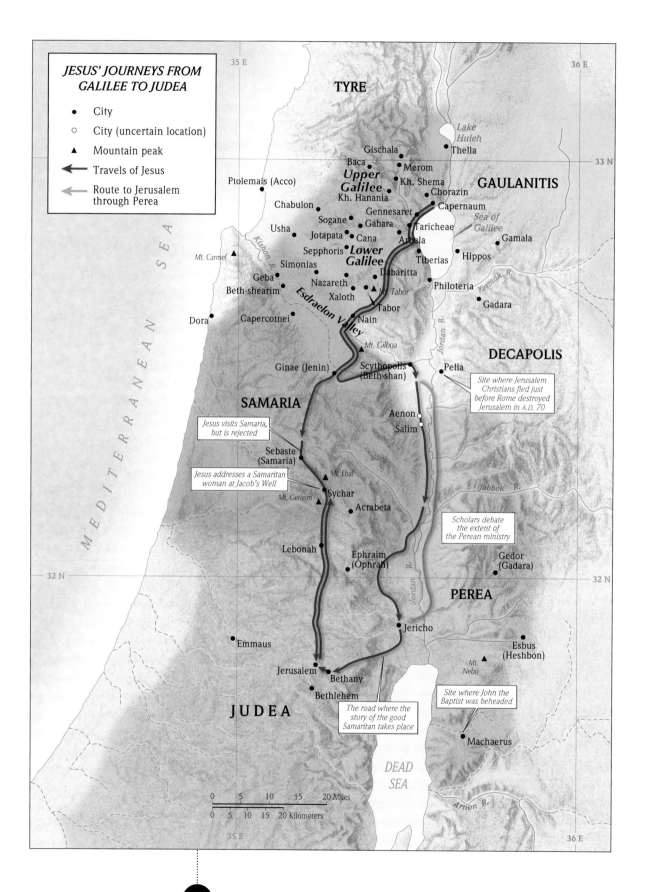

JESUS' JOURNEYS FROM GALILEE TO JUDEA

- ● City
- ○ City (uncertain location)
- ▲ Mountain peak
- ← Travels of Jesus
- ← Route to Jerusalem through Perea

TYRE

Lake Huleh

GAULANITIS

35 E

36 E

33 N

Gischala

Thella

Baca

Merom

Upper Galilee

Kh. Shema

Ptolemais (Acco)

Chorazin

Kh. Hanania

Capernaum

Chabulon

Gennesaret

Sea of Galilee

Usha

Sogane

Gabara

Taricheae

Jotapata

Cana

Arbela

Gamala

Sepphoris

Lower Galilee

Tiberias

Hippos

Simonias

Dabaritta

Mt. Carmel ▲

Geba

Nazareth

Mt. Tabor ▲

Philoteria

MEDITERRANEAN SEA

Beth-shearim

Xaloth

Tabor

Yarmuk R.

Kishon R.

Esdraelon Valley

Nain

Gadara

Capercotnei

Mt. Gilboa ▲

DECAPOLIS

Dora

Jordan R.

Ginae (Jenin)

Scythopolis (Beth-shan)

Pella

Site where Jerusalem Christians fled just before Rome destroyed Jerusalem in A.D. 70

SAMARIA

Jesus visits Samaria, but is rejected

Aenon

Salim

Sebaste (Samaria)

Jesus addresses a Samaritan woman at Jacob's Well

Mt. Ebal ▲

Mt. Gerizim ▲

Sychar

Acrabeta

Jabbok R.

Scholars debate the extent of the Perean ministry

Lebonah

Ephraim (Ophran)

Gedor (Gadara)

Jordan R.

32 N

PEREA

32 N

Jericho

Emmaus

Esbus (Heshbon)

Mt. Nebo ▲

Jerusalem

Bethany

Bethlehem

JUDEA

The road where the story of the good Samaritan takes place

Site where John the Baptist was beheaded

Machaerus

DEAD SEA

Arnon R.

| 0 | 5 | 10 | 15 | 20 Miles |

| 0 | 5 | 10 | 15 | 20 Kilometers |

Travel in Judea

After this, Jesus stayed "on the move." Luke 10—17 appears to be the most complete account of these travels. Jesus now sent seventy-two disciples out to preach and to cast out demons. Galilee had heard the message of the kingdom. Judea was now the recipient of a tremendous outreach that Jesus organized. A number of Jesus' best-loved parables belong to this phase of ministry. During this time, also, Jesus had dinner in Bethany (near Jerusalem) at the house of Mary, Martha, and Lazarus (Luke 10:38-42) and healed ten men of leprosy (Luke 17:11-19).

At the Feast of Dedication

According to John 10:22-42, Jesus visited Jerusalem yet again. This time He participated in the Feast of Dedication (Hanukkah), the annual Jewish celebration of the Maccabean victory. It was now December before the crucifixion, and the climate of hostility against Jesus was becoming more intense. He became the subject of another stoning attempt. This time when He withdrew from the city He would no longer stay in Judea. He crossed the Jordan to Perea for a number of weeks.

Courtyard of Church of the Holy Sepulchre in Jerusalem.

Traditional site of Lazarus' tomb.

THE MINISTRY IN PEREA (LATE WINTER AND EARLY SPRING A.D. 30)

Jesus' ministry in Perea may be thought of as the calm before the storm. Many people still came to Him however (Matt. 19:1; John 10:41). He continued to teach and heal, and apparently He would have stayed there quietly until the Passover season. The death of Lazarus interrupted Him.

RAISING LAZARUS

Jesus' raising Lazarus four days after he died was the most important of all His miracles (John 11). First, it showed in a compelling way God's wonderful power at work through Jesus. Critics may have explained away His other healings, but this one could not be denied or ignored. Second, this miracle was a kind of preview of Jesus' own resurrection. Third, the event so infuriated the Jewish leadership that the Sadducee high priest Caiaphas organized a plot to kill Jesus. From a human viewpoint Jesus was doomed from this point.

An olive grove at the modern church of St. Lazarus at Bethany. The church was built in close proximity to the traditional site of Lazarus' tomb.

JOURNEY TOWARD JERUSALEM

As the time of the Passover season approached, Jesus joined travelers from Galilee that were heading south toward Jerusalem. They were using the roads east of the Jordan Valley. The sense of anticipation was palpable. He continued to review His teachings. (The third passion prediction was made during this time.) He unsuccessfully challenged the "rich young ruler" to give up his wealth and become a disciple (Mark 10:17-22).

Sadducees

The name may be related to a Hebrew verb meaning "to be righteous" or else to the name Zadok. The Sadducees were the Jewish sect of the aristocratic priests for more than two centuries, from the time of the Maccabees to the fall of Jerusalem. Under the Romans the Sadducees approved of the status quo. Like the Samaritans, the Sadducees accepted only the five Books of Moses as Scripture. Satisfied with the present, they did not look forward either to existence after the body died or to a future messianic age. They did not have favor with the general Jewish population and did not survive the destruction of Jerusalem in A.D. 70.

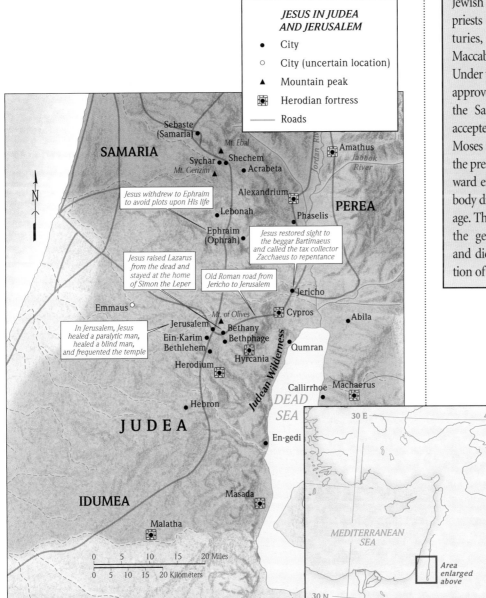

JESUS IN JUDEA AND JERUSALEM

- • City
- ○ City (uncertain location)
- ▲ Mountain peak
- ▣ Herodian fortress
- — Roads

Sebaste (Samaria)
SAMARIA
Mt. Ebal
Sychar Shechem
Mt. Gerizim Acrabeta
Amathus
Jabbok River
Jordan River

Jesus withdrew to Ephraim to avoid plots upon His life

Alexandrium
PEREA
Lebonah
Phaselis

Ephraim (Ophrah)

Jesus restored sight to the beggar Bartimaeus and called the tax collector Zacchaeus to repentance

Jesus raised Lazarus from the dead and stayed at the home of Simon the Leper

Old Roman road from Jericho to Jerusalem

Jericho
Emmaus
Mt. of Olives
Cypros
Abila
Jerusalem Bethany
Ein-Karim Bethphage
Bethlehem
Qumran
Hyrcania
Judean Wilderness

In Jerusalem, Jesus healed a paralytic man, healed a blind man, and frequented the temple

Herodium

DEAD SEA
Callirrhoe Machaerus

Hebron

JUDEA

En-gedi

IDUMEA
Masada

Malatha

0 5 10 15 20 Miles
0 5 10 15 20 Kilometers

30 E 40 E 40 N

MEDITERRANEAN SEA

Area enlarged above

30 N 30 N

30 E 40 E

The travelers eventually turned west, forded the Jordan River, followed the road through Jericho, and climbed the last seventeen-mile uphill stretch to Jerusalem. The two events recorded from Jesus' time in Jericho summarize all He had been doing since John baptized Him.

- He gave sight to two blind men, one of them named Bartimaeus. This summarizes Jesus' ministry to the physical bodies of people (Matt. 20:30; Mark 10:46)

- He gave salvation to Zacchaeus, the short but rich chief tax collector of Jericho. This summarizes Jesus' ministry to the hearts of people (Luke 19:1-10)

As Jesus traveled on toward Jerusalem, He stopped in Bethany to visit Lazarus, whom He had lately raised to life. From that point He was within a week of being killed.

SUFFERING SERVANT AND SON OF DAVID:
DEATH, RESURRECTION, AND
EXALTATION OF JESUS (A.D. 30)

Because of the stark contrast between Jesus' humiliation and exaltation, two titles are necessary to summarize this part of the Kingdom Story. On one hand He was revealed as the Suffering Servant prophesied in Isaiah 53:10-11. On the other hand He was acknowledged as the glorious Son of David, the triumphant King over the people of God. **MATTHEW 21—28, MARK 11—16, LUKE 20—24**, and **JOHN 12—21** describe this.

Jesus' crucifixion redeemed His people to God for eternity, just as the exodus had redeemed the people of Israel for time. According to His own words, Jesus' death secured the new covenant relationship of God with His people, the one Jeremiah had prophesied. Jesus' bodily resurrection and exaltation by His Father demonstrated that His sacrifice was satisfactory. The dates of Jesus' crucifixion and resurrection, using modern calendar notation, were almost certainly Friday, April 7, and Sunday, April 9, of A.D. 30.[3]

THE DAY OF ANOINTING
SATURDAY, APRIL 1, A.D. 30

There is no record about whether Jesus taught in the synagogue of Bethany on the Sabbath before His crucifixion. After sundown it was no longer the Sabbath, and He enjoyed a good meal. His first miracle had been at a wedding feast, and now on His way to Passover He was the guest of honor at Bethany at the house of a certain Simon. Mary the sister of Martha and Lazarus took this occasion to break social custom by pouring an exceptionally expensive perfume on Jesus while He was eating.

Gospel According to Matthew

This Gospel presents Jesus' life from the angel's announcement of His birth to His resurrection. From the earliest days Matthew, the former tax collector and apostle, has been recognized as its author. Matthew wrote more self-consciously from a Jewish perspective concerning Jesus' fulfillment of prophecy than the other evangelists did. The first readers were Jewish Christians, probably in the late A.D. 50s. The keyword for the book is "Messiah"; the key text is Matthew 16:16,18. **One-Sentence Summary:** *In His life, death, and resurrection, Jesus fulfilled the prophecies about the Jewish Messiah and began the new people of God, the church.*

Jesus welcomed this act of love and devotion, remarking that it was a way of preparing His body for burial. (John's Gospel specifically dated this as occurring the day before Jesus' royal entry. Matthew and Mark described this in a logical place nearer Jesus' death. Luke reported that a "sinful woman" anointed Jesus with perfume much earlier, Matt. 26:6-13; Mark 14:3-9; Luke 7:36-50; John 12:1-8.)

THE DAY OF THE ROYAL ENTRY
SUNDAY, APRIL 2, A.D. 30

Passover was the most exciting time of the year for Jerusalem. The population swelled so much that people were everywhere, often staying at campsites outside the city walls. The Roman governor came to town, accompanied by Roman troops, to keep order. He kept a watchful eye from the Fortress of Antonia adjacent to the temple courts.

Jesus came to the city as well. This was now the fourth Passover since His baptism. All four Gospels describe His entrance. He could have slipped in unnoticed, but He staged a dramatic demonstration. The five-mile parade route from Bethany over the Mount of Olives and down into the city must have taken all afternoon. He chose as His royal mount a donkey, an honorable animal ridden by kings, yet an animal unsuited for riding into battle. Jesus was deliberately offering Himself as the King of the kingdom of God (but not as a military leader). He was also deliberately fulfilling the prophecy of Zechariah 9:9 about the King coming to Zion riding a donkey.

Top of the Mount of Olives in Jerusalem.

Herod's Temple

The Jerusalem temple in the first century was an extraordinary expansion of Zerubbabel's temple, the modest structure that the returning exiles had completed in 516 B.C. After gaining the approval of the Jewish leaders, Herod the Great authorized the reconstruction project in 20 B.C. The main temple building was fifteen stories tall, gleaming with white marble and gold. The courtyards were expanded, with rows of marble columns and covered porches contributing to the magnificence of the temple complex. In A.D. 70 not one stone was left standing of this temple, just as Jesus had said. The Wailing Wall in modern Jerusalem was constructed originally in Herod's day as a retaining wall to hold up one end of the courtyard.

The Passover crowds from Galilee were quick to recognize and revel in the situation. They praised Jesus as "Son of David" and "He who comes in the name of the Lord," high messianic acclaim. They even shouted "hosanna," a cry for salvation. The salvation they wanted (freedom from the Romans) and the salvation He provided (freedom from sin) were different indeed. After publicly entering the city, Jesus looked over the temple courts, making a plan for the next day's activities (Mark 11:11). Then He and the apostles left to spend the night at their campsite on the Mount of Olives.

THE DAY OF CLEANSING THE TEMPLE
MONDAY, APRIL 3, A.D. 30

Three years earlier, before He was well-known, Jesus had cleared the temple courts of animals and money changers. Now He did it again. The courtyard was massive. Several football fields would fit. The Jewish people needed to be able to purchase animals acceptable for sacrifice, but this did not have to be done within the temple precincts. No doubt a great deal of price gouging went on. Surely it was hard to pray and worship the Lord with the sounds and smells of a stockyard at hand.

Jesus created absolute havoc single-handedly, a superb example of His authority. He was, in a sense, rejecting the current worship system—led by the Sadducee chief priests—as unacceptable. He was also fulfilling Scripture that the Messiah would come to the temple dramatically (Mal. 3:1-3). Further, He was defying the religious authorities, mounting a challenge concerning how they would deal with His threat to their security.

Jesus turned the temple courts from a barnyard to a playground. The children offered their praise. He also healed the sick—His final miracles of healing (except for the restoration of a severed ear when He was arrested). That night He and the apostles returned to their campsite once again.

THE DAY OF TEACHING
TUESDAY, APRIL 4, A.D. 30

The day after He cleared the temple, Jesus held forth as a teacher in the temple courts and later on the Mount of Olives. Matthew 21:23—25:46 is the most extensive account of this teaching. What He said shows the great variety of both His content and His methods.

Parables: With important parables Jesus accused the Jewish religious leaders of utterly rejecting God's purposes (Matt. 21:28—22:14).

Debates: In a four-round verbal sparring match Jesus bested His religious enemies on any issue they proposed (Matt. 22:15-46).

Woes: In a stinging critique of legalism Jesus pronounced "woe to you" (the opposite of "blessed are you") against the Pharisees. Their chief fault was that they cared more about what they looked like before others than in being righteous (Matt. 23).

A model of the temple in a Jerusalem model at the Holyland Hotel, Jerusalem.

Prophecies: After leaving the temple courts Jesus taught about the future from the Mount of Olives. The Olivet Discourse, as it is known, answered two distinct questions from the apostles: "When will the temple be destroyed?" and "What is the sign of your coming?" Jesus' teaching included information both about the Roman destruction of Jerusalem forty years later (A.D. 70) and about His glorious return at the end of the age (Matt. 24—25).

THE DAY OF SILENCE AND TREACHERY
WEDNESDAY, APRIL 5, A.D. 30

The Gospels did not report any of Jesus' activities on this day. It was, however, the day that Caiaphas the high priest was able at last to put together the piece he needed to get rid of Jesus. Judas, an insider, volunteered to hand over Jesus when the time presented itself. Hardly more than twenty-four hours later, he stuck—evidently sooner than Caiaphas expected, given all the maneuvering behind the scenes after Jesus was arrested.

Although Caiaphas was the chief plotter, Judas was the most to blame because of his treachery. No satisfactory answers have ever been given as to why he betrayed Jesus. It's hard to believe his motive was merely financial. He had already been stealing from the common treasury of the apostles, and the thirty silver coins that he received were not that large a sum. Forever the name Judas Iscariot has become associated with the worst kind of personal treason.

THE DAY OF THE LAST SUPPER
THURSDAY, APRIL 6, A.D. 30

The time for which Jesus had come to the world had at last arrived (John 13:1). Jesus planned the day before His crucifixion to be filled with meaning and with final instruction for the apostles.

Jesus entrusted Peter and John with the responsibility of preparing the Passover dinner. This required elaborate care, for the menu was fixed. The man who provided an upstairs dining room large enough for a formal dinner for thirteen must have had a certain amount of affluence. He may have been a follower of Jesus, for apparently the same upstairs room became the gathering place for all the disciples after Jesus' crucifixion.

Only John's Gospel describes that Jesus washed the feet of His disciples before dinner. This was a menial task, usually assigned to the household servant with the lowest status. What He was doing, of course, was to illustrate what true humility in action looks like. This was the only time that Jesus specifically called Himself an example for His followers to copy (John 13:15).

Sometime during the meal Jesus made two startling predictions, which must have added to the anxiety already present. Jesus announced that He would soon be betrayed by one of those present. He identified Judas as the traitor by a symbolic gesture that only John recognized at the time (John 13:25-26). Judas soon left the meal. Jesus also announced that Peter would deny Him three times before morning.

The Wailing Wall where a large crowd gathers during a Jewish holiday.

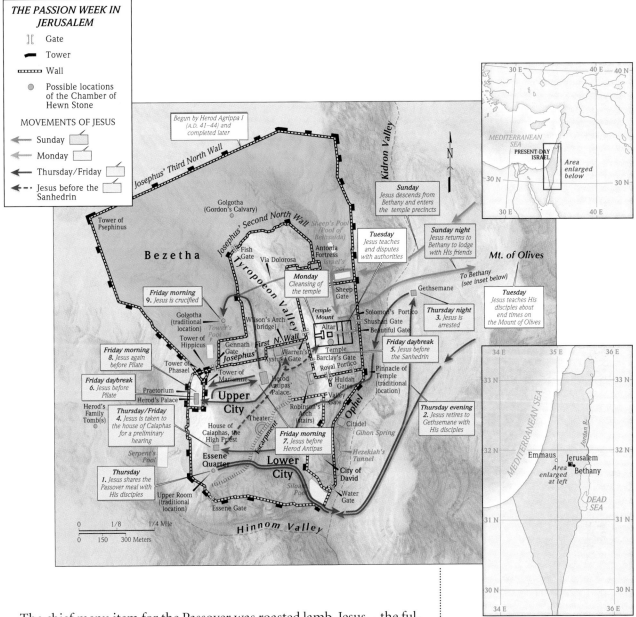

THE PASSION WEEK IN JERUSALEM

Legend:
- Gate
- Tower
- Wall
- Possible locations of the Chamber of Hewn Stone

MOVEMENTS OF JESUS
- Sunday
- Monday
- Thursday/Friday
- Jesus before the Sanhedrin

Begun by Herod Agrippa I (A.D. 41–44) and completed later

Josephus' Third North Wall

Kidron Valley

MEDITERRANEAN SEA

PRESENT-DAY ISRAEL

Area enlarged below

Golgotha (Gordon's Calvary)

Sunday Jesus descends from Bethany and enters the temple precincts

Josephus' Second North Wall

Sheep's Pool (Pool of Bethesda)

Sunday night Jesus returns to Bethany to lodge with His friends

Bezetha

Fish Gate

Via Dolorosa

Antonia Fortress

Israel's Pool

Tuesday Jesus teaches and disputes with authorities

Mt. of Olives

To Bethany (see inset below)

Gethsemane

Monday Cleansing of the temple

Sheep Gate

Tuesday Jesus teaches His disciples about end times on the Mount of Olives

Friday morning 9. Jesus is crucified

Golgotha (traditional location)

Wilson's Arch (bridge)

Temple Mount

Altar

Solomon's Portico

Shushan Gate

Beautiful Gate

Thursday night 3. Jesus is arrested

Tower's Pool

Friday morning 8. Jesus again before Pilate

Tower of Hippicus

Gennath Gate

Josephus' First N. Wall

Warren's Gate

Xystus Gate

Temple

Barclay's Gate

Royal Portico

Huldah Gates

Pinnacle of Temple (traditional location)

Friday daybreak 5. Jesus before the Sanhedrin

Tower of Mariamne

Friday daybreak 6. Jesus before Pilate

Tower of Phasael

Herod Antipas' Palace

Robinson's Arch (stairs)

Valley Gate

Ophel

Thursday evening 2. Jesus retires to Gethsemane with His disciples

Praetorium

Herod's Palace

Upper City

Herod's Family Tomb(s)

Thursday/Friday 4. Jesus is taken to the house of Caiaphas for a preliminary hearing

Theater

Citadel

Gihon Spring

Serpent's Pool

House of Caiaphas, the High Priest

Friday morning 7. Jesus before Herod Antipas

Hezekiah's Tunnel

Essene Quarter

Lower City

City of David

Thursday 1. Jesus shares the Passover meal with His disciples

Upper Room (traditional location)

Siloam Pool

Water Gate

Essene Gate

Hinnom Valley

0 1/8 1/4 Mile
0 150 300 Meters

MEDITERRANEAN SEA

Jordan R.

Emmaus

Jerusalem

Bethany

Area enlarged at left

DEAD SEA

The chief menu item for the Passover was roasted lamb. Jesus—the fulfillment of what the Passover lambs had pointed to at the time of Israel's exodus from Egypt—was ready to do His work as the Lamb of God. Yet it was two other items from the dinner table to which He gave new meaning. He took the flat bread made without yeast and the customary wine and said that they were His body and blood, given for them and to be eaten regularly to remember Him. When He said that the cup was the "new covenant" (Luke 22:20), Jesus was making the astonishing claim that what God had promised in Jeremiah 31:31-34 was now being fulfilled.

Olive trees in the traditional site of the Garden of Gethsemane.

New Covenant

Jeremiah had prophesied the coming of a new covenant (Jer. 33:31-34) that would be qualitatively different from the old, Sinaitic covenant. At His last supper, Jesus announced that this unconditional covenant was secured by His death. All blessings of the new covenant come to all that are "in Christ." In a sense the new covenant is a wonderful extension of the Abrahamic covenant and the Davidic covenant, and its blessings come to those who become Kingdom People by faith. The divinely given sign of the new covenant is the memorial observance of the Lord's Supper.

After the meal was over, Jesus taught one final time before His suffering began. John 14—17 reports what He said. He included important teaching about the Holy Spirit, teaching about Himself as the true vine, and an extensive prayer for the disciples.

It must have been near midnight when Jesus and the Eleven finally arrived at their campsite on the Mount of Olives. There at Gethsemane ("Olive Press") He prayed earnestly. Once again John was in a privileged place, along with Peter and James. Jesus' suffering began with this "agony in the garden." His grief may be understood on at least three levels. First, physically crucifixion was the most horrible, painful way to die ever devised. Second, emotionally crucifixion was shameful, a sign that the victim was especially cursed. Third, spiritually Jesus faced the weight of bearing human sin—and separation from His Father. His prayers were very intense, but in the end He settled on completing the mission that God had given Him.

When the arrest finally came, it was perhaps two in the morning. The soldiers that came with Judas were Jewish temple police (Roman soldiers did not carry clubs, Luke 22:52). After a momentary skirmish all the apostles ran off into the night. Jesus was bound and taken away to the house of Annas, the previous high priest (and father-in-law of Caiaphas).

THE DAY OF THE CRUCIFIXION
FRIDAY, APRIL 7, A.D. 30

THE JEWISH TRIAL

Both Jews and Romans put Jesus on trial. What the Jews started, the Romans finished. When all four Gospels are read carefully, it appears that the Jewish trial had three distinct phases.

1. **THE HEARING BEFORE ANNAS**. Annas had no real authority since he was the former high priest. His harassment of Jesus was perhaps a matter of "killing time" while Caiaphas gathered enough members of the Jewish Sanhedrin (council) together to convene a hearing (John 18:12-24).

2. **THE NIGHTTIME HEARING BEFORE THE SANHEDRIN**. This was held in haste at Caiaphas's house. Caiaphas had not had time to coach false witnesses, so their testimony conflicted. Jesus remained silent until He was illegally forced under oath. After Jesus testified to being the Son of God, a conviction of blasphemy was inevitable. During this time Peter was out in the courtyard, where he regrettably fulfilled Jesus' prophecy of a few hours earlier. After this hearing they began physically torturing Jesus (Mark 14:53-72).

3. **THE MORNING HEARING BEFORE THE SANHEDRIN**. At daybreak the council met again, making official what they had established during the night. This may have occurred in their chambers in the temple complex. As a result of this hearing, Judas changed his mind about Jesus and tried to take back his betrayal. When that failed, he committed suicide (Matt. 27:1-10; Luke 22:66-71).

THE ROMAN TRIAL

Because the Sanhedrin did not have the right to impose capital punishment, they took Jesus to the Roman governor. The charge would not be blasphemy (which Pontius Pilate could not have cared about) but treason against Rome. Like the Jewish trial, the Roman trial had three phases.

1. **THE FIRST HEARING BEFORE PILATE**. Pilate was not inclined to grant the Sanhedrin's request and indeed wanted to thwart the Jews. This hearing at the governor's Jerusalem residence, the Fortress of Antonia, was cut short when Pilate learned that Jesus was a Galilean. Since the ruler of Galilee, Herod Antipas, was in town for the holiday, he could decide what to do with Jesus (Luke 23:1-7).

2. **THE HEARING BEFORE HEROD ANTIPAS**. King Herod was probably at the family palace in Jerusalem. He had long wanted to see Jesus, but he suffered from a guilty conscience over the death of John the Baptist. He refused to have anything to do with condemning Jesus. Therefore, after mocking and torturing Jesus, Herod sent Jesus back to the governor (Luke 23:8-12).

According to 4th century tradition, this is where Jesus was scourged by Pilate.

3. THE SECOND HEARING BEFORE PILATE. When Jesus appeared before Pilate the second time that terrible morning, the governor knew Jesus had been set up. He tried two maneuvers to get Jesus released, both of which backfired. He gave the crowd the choice of Jesus or the thoroughly vile Barabbas—and the crowd was persuaded by the chief priests to ask for Barabbas. He then had Jesus scourged, a gruesome ordeal that left a man barely alive. The Jewish leaders finally won Pilate over by blackmail: they threatened to end his political career. Pilate was cornered and agreed to sign the death warrant (John 18:28—19:16).

THE CRUCIFIXION

The Gospels did not describe many details of Jesus' crucifixion. About nine in the morning, He was nailed to a cross between two robbers. The capital charge of which He was convicted ("King of the Jews") was placed above His head. The verbal abuse was unrelenting. At noon an unnatural darkness spread over the land, lasting until Jesus' death at three in the afternoon. The nature of crucifixion makes drawing a breath sheer agony, so the words of a crucifixion victim were noteworthy. Jesus spoke seven times from the cross; perhaps the most important was, "It is finished!" (meaning "I have completed my mission"; John 19:30.)

Some crucifixion victims lingered alive for days. Jesus died mercifully quickly. When the leg bones of the two robbers were broken to hasten their death (to disable them from pushing up with their feet to draw breath), Jesus had already died. This was confirmed by the spear thrust to His side, for His blood had already separated into its component parts.

THE BURIAL

For a crucified criminal to be buried decently was unusual. Jesus had two influential supporters who worked quickly. They were able to get the corpse wrapped, buried, and sealed in a nearby cavelike tomb before sundown (when the Sabbath began and work was no longer permitted). Pilate allowed a guard to be kept at the gravesite. Whether these were Roman soldiers or Jewish temple police is not certain, but in any event they were doomed to fail in their task.

THE DAY OF THE TOMB
SATURDAY, APRIL 8, A.D. 30

Saturday (daylight hours) was the time of mandatory rest for the followers of Jesus. They were overwhelmed with fear, grief, and questions. The upstairs room where they had met with Jesus for the Passover dinner became their gathering place. After sundown, some of the women went out and bought burial spices so that they could grieve more completely.

THE DAY OF THE RESURRECTION
SUNDAY, APRIL 9, A.D. 30

The resurrection of Jesus is never described in the Gospels. The report is of ordinary people faced with two striking kinds of evidence on Easter day: the tomb was empty and Jesus appeared alive to selected witnesses. The emphasis is on the resurrection appearances more than on the empty tomb. Jesus appeared five times on Easter:

- To Mary Magdalene (John 20:10-18)

- To a group of women (Matt. 28:9-10)

- To Simon Peter (Luke 24:34; 1 Cor. 15:5)

- To two disciples traveling to Emmaus (Luke 24:13-35)

- To ten apostles locked in the upstairs room (John 20:19-23)

The Easter appearances were all short, sudden, and mysterious. Jesus did not return to normal life. Although He could be touched and ate food, He appeared and disappeared at will. He chose to appear as not strikingly different from other people, although He selected only certain persons to witness His resurrection form (Acts 1:3).

Tomb of Jewish Sanhedrin. The Sanhedrin was the governing body of the Jews in the Greek and Roman periods. It consisted of 70 members plus its leader, the high priest. Jesus was brought before a hastily called Sanhedrin for trial.

THE POSTRESURRECTION MINISTRY
APRIL–MAY, A.D. 30

For forty days Jesus appeared in various places and situations to a variety of individuals. Six more incidents are reported:

- To eleven apostles locked in the upper room with Thomas present (John 20:24-29)

- To eleven apostles on a mountain in Galilee (Matt. 28:16-20)

- Beside the Sea of Galilee after a miraculous haul of fish (John 21:1-14)

- To more than 500 witnesses at one time as reported by the Apostle Paul (1 Cor. 15:6)

- To His brother James as reported by the Apostle Paul (1 Cor. 15:7)

- To the apostles on the Mount of Olives when He ascended to heaven (Acts 1:6-11)

This makes a total of eleven appearances of the risen Lord. The Apostle Paul insisted that there was a final appearance—when he saw Jesus at the time of his own conversion and call (1 Cor. 15:8; Acts 9:1-6). Thus, the man crucified as a blasphemer and traitor was vindicated and approved by God through His resurrection (Rom. 1:4). The resurrection demonstrated that all Jesus' claims about Himself and His mission were true.

Luke was the only writer that told of Jesus' bodily ascent from earth to heaven (Luke 24:50-51; Acts 1:4-11). The apostles now knew that they would no longer see Him in a bodily form. According to the Epistles Jesus was seated at the right hand of God, the greatest place of prestige and authority imaginable. The exaltation of Jesus proved to be critically important for the next chapter of the Kingdom Story. From such a place of glory He sent the Holy Spirit to indwell and empower believers.

A tomb with a rolling stone at Bethphage.
Bethphage is on the Mount of Olives and was where
Jesus asked two disciples to go find a colt for Him
before His entrance into Jerusalem on Palm Sunday.

CONCLUSION

In the space of less than forty years, God brought about the climax of His Kingdom Story by redeeming His people and establishing the kingdom of God through Jesus.

1. Beginning with His miraculous conception, Jesus came to the world as "God with Us," growing into adulthood as the son of Mary (6 B.C.–A.D. 26).

2. After He was anointed and empowered at His baptism, Jesus fulfilled the work of the Son of Man through His teaching—especially about the kingdom of God—and through His mighty signs (A.D. 26–30).

3. Jesus suffered and died to fulfill His mission to redeem sinners, but God raised Him and exalted Him. He now rules as the King, the everlasting Son of David (A.D. 30).

The grand summary of the Bible is, *The Lord God through His Christ is graciously building a kingdom of redeemed people for their joy and for His own glory.* We have seen now that God fully succeeded purchasing redemption and beginning the kingdom. In the next chapter in the Kingdom Story, God will succeed in His purpose of spreading the message of the kingdom through the church.

REFLECTIVE QUESTIONS

1. What names for Jesus other than Immanuel (God with Us) would you use to characterize the birth and growth of Jesus?

2. Could God have chosen to enter the world as a human in a way other than the virgin birth? Why? If your answer is yes, what other means might He have chosen?

3. What would you like to know about the years of Jesus' life about which nothing is recorded? List four or five questions.

4. What titles in addition to Son of Man would you use to characterize the period of Jesus' public ministry?

5. Summarize the role that John the Baptist fulfilled in the Kingdom Story. Why was he so important that all four Gospels all tell about him?

6. What were some of the purposes of Jesus' baptism?

7. Which statement do you believe is true: "Jesus became the Messiah (Anointed One) at His baptism" or "Jesus was empowered to do the work of the Messiah at His baptism"? Why?

8. Why was it important for Jesus to be tempted so severely?

9. During His early period of ministry Jesus encountered two distinctly different individuals, Nicodemus and the Samaritan woman. Compare the way He interacted with them (John 3 and 4).

10. Summarize Jesus' teaching about the kingdom of God in your own words.

11. Summarize Jesus' teaching about His mission in your own words.

12. Jesus' ministry in Galilee often included His commands that people not tell others who He was. Why did He do this if the goal was to give His message maximum exposure?

13. Interact with the following: "Jesus' miracles were signs of the kingdom and evidence of His compassion. We should therefore expect miracles to be done in Christ's name today."

14. What makes the Sermon on the Mount such a powerful message? Was it really the most important sermon ever preached? Why or why not?

15. Why were Jesus and the Pharisees such an explosive combination?

16. Which of Jesus' parables is your favorite? Explain your choice.

Emmaus (Imwas). According to the Sinai manuscript Emmaus is thought to be the site of the house of Cleopas.

17. If the (future) church was so important to Jesus, why do you suppose He taught about it only twice?

18. What function did the transfiguration serve for Jesus? For the apostles?

19. Why did the raising of Lazarus cause the Sadducees to enter the plot against Jesus?

20. Both Jesus' royal (triumphal) entry and His cleansing of the temple included symbolic actions. Which symbol interests you the most? Why?

21. What was the significance of Jesus' language about the new covenant at His Last Supper?

22. Contrast the Jewish and the Roman phases of Jesus' trial. Which represented the greatest injustice? Why?

23. Which of Jesus' sayings from the cross is the most meaningful to you? Why?

24. Why does the New Testament emphasize Jesus' postresurrection appearances more than the empty tomb as evidences of His resurrection?

25. How does God's redemption of His people work itself out in Chapter Four of the Kingdom Story?

26. What evidences of God's glory are evident in Chapter Four of the Kingdom Story?

27. What evidences of joy in the lives of God's redeemed people do you see in Chapter Four of the Kingdom Story?

[1] An oddity of the calendar system is that Jesus was born several years "before Christ." After Christianity became powerful and pervasive enough to warrant dating events in Europe from the year of His birth, scholars were put to the task of determining just when that had occurred. More modern historical research has showed that these medieval scholars missed the date by a few years. Rather than redate all events of the past twenty centuries, we live with this miscalculation. The traditional designations B.C. and A.D. are now being replaced by B.C.E.(before the common era) and C.E. (common era) by some historians.

[2] Evangelical Bible students are not entirely agreed on how to interpret the chronological data for Jesus' public ministry. The length noted for each stage of Jesus' ministry suggested here is plausible and fits all the data.

[3] Not all Bible students have concluded that the year of the crucifixion was A.D. 30. The possible years are either 30 or 33 (the years during Pontius Pilate's governorship when Passover fell on a Friday). The year 33 appears too late because (1) it would mean Jesus was 39 or 40 at the time of His death (compare Luke 3:23) and (2) it does not seem to allow enough time between the crucifixion and the conversion of Saul of Tarsus (probably as early as A.D. 33; not later than A.D. 35).

God Spreads the Kingdom through the Church

Sections of the eastern wall of the old city of Jerusalem.

The Current Age, A.D. 30–?

(Acts and the Epistles)

With Chapter Five in the Kingdom Story, we come to the part of the story that includes our times. We belong here. This is the period of Christ's disciple-making mandate, when God's plan has moved from focusing on persons of a single ethnic group in a single place (Israel) to redeeming persons out of every ethnic group in every place (church).

Wherever and whenever God's people are meeting, they meet as churches, worshiping communities under the terms of the new covenant. From Pentecost until the end-time scenario unfolds, God is about the business of spreading the message of the kingdom through Christ's church.

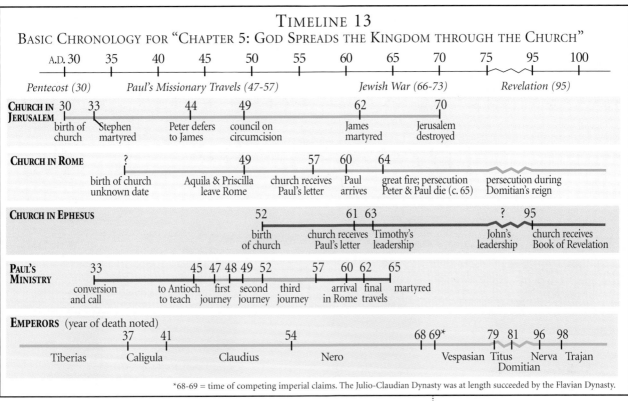

TIMELINE 13
BASIC CHRONOLOGY FOR "CHAPTER 5: GOD SPREADS THE KINGDOM THROUGH THE CHURCH"

A.D. 30   35   40   45   50   55   60   65   70   75   95   100

Pentecost (30)   *Paul's Missionary Travels (47-57)*   *Jewish War (66-73)*   *Revelation (95)*

CHURCH IN JERUSALEM
- 30 birth of church
- 33 Stephen martyred
- 44 Peter defers to James
- 49 council on circumcision
- 62 James martyred
- 70 Jerusalem destroyed

CHURCH IN ROME
- ? birth of church unknown date
- 49 Aquila & Priscilla leave Rome
- 57 church receives Paul's letter
- 60 Paul arrives
- 64 great fire; persecution Peter & Paul die (c. 65)
- persecution during Domitian's reign

CHURCH IN EPHESUS
- 52 birth of church
- 61 church receives Paul's letter
- 63 Timothy's leadership
- ? John's leadership
- 95 church receives Book of Revelation

PAUL'S MINISTRY
- 33 conversion and call
- 45 to Antioch to teach
- 47 first journey
- 48 second journey
- 49
- 52 third journey
- 57 arrival in Rome
- 60 final travels
- 62
- 65 martyred

EMPERORS (year of death noted)
- 37 Tiberias
- 41 Caligula
- 54 Claudius
- Nero
- 68 Vespasian
- 69* Titus
- 79 Domitian
- 81
- 96 Nerva
- 98 Trajan

*68-69 = time of competing imperial claims. The Julio-Claudian Dynasty was at length succeeded by the Flavian Dynasty.

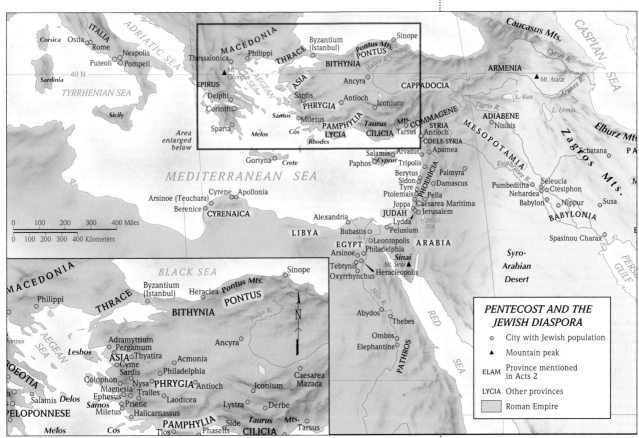

PENTECOST AND THE JEWISH DIASPORA
- ○ City with Jewish population
- ▲ Mountain peak
- ELAM Province mentioned in Acts 2
- LYCIA Other provinces
- Roman Empire

An overview of a Jerusalem model found at the Holyland Hotel in Jerusalem.

The Book of Acts

This book is a selective narrative of the church's first three decades, from about A.D. 30 to 61. From the earliest days Luke, the Gentile physician and friend of Paul, has been recognized as its author. Luke continued to write self-consciously as a historian just as he had done in his Gospel. The first reader was Theophilus, an unknown friend of Luke, probably about A.D. 62. The key word for the book is "Spirit"; the key text is Acts 1:8. **One-Sentence Summary:** *Christianity spread from Jerusalem to Rome and from Jews to Gentiles by the power of the Holy Spirit, working especially through Peter and Paul.*

As the Introduction noted, the grand summary of the Bible is, *The Lord God through His Christ is graciously building a kingdom of redeemed people for their joy and for His own glory.* Chapter Five in the Kingdom Story is the part of the story that has taken the longest. It includes not only the biblical record of everything God did to establish the church (Acts through Jude), but also everything in church history. Everything that has happened for the past nineteen centuries reflects God's plan to spread the kingdom through the church.

THE FIRST CHRISTIANS IN JERUSALEM:
THE CHURCH AS A JEWISH SECT (A.D. 30–45)

With the experience of the day of Pentecost, the church of Jesus was finally and fully thrust into existence (Acts 2). A new era began, the age of the Spirit, when every redeemed person receives the gift of the Spirit. Although Christianity soon moved beyond its nest in Jerusalem, the congregation there was a critical foundation. The church was born on Pentecost in the spring of A.D. 30. Although Christianity took "baby steps" toward becoming the worldwide movement that Jesus entrusted to the apostles, for about fifteen years the church existed essentially as a sect ("denomination") within Judaism. The biblical materials that describe this are **ACTS 1—12** and the **EPISTLE OF JAMES**.

Birth and Babyhood of the Church

During the last year that He discipled the Twelve, Jesus told them that He planned to build His church (assembly). He even explained the procedure for maintaining discipline and invoking His presence within the various congregations (Matt. 18:15-20). Yet the account of Jesus' post-Easter ministry shows that the disciples followed no regular pattern of worship or witness. He told them simply to wait for the power of the Spirit (Acts 1:5). After the Spirit empowered all believers on the day of Pentecost, everything was different. We may say that the church existed in embryonic form before Pentecost; afterwards it had an independent existence, "breathing on its own."

What was the significance of the coming of the Holy Spirit in the birth of the church? This event represents a huge advance in the Kingdom Story. Here is a new kind of relationship of redeemed people to the Spirit of God, evidence of the new covenant blessings Jeremiah had foreseen (Jer. 31:33-34). For the first time, all redeemed people were occupied by and empowered with the Holy Spirit, fulfilling Joel 2:28-32 (Acts 2:16-21). (Under the Sinaitic covenant, only a few—judges, kings, and prophets—were empowered by the Spirit.) In fact, later on the apostles taught that the indwelling presence of the Holy Spirit is the identifying feature of kingdom people (Rom. 8:9; 1 Cor. 12:13). Those indwelt by the Spirit began enjoying the victory that Jesus secured through His death and resurrection.

Peter's preaching on Pentecost, the first post-Easter sermon, established his role as the leader of Jesus' disciples. This was also the occasion when he first discharged his duty as the one entrusted with the "keys of the kingdom" (Matt. 16:18-19). On Pentecost Jews who believed in Jesus through the ministry of Peter received the Spirit, signaling that the long-awaited messianic age had arrived through Jesus. (After Pentecost all Jews—wherever they were—who believed in Jesus received the Spirit. Peter was simply the Christ-appointed "door opener" of the Spirit for Jews.)

Feast of Pentecost

Pentecost was the Greek name ("fiftieth day") for the annual Jewish Feast of Weeks, occurring seven weeks after Passover. Along with Passover and Tabernacles, it was one of the three great annual Jewish festivals. It celebrated the first of the grain harvest (late spring). During the first century thousands of out-of-town Jews gathered at the Jerusalem temple for this celebration. Thus, the events attending the birth of the church received great publicity. After the Holy Spirit came on Jesus' followers, Pentecost was taken over as an annual Christian celebration (just as Passover was taken over in the events celebrated annually as Good Friday and Easter).

Roman forum and Arch of Severus in Rome, Italy. The forum dates from the 1st century B.C. and the arch from A.D. 203. The arch is at the western end of the forum.

Baptismal in the baptisterion of the Church of St. John at Ephesus.

 # Baptism (Christian)

The ceremonial washing (immersion) of those who confess faith in Jesus has always been a sign of initiation into Christianity. The risen Jesus commanded that those who became Hhis disciples were to be baptized in the name of the Father, Son, and Spirit (Matt. 28:19). Although John the Baptist baptized as a sign of repentance, Christian baptism adds the specific symbolism of the believer's participation in Jesus' death, burial, and resurrection (Rom. 6:2-4). Further, baptism in water signifies the "baptism in the Holy Spirit" (receipt of the gift of the Spirit) that began on Pentecost (Acts 10:47).

Three thousand responded to Peter's message and were baptized in the name of Jesus, the first time Christian baptism was given to persons who repented and believed. From the very beginning the first Christians that met in Jerusalem dedicated themselves to the essential ingredients for a true church (Acts 2:42):

- *Apostles' teaching* (Christian doctrine; later written in the New Testament)

- *Fellowship* (genuine commitment to the second great commandment)

- *Breaking bread* (frequent ritual repetition of the Lord's Supper)

- *Prayer* (worship; genuine commitment to the first great commandment)

Acts 3—7 record a series of "first things" for the infant church. This fascinating record shows a congregation coming to terms with its identity. On the one hand, the believers were clearly Jewish in most of their practices—praying at the time of the temple sacrifice, for example (Acts 3:1)—and therefore under the umbrella of Judaism. On the other hand, they recognized in Jesus' resurrection divine proof that He was now the exalted Lord who must be believed (Acts 4:12). Here are some of the "first things," which all occurred over the space of about three years (A.D. 30 to A.D. 33[1]).

- First miracle performed after Jesus' ascension (Acts 3)

- First arrest of Peter and John for proclaiming Jesus as victorious Lord (Acts 4)

- First exercise of church discipline over Ananias and Sapphira's falsehoods (Acts 5)

- First experience of serious persecution, with all the apostles beaten (Acts 5)

- First organizational structure, possibly the historical origin of deacons (Acts 6)

- First Christian to preach that the gospel implied an end to temple sacrifices (Acts 7)

- First Christian (Stephen) to be martyred for his faithfulness to Jesus (Acts 7)

Eucharist

The ceremonial meal shared regularly by those who confess faith in Jesus has always been a sign of ongoing fellowship with Jesus, signaling that those who participate draw their spiritual nourishment from Him. Many Christians call it the Eucharist (from the Greek word for "thanksgiving") because of the prayers of thanks offered before believers participate in the bread and the cup. The Lord's Supper is the central act of worship for gathered Christians (Acts 20:7). Just as God gave participants in His earlier covenants a sign of the covenant, so Jesus commanded that those who participate in the new covenant partake of the Lord's Supper on a regular, ongoing basis (1 Cor. 11:25-26).

Close-up of bread for sale in old Jerusalem.

Stephen

A Hellenistic (Greek speaking and Greek in cultural outlook) Jewish Christian, Stephen was one of the seven chosen to assist the apostles in Jerusalem. His responsibility at first was tending to the needs of the widows among the church members. Yet he was soon doing the same ministry as the apostles, both performing miracles of healing and proclaiming the message about Jesus. Stephen's speech before he was martyred (Acts 7) is a masterful review of the Kingdom Story until his own times. Stephen was evidently the first Christian teacher to grasp that Judaism (with its animal sacrifices) became obsolete with the coming of Christ. Stephen is honored as the first Christian martyr.

Much of this shows a continuation of the hostility that had begun as a conflict between Jesus and the Sanhedrin. The Jewish leaders only thought they could stop the message of the kingdom of God by killing the King and the founder of the message. His followers were empowered by the same Spirit that He had manifested; yet the Sanhedrin continued to reject this message despite evidence that it was undeniable.

At last they resorted to stoning to death one of Jesus' followers, in hopes of stopping the troublesome messianic sect whose first name seems to have been "The Way" (Acts 9:2; 22:4; 24:14). Presumably the Sanhedrin succeeded in stoning Stephen (when they had been frustrated in their effort to kill Jesus by their own authority) because Pilate, the governor, was in Caesarea rather than in Jerusalem.

FIRST STEPS OUTSIDE THE NEST OF JUDAISM

The fledgling church was forced out of the nest of Jerusalem because of officially endorsed persecution of believers in Jesus. The apostles managed to keep at least some semblance of the church's presence in Jerusalem. They must have rebuilt the congregation, because throughout the rest of Acts the congregation in Jerusalem was still viewed as the mother church.

The first non-Jerusalem Christian assembly arose in a city of Samaria (probably Sebaste, recently rebuilt on the site of the Old Testament city of Samaria), where Philip proclaimed that the Messiah had come.

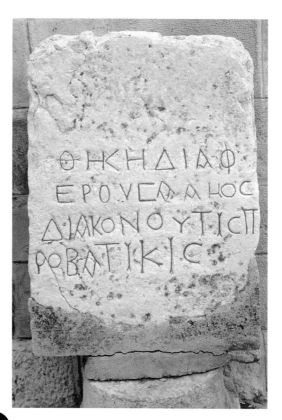

Although many historians believe that the Samaritans were biologically Jewish, nevertheless "pure" Jews did not accept them as such, even though Samaritans accepted the five Books of Moses as Scripture.

The really interesting thing as far as the Kingdom Story is concerned is that Peter—not Philip—was the "key man" to open the door for Samaritans to receive the Holy Spirit. This was similar to what had happened for Jews three years earlier on Pentecost (Acts 8:17).

Tombstone of a deacon attached to the Probatica (Pool of Bethesda) in Jerusalem.

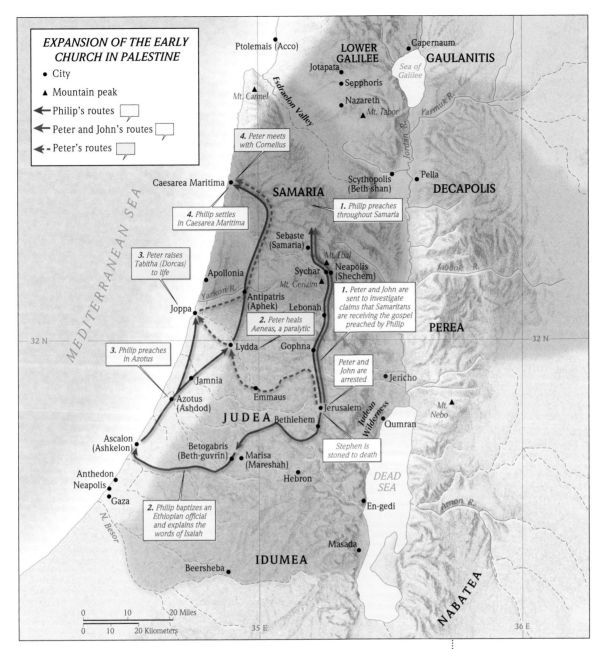

EXPANSION OF THE EARLY
CHURCH IN PALESTINE

- • City
- ▲ Mountain peak
- ← Philip's routes
- ← Peter and John's routes
- ◄- Peter's routes

4. Peter meets
with Cornelius

4. Philip settles
in Caesarea Maritima

1. Philip preaches
throughout Samaria

3. Peter raises
Tabitha (Dorcas)
to life

1. Peter and John are
sent to investigate
claims that Samaritans
are receiving the gospel
preached by Philip

2. Peter heals
Aeneas, a paralytic

3. Peter preaches
in Azotus

Peter and
John are
arrested

Stephen is
stoned to death

2. Philip baptizes an
Ethiopian official
and explains the
words of Isaiah

Ptolemais (Acco)
LOWER GALILEE
GAULANITIS
Capernaum
Jotapata
Sea of Galilee
Sepphoris
Mt. Carmel
Nazareth
Mt. Tabor
Caesarea Maritima
SAMARIA
Scythopolis (Beth-shan)
Pella
DECAPOLIS
Sebaste (Samaria)
Mt. Ebal
Neapolis (Shechem)
Apollonia
Sychar
Mt. Gerizim
Antipatris (Aphek)
Lebonah
Joppa
PEREA
Lydda
Gophna
Jamnia
Emmaus
Jericho
Azotus (Ashdod)
JUDEA
Bethlehem
Jerusalem
Qumran
Mt. Nebo
Ascalon (Ashkelon)
Betogabris (Beth-guvrin)
Marisa (Mareshah)
Anthedon
Neapolis
Hebron
DEAD SEA
Gaza
En-gedi
Masada
IDUMEA
NABATEA
Beersheba

MEDITERRANEAN SEA
Esdraelon Valley
Jordan R.
Yarmuk R.
Jabbok R.
Yarkon R.
Judean Wilderness
Arnon R.
N. Besor

32 N   32 N
35 E   36 E

0   10   20 Miles
0   10   20 Kilometers

On Pentecost Jews who believed in Jesus through the ministry of Peter had received the Spirit, signaling that the messianic age had arrived through Jesus. (After this "Samaritan Pentecost," all Samaritans—wherever they were—who believed in Jesus received the Spirit; Peter was simply the Christ-appointed "door opener" of the Spirit for Samaritans.) Peter's role as "door opener" to the Samaritans was critical at this time because it ensured the essential unity of the early church. There would be no Jewish versus Samaritan Christianities. The same Peter who had been present and instrumental when Jews first received the Holy Spirit was also present when Samaritans received the Spirit.

Acts 8—10 reports three remarkable conversions to Jesus, all of them unexpected illustrations of God's surprising grace reaching a variety of persons in a variety of life situations.

CONVERT	PREACHER	CONVERT'S ORIGIN AND STATUS	PLACE OF BAPTISM
an Ethopian friendly to Judaism	Philip, a "deacon" who was preaching in Samaria	Ethiopia—a high ranking government official	a pool beside the road from Jerusalem to Gaza
Saul, a Pharisee Jew	Ananias, a disciple of Damascus who was minding his own business	Tarsus—a religious zealot officially tormenting believers	house of Judas on Straight Street in Damascus
Cornelius, a God-fearing Gentile	Peter, an apostle who was preaching and healing in Joppa	Italy—a career officer in the Roman army	house of Cornelius in Caesarea

The conversions of both Saul and Cornelius were extremely important for the future of Christianity. These are the only two that Luke recorded more than once in Acts (for Saul, see Acts 9; 22; 26; for Cornelius, see Acts 10–11). Saul of course became the Apostle Paul and was mightily used by God during the next phase of Chapter Five. Cornelius was the first true Gentile (one that was not already a proselyte to Judaism) to believe in Jesus and be baptized.

Roman arches at Caesarea Maritima. These arches date from the 1st century A.D.

FIRST GENTILE CONVERT AND
FIRST INTERRACIAL CONGREGATION

In God's plan Peter once again fulfilled his responsibility as the "key man." It took a divinely inspired vision to get Peter to go to Cornelius's house, and even so he could barely bring himself to tell the good news of Jesus' victory to a Gentile. Yet, even before he finished his sermon, the Holy Spirit was poured out on Cornelius and his household. The same evidence that was present when Jews first received the Holy Spirit (miraculously speaking in other languages) now occurred when Gentiles first received the Spirit. (After this "Gentile Pentecost," all Gentiles— wherever they were—who believed in Jesus received the Spirit; Peter was simply the Christ-appointed "door opener" of the Spirit for Gentiles.)

When Peter was called to defend his actions to the Jewish Christians of Judea, he explicitly understood that Cornelius's experience was identical to what had happened "at the beginning" of the church (Acts 11:15-17). This was an unexpected turn of events in the minds of these Jewish Christians, and they could not have known that this was the beginning of the church becoming a Gentile-majority expression of God's Kingdom. Once again Peter's role as "door opener" to the Gentile was critical at this time because it ensured the essential unity of the early church. There

Antioch of Syria

Antioch was third largest city in the Roman Empire, after Rome and Alexandria, and it may have had a population of half a million in the first century. It was the capital of the province of Syria and former capital of the Seleucid Empire (during the time of the Maccabees). Antioch was the city where the nickname "Christian" was given. Each of Paul's three missionary journeys began in Antioch. The church there continued to exert a strong influence for centuries.

would be no Jewish versus Gentile Christianities because the same Peter who had been present when Jews and later the Samaritans first received the Holy Spirit was also present when Gentiles received the Spirit, although this issue was not officially settled until the Jerusalem Council of A.D. 49.

This incident shows Peter continuing to use the pattern of gospel preaching or "Kingdom Proclamation" that was evidently standard for him and others whose presentations have been preserved (Acts 2–4; 10; 13). The standard outline the early Christian preachers used included all or most of the following elements:

- Jesus lived on earth, teaching and doing good deeds

- Jesus was crucified

- God raised Jesus from the dead as the victorious Lord

- These events fulfilled the prophecies of Scripture

- You must repent and believe in Him

- Those who do so will receive the gift of the Spirit

For about ten years (34–44) few details of the spread of the church are known. Jewish believers went to Phoenicia and the island of Cyprus (both north of Palestine), where they shared with other Jews that the Messiah had come (Acts 11:19). A few of these, however, tried a new experiment in the city of Antioch. These Jewish believers tried telling the message of Jesus to Gentiles directly, and the results were a surprising number of converts.

Ruins of Antioch of Syria on hill above the modern town of Antakya, Turkey.

When the Jerusalem church learned about this, they dispatched one of their capable leaders, Barnabas, to keep an eye on things. He discovered that these Gentile converts needed to be instructed properly. Barnabas remembered Saul, the brilliant young scholar and convert who had disappeared to his home city of Tarsus years before. Barnabas successfully retrieved Saul, and together they taught the church there for a year (probably A.D. 45–46, Acts 11:26).

Although the original congregation in Jerusalem practiced the essential elements for a true church, the Antioch church successfully added a number of ingredients that have also been very important throughout Christian history for a healthy local congregation:

• Welcoming all ethnic and racial groups as full participants (Acts 11:21; 13:1)

• Adopting the name Christian or "partisan of Christ" (Acts 11:26)

• Sending financial aid to support needy believers elsewhere (Acts 11:29-30)

• Commissioning (and funding?) missionaries from their number (Acts 13:1-3)

Peter had exercised oversight of the expanding Christian movement. He traveled throughout Palestine (Acts 9:32-42). Around A.D. 44, however, Peter's public leadership—at least in Jerusalem—ended, as Acts 12 reports.

The political situation in Judea had changed (yet again) after Claudius Caesar became emperor in A.D. 41. That year he appointed Herod the Great's grandson, Herod Agrippa I (called "King Herod" in Acts) as king of Judea. Because his grandmother was a Hasmonean princess, the Jews generally accepted Herod Agrippa's rule, and he courted the approval of his subjects.

He discovered that persecuting the church was a good way to gain favor with the Jewish religious leaders. He even went to the extent of having the Apostle James arrested and killed, and soon Simon Peter was in line for the same treatment. He was arrested and held during the Passover season. (This was probably the Passover of A.D. 44, fourteen years after Jesus' death.) Peter, however, was divinely rescued from his predicament. He realized that it was best to relinquish his leadership in Jerusalem, which now fell to James, the half-brother of Jesus (Acts 12:17).

James proved to be an outstanding leader for the Jewish followers of Jesus in Jerusalem, as the account of his expert leadership of the Jerusalem Council later demonstrated (Acts 15). He also exercised pastoral concern for Jewish Christian assemblies that had sprung up in places such as Phoenicia and Cyprus (Acts 11:19). The epistle that he wrote to some of these believers was almost certainly the first part of the New Testament to be composed.

Epistle of James

This letter was sent to Jewish believers that were being harassed because of their commitment to Jesus as the Messiah. They were meeting in synagogues led by elders, an indication that the letter pre-dates Paul's travel, probably around A.D. 45. James was the younger half-brother of Jesus, converted after the resurrection. The key word for the book is "works" or "deeds"; the key text is James 2:26. **One-Sentence Summary:** *True faith must be lived out in everyday life by good deeds, especially in the face of trials or persecution, and such good works demonstrate the presence of faith and justification before God.*

The incident of Peter's escape shows God's vindication of Peter as representative leader of the church; the same chapter of Acts shows God's judgment on King Herod as representative leader of the Jews. This arrogant king was struck down and killed by an angel of the Lord, presumably the same angel that released Peter from prison (Acts 12:7,23). The Jewish historian Josephus provides striking corroboration of the date and nature of this event. In Acts Herod's death was divine judgment both for his claim to divine status and for his persecution of the church. (Similar judgment later fell on the entire Jewish State when the Romans utterly destroyed Jerusalem in A.D. 70.)

Little more is known about Peter's activities, although some twenty years later he wrote letters to churches. Peter, it seems, had fulfilled the duty Jesus had given him of using the "keys of the kingdom." He was the instrument through whom the Holy Spirit came at first to Jews, Samaritans, and Gentiles (Acts 2; 8; 10). From then on, others took the lead. Even so, until his death around A.D. 65, he continued to be Christ's beloved "apostle to the Jews" (Gal. 2:8).

Thus, in the space of about fifteen years (A.D. 30 to 45), communities committed to God's Kingdom had spread throughout Judea and other areas where Jews might be exposed to the message about Jesus. There were already hints, however, that Judaism was not large enough to contain Christianity within its boundaries. Already the conversion of Cornelius showed that Gentiles could receive the Holy Spirit without becoming Jewish proselytes first. The multi-ethnic church in Antioch was about to take the step of sending a mission team to provinces that had not heard about the Kingdom of God.

Ministry of the Apostle Paul:
The Church Reaching More Gentiles than Jews
(A.D. 46–65)

Paul discharged the unique calling and contribution of serving as Jesus' apostle to Gentiles. Through his ministry of traveling evangelism and extensive letter writing, the church expanded greatly, both quantitatively and qualitatively. In numbers the church grew to include congregations all over the Roman Empire. Further, the church's theology grew to embrace both Jew and Gentile as one body of Christ. Two of the letters Paul wrote during this period have proved to be exceptionally important. First, the message of Romans is his great work revealing the meaning of Jesus' death and how it provides righteousness for all that believe. Second, the message of Ephesians is Paul's great work explaining the "mystery" of the church. **Acts 13—28** and Paul's epistles, **Romans through Philemon**, are the primary Scriptural evidence for this phase of God's Kingdom Story.

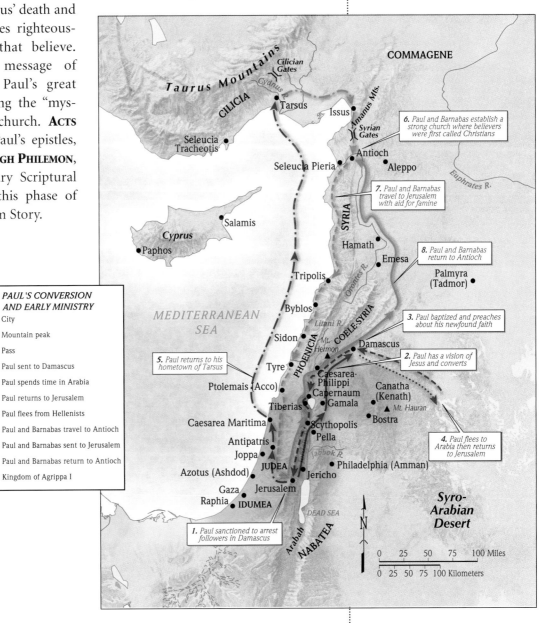

PAUL'S CONVERSION AND EARLY MINISTRY

- • City
- ▲ Mountain peak
- ⟩⟨ Pass
- ← Paul sent to Damascus
- ◄···· Paul spends time in Arabia
- ← Paul returns to Jerusalem
- ← Paul flees from Hellenists
- ← Paul and Barnabas travel to Antioch
- ← Paul and Barnabas sent to Jerusalem
- ← Paul and Barnabas return to Antioch
- ▢ Kingdom of Agrippa I

COMMAGENE

Taurus Mountains

Cilician Gates

Cydnus

CILICIA

Tarsus

Issus

Amanus Mts.

Syrian Gates

6. Paul and Barnabas establish a strong church where believers were first called Christians

Seleucia Tracheotis

Antioch

• Aleppo

Seleucia Pieria

SYRIA

Euphrates R.

7. Paul and Barnabas travel to Jerusalem with aid for famine

Cyprus

Salamis

Hamath

Paphos

8. Paul and Barnabas return to Antioch

Emesa

Palmyra (Tadmor) •

Tripolis

Orontes R.

Byblos

3. Paul baptized and preaches about his newfound faith

MEDITERRANEAN SEA

COELE-SYRIA

Litani R.

Sidon

PHOENICIA

Mt. Hermon

Damascus

5. Paul returns to his hometown of Tarsus

Tyre

Caesarea-Philippi

2. Paul has a vision of Jesus and converts

Ptolemais (Acco)

Capernaum

Canatha (Kenath)

Tiberias

Gamala

▲ Mt. Hauran

Caesarea Maritima

Scythopolis

• Bostra

Antipatris

Pella

4. Paul flees to Arabia then returns to Jerusalem

Joppa

JUDEA

Jabbok R.

Azotus (Ashdod)

Jericho

• Philadelphia (Amman)

Gaza

Jerusalem

Raphia • IDUMEA

DEAD SEA

Syro-Arabian Desert

N

1. Paul sanctioned to arrest followers in Damascus

Arabah

NABATEA

0 25 50 75 100 Miles

0 25 50 75 100 Kilometers

Paul

His birth name (Saul) was used in Jewish contexts; in all his letters he called himself Paul. A native of Tarsus, this brilliant Pharisee realized the threat that belief in Jesus made to first-century Judaism. After his dramatic encounter with the risen Christ on the road to Damascus, he became a passionate Christian, the single most influential human figure for the first century of the church. The thirteen letters that bear his name have essentially defined the message of Christianity. According to unbroken Christian tradition, Paul was beheaded in the city of Rome during the reign of Nero Caesar. His life spanned from about A.D. 5 to A.D. 65.

The Via Sacra or Sacred Way is the main street that runs through the Roman Forum, the birthplace and epitome of Roman culture. Returning military heroes marched in triumph along this road leading prisoners of war and showing off the spoils of victory.

PAUL'S FIRST MISSIONARY JOURNEY

The risen Jesus had commissioned Saul of Tarsus at the time of his conversion and call to be the apostle to the Gentiles (A.D. 33). Three years later he visited the church in Jerusalem, which still was afraid to trust him (Acts 9:26-30; Gal. 1:18-23), so he went back home to Tarsus into relative obscurity. During his one-year leadership and teaching opportunity in Antioch he evidently mastered the art of making disciples of Gentiles.

Fourteen years after his conversion (A.D. 46, Gal. 2:1), the Antioch church entrusted Saul[2] and Barnabas with an offering to take to the impoverished church in Jerusalem. They took with them the Gentile convert Titus, who had become such a devout disciple that no Jewish Christian in Jerusalem asked him to convert to Judaism and submit to circumcision (Acts 11:27-30; 12:25; Gal. 2:1-10). The leaders of the church in Jerusalem approved of Saul's desire to preach further to Gentiles (Gal. 2:9).

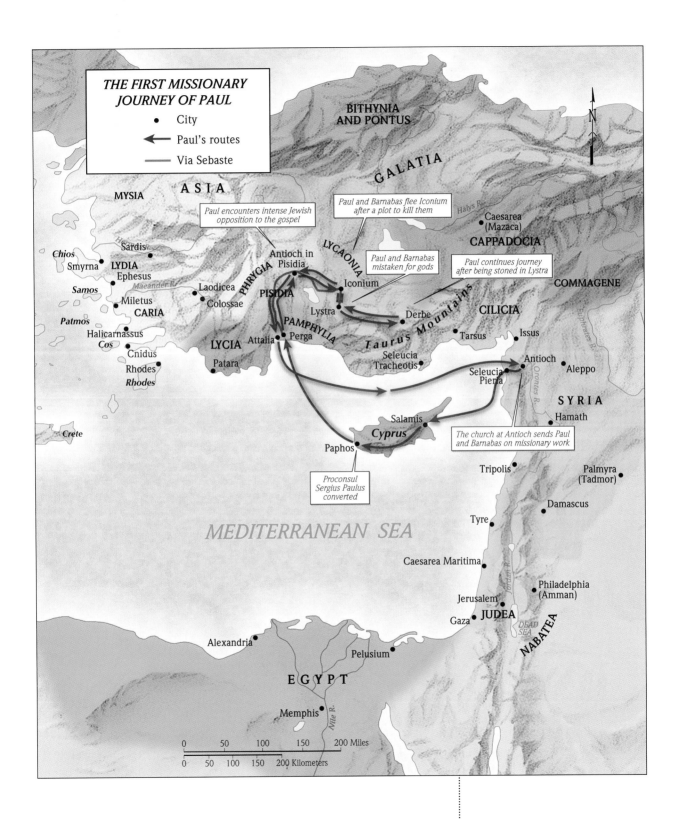

THE FIRST MISSIONARY
JOURNEY OF PAUL

● City

← Paul's routes

— Via Sebaste

BITHYNIA
AND PONTUS

GALATIA

MYSIA

ASIA

Chios
Smyrna
Sardis
LYDIA
Ephesus
Samos
Miletus
CARIA
Patmos
Halicarnassus
Cos
Cnidus
Rhodes
Rhodes

Crete

Maeander R.
Laodicea
Colossae

PHRYGIA
Antioch in
Pisidia

PISIDIA

LYCIA
Attalia
Perga
PAMPHYLIA

LYCAONIA

Iconium

Lystra

Derbe

CAPPADOCIA
Caesarea
(Mazaca)

COMMAGENE

Halys R.

*Paul and Barnabas flee Iconium
after a plot to kill them*

*Paul encounters intense Jewish
opposition to the gospel*

*Paul and Barnabas
mistaken for gods*

*Paul continues journey
after being stoned in Lystra*

Taurus Mountains

CILICIA

Tarsus

Issus

Euphrates R.

Seleucia
Tracheotis

Seleucia
Pieria

Antioch

Aleppo

SYRIA

Hamath

Orontes R.

Salamis

Cyprus

Paphos

*The church at Antioch sends Paul
and Barnabas on missionary work*

*Proconsul
Sergius Paulus
converted*

Tripolis

Palmyra
(Tadmor)

Damascus

Tyre

MEDITERRANEAN SEA

Caesarea Maritima

Jordan R.

Philadelphia
(Amman)

Jerusalem

Gaza
JUDEA

DEAD
SEA

NABATEA

Alexandria

Pelusium

EGYPT

Memphis

Nile R.

0   50   100   150   200 Miles

0   50   100   150   200 Kilometers

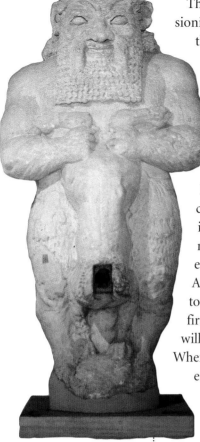

Colossal statue of Bes. Bes originally was a semi-god of ancient Egypt. He was a popular god in Cyprus and was often confused with Herakles.

The church in Antioch soon took the momentous step of commissioning Barnabas and Saul to go out as their ambassadors. Thus began the first of what is usually called the three missionary journeys of the Apostle Paul. The first journey lasted about two years, A.D. 47–48 (Acts 13:4—14:26). The first leg of the trip took the missionaries to the island of Cyprus, a logical step since this was Barnabas's home area and a place where a gospel witness had already been established. The success of the message was mixed—as Luke always reported.

The next leg of the journey took the missionaries to the mainland of the province of Galatia. Here Paul took the lead in planting churches. His pattern was to begin, whenever possible, by proclaiming in the city synagogue that the Messiah had come and that His name was Jesus. Since Jews already believed in one God and accepted Scripture as His Word, many were ready to embrace the message. After Paul wore out his welcome in the synagogue, however, he turned to preach to Gentiles. Here the task was more challenging, since he first had to present the message of a single Creator (by whom people will be judged) before he proclaimed Jesus as the Lord and Savior. When he preached to Gentiles, Paul offered the gospel free of charge. He emphasized the gift of salvation without regard to good works or keeping the law of Moses.

Four congregations in Galatia were established on this basis. First there was Antioch (not to be confused with the city from which Paul had set out). Then there were the cities of Iconium, Lystra, and Derbe. Two of these show the amazing diversity of situations that Paul and Barnabas dealt with.

- In Iconium Paul confronted Jewish legalism—and they wanted to stone him to death (Acts 14:1-7).

- In Lystra Paul confronted primitive polytheism—and they stoned him to the point that they thought he had died (Acts 14:8-19).

The missionaries returned to Antioch and resumed the role they had previously enjoyed as teachers and leaders. Word reached Jerusalem that Paul was establishing whole congregations of believers that were uncircumcised Gentiles. Some were alarmed, persuaded that the church must operate as a sect within Judaism. Without official authority certain Jewish believers traveled north to Antioch and then on to the new churches in Galatia. They argued that God's law could not be trampled on, and that the law—at least in some measure—must be followed by the Gentile converts. At the least they must be circumcised. This issue became contentious in Antioch (Gal. 2:11-21), and even Simon Peter behaved inconsistently concerning the issue.

The tell of Lystra near the Turkish village Khatyn Serai.

In Galatia there was utter confusion. When word reached Paul back in Antioch that the "Judaizers" (Jewish Christians who argued that Gentile Christians should live as Jews) had gone there, he was livid. This prompted the first epistle to come from his pen, Galatians. In it he argued that the gospel comes to all people, Jew and Gentile alike, by God's grace without any reference at all to keeping the law.

THE JERUSALEM COUNCIL

This issue finally became a serious problem for the mother church in Jerusalem. Many law-keeping Jews in Jerusalem heard that some of Jesus' followers had discarded the law. It was becoming difficult to evangelize such Jews with the message that this Jesus was their longed-for Messiah. Further, Pharisees of Jerusalem who had embraced Jesus as the Messiah were having tremendous difficulty in seeing how the requirements of God's law could be ignored by Gentile converts to the Messiah (Acts 15:5).

The council in Jerusalem, convened in A.D. 49 by the church, thus pitted Paul the Pharisee against other Pharisees. The report of the proceedings (Acts 15:6-29) shows Peter, Paul, and Barnabas as major speakers. Yet James—secure in his role as pastor of the Jerusalem church—was the one who summarized matters and guided the assembly toward the right conclusion. In the end the Judaizers conceded that God accepts Gentiles without circumcision or keeping the law. This decision made it possible for Christianity to become separate from Judaism. On the other hand, Paul conceded that Gentile Christians should keep certain regulations for the sake of morality (for example, sexual purity) and other regulations for the sake of Christian unity (for example, sensitivity to Jewish scruples by avoiding certain foods, Acts 15:20,29).

Epistle to the Galatians

Paul sent this passionate letter, written about A.D. 49, from Antioch to Gentile believers being harassed (by "Judaizers") because of their commitment to Jesus as the Messiah yet without being circumcised. Paul had established churches in Galatia during his first missionary journey based on preaching the law-free gospel of grace. The key word for the book is "faith"; the key text is Galatians 2:16. **One-Sentence Summary:** *Sinners are justified (and live out a godly life) by trusting in Jesus Christ alone, not by keeping the law or by counting on good works.*

PAUL'S SECOND MISSIONARY JOURNEY

Armed with this official decision, Paul was jubilant and returned to Antioch with Barnabas to share news from the council. The apostle, however, was soon ready to begin another missionary journey. After all, the Galatian Christians needed to hear the outcome of the proceedings, and there were more cities to be reached with the news of the kingdom of God. The second missionary journey lasted about three years, A.D. 49–52 (Acts 15:40—18:22).

Paul establishes churches in Philippi, Thessalonica, and Berea

Paul imprisoned

Luke joins Paul

Paul receives vision that encourages him to travel to Macedonia

Paul brought on charges before Gallio

Paul speaks to the Areopagus

Paul asks Timothy to join him in his work

Paul returns from Jerusalem to plan his next venture

Jerusalem Conference, A.D. 49, (Acts 15:1–30; Gal 2:1–21)

THE SECOND MISSIONARY JOURNEY OF PAUL

- ● City
- ▲ Mountain peak
- — Via Egnatia
- ⋈ Pass
- ← Route of Paul and Silas

THE MOVE INTO MACEDONIA

Taking a new missionary partner named Silas, Paul left Antioch and visited the Galatian churches. In Lystra he asked Timothy, a promising young convert, to join them. Their way progressed west to the coastal city of Troas. While pondering the next move, Paul had a vision of a Macedonian man asking for help and knew that Jesus had shown him the next step for their travel. Luke probably joined the party in Troas (note the "we" of Acts 16:10).

After crossing the Aegean Sea, Paul and his team established three congregations in the province of Macedonia:

- **PHILIPPI:** an important commercial center. Three individuals were especially changed by the good news (a rich businesswoman named Lydia, a slave girl, and the town jailer). Luke evidently stayed behind in Philippi, so the account of this church's founding is rich with his eyewitness memory.
- **THESSALONICA:** the capital city of Macedonia. A riot started because Paul was preaching about a rival King, named Jesus, and His glorious victory.
- **BEREA:** a city in southwest Macedonia. Paul had a highly successful ministry, but he was eventually forced to leave for Athens for his own safety. Timothy and Silas followed later.

MINISTRY IN ATHENS AND CORINTH

Alone in Athens, the intellectual center of the world, Paul successfully preached to the philosophers and religious council of the city. The Epicureans and Stoics—followers of opposing worldviews and lifestyles—heard how Jesus and His resurrection fulfilled what was missing in their religion. Although most refused the message, some responded. In Athens Timothy reported to Paul about the situation in Macedonia, and Paul felt it best for Timothy to return there immediately, particularly to work in Thessalonica (1 Thess. 2:17—3:5).

Paul moved west to Corinth, the bustling, immoral capital of the Roman province of Achaia. For the first time since he began his extensive travel schedule, Paul settled down in a single city to disciple the converts. He stayed there about a year and a half (autumn of A.D. 50 to spring of A.D. 52, Acts 18:11). In Corinth Paul received more than a little encouragement from several able assistants:

- **AQUILA AND PRISCILLA:** a Jewish Christian couple who were expelled from Rome by Claudius's decree (of A.D. 49) and who shared with Paul the skill of tent making

Lydia

Lydia ("woman from the Lydian region") was a wealthy Gentile woman who became Paul's first convert to Christ in Macedonia. She lived in Philippi as a seller of the purple fabric for which her native city, Thyatira (in the territory of the old Lydian Empire), was famous. She first heard the gospel when Paul and his associates came to the river where she and others gathered for worship. After she became a believer, she invited the group to come to her home to stay, and they did so (Acts 16:14-15). Her home thus became the first meeting place for the church in Philippi. Lydia is representative of the many influential women reached by the gospel in the early decades of Christianity.

Aquila and Priscilla

This Jewish husband-and-wife team is one of a very few Christian couples who are both named in the Bible; in fact, they are always mentioned together. They were from the province of Pontus but moved to Rome where apparently they were converted. Later they opened a tent-making business in Corinth, where they worked with Paul. Next they moved to Ephesus where they laid the groundwork for the church there, particularly by discipling Apollos. They eventually returned to Rome, for Paul praised them in the Epistle to the Romans for risking their lives for his sake (Rom. 16:3-4). Priscilla was perhaps more outgoing than Aquila, for her name usually precedes that of her husband.

- **TIMOTHY AND SILAS:** Paul's missionary friends who finally arrived from Macedonia, probably with a financial gift from the Philippian church (Acts 18:5; Phil. 4:15-16)

The report Timothy brought to Paul concerning the Thessalonian congregation was mainly positive. However, one serious issue had come up. Some believers had died and "King Jesus" had not yet come back to set up His visible kingdom. Was His victory real or sham? Had such Christians missed out entirely on Christ's coming? Paul's first epistle to the Thessalonian church addressed this and other issues.

Paul soon received further word about the church in Thessalonica. Far from being at peace, they were in more of an uproar than ever. Although the details have become lost to us, the Christians had evidently received a letter that they wrongly assumed had come from Paul. In it was news that "the day of the Lord" was about to be completely fulfilled. Because Jesus' visible kingdom was at hand, some Thessalonians had stopped working for a living and were idly waiting for the end.

The church was now being expected to support these people. Paul's second letter to the church, probably written only a few months after the first letter, was his attempt to restore calm to the church and to correct their faulty understanding about the coming "day of the Lord."

First Epistle to the Thessalonians

Paul sent this letter, written about A.D. 50 while staying in Corinth, to believers facing harassment because of their commitment to Jesus as the King. At the same time they were confused concerning the nature of the second coming. Paul established the church in Thessalonica during his second missionary journey. The key word for the book is "coming"; the key text is 1 Thessalonians 4:16-17. **One-Sentence Summary:** *Whatever difficulties and sufferings believers experience in this life, the coming of Christ is the true hope of the Christian.*

Second Epistle to the Thessalonians

Paul had established the church in Thessalonica during his second missionary journey. While in Corinth he sent this letter, written about A.D. 51, to believers under the illusion that the "day of the LORD" was upon them. The letter is shorter, but more intense, than the first epistle. The key term for the book is "stand firm"; the key text is 2 Thessalonians 2:15. **One-Sentence Summary:** *Whatever difficulties believers face, they should stand firm and continue living useful lives, since Christ's return may be in the distant future.*

Overlooking the city of NT Berea in Macedonia. This is the city to which Paul escaped after the Jews of Thessalonica sought to harm him.

The Thessalonian Christians must have responded well to Paul's letters, for representatives of the church later accompanied Paul on his final trip to Jerusalem (Acts 20:4; 27:2).

At length Jews hostile to Paul's message stirred up trouble in Corinth. The brief account of Paul brought before Gallio,[3] the Roman consul of Achaia, shows official government neutrality toward the Christians, a situation which changed only after the great fire of Rome in A.D. 64.

When Paul left Corinth, he crossed the Aegean Sea east to Ephesus, the leading city of the Roman province of Asia. Because of his success in planting Christianity on the west side of the Aegean (Corinth), he planned to follow this pattern on the east side. Thus he took Aquila and Priscilla to Ephesus and left them there to lay a foundation for his return. This second missionary journey concluded with a brief visit (and report) to the church in Jerusalem, and a longer visit (and report) to his home base church in Antioch (Acts 18:22-23). Like the first journey, this one began and ended in the city of Antioch.

The following labels appear on the map:

Amastris
Heraclea
Pompeiopolis
Pontus Mts.
Amisus
THRACE
Byzantium (Istanbul)
Perinthus
BLACK SEA
BITHYNIA AND PONTUS
Hadrianopolis
Amaseia
MACEDONIA
Philippi
Amphipolis
Neapolis
Porsule
Doriscus
Chalcedon
Bosporus R.
MARMARA SEA
Pella
Apollonia
Thessalonica
Samothrace
Ancyra (Ankara)
GALATIA
Tavium
Berea
Mt. Olympus
Lemnos
Troas
MYSIA
Paul restores life to young Eutychus
Parnassus
Halys R.
Caesarea (Mazaca)
Larissa
Paul revisits the troubled church at Corinth
Assos
Adramyttium
ASIA
Ancyra
Anatolian Plateau
CAPPADOCIA
Lesbos
Pergamum
Mitylene
Thyatira
Archelais
Delphi
Euboea
AEGEAN SEA
Chios
Sardis
Philadelphia
PHRYGIA
LYCAONIA
Antioch in Pisidia
ACHAIA
Corinth
Athens
Smyrna
LYDIA
Ephesus
Tripolis
Hierapolis
Seleucia
Iconium
Cicilian Gates
CILICIA
Cenchreae
Epidaurus
Sounion
Paul establishes churches and writes 1 and 2 Corinthians
Samos
Priene
Hermus R.
Maeander R.
Laodicea
Colossae
PISIDIA
Cremna
Derbe
Lystra
Paul revisits the churches of Galatia
Tarsus
Issus
Syrian Gates
Sparta
Patmos
Miletus
Aphrodisias
CARIA
Halicarnassus
LYCIA
Attalia
PAMPHYLIA
Perga
Taurus Mountains
Seleucia Tracheotis
Amanus Mts.
Cyclades Islands
Cos
Cnidus
Xanthus
Patara
Seleucia Pieria
Antioch
Rhodes
Rhodes
Paul resumes his missionary travels
Hamath
Crete
Cyprus
Salamis
Fair Havens
Paphos
Tripolis
Byblos
Sidon
MEDITERRANEAN SEA
Cyrene
Tyre
Ptolemais (Acco)
CYRENAICA
Caesarea Maritima
Antipatris
Phila (Amm)
Jordan R.
Jerusalem
Gaza
JUDEA
DEAD SEA
Alexandria
EGYPT
Pelusium
Qattara Depression
Memphis
Nile R.

THE THIRD MISSIONARY JOURNEY OF PAUL
- • City
- ◻ Site of the Seven Churches of Asia
- ▲ Mountain peak
- — Roads
- ⋈ Pass
- ← Paul's routes

PAUL'S THIRD MISSIONARY JOURNEY

During his third missionary journey, Paul did not travel very much to establish new churches. Instead, he planted himself in a single city (Ephesus) for an extensive ministry. His travel after he left Ephesus was for the purpose of visiting established churches and gathering a financial collection from them. The details of this period are told in Acts 18:23—21:19. The time frame was from the autumn of A.D. 52 to the spring of A.D. 57, some four and a half years.

View looking west down a major street in Ephesus.

MINISTRY IN EPHESUS

After visiting the Galatian churches again, Paul used the Roman road system to travel directly west to Ephesus. His ministry there was to last three years (autumn of 52 to summer of 55). As far as the record shows, this was the time when more people heard the gospel and responded than any other period of Paul's life.

The church in Ephesus benefited from the extensive healing and teaching ministry of Paul. For the first time in a Gentile city, a public lecture hall became the center of Christian ministry. From this place scores must have gone out as ambassadors for Christ, because the entire province of Asia—more than a million persons—heard the gospel (Acts 19:10). The lifestyles of former pagans changed drastically; in particular those who had practiced the occult destroyed the paraphernalia associated with their evil deeds.

Among the daughter congregations planted at this time was the church in Colosse. Two men Paul had discipled, Epaphras (a preacher of some skill) and Philemon (a family man of some wealth), became leaders in this congregation. Paul later had opportunity to interact with both of them from his Roman imprisonment.

Looking through a gate into the ancient city of Corinth.

First Epistle to the Corinthians

While in Ephesus Paul sent this letter, written about A.D. 54, to believers facing a number of difficulties, such as abuse of worship, division, and immorality. Paul had established the church in Corinth during his second missionary journey. The key word for the book is "love"; the key text is 1 Corinthians 15:58. **One-Sentence Summary:** *The many problems a congregation may have, whether doctrinal or practical, will be resolved as that church submits properly to the lordship of Christ and learns to love one another genuinely.*

DEALING WITH THE CORINTHIANS

Acts does not describe the difficulties that Paul had during this time with the Corinthian church. Studying 1 and 2 Corinthians, however, demonstrates that the apostle exerted a great deal of energy to help that congregation solve its many problems. This even involved a brief interruption of his Ephesian ministry so that he could go in person to Corinth.

Sometime around the spring of A.D. 54 Paul received at least two sets of visitors from the church of Corinth that gave him news of trouble among the Christians there. People from the house of a Corinthian woman named Chloe informed him of serious divisions in the church. In addition, a church committee of three men came to Paul with a list of questions, as well as a report of serious sexual immorality that the church was tolerating (1 Cor. 1:11; 5:1; 16:17).

Paul wrote 1 Corinthians with extensive advice concerning how to correct these problems. Timothy was evidently the letter carrier, on whom Paul was relying to urge his teachings on the Corinthian Christians (1 Cor. 4:17). Timothy, however, was not well received by the church, and he returned to Paul in Ephesus with a negative report. Things were getting even more out of hand, to the extent that Paul concluded he must personally visit Corinth. Sometime around the autumn of A.D. 54, he made what he called a painful visit to see them (2 Cor. 2:1) in which he—like Timothy—was not well received.

Paul discovered that the church had been infiltrated by Jewish-Christian teachers that he later called "false apostles" or, sarcastically, "super apostles" (2 Cor. 11:5,13; 12:11). The exact nature of their teaching is unclear. They may have been like the Judaizers he had dealt with in Galatia, or they may have emphasized ecstatic experiences (speaking in tongues, healing, prophecy). In any event these teachers had gained the upper hand, and Paul left Corinth in sorrow.

After returning to Ephesus, Paul sent the Corinthians another epistle, which has not been preserved, delivered by Titus (2 Cor. 7:6-8). In this letter he blasted his opponents and demanded that the church pay attention to Titus, evidently a more vigorous leader than Timothy. Paul later discovered that the ministry of Titus largely achieved its objectives. Meanwhile Paul was concluding his ministry in Ephesus.

Panorama from atop ancient Corinth. Roman walls are joined with walls from the period of the Crusades.

A view of Ephesus, showing Curetes Street descending down to the Library of Celsus.

THE COLLECTION AND THE EPHESIAN RIOT

Paul was determined to maintain the unity of the worldwide church—Jewish and Gentile congregations—at all costs. In Ephesus he concluded that one way to demonstrate this would be for Gentile churches to collect and send a significant financial gift to the mother church in Jerusalem. As early as the writing of 1 Corinthians, he asked that church to participate in this collection (1 Cor. 16:1-2). Later on, he dispatched two assistants to Macedonia as his "advance men" for the offering (Acts 19:21-22). This proved to be highly effective, and when he later arrived there, he discovered that the congregations had given sacrificially and joyfully to this cause (2 Cor. 8:1-5).

In Ephesus the church had so affected the pagan culture that business for the world-renowned shrine of the Ephesian patron divinity was alarmingly down. (A huge temple in the city was devoted to Artemis, a fertility goddess, and the Artemis tourist trade supported many workers.) The resentment against Paul and the Christians finally reached a boiling point, and the pro-Artemis forces started a citywide uproar. People flooded into the public open-air theater, and for two hours people screamed their support for Artemis. Government officials friendly to

The theater at Ephesus was built in the 3rd century B.C.

Paul finally persuaded him not to appear before the crowd, and at last the city clerk was able to regain control of the immediate situation.

The riot (summer of 55) made Paul a marked man in Ephesus. It was important for the safety of the Christians there for him to leave the city. Thus he said goodbye and set out for the city of Troas, where he hoped to see Titus with news from Corinth.

TRAVEL FOR THE COLLECTION AND ON TO JERSUALEM

Paul and Titus did not meet in Troas, so he crossed the Aegean to Macedonia again. His primary purpose was to encourage the churches and gather the collection (Acts 20:1-2; 2 Cor. 8:1-5). It is possible, however, that during those days he preached in Illyricum, the province northwest of Macedonia (Rom. 15:19).

Somewhere in Macedonia Paul and Titus finally reunited, perhaps in the spring of 56. It had been at least a year since Paul had sent Titus to Corinth with his severe letter. There was good news. The severe letter and the ministry of Titus had accomplished much. The false apostles had been routed, and a majority of the Corinthians had repented and come back to the true gospel.

The Second Epistle to the Corinthians

While in Macedonia Paul sent this letter, written about A.D. 56, to a church that had recently repented of its shameful treatment of him as an apostle. The last four chapters appear to be addressed to those who had not repented. The key word for the book is "defense"; the key text is 2 Corinthians 12:9. **One-Sentence Summary:** *True Christian ministry, although it may have to be defended against false attacks, is commissioned by Christ and empowered by His Spirit.*

Epistle to the Romans

While in Corinth Paul sent this letter, written early in A.D. 57, to a church that he had not established. This epistle is the greatest summary of Christian doctrine found in the Bible, and it has been more important in subsequent Christian history than any other book of the Bible. Its central message is that the just shall live by faith. The key word for the book is "righteousness"; the key text is Romans 1:16-17. **One-Sentence Summary:** *Righteousness with God is given freely (imputed) to all those who have faith in Jesus Christ for salvation according to God's eternal plan.*

Paul was so relieved that he wrote them another letter, sending it back by Titus (2 Cor. 8:23-24). In it he expressed his joy and at the same time warned those who had still not changed their minds that he would come to deal with them. This letter, now known as 2 Corinthians, also asked the church to finish their financial collection for the poor Jewish Christians of Jerusalem (2 Cor. 8—9).

At last Paul left Macedonia and traveled south, arriving in Corinth late in A.D. 56. (This was now his third visit, a fulfillment of the promise of 2 Cor. 13:1.) The church in Corinth was the final congregation from which he expected to receive an offering for the collection, and he planned to sail from Corinth to Jerusalem as soon as the winter passed and the Mediterranean could be safely navigated.

Paul's thoughts already had shifted to what would happen after he completed his mission to Jerusalem. He had long wanted to preach in Rome and to teach the Christians there. Thus, from the enforced quiet of a winter spent in Corinth, Paul composed the longest and most important of his letters, the great Epistle to the Romans. In it, he not only gave them an extensive summary of his teachings, he addressed a number of practical issues to encourage them in Christian living.

When Mediterranean navigation reopened early in A.D. 57, Paul changed his travel plan to avoid an assassination attempt on his life (Acts 20:3). Accompanied by seven men representing the churches he had established during each of his three missionary journeys, Paul finally arrived in Jersualem sometime after Easter of A.D. 57. Acts emphasizes the joy of the believers there when they heard about the success of Paul's ministry among the Gentiles. Their joy was no doubt increased because of the substantial offering that Paul brought with him from the Gentile churches.

PAUL'S FOUR YEARS OF IMPRISONMENT

Within a week of his arrival in Jerusalem, Paul was arrested in the temple precincts on the false charge that he had taken a Gentile into the area of the temple reserved only for Jews. His arrest provoked a riot among the anti-Christian Jews of the city. People flooded into the temple courts, screaming for Paul's life. (The irony was surely not lost on Paul. Two years earlier he had caused *Gentiles* to riot in Ephesus because he had proclaimed a *Jewish* Messiah to worshipers at the temple of Artemis. Here he was in Jerusalem causing *Jews* to riot because he supposedly brought a *Gentile* to worship at the temple of the Lord.) The intervention of a Roman army officer spared Paul's life.

Paul was soon given opportunities to defend his beliefs about Jesus in a variety of situations:
- To the Jewish crowd at the temple courts after he was arrested (Acts 22)
- To the Jewish Sanhedrin the next day (Acts 23)
- To the Roman governor, Antonius Felix,[4] several days later in Caesarea (Acts 24)

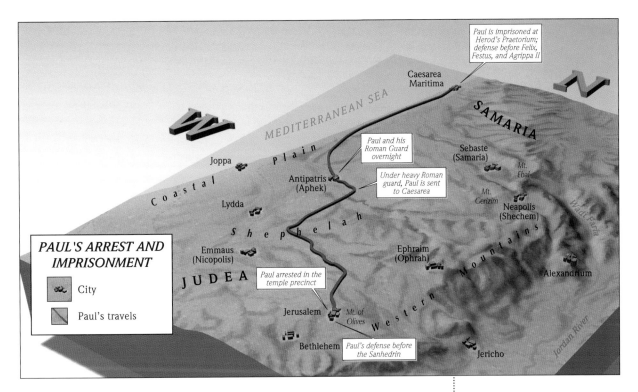

PAUL'S ARREST AND IMPRISONMENT

- 🐌 City
- Paul's travels

Paul is imprisoned at Herod's Praetorium; defense before Felix, Festus, and Agrippa II

Caesarea Maritima

MEDITERRANEAN SEA

SAMARIA

Joppa

Paul and his Roman Guard overnight

Sebaste (Samaria)

Mt. Ebal

Antipatris (Aphek)

Under heavy Roman guard, Paul is sent to Caesarea

Mt. Gerizim

Neapolis (Shechem)

Wadi Fara'a

Lydda

Shephelah

Western Mountains

Ephraim (Ophrah)

Alexandrium

Emmaus (Nicopolis)

JUDEA

Paul arrested in the temple precinct

Jerusalem

Mt. of Olives

Bethlehem

Paul's defense before the Sanhedrin

Jericho

Jordan River

Two Years in Caesarea

The outcome of these defenses was that Felix kept Paul in prison in Caesarea for two years (A.D. 57–59). The governor had enough evidence to release Paul, but he was greedy for a bribe. He kept Paul in custody.

During this time Luke was near Paul (compare Acts 21:17 and 27:1). It is entirely likely that he used these two years to do the research necessary to publish his Gospel (Luke 1:1-4).

When Festus became the next governor of Judea in A.D. 59, he had to decide what to do with the prisoners left over from his predecessor. He invited Paul to make his case, giving Paul two more splendid opportunities to defend his beliefs:

- To the Roman governor, Porcius Festus, shortly after he began ruling (Acts 25)

- To King Herod Agrippa II, who was enjoying a state visit to Caesarea (Acts 26)

The hippodrome at Caesarea Maritima.

Nero Caesar

Not directly named in the New Testament, Nero's reign as emperor (A.D. 54–68) affected a number of the most important events for the foundation of the church. His personal immorality and excesses offended even the most callous Romans. Because his first years were peaceful, Paul was secure in appealing to Nero (A.D. 59) when he believed Roman justice was impossible at the local level. After the great fire of Rome (A.D. 64), however, Nero blamed the Christians and ordered a vicious persecution in the city of Rome. Both Peter and Paul perished under Nero. When the Jewish War broke out in A.D. 66, Nero ordered his best general, Vespasian, to stop the revolt. Nero died by his own hand before the war ended, thus ending the family dynasty that began with Julius Caesar.

Head of Nero, Roman emperor from A.D. 54–68.

When he appeared before Festus, Paul invoked his Roman citizenship right of having his case heard directly by the emperor, by this time Nero Caesar. (During the first few years of his rule, Nero had a reputation for justice.) Thus, when Paul spoke to King Agrippa, he already knew he would be going to Rome. His defense before the king was a brilliant account of his conversion and travels, but Agrippa refused to take Paul seriously.

Paul sailed for Rome late in A.D. 59 for his case to be heard. He was caught in a furious storm on the Mediterranean, which delayed his arrival in Rome until early in A.D. 60. At last he reached the city where he had longed to preach, but under entirely different circumstances than he had supposed when he had written to the Roman church three years earlier.

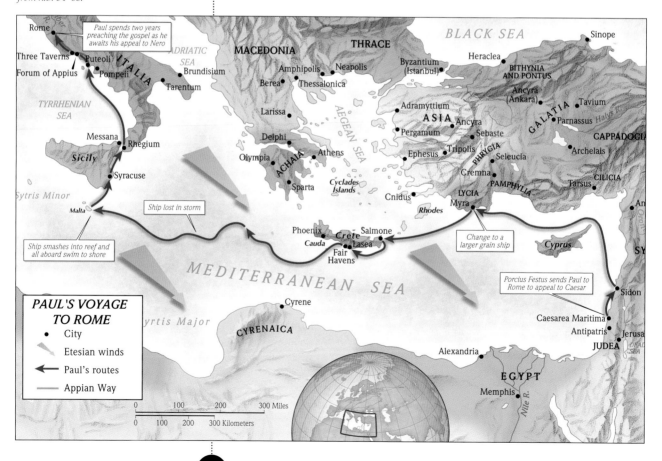

TWO YEARS IN ROME

Paul lived under house arrest for two years (A.D. 60–62), waiting for his case to come before Caesar. Luke had traveled with him and probably published Acts from Rome before Paul's verdict was reached, thus accounting for the abrupt ending for Acts.

When word reached the Gentile churches that Paul was in Rome, his rented house became a beehive of activity. He received many guests and answered a number of questions. One who found him in Rome was Onesimus, a slave who had run away from his master Philemon in Colosse. Onesimus had now become a disciple, and Paul faced the delicate responsibility of sending Onesimus home and of begging Philemon to treat his slave gently. The result was Paul's shortest letter, the Epistle to Philemon.

About the same time Paul received a visit from Epaphras, a leader in the church of Colosse. He reported many good things about the congregation but informed Paul about a dangerous teaching that was making headway in Colosse. Apparently a mixture of Jewish (religious) and Hellenistic (philosophical) beliefs, the "Colossian heresy" was in danger of leading the church away from total commitment to Christ. Tychicus carried Paul's letter to the church. He was also responsible for delivering a letter and the slave Onesimus to Philemon at the same time (Col. 4:7-8). (The church in Colosse met in Philemon's home; see Philem. 2.)

As Paul reflected on the truths he had written to the church in Colosse, he realized that much of what he said would be beneficial to other churches. Shortly after he wrote to the Colossians, therefore, he expanded and rewrote the letter, sending it out to his beloved friends in and around Ephesus. Paul's great letter, now known as the Epistle to the Ephesians, is his finest thinking about the church

Epistle to Philemon

Paul sent this letter, written about A.D. 61, from his first Roman imprisonment to a friend who lived in Colosse. Its focus is to urge Philemon to treat his now-converted slave Onesimus in a gentle manner, as a brother rather than as an inferior. The key word for the book is "brother"; the key verse is Philemon 16. **One-Sentence Summary:** *Everyone who has repented of sin and come to Christ should be welcomed as a brother (or sister), treated gently, and forgiven by other believers.*

Epistle to the Colossians

Paul sent this letter, written about A.D. 61, from his first Roman imprisonment to the Christians in Colosse. It was directed primarily against the false teaching in Colosse now called the "Colossian heresy." Paul especially emphasized the supremacy of Christ in all things. The key word for the book is "supremacy" (or "preeminence"); the key text is Colossians 1:18. **One-Sentence Summary:** *Jesus Christ is supreme Lord of the universe and Head of the church and therefore He is the only One through whom forgiveness is possible, making legal obligations or philosophical studies irrelevant in matters of salvation.*

Epistle to the Ephesians

Paul sent this letter, written about A.D. 61, from his first Roman imprisonment to the Christians in Ephesus (and perhaps in surrounding cities). This epistle is the greatest summary of the doctrine of the church found in the Bible, and it has been more important in subsequent Christian history than any of Paul's letters except Romans. The key word for the book is "unity"; the key text is Ephesians 3:10-11. **One-Sentence Summary:** *In God's eternal plan, His great masterpiece, the church, has now been manifested, in which Christ is united with all the redeemed, whether Jew or Gentile, transforming relationships in this life and leading to a glorious future.*

The Illustrated Guide to Biblical History **243**

Overlooking ruins of Philippi from atop the theater.

Epistle to the Philippians

Paul sent this letter, written about A.D. 62, from his first Roman imprisonment to the Christians in Philippi. He wrote a joyful letter that includes wonderful doctrinal teachings, especially about Jesus Christ and salvation by faith. He also expressed thanks for the Philippians' gift. The key word for the book is "joy"; the key text is Philippians 3:10. **One-Sentence Summary:** *Knowing Jesus Christ is much more joyful and important than anything else because God has exalted Jesus, the crucified Servant, with the name above every name.*

as the greatest expression of God's kingdom. In this letter he demonstrated that God's eternal plan has always been to bring praise to himself forever through two agents: the church and Christ Jesus (Eph. 3:21).

One visitor that came to Paul was especially welcome, Epaphroditus from the congregation in Philippi. He came with a large financial gift that the church had gathered for Paul's use. Much to Paul's dismay, however, Ephaphroditus had fallen so ill that he had nearly died (Phil. 2:25-30). At last, however, he was well again and able to return home. Paul wrote the beautiful Epistle to the Philippians to express his thanks for the gift, his joy over Epaphroditus's recovery, and to give them important instructions. Because he expressed in this letter that he expected to be set free soon, he probably wrote this letter at the end of his two-year imprisonment in Rome.

PAUL'S FINAL TRAVELS AND LAST IMPRISONMENT

The New Testament does not describe Paul's acquittal before Nero (around A.D. 62), but the last letters he wrote show that he traveled to see a number of his churches again. One place that he visited was the island of Crete. Paul had stopped there briefly as a prisoner on the way to Rome at least two years earlier. Now he took his long-term disciple Titus—who had been so effective in helping the Corinthians—and left him in Crete

The palace of Knosos on Crete.

Epistle to Titus

Paul sent this letter, written about A.D. 63, to his close friend Titus from an unknown location. Titus was on the island of Crete to consolidate the work of the Kingdom in a challenging situation. The key word for the book is "doctrine"; the key text is Titus 2:1. **One-Sentence Summary:** *Whatever challenges they face in life and ministry, Christian leaders are to maintain order in the congregation, but only according to sound doctrine.*

as his ambassador. The churches there needed guidance, particularly in returning to good order, and Titus was the right sort of leader to get the job done. Sometime later Paul wrote a brief letter to Titus reminding him of his duties on Crete.

Another place to which Paul returned was Ephesus. This church that had been so successful had now experienced a number of difficulties that required immediate attention. Once again false teachers were challenging the truth of the gospel. He left his closest friend Timothy there to meet the ongoing needs of the situation. Sometime later Paul wrote a letter to Timothy reminding him of his personal responsibility to live a godly life as well as to fulfill his duties to the church in Ephesus.

Domitian Square at Ephesus.

First Epistle to Timothy

Paul sent this letter, written about A.D. 63, to his closest friend Timothy from an unknown location. Timothy was in Ephesus to consolidate the work of the kingdom and to combat the threat of false teachers. The key word for the book is "godliness"; the key text is 1 Timothy 6:11. One-Sentence Summary: *Whatever challenges Christian leaders face in life and ministry, they are to make progress in godliness and help maintain order in congregational life.*

Throughout Paul's travels, Roman authorities treated him more fairly than Jewish authorities had. In none of his letters was there a suggestion that Christians ought to subvert the (pagan) political system. So far, the churches had largely benefited from Rome's commitment to justice. Paul himself had been acquitted when his appeal case reached Nero around 62. In A.D. 64, however, the situation changed drastically, at least for Christians in and around Rome. The great fire that swept through Rome—possibly at Nero's suggestion—needed a scapegoat. Nero viciously arranged to accuse the growing Christian movement for starting the fire. (After all, the Christians would not acknowledge the divine status of the emperor, and they apparently drank the blood and ate the flesh of their God, whom they claimed was a victorious King superior to Caesar.) A number of Christians were arrested. Some were killed. From this time on, the Christian movement was suspect.

St. Paul's outside the wall where Paul was buried.

Mamertinum Prison, the likely place of Paul's second imprisonment in Rome and from where he wrote 2 Timothy.

Paul was arrested again, perhaps in A.D. 64, and taken back to Rome. This time his situation was entirely different. At his preliminary hearing he realized that he would not be released. He would soon be convicted of a crime against the state and face death by beheading. He was probably being held in a dismal prison cell. With only Luke available to him, Paul was lonely for more Christian companionship. He wanted to see his dearest friend Timothy once more before he died. Thus, he wrote one final letter, asking Timothy to come at once. In the letter, however, he expressed his final thoughts, just in case Timothy did not arrive in time. Nobody knows whether Timothy came.

Thus, in the space of about twenty years (A.D. 45 to 65), communities committed to God's Kingdom spread throughout many provinces in the eastern part of the Roman Empire through Paul's ministry. Many more Gentiles than Jews responded to the message of God's Kingdom. Official church policy had established that Paul's law-free gospel was legitimate. Events in Palestine, however, were about to bring the Jewish temple to an end. The Christians would forge ahead as an entity entirely separate from Judaism. The church, separate from the synagogue after a forty-year transition, moved ahead as the single expression of the people of God on earth.

Second Epistle to Timothy

Paul sent this letter, written about A.D. 65, to his closest friend Timothy from a prison in Rome where he was waiting for the trial that would end in his death. Paul wrote his "last will and testament" as a charge for Timothy to carry on with the work of the kingdom. The key word for the book is "committed"; the key text is 2 Timothy 2:2. **One-Sentence Summary:** *Christian leaders are to be unashamed of the gospel and to carry on faithfully with the message about Christ entrusted to them.*

The opening presentation and reading of the Torah (law) for a Bar Mitzvah ceremony at the Western (Wailing) Wall at Jerusalem.

SOLIDARITY OF THE CHRISTIAN MOVEMENT:
THE CHURCH AS SEPARATE FROM THE SYNAGOGUE
(A.D. 65–100)

The thirty-five year period from Paul's death to the end of the first century is not known nearly as well as the earlier period. No historian such as Luke recorded the key events. What we know is essentially limited to the facts that can be gathered from later epistles and the Book of Revelation. Jesus had prophesied the critical event—the destruction of the temple— but the fulfillment is not described in the New Testament.

The final biblical portrait of the spread of God's Kingdom through churches is Revelation 2—3. The seven churches of Asia show the strengths and weaknesses that were exhibited by churches at the end of the first century. The story of the church as separate from the synagogue is told in **HEBREWS, PETER'S EPISTLES, JOHN'S EPISTLES,** and **JUDE.**

EPISTLES OF THE A.D. 60S

The (non-Pauline) epistles written in the A.D. 60s show in one way or another that the Christians were increasingly asked to think of themselves as separate from Judaism. Four epistles belong in this category.

First, the only completely anonymous epistle of the New Testament was written to Jewish followers of Christ undergoing serious suffering for their faith. They may have been subject to the persecution that Nero prompted after the fire in Rome of A.D. 64. When the author learned that these people were considering giving up the church and going back to the synagogue—or, putting it another way, giving up Christianity and returning to Judaism—he wrote a forceful letter arguing for the utter superiority of Christ. He understood that the way of Judaism, expressed by living under the Sinaitic covenant, was meant as a temporary measure. The old system was obsolete; the new covenant had arrived (Heb. 8:13; 12:24).

Second, Simon Peter—the "apostle to the Jews"—wrote a wonderfully argued letter to Gentile churches that he had become acquainted with during his extensive travels. These Christians may also have been subject to the persecution that Nero prompted after the fire in Rome of A.D. 64. In his letter Peter particularly addressed the question of how to suffer as a Christian. In developing this, however, he expressed that the church, not Israel, was now God's chosen people, royal priesthood, and holy nation (1 Pet. 2:9). In other words, language that was appropriate for Israel in Chapters One, Two, and Three of the Kingdom Story was now fully applicable to the church.

Third, in the letter composed shortly before his death, Peter wrote a brief letter to combat false doctrine. In it he reminded the believers that

Epistle to the Hebrews

This anonymous letter was written probably around A.D. 65 to Jewish believers undergoing serious persecution. This teaches the superiority of Jesus Christ and the new covenant and warns against apostasy. Its central message is that Christ is better than the old way. The key word for the book is "better"; the key text is Hebrews 1:1-3. **One-Sentence Summary:** *Jesus Christ, who is better than the angels, Moses, Joshua, and the Hebrew high priests, made a better sacrifice and established a better covenant, ensuring that the old way is obsolete and that faith is the better way to live.*

First Epistle of Peter

Peter sent this letter from Rome, written about A.D. 65, to persecuted churches scattered through- out five Roman provinces. This epistle is an outstanding blend of doctrinal instruction and practical advice for Christians that were suffering persecution. The key word for the book is "hope"; the key text is 1 Peter 4:13. **One-Sentence Summary:** *As Christians grow in understanding their privileges in salvation, their blessings of election, and the theology of suffering, they will live in holiness and humility, waiting for their great future hope of sharing Christ's glory.*

Second Epistle of Peter

Peter sent this letter from Rome, about A.D. 66, shortly before his death. He wrote to Christians dealing with certain false teachings. Its content and style are substantially different from his earlier letter. The key word for the book is "return"; the key text is 2 Peter 1:12. **One-Sentence Summary:** *As Christians grow in understanding, they will be safeguarded from false teachers, especially those who deny the return of Christ and the end of the world as it now exists.*

they must not give up expecting the return of Christ. The day of the Lord that the Old Testament prophets had long foreseen would come at last. The universe will melt and Christians will live forever in a new heaven and new earth (2 Pet. 3:12-13). He made no reference to any Israelite future separate from the church's future.

Epistle of Jude

Jude, the brother of James and half-brother of Jesus, wrote this letter. He probably composed it in the A.D. 60s, and the letter has many parallels to 2 Peter. It warns particularly against false teachers. The key word for the book is "contend"; the key verse is Jude 3. **One-Sentence Summary:** *Christians must defend the faith against false teachings and false teachers, and at the same time they must build up their own faith in Christ.*

Fourth, Jude—a half-brother of Jesus who became a disciple after the resurrection—composed a short letter to Christians living at a time and place that cannot now be definitely determined. His letter has many similarities to 2 Peter, including the warning against false teachers and the hope of Christ's coming (Jude 4,21).

All four of these letters, then, contribute to the growing sense that Christianity as a religion was now entirely separate from Judaism. The event that finalized this, however, was the Jewish War that resulted in the destruction of the temple and the end of animal sacrifices.

THE JEWISH WAR AND THE DESTRUCTION OF THE TEMPLE

As a part of Chapter Three of the Kingdom Story, Daniel 11 had predicted events surrounding the Maccabean revolt in the time of Greek dominion (the "belly of bronze" of Nebuchadnezzar's dream, Dan. 2:39). This prophecy was fulfilled, including the dreadful abomination of desolation (Dan. 11:31), yet the fulfillment was not described in any Old Testament book. Abundant historical documentation (such as 1 Maccabees in the Apocrypha) shows how Daniel's words came true.

Likewise, as part of Chapter Four of the Kingdom Story, Jesus had predicted events surrounding the Jewish War during the time of the Roman dominion (the "legs of iron" of Nebuchadnezzar's dream, Dan. 2:40). This prophecy was just as clearly fulfilled, including the other dreadful abomination of desolation that Daniel had predicted and that Jesus confirmed was still future (Dan. 9:27; Mark 13:14). The fulfillment was not described in any New Testament book, but again, abundant historical documentation (such as Josephus's *The Jewish War*) shows how Jesus' prophecy came true. Not one stone of the temple was left standing after the war of A.D. 70 (Mark 13:2).

Column bases with pedestals from the Temple Mount area in Jerusalem, dating to the period of Herod's Temple (20 B.C. to A.D. 69).

The bitter events of A.D. 66–73 brought untold suffering to thousands of Jews. The temple and sacrificial system were utterly ended, however, as divine confirmation that God no longer accepted animal sacrifices. The Sinaitic covenant had completely run its course. The facts of the story may be told briefly.

The Roman governor appointed over Judea in A.D. 64 was Gessius Florus, a corrupt and cruel man. After he raided the treasury of the temple in Jerusalem, Jewish resentment finally boiled over. The Pharisees joined forces with a rejuvenated Zealot movement in organizing a revolt. Herod Agrippa II—the king before whom Paul had appeared some seven years earlier—urged the Jews to be at peace, but he was rejected. (He stayed loyal to Rome.)

A rebel leader named Menahem led a band of men to capture the Roman military fortress at Masada (near the Dead Sea). Then, using the weapons from Masada, he went on to capture the Roman garrison in Jerusalem next to the temple (the Fortress of Antonia). Menahem, however, was killed in August of A.D. 66. The early successes of the rebels caused revolution fever to spread throughout the countryside. Many expected a complete victory, as in the days of the Maccabean revolt more than two centuries earlier. This seemed to be guaranteed in November A.D. 66, when the Jewish rebels defeated a Roman legion sent from Syria.

Rome's might, however, was a more ominous threat than the Seleucid power that the Maccabeans overcame. Nero Caesar sent his best general, Vespasian, with three legions from Rome to Palestine. They arrived in Galilee early in A.D. 67 and began by subduing Galilee. (Josephus, who became the historian of the war, poorly defended it.) Vespasian's forces began consolidating his gains and approached Jerusalem.

An overview of the storerooms and watchtower at Masada. The storerooms are on the left and the watchtower is on the right. Masada was one of the best known Herodian fortresses.

Roman Emperor Vespasian.

The war was interrupted briefly by Nero's suicide (A.D. 68) and the civil unrest in Rome following his death. Vespasian resumed his military offensive in June of 69 and quickly took all of Palestine except for Jerusalem and three other Jewish fortresses. After he was proclaimed emperor, however, Vespasian himself left Palestine for the city of Rome in order to take control of the Roman Empire.

In the spring of A.D. 70, Vespasian sent his son Titus to crush the Jews. Titus had several Roman legions at his disposal. His troops laid siege to Jerusalem in April; the Jews were able to endure for five months. The last animal sacrifice was offered on the great altar August 6; the temple was burned on August 28. The destruction of the entire city soon followed and was made into heaps of rubble by the end of September. It is reported that after the fires cooled, the Roman troops literally pried apart the stonework of the temple in order to retrieve the gold that had melted between the cracks. This was a grim fulfillment of Jesus' words in Matthew 24:2.

The Romans then proceeded to subdue the three remaining rebel fortresses. The last one was Masada, which finally fell in May of A.D. 73, after its defenders committed mass suicide. The Romans ruled Judea with an iron fist, treating it as an occupied hostile territory.

Roman siege ramp on the western side of Masada. The Romans built the siege ramp in their efforts to overtake the Jews at Masada in A.D. 70.

Although the Jewish population in Judea remained intact, everything about Judaism as a religion changed with the loss of the temple. The Sadducees and the priesthood disappeared as factors in society. The Pharisees came to dominate official Judaism. A new Sanhedrin was established in Jamnia (western Judea), mainly as an institution to study the Scriptures. The synagogues continued to be the institution by which Judaism was sustained. There was no toleration of the Christian movement within Judaism any more. Judaism without the temple and rejecting the message of Jesus had become a religion without its heart and soul.

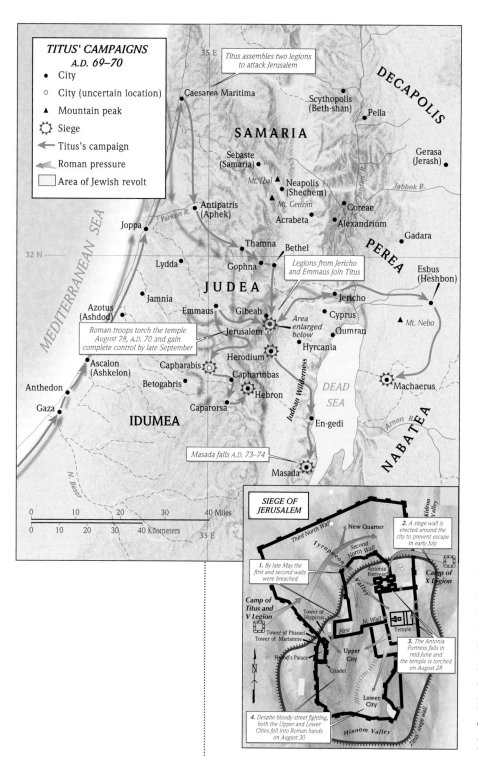

TITUS' CAMPAIGNS
A.D. 69–70

- • City
- ○ City (uncertain location)
- ▲ Mountain peak
- ✺ Siege
- → Titus's campaign
- → Roman pressure
- ☐ Area of Jewish revolt

Titus assembles two legions to attack Jerusalem

DECAPOLIS

Caesarea Maritima

Scythopolis (Beth-shan)

Pella

SAMARIA

Gerasa (Jerash)

Sebaste (Samaria)

Mt. Ebal ▲ Neapolis (Shechem)

▲ Mt. Gerizim

Jabbok R.

Antipatris (Aphek)

Coreae

Acrabeta

Alexandrium

Joppa

Thamna

Bethel

PEREA

Gadara

32 N

Lydda

Gophna

Legions from Jericho and Emmaus join Titus

Esbus (Heshbon)

Jamnia

JUDEA

Jericho

Azotus (Ashdod)

Emmaus

Gibeah

Cyprus

Mt. Nebo ▲

Roman troops torch the temple August 28, A.D. 70 and gain complete control by late September

Jerusalem

Qumran

Area enlarged below

Hyrcania

Ascalon (Ashkelon)

Herodium

Capharabis

Caphartobas

DEAD SEA

Betogabris

Hebron

Judean Wilderness

Anthedon

Caparorsa

En-gedi

Arnon R.

Gaza

IDUMEA

Machaerus

NABATEA

Masada falls A.D. 73–74

Masada

MEDITERRANEAN SEA

Yarkon R.

N. Besor

0 10 20 30 40 Miles
0 10 20 30 40 Kilometers

35 E

SIEGE OF JERUSALEM

Third North Wall

New Quarter

Tyropoeon

Second North Wall

Kidron Valley

2. A siege wall is erected around the city to prevent escape in early July

1. By late May the first and second walls were breached

Antonia Fortress

Camp of X Legion

Camp of Titus and V Legion

Tower of Hippicus

N. Wall

First

Temple

Tower of Phasael
Tower of Mariamne

Herod's Palace

Upper City

Citadel

3. The Antonia Fortress falls in mid-June and the temple is torched on August 28

Lower City

N

4. Despite bloody street fighting, both the Upper and Lower Cities fell into Roman hands on August 30

Hinnom Valley

Titus siege wall

THE PERSPECTIVE OF THE APOSTLE JOHN

Not much is known about the reaction of the Christians to the fall of the temple. On one hand, surely there was great sorrow that, once again, the Roman army had brutally destroyed a native population, particularly the people who had brought forth Jesus Christ. On the other hand, they could not help but interpret these events first, as proof that Jesus was truly a prophet of God, and second, as evidence that God had rejected Judaism as a valid means of approaching Him. The only way to be acceptable with God was through Jesus.

The final composer to contribute to the New Testament was the apostle John. According to Christian tradition, he spent many years in the city of Ephesus helping the church in that city, a generation after Paul had labored there. The challenge for Christians of the A.D. 80s and 90s was no longer how to relate to Judaism, but how to relate to the current challenges of Greco-Roman philosophical speculation. As long as the church had existed within the nest of Judaism, there was no need to debate whether Jesus was a historical figure. There had been plenty of eyewitnesses. The question at that time was "What was the meaning of the death of Jesus, who appeared to have died under God's curse?" (The answer, of course, was that God vindicated Him in the resurrection.)

Now, however, the question became "Did Jesus even come in the flesh?" The church would deal with this devastating challenge (Gnosticism) during the second and third centuries. John's letters show that the church near the end of the first century was dealing with an agenda that had little to do with its former relationship to Judaism. (First John did, of course, note that Jesus is "the Christ" or "the Messiah" who had been prophesied in Scripture of old.)

Individual Christian families needed this same message. Through his travels John had become acquainted with a woman he called only "the elect lady." The apostle encouraged her with a short note similar to the longer epistle he had sent to a larger audience.

John was extensively involved in sending out traveling bands of preachers, and one of the last snapshots we have of Christianity in the New Testament is John's advice to a Christian leader (Gaius) about how to respond to the preachers and to a contrary church leader named Diotrephes. What is interesting in the letter is that the name Jesus does not appear at all; rather He is referred to as "the Name" (3 John 7). The designation by which Jews often referred to God in the Old Testament had been taken over by Christians as a reference to Jesus.

First Epistle of John

This letter was sent to believers that were probably living in or around Ephesus in the Roman province of Asia. They were coming to terms with challenges to their faith in Jesus based on the argument that He did not come "in the flesh." The letter was probably written in the A.D. 80s, about the same time as the Gospel according to John. John was the beloved disciple of Jesus, early leader of the church, and at this time probably the last surviving apostle. The key word for the book is "fellowship"; the key text is 1 John 1:3. **One-Sentence Summary:** *Christians have fellowship with Christ, who is God incarnate, through walking in the light and through living in love, and as a result they are secure in the eternal life that Christ has given them.*

Second Epistle of John

This letter was sent to a Christian woman probably living in or around Ephesus in the Roman province of Asia. The letter was probably written in the A.D. 80s, about the same time as the First Epistle of John. The key idea for the book is "faithful"; the key text is 2 John 8. **One-Sentence Summary:** *Those who are faithful to the "doctrine of Christ" know the Father and the Son and will one day be fully rewarded.*

Third Epistle of John

This letter was sent to a Christian leader named Gaius, probably living in or around Ephesus in the Roman province of Asia. The letter was probably written in the A.D. 80s, about the same time as the First Epistle of John. The key idea for the book is "truth"; the key text is 3 John 8. **One-Sentence Summary:** *Christians are to recognize and to work for the truth of the gospel, and one way they do this is to show hospitality to Christian ministers that are hard at work.*

The stairway leading up to the Temple of Domitian (background, left) as viewed through the reconstructed arch (foreground) of the Fountain of Pollio at Ephesus.

The last portrait of the church told in Chapter Five of the Kingdom Story is the description of seven congregations of Asia (Rev. 2—3). Perhaps a decade had passed since John had written his three epistles. He was now exiled on the tiny island of Patmos out in the Aegean Sea off the coast of Ephesus.

Although the primary focus of the visions he received belong to Chapter Six of the Kingdom Story, the messages addressed to the seven struggling, persecuted churches show these Christians as having the same kinds of strengths and weaknesses that Christians down through the ages have shared. They were an entity separate from a hostile Judaism, now "the synagogue of Satan" (Rev. 2:9; 3:9). Further, they were a separate entity from a hostile Roman Empire, now "the throne of Satan" (Rev. 2:13).

Each of the seven messages ended on a threefold note. First, the Holy Spirit is the one who speaks to Christ's churches—a reminder that Chapter Five may rightly be called "the era of the Spirit." Second, believers in churches are reminded of the need to be "overcomers" throughout this life. Finally, the victorious Jesus promises all His overcoming people the great ultimate reward of sharing in His victory. This, then, is the note on which Chapter Five ends.

CHRISTIAN HISTORY:
NINETEEN CENTURIES OF KINGDOM EXPANSION
(A.D. 100–?)

The details of the Kingdom Story for nineteen centuries (second through the twentieth centuries) are told not by Scripture but by church historians. The Book of Acts and the Epistle to the Hebrews, however, demonstrate that in God's kingdom purposes for the current age both the Jewish temple and Israel as a national entity have been rendered obsolete. Thus the destruction of the temple and Jerusalem in A.D. 70 by the Romans serves as important historical evidence that the former way of (national, ethnic) Israel has been supplanted by the new way of (inter-national, multiethnic) Christianity.

Although the current book is not designed to tell the Kingdom Story after the conclusion of the New Testament, it is generally understood that Christian history may be organized into the following eras:

- The era of the classic church (A.D. 100–600)

- The era of medieval catholicism (A.D. 600–1500)

- The era of the Reformation (A.D. 1500–1750)

- The era of modern (Enlightenment based) Christianity (A.D. 1750–1980)

- The era (informed by postmodernism) currently emerging (A.D. 1980–?)

Clay tile has LXF symbol of the 10th Legion of Titus. Tile was excavated west of the temple at Jerusalem.

Overview of Patmos.

CONCLUSION

In the space of about sixty years, God fully established the church as His means of spreading God's kingdom. The biblical record of this period, told in the Book of Acts and the epistles, emphasized the following as Chapter Five of the Kingdom Story.

1. For about fifteen years after its birth on the day of Pentecost, the church existed as a part of Judaism. Under Simon Peter's leadership, however, the Holy Spirit was given successively to Jews, Samaritans, and Gentiles. The church in Antioch became the first congregation successfully to reach Gentiles (A.D. 30–45).

2. Through the traveling and letter-writing efforts of Paul the apostle, the message of the kingdom of God rapidly spread to Gentiles. The Jerusalem Council determined that the good news was a gospel of grace apart from law or works. Although the church became a Gentile-majority entity during this time, Paul labored to preserve the Jew-Gentile unity of the kingdom people through his writings (especially Ephesians) and through his collection for the poor Christians of Jerusalem. This period lasted about twenty years (A.D. 46–65).

3. The destruction of the temple in A.D. 70 in fulfillment of Jesus' prophecy left the church no choice but to believe that God had rejected temple and animal sacrifice as a way to approach Him. Israel as a nation was no more. During the last decades of the first century, the church was entirely separate from Judaism, setting the stage for the centuries of kingdom growth that is a part of Christian history (A.D. 66–100).

The grand summary of the Bible is, *The Lord God through His Christ is graciously building a kingdom of redeemed people for their joy and for His own glory.* We have seen now that God established the church as His instrument for spreading the message of the kingdom. In the next (and final) chapter in the Kingdom Story, God will succeed in His purpose of consummating redemption and confirming His eternal kingdom.

REFLECTIVE QUESTIONS

1. What was really different about the "era of the Spirit" that began on Pentecost?

2. Summarize the role that Simon Peter had in the years immediately following Pentecost.

3. How were the first members of the mother church in Jerusalem like the other Jews of the city? How were they different?

4. Why did Stephen, a Hellenistic Jewish Christian, realize the worldwide implications of the gospel more quickly than the apostles did?

5. Was the experience of Saul on the Damascus Road a conversion (change to a different religion) or a clarification of his old religion? Why do you say so?

6. What made the church at Antioch different from the church in Jerusalem? Which congregation would you prefer to be a part of? Why?

7. Paul's enduring ministry was twofold: church planting and letter writing. What factors account for his success at each of these?

8. What difference did the Jerusalem Council make to the future of Christianity (Acts 15)?

9. The two cities in which Paul lived the longest as a church planter were Corinth and Ephesus. Contrast his ministry in these cities.

10. Much more is known about Paul's ministry than any other early Christian leader. How does this impact our understanding of the Kingdom Story?

11. The early church separated far from Judaism. Was this a good thing or an unnecessary detour? Why do you say so?

12. The Jewish War of A.D. 66–73 was pivotal for first-century Christians, yet it is not reported in the Bible. Why?

13. If Hebrews was originally written for Jewish Christians, what makes its message so important for Gentile Christians?

14. Why is it important to remember that the Kingdom Story includes nineteen centuries of Christian history?

15. If you could choose to live in a Christian age of the past, which would you choose: the era of the classic church (A.D. 100–600); the era of medieval catholicism (A.D. 600–1500); or the era of the Reformation (A.D. 1500–1750)? Why?

16. Do you think it likely that the age of the Spirit (the current church age) will last through the twenty-first century? Why or why not?

17. How does God's redemption of His people work itself out in Chapter Five of the Kingdom Story?

18. What evidences of God's glory are evident in Chapter Five of the Kingdom Story?

19. What evidences of joy in the lives of God's redeemed people do you see in Chapter Five of the Kingdom Story?

---

[1] Saul's conversion probably happened in A.D. 33. In Galatians 2:1 he wrote of his second post-conversion trip to Jerusalem as occurring fourteen years after he was converted. This is most likely a reference to the famine-relief visit in which he and Titus went to Jerusalem with money from the Antioch church, almost certainly occurring in A.D. 46 (Acts 11:27-30).

[2] The apostle's Hebrew name was "Saul," in honor of first Israelite monarch, also from the tribe of Benjamin. In Gentile settings he used the Greek name "Paul."

[3] Secular Roman records indicate that Gallio became proconsul of Achaia in the spring or summer of A.D. 52. This date, then, becomes one of the fixed points of reference for a chronology of Paul's ministry. Ruins of the judgment seat of Corinth, where Paul appeared before Gallio, are still visible.

[4] After the death of King Herod Agrippa I in A.D. 44, Judea had once again become a province ruled by a Roman governor. By the time of Paul's arrest, however, Herod's young son, Herod Agrippa II, was ruling as a king over a section of northern Palestine. This is the one Paul later referred to as "King Agrippa."

God Consummates His Eternal Kingdom

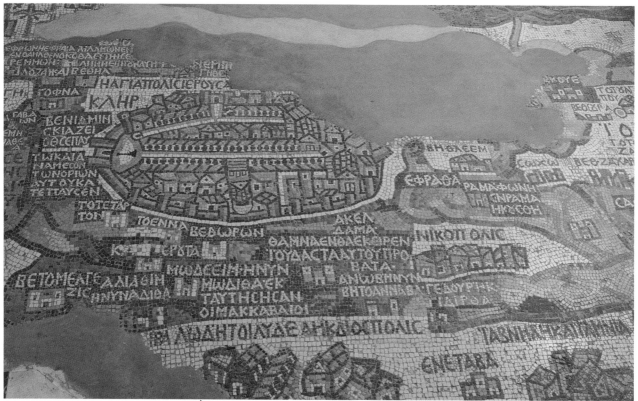

Oldest known mosaic map of Jerusalem at the Church at Madeba. The mosaic dates from the 6th century A.D.

Redemption Completed

(Revelation and Other Scriptures)

In Chapter Six, God's plan to build an everlasting kingdom of redeemed people through His Christ for their joy and for His own glory is fully realized at last. Although Bible students often disagree about how to interpret some details of this chapter, the main points are clear. There will be violent hostility against God's people in the end times. Yet God will prevail through the personal, bodily, glorious return of Jesus. When He returns, the world's kingdoms will become the kingdom of Christ forever under His visible rule. Chapter Six carries the plot of the Kingdom Story from the present age to the Day of the Lord and on through the final judgment of all mankind.

TIMELINE 14
BASIC CHRONOLOGY FOR "CHAPTER 6: GOD CONSUMMATES HIS ETERNAL KINGDOM"

tribulation saints sealed	harvest of saints; "rapture" Christ as Bridegroom	winepress of wrath Christ as General	last judgment Christ as Judge
SEALS broken, church history *more than 19 centuries*	TRUMPETS blown; tribulation; antichrist; Babylon *"time, times, half a time;"* *"42 months"*	BOWLS poured; Day of the Lord *"one hour"*	martyrs rewarded *"1000 years"*	new creation *eternity*

Time in quotation marks may be figurative rather than literal. The "second coming of Christ" includes everything from the harvest of saints (Christ as Bridegroom) through the wrath of God (Christ as General) and perhaps even on through the last judgment (Christ as Judge).

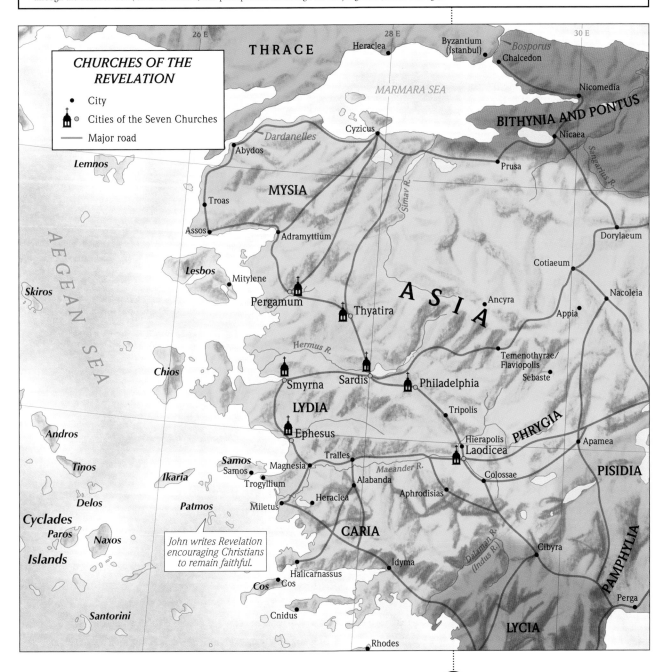

CHURCHES OF THE REVELATION

- • City
- • Cities of the Seven Churches
- — Major road

THRACE

MARMARA SEA

Bosporus

Heraclea

Byzantium (Istanbul)

Chalcedon

Nicomedia

BITHYNIA AND PONTUS

Dardanelles

Cyzicus

Abydos

Nicaea

Lemnos

Prusa

Sangarius R.

MYSIA

Simav R.

Troas

Dorylaeum

Assos

Adramyttium

Cotiaeum

AEGEAN

Lesbos

Mitylene

A S I A

Ancyra

Nacoleia

Pergamum

Appia

Skiros

Thyatira

SEA

Hermus R.

Temenothyrae/
Flaviopolis

Chios

Sardis

Philadelphia

Sebaste

Smyrna

Tripolis

LYDIA

PHRYGIA

Andros

Ephesus

Hierapolis

Apamea

Tinos

Samos

Tralles

Laodicea

PISIDIA

Ikaria

Samos

Magnesia

Maeander R.

Colossae

Delos

Trogyllium

Alabanda

Aphrodisias

Cyclades

Heraclea

Dalaman R.
(Indus R.)

Paros

Patmos

Miletus

CARIA

Cibyra

Naxos

Islands

John writes Revelation encouraging Christians to remain faithful.

Idyma

PAMPHYLIA

Halicarnassus

Cos

Cos

LYCIA

Perga

Santorini

Cnidus

Rhodes

The Book of Revelation

This book self-consciously calls itself a prophecy at both its beginning and its end (1:3; 22:18-19) and is the only New Testament book that is mainly prophetic. From the earliest days its author, John, was believed to be the apostle of Jesus. The book was written in response to visions that John received and was commanded to write down. The first readers were persecuted, struggling Christians in seven cities in the Roman province of Asia, probably about A.D. 95. The key word for the book is "prophecy"; the key text is Revelation 1:7. **One-Sentence Summary:** *Jesus the Lord of history will return to earth, destroy all evil and all opposition to Him, and bring the kingdom of God to its glorious culmination.*

As the Introduction noted, the grand summary of the Bible is, *The Lord God through His Christ is graciously building a kingdom of redeemed people for their joy and for His own glory.* Chapter Six in the Kingdom Story is the last chapter. When its tale has been told, heaven and earth as we know it will be renewed. Christ will rule forever and ever, and the glory of God and the joy of the redeemed will extend throughout eternity.

THE LAMB, THE CHURCHES, AND THE MARTYRS: PREVIEW OF THE LAST DAYS ("SEALS")

This piece of ivory, decorated with a shepherd and his flute with sheep around him, comes from Khirbet el-Karmel.

As we saw in Chapter Five, God established the church to be the agency through which the kingdom of God expands during the present era. This is the time in which Christ's Great Commission actively functions. The story of Christian history is not prophesied in any detail in Scripture. On the other hand, **REVELATION 1—6** describes the kinds of things that, indeed, have happened and will continue to occur in the period between the end of the first century and the arrival of the Day of the Lord. In a sense, these Bible chapters serve as a precursor of the last days because they recognize that in fact the last times have begun already.

In a number of New Testament passages, the author recognizes that the "last day" or "last hour" or "last time" arrived with Chapter Four of the Kingdom Story—the first coming of Christ and the completion of His mission. (See Acts 2:16-17; 2 Tim. 3:1; James 5:3; 1 Pet. 1:20; 2 Pet. 3:3; Jude 18; above all, see Heb. 1:2; 1 John 2:18.) Thus, the entire period of Christianity is already the "last times." John's visions on the island of Patmos not only described the distant future, but also things that were present (Rev. 1:9,19).

THE EXALTED LORD

The Gospels nowhere gave any hint of the physical appearance of Jesus. Yet Revelation 1 and 5 offer two symbolic portraits of Jesus as the exalted Lord of glory. He appeared to John on Patmos as a glorious figure so dazzling that the only proper response was worship (Rev. 1:16-17). Further, He appeared in heaven as the slaughtered Lamb seated on heaven's throne and worthy to unleash judgment on sin and evil (Rev. 5:6-11).

Christian history shows many challenges to the growth of the kingdom and the success of the church in carrying out its Great Commission. Yet Christians who have read Revelation 1—6 understand that Jesus Christ, the exalted Lord, is sovereign over all the affairs of people and nations. None can doubt that He has planned both the course of His church and the course of world affairs down through the ages.

THE STRUGGLING CHURCHES

The famous seven churches of Asia were the first to receive and read the written contents of the Book of Revelation (Rev. 1:11). They were under attack by the Babylon of their day, Rome. Under Domitian, who wanted to be worshiped as God, many martyrs had been made. Rome, the city of seven hills, was a horrible threat that appeared likely to snuff out the churches (Rev. 17:9).

Marketplace of Rome.

Large peristyle with Stadium of Domitian in background.

Rome

The Italian peninsula, home to Rome, had been a growing civilization for several centuries before Jesus' birth. The Romans rose to superpower status during the first century B.C. and during that time moved from a Republic (led by the Senate) to an Empire (ruled by Caesar). The first Roman emperor was Augustus, during whose rule Jesus was born. Rome—in the person of Domitian, emperor from A.D. 81 to 96—was the sixth oppressor kingdom bent on destroying the people of God (after Egypt, Assyria, Babylonia, Persia, and Greece). This period is alluded to prophetically in Daniel 11 as well as in the Book of Revelation.

To each congregation, the exalted Lord addressed a specific word (Rev. 2—3). Just as every New Testament epistle had an *immediate* local message and an *ongoing* universal message, so it is with the short letters addressed to the churches of Asia.

The essence of these letters is as follows:[1]

• To Ephesus: "Love one another greatly."

• To Smyrna: "Be steadfast in persecution."

- To Pergamum: "Hold to the truth."
- To Thyatira: "Be morally pure."
- To Sardis: "Return to spiritual life."
- To Philadelphia: "Be sure of the kingdom."
- To Laodicea: "Repent of self-sufficiency."

As the previous chapter of the present book noted, the messages addressed to these seven struggling, persecuted churches show that first-century churches had the same strengths and weaknesses that churches down through the ages have shared. This last glimpse of congregational life in the Bible is at once a comfort and a challenge.

Church

The primary manifestation of God's kingdom since the day of Pentecost has been local assemblies of Jesus' followers— "churches." The seven churches of Revelation 2—3 demonstrate both Christ's care for His churches and the churches' responsibility to respond to His guidance. A number of New Testament texts use such images as body of Christ to refer to the church in its global aspect, enduring throughout time (and eternity). Revelation 19:7 speaks of the church as the bride of the Lamb (Christ), and the last two chapters of Revelation describe the New Jerusalem—God's glorified people—as His everlasting treasure (Eph. 3:21).

The colonnaded forum in Smyrna dates from the first centuries B.C. and A.D.

(Above) Columns from the Temple of Trajan at ancient Peregamum. The temple was built in the 2nd century A.D. to honor the emperor Trajan.

(Below) Modern Turkish boys sitting amidst the ruins of Philadelphia of the Revelation.

The risen Christ who walks among His churches (Rev. 1:13,20; 2:1) charged five of these seven historical congregations with the need to repent of specific sins. Although Christ is Lord of history and Lord of His churches, His people must continue their fight against unrighteous behavior until He returns. Christ's last appeal to the seventh church is that they invite Him in for fellowship (Rev. 3:20).

House in ancient Laodicea.

THE "SEALS" BROKEN

The Book of Revelation is famous because of the frequency with which the number seven occurs. One of the most important is the seven seals that appeared on the judgment scroll that the Lamb received (Rev. 5:7).

Because these seals were on the outside edge of the scroll, the scroll could not be opened until all seven seals were broken. Thus, the events described in Revelation 6—the breaking of the seals—appear to be precursors of the last days (that is, belonging to church history) rather than to the final Day of the Lord sequence that ends in Christ's return.

The "Four Horsemen of the Apocalypse" revealed when the first four seals were broken have ridden throughout the centuries since Revelation was composed (Conquest, War, Famine, and Death, Rev. 6:1-8). These surely indicate that military, political, and economic concerns are the broad context within which Christian history must be understood.

Stone seal from the Hellenistic period: 330–30 B.C.

THE WAITING MARTYRS

The fifth seal shows that Christianity is fundamentally the story that many martyrs for Christ are being made throughout the years (Rev. 6:9-12). From the first Christian martyr (Stephen) to the first murdered apostle (James) and on to the martyr from the church in Pergamum (Antipas), the story of God's people has been about those who are faithful until death (Acts 7:59-60; 12:2; Rev. 2:13).

The emphasis on martyrs in the early chapters of Revelation serves as good preparation for the later chapters, in which many more martyrs are described.

Rider on horse in glass from Syria-Palestine. Dates to the 1st century A.D.

Angels

Angels appear in the Bible from Genesis to Revelation, although they are more prominent in Revelation than any other book. They are supernatural beings that are the opposite of the fallen angels. They exhibit the traits of personality such as intellect and will. Angels are God's servants, but one of their chief functions is to bring God's messages to selected individuals. (The Greek word "angel" meant "messenger.") There are several categories of supernatural beings who serve God, such as "cherubs," "seraphs," "archangels," and "living creatures." The only holy angels named in the Bible are Gabriel and Michael.

One striking feature is that a predetermined number of martyrs, known only to God, must be made before the end of all things (Rev. 6:11). (This is parallel to another predetermined number mentioned by Paul—the full number of Gentile converts to be made before the end of all things, Rom. 11:25.)

Thus, these chapters at the opening of Revelation, heralding the last days, suggest that Christian history is to be understood as an ongoing saga of churches both weak and strong. The exalted Lord Jesus is seated on heaven's throne, yet present among His churches. He holds the scroll of future judgment, yet has planned for many martyrs to be made during the present era.

SATANIC RAGE AGAINST GOD AND GOD'S PEOPLE: GREAT TRIBULATION ("TRUMPETS")

Throughout the Kingdom Story wicked rulers often rose to oppose God and the people of God. In Chapter One the wicked ruler was pharaoh, king of Egypt. In Chapter Two of the Kingdom Story, Nebuchadnezzar, the king of Babylon, succeeded in destroying Jerusalem. In Chapter Three Daniel predicted the coming of Antiochus Epiphanes, whose abomination of desolation brought about the victory of the Maccabees. Each of these evil men, of course, was acting as the agent of the devil, vainly attempting to thwart God's Kingdom Story.

Thus, it is not surprising to find that this pattern will be repeated and intensified at the time of the Day of the Lord. **REVELATION 7—14** depicts one final evil kingdom that will arise to oppose God's people. This kingdom will be under a particularly wicked ruler that will be directly empowered by the devil himself. This is described by using another sequence of seven—the angelic blowing of judgment trumpets.

THE ANTICHRIST

Other biblical texts besides Revelation speak of one last horrible ruler to rise up against God. Before noting the descriptions in Revelation, we should note his presence in other texts.

IN THE OLD TESTAMENT

Some students of Scripture have found antichrist's footprints in the Book of Daniel. Daniel referred to three powerful figures that may be direct prophecies of the last opponent of God's people. These are the little horn of Daniel 7:8-28, the anointed one that will come in Daniel 9:25-27, and the "king" of Daniel 11:36-46. Much of what is predicted about these figures was fulfilled by the ancient wars between the Ptolomies and the Seleucids, in particular the evil Seleucid king Antiochus Epiphanes. Yet Daniel's prophecies were not precisely fulfilled, leaving some to believe they refer to the final antichrist. Even if these figures are only a pattern of the final antichrist, they show the viciousness with which the final military-political-religious opponent of God will strike out.

Tetradrachm of Antiochus IV Epiphanes. Obverse: Head of Antiochus IV.

IN SECOND THESSALONIANS

The Christians in Thessalonica were upset because they thought that the Day of the Lord was already upon them (2 Thess. 2:2). Paul told them that this day was not yet present, but that the time would finally come for the revelation of a "lawless one." Paul focused more on this one's satanic inspiration than his military might. He will deceive people so that they perish, using the power of Satan to do miracles (2 Thess. 2:9-10). He will be overthown personally by the Lord Jesus, destroyed by the glory of Christ's return (2 Thess. 2:8).

The most puzzling element of Paul's portrait is that this monster will set himself up in God's temple (2 Thess. 2:4). Many Bible students have argued that this refers to a literal (future) Jewish temple in Jerusalem. Others have thought that "God's temple" refers to the church, which Paul described elsewhere as a holy temple (Eph. 2:21). According to this perspective, antichrist will work his devilry within Christianity. A third view is that antichirst will assault the very heavenly glory of God, attempting to take over God's heavenly temple. No Bible student can be absolutely certain about the right interpretation of this. The future will make it clear.

IN FIRST AND SECOND JOHN

Only four verses in the entire Bible use the term "antichrist" (1 John 2:18,22; 4:3; 2 John 7). The Apostle John expected that antichrist would come in the last hour (1 John 2:18, "anti" = "in place of"; "christ" = "anointed one"; thus, one who offers himself in place of the true Christ).

Antichrist

The word "antichrist" means either an enemy of Christ or one who usurps Christ's name and rights. Jesus warned against the false Christs and the false prophets that would lead astray, if possible, even the elect (Matt. 24:24; Mark 13:22). The beast of Revelation 17:8 will claim worship and make war on God's people. For a limited period he will rule the earth but will finally be destroyed by the Lord in battle. With his defeat the age-long contest between good and evil will come to its final conclusion.

Yet the last hour in some sense was already upon John and his readers.

These verses show that the work of antichrist is to stamp out the truth about Jesus, rejecting that He is the Messiah or that He came as God in the flesh. Although John clearly expected a single, dangerous antichrist figure, his main concern was to warn that many antichrists were already present (1 John 2:18). He spoke of the spirit of antichrist already at work (1 John 4:1-3). Thus, throughout Christian history evil men have been identified as the antichrist (Nero, Mohammed, popes, Hitler), yet the best one can say is that such persons have come with the spirit of antichrist.

The Beast from the Sea

In Revelation 13 a monstrous figure arises from the sea. He is the very embodiment of evil, called forth by the dragon (Satan). Some Bible students have seen this figure as symbolic of all political opposition against God and His people throughout the ages. On the other hand, a number of features suggest that he is the final great enemy.

- Empowered by Satan (the dragon) as a conqueror (13:4)

- Defiance of God and His people for a specific time period (13:5-6)

- Receiving the worship of all the world's peoples (13:8)

- Deception of all the world's peoples (13:14)

- Served by a powerful beast from the earth (13:11-5)

The power of this beast will become so great that he will force his followers to accept his mark, the infamous 666, as a sign of loyalty and economic control (Rev. 13:18). In the first century brands were sometimes burned on slaves as a mark of ownership and servitude, but the mystery of 666 has continued to be a puzzle. When ancient languages did not have a system of digits for numbers, they substituted letters, for example, A = 1; B = 2; C = 3. Thus the numerical value of a word could be counted by adding up the value of the letters in the name. The Hebrew total for "Nero Caesar" is 666; so is the Latin total for "Latin Empire." (The Greek total for "Jesus" is 888.) Nobody has yet solved this mystery, but when the time comes, its meaning will be clear.

Tile (glazed brickwork) dragon from early 6th century Babylon. Tile reliefs including this one repeated at regular intervals along the Ishtar Gate and its walls which adjoined Procession Street, the main highway to the city.

The beast from the sea (antichrist, who in parody of Jesus will apparently have a kind of death and resurrection, Rev. 13:3-4) and the beast from the earth (a false prophet, Rev. 13:11-15) are agents of the dragon (Satan or the devil, Rev. 12:17). These three form a vile "unholy trinity."

GREAT TRIBULATION

Scripture abounds with references that God's plan for His people includes suffering and distress (see John 16:33; Acts 14:22; Rom. 5:3; 2 Cor. 4:17; Rev. 2:10). Tribulation is a general term that refers to pressure on God's people brought by a hostile world. Revelation 7:14 mentions a large multitude of God's people that come out of *great* tribulation. This seems to refer directly to Jesus' teaching about a horrible time of *great* tribulation more severe than anything else in history, from which hardly anyone will survive (Matt. 24:21). These are the only specific biblical uses of the phrase "great tribulation" in an end-time sense. (See Acts 7:11 and Rev. 2:22 for two other unrelated instances of the phrase.)

INTENSE SUFFERING

Daniel's prophecy identified a coming terrible time of trouble—whether near to him or in the distant future is debated—using the phrase "time, times, and half a time" (Dan. 7:25; 12:7). Many Bible students agree that he meant three and a half years. If 30 days are allowed for a month, this totals 1260 days or 42 months (Rev. 11:3; 12:6,14; 13:5). John may have been using these same numbers as a conventional figure of speech to refer to the *intense but limited time of suffering* that will come at the end. He may not have meant to specify an exact number of days, any more than the figure of speech "seven-year itch" does. (Jesus may have referred similarly to the famine of Elijah's time as three and a half years, even though the Old Testament never actually stated the length of this time of suffering, Luke 4:25.)

Of course, it is possible that the time references in Revelation are meant to be precisely literal, but until they are fulfilled, no one should insist that God has revealed the exact length of the great tribulation in advance. In His only specific reference to this great tribulation, Jesus mentioned that this time of suffering would in fact be cut short, surely a warning against trying to mark its duration on a calendar (Matt. 24:22).

THE TRUMPETS BLOWN

The intensity of this period of suffering is described in Revelation 8—9 under the symbol of blowing the first six of God's judgment trumpets. Although none can know exactly what is predicted, the language alone is terrifying:

• first trumpet: a third of earth's surface vegetation destroyed (8:7)

• second trumpet: a third of earth's oceans destroyed or poisoned (8:8-9)

A 9th century B.C. shofar. This trumpet was made of conch.

- third trumpet: a third of earth's fresh water destroyed or poisoned (8:10-11)
- fourth trumpet: a third of the sky destroyed or darkened (8:12)
- fifth trumpet: a painful five-month plague of locustlike demons (9:1-12)
- sixth trumpet: a third of human beings killed by horselike demons (9:13-21)

GOD'S PEOPLE: PRESENT OR ALREADY "RAPTURED"?

One of the most emotionally charged of all the parts of the Kingdom Story is the ongoing debate concerning the time of the event Paul described in 1 Thessalonians 4:16-17. He plainly stated that a group of believers in Christ would be alive at His coming. They will be caught up alive to meet Him. (The term rapture is taken from the Latin for "caught up.") The interpretive question for so many is whether the event Paul described is a kind of secret rapture of the church before the glorious return of Christ.

Certainly some believers will be present on earth during this time of great tribulation. The famous sealing of 144,000 from Israel is noted in Revelation 7:1-8, the divine counterpart to the "666" mark on the beast's people. Further, John saw a multitude of saints who had been victims (and martyrs) of the great tribulation (7:9-17). Even more striking, the sealed saints are spared the horrible pains of the locust plague (9:4).

Direct evidence in Revelation that the church will be raptured before the great tribulation is difficult to find. Some Bible students find it in Christ's promise to the church of Philadelphia that it will be kept out of the coming worldwide hour of trial (Rev. 3:10). This, however, was a promise to members of a specific historical congregation.

Others find it in Christ's personal command to John to come up to heaven before the tribulation is announced (Rev. 4:1). In this verse, however, the command is singular—referring to John alone—rather than plural, which could include others.

On the other hand, many note the presence of the church during the tribulation in such texts as Revelation 12:17. Here, the objects of satanic wrath during the "time, times, and half a time" are said to be those who obey God's commandments and hold to the testimony of Jesus. In other Revelation passages, this language is applied to members of the church, for example, Rev. 6:9; 12:11; 20:4.

Thus, as far as the Book of Revelation itself is concerned, there is no direct evidence that removes Christians (the church) from the time of satanic wrath against God and God's people described as the great tribulation. While this may indeed occur, those who affirm it base their beliefs on something other than the direct teaching of Revelation (or other New Testament texts).

GOD'S VENGEANCE AGAINST SATAN AND ALL EVIL: THE DAY OF THE LORD ("BOWLS")

As we have seen, Revelation 7—14 tells about how the wrath of the devil and of evil men will wreak havoc on God's people during the days of the "seven trumpets." At last the appointed time for God's wrath has come. **REVELATION 15—18** describes the holy justice of God erupting on behalf of His kingdom people, at long last fulfilling the many biblical prophecies about the Day of the Lord.

THE DAY OF THE LORD AS DIVINE WRATH

IN THE OLD TESTAMENT

Many of the prophets who warned God's ancient people living in Israel or Judah foresaw the coming of the Day of the Lord. It would be a decisive intervention of God in which the enemies of God would receive His blazing judgment and His people would be delivered. Sometimes this Day of the Lord—alternately called "that day"—referred to an intermediate intervention of God, such as divine wrath poured out on Egypt through the Babylonians (see Jer. 46:10).

Often, however, the references point beyond the times of the prophets to the final end time of divine vengeance on God's enemies. It will ultimately bring rest and relief to God's people. Found only in the

Day of the LORD

Old Testament prophets first used "Day of the LORD" to describe a coming time of the Lord's judgment and triumph over the enemies of His people. The New Testament use of the phrase shows that its final fulfillment is yet future. As 2 Corinthians 1:14 shows, the "Lord" of this day is the Lord Jesus. The people whom God will judge are the enemies of Christians (2 Thess. 1:6—2:2). The great tribulation in Revelation is described as evil coming against God's people, while the "great day of God" is the outpouring of God's wrath against both human and supernatural evil (Rev. 16:14). The events surrounding the wrath of God culminate in the second coming of Christ.

prophetic books, the phrase "the Day of the Lord" may be traced in the following Old Testament books:

- Isaiah (13:6,9)
- Ezekiel (13:5; 30:3)
- Joel (1:15; 2:1,11; 2:31; 3:14)
- Amos (5:18,20)

- Obadiah (15)
- Zephaniah (1:7,14)
- Zechariah 14:1
- Malachi (4:5)

Modern Tekoa. Tekoa was the home of the Old Testament Prophet Amos.

IN THE NEW TESTAMENT

The two New Testament apostles that used the specific phrase "the Day of the Lord" were Peter (Acts 2:20; 2 Pet. 3:10) and Paul (1 Cor. 5:5; 2 Cor. 1:14; 1 Thess. 5:2; 2 Thess. 2:2). They clearly took the Old Testament term and applied it to the end time outpouring of wrath and judgment connected with the return of Christ. Parallel phrases are "that day" (Matt. 7:12; 2 Tim. 4:8) and "day of God" (2 Pet. 3:12).

THE DAY OF GOD ALMIGHTY IN REVELATION

Throughout the history of human sin, divine wrath has always been revealed (Rom. 1:18) This is as much an attribute of God as is His righteousness or love. In Revelation 1—14 His full wrath was announced but not yet unleashed (6:16-17; 11:18; 14:10). When the contents of the seven bowls of wrath are poured out in Revelation, His wrath will be fully expressed—and exhausted—on evil (15:1). This culminates in the great day of God's wrath against all the world's kings (16:14).

This outpouring of wrath appears to overcome the world as quickly as the waters of a ruptured dam flood everything downstream. Four times in Revelation 18 the wrath of God on the harlot city Babylon is described as taking place in "one hour" or "one day" (Rev. 18:8,10,17,19).

DIVINE WRATH ON THE HARLOT CITY

So far in previous parts of the Kingdom Story, six evil kingdoms tried without success to eliminate God's kingdom and God's people (Rev. 17:10). The triumph of God's plan throughout time has been that God worked so that His people overcame these six horrible threats:

- Egypt, at the time of Moses and the exodus, 1446 B.C. (Exod. 14)

- Assyria, at the time the Northern Kingdom of Israel fell, 722 B.C. (2 Kings 17)

- Babylon, at the time the Southern Kingdom of Judah fell, 586 B.C. (2 Kings 25)

- Persia, at the time of Esther and the assault of Haman, 474 B.C. (Esther 9)

- Greece, at the time of Antiochus Epiphanes, 168 B.C. (Daniel 11)

- Rome, at the time Revelation was written, A.D. 95 (Revelation 6)

Each of these empires ultimately fell under divine judgment and is no more. On the Day of the Lord, wrath will fall on the seventh kingdom (the harlot city Babylon).

Wrath of God

The wrath of God is His display of righteous anger because His holiness has been insulted by sin. Believers in Christ have been spared the wrath of God because God's wrath fell on His Son at the cross (Rom. 5:9; 1 Thess. 5:9). In the present age, God's wrath against sin is not fully displayed in order that people may repent. In the New Testament, however, the consistent teaching is that at the end of the age, God's wrath will be fully expressed against evil (Rom. 2:5; 9:22; 1 Thess. 2:16; Rev. 16:19).

Murals connected with the tomb of Darius, a Persian king.

BABYLON, THE HARLOT CITY

In the end times—when Chapter Six of the Kingdom Story at last unfolds—the seventh and worst kingdom of all will arise (Rev. 17:10). One more time an evil kingdom will attempt to destroy God's people from the earth. The gruesome image in Revelation for this evil kingdom is the harlot city Babylon (Rev. 17). Just as the ancient city of Babylon represented everything wicked, and just as first-century Christians used "Babylon" as a code name to refer to Rome as the representation of everything wicked, so the last wickedness can be called Babylon.

Babylon, drunk on the blood of God's people (Rev. 17:6), will work in cooperation with the beast from the sea (antichrist), on whose back she rides (Rev. 17:3). As the eighth kingdom/king, antichrist's nature is like that of the previous seven, and he too, like them, will go to destruction (Rev. 17:11).

THE BOWLS POURED OUT

The bitter laments for Babylon's destruction by divine wrath are reported in Revelation 18. This wailing reflects the terrible wrath of God as reflected in Revelation 16, where the seven bowls of divine wrath are poured on all the earth. As in the case of the judgment trumpets, none can know exactly what is predicted. The language concerning the bowls being poured out is so horrible that it must be describing the end of the world as we know it.

- first bowl: sores on the beast's people (16:1-2)

- second bowl: earth's oceans completely destroyed (16:3)

- third bowl: earth's fresh water completely destroyed (16:4-7)

- fourth bowl: the sun scorches the beast's people (16:8-9)

- fifth bowl: darkness on the beast's kingdom (16:10-11)

- sixth bowl: armies gather for worldwide battle (16:12-16)

- seventh bowl: most severe earthquake ever (16:17-21)

Fluted pottery bowls from the 16th–15th centuries B.C.

HARVEST VERSUS WINEPRESS

Just as the Israelites in Egypt experienced the wrath of pharaoh but did not experience the divine plagues, so it will be on the Day of the Lord. The people of God will experience the wrath of the "unholy trinity" but will be spared God's wrath described as the pouring out of seven bowls.

Revelation 14:14-16 depicts a divine harvest of grain just prior to the outpouring of the bowls, almost certainly the event referred to by some as the "rapture." Note, for example, the similarity of this description to Jesus' parable in Matthew 13:24-30, in which the righteous are gathered like good grain. Further, Revelation 15:1-4 portrays these "raptured" saints in heaven singing "beside the sea," just as the redeemed Israelites sang with Moses "beside the sea" (Exod. 15). The people of Christ will be harvested like good grain, but the people of antichrist will soon be thrown into the winepress of God's wrath (Rev. 14:17-20). This horribly graphic image of judgment is found in other passages of Scripture, for example Isaiah 63:3.

The Mediterranean Sea on the coast of Israel near the border with Lebanon. As John came close to the end of his vision he said, "Then I saw a new heaven and a new earth, for the first heaven and the first earth had passed away, and the sea existed no longer (Rev. 21:1, HCSB)." The surging oceans had been a metaphor for the wicked of Isaiah's day (Is. 57:20).

Marriage Supper

The notion of a king's wedding celebration as a symbol of the messianic age is found in Isaiah 25:6-9 and in Jesus' teaching about the future feast with Abraham, Isaac, and Jacob in the kingdom of heaven (Matt. 8:11; 22:2-14). Thus, Revelation describes the wonderful intimacy between God and His people in terms of the marriage supper between the Lamb (Christ) and His bride (the saints), Rev. 19:7-9. This contrasts with the horrible supper for the birds as the picture of divine destruction (Rev. 19:17-18).

CHRIST'S COMING IN GLORY: FULFILLMENT OF THE BLESSED HOPE

Many texts in both Testaments point to the future glorious, visible return of Christ. **REVELATION 19—20** is the only passage that actually portrays the second coming of Christ. Three images of Christ predominate: the Bridegroom; the General; and the Judge.

THE RETURN OF CHRIST AS THE BRIDEGROOM

For the redeemed people of God, Jesus' return is compared to a bridegroom at last joining His beloved in marriage. The language of Revelation 19 certainly supports this view, as does Paul's teaching on the church as the bride of Christ in Ephesians 5:25-27. At long last the "blessed hope" of believers, the glorious appearing of Christ as the bridegroom, will be fulfilled (Titus 2:12-14).

The greatest passage on the resurrection of believers is 1 Corinthians 15, particularly verses 35-49. There Paul uses the language of grain which, after having been planted in the earth, is raised as something different than (but in continuity with) the seed that was sown.

THE RETURN OF CHRIST AS THE GENERAL

In the Old Testament Israel's king led the battles against the enemies of God. The New Testament adapts this same image to speak of Christ's return as God's agent in conquering all evil. We have already seen that the wrath of God will be poured out against sin at the end of the age. In Revelation 19 Jesus' coming is pictured as a blood-spattered general riding a white horse, with victorious armies coming behind Him.

The earth's kings may all join together for one last battle. The mysterious place called "Armageddon," or "Har-Magedon" (Rev. 16:16), will not be the scene of any battle but rather a complete rout by the general who will simply strike them down (Rev. 19:15; 2 Thess. 1:6-10). The terrible Old Testament imagery of God treading the winepress of His wrath (Isa. 63:3) will be fulfilled by Christ as the general of the Lord.

THE RETURN OF CHRIST AS THE JUDGE

When Jesus Himself taught about His return, He spoke of Himself as God's righteous judge (Matt. 25:31-46). All the people of the world will stand before Him and be evaluated on the basis of their deeds. The righteous ("sheep") will go into eternal life; the wicked ("goats") would go into eternal punishment. The Book of Revelation speaks of Christ as God's righteous judge as well (Rev. 20:11-15). From a great white throne, He will judge all people. Those who have done good deeds (and whose names are in the book of life) will go into eternal life; the wicked (whose names are not in the book) will go into a fiery lake.

It may be debated as to the exact number and times of judgment to come at which Christ will preside. It is, however, abundantly clear that Scripture teaches that all persons will one day stand before Christ as their judge.

A seat of judgment possibly from a Jewish synagogue.

THE THOUSAND-YEAR RULE: HOW LITERAL?

Revelation 20:4-6 is famous for its teaching that certain martyrs from the end of the age will come to life and reign with Christ for a thousand years. These verses have been a battleground of interpretation for more than a thousand years.

On one hand, those generally calling themselves premillennialists believe that these verses point to a literal, long period of time after Christ's coming during which He will rule on the earth, after which time His rule will be (temporarily) usurped before the final appearing of the new creation. In a nutshell, Christ will rule for an intermediate period on the earth.

On the other hand, those generally calling themselves amillennialists believe that these verses say nothing about an earthly rule of Christ and argue that everywhere else in Scripture the teaching about the Messiah's visible rule after His second coming is that it will be uninterrupted, that it will endure forever. Thus, amillennialists typically believe that the rule of the martyrs spoken of in these verses is their current victory in heaven as they wait for Christ's return.

Both views in fact take Revelation 20:4-6 figuratively. Premillennialists take the thousand years literally but believe that the reference to reigning martyrs extends figuratively to all the resurrected saints of the ages. Amillennialists take the reference to reigning martyrs literally but believe the thousand years is figurative. It may be better to take the stance of "promillennialists." This view affirms that Revelation 20:4-6 speaks essentially about the exceedingly great reward that Christ will give specifically to His faithful martyrs after His return but without specifying its chronological duration. The teaching in Revelation about the thousand years is meant to encourage believers to be faithful until death so that they may receive the crown of life (see Rev. 2:10).

A portion of the Dead Sea Scrolls dating from the 1st century B.C. found at Qumran. Thought to be from Lamentations.

CONCLUSION

At some time known only to God, He will usher in the end of the age. God will conclude His Kingdom Story through the events that culminate in the glorious return of Jesus to earth.

1. The kinds of things that have happened and will continue to occur between the end of the first century and the arrival of the Day of the Lord are described as the breaking of seals on God's judgment scroll.

2. One final evil kingdom will arise to oppose God's people. This time of great tribulation will feature the wickedness of Satan (the dragon) and the antichrist (the beast from the sea). This evil time is described as the blowing of trumpets by God's angels.

3. The prophecies about the Day of the Lord will all come true as God's vengeance against all evil is at least unleashed against the harlot city Babylon and the beast she rides (antichrist). The day of wrath is described both as the time of the winepress of wrath and as the outpouring of seven bowls of wrath.

4. Christ will come in power and great glory just as He promised. The pictures that Revelation uses focus on Christ as the Bridegroom, the General, and the Judge.

The grand summary of the Bible is, *The Lord God through His Christ is graciously building a kingdom of redeemed people for their joy and for His own glory*. We have seen now that God will fully succeed in completing redemption culminating in the second coming of Christ. With this, all the chapters in the Kingdom Story have been completed. The only thing that remains is the Epilogue in which the curtains are (briefly) parted and we see something of everlasting life in the new creation.

REFLECTIVE QUESTIONS

1. What is the basis for believing that the breaking of the seals in Revelation refers to events of church history? Do you agree? Why?

2. How do the seven churches of Asia (Rev. 2—3) reflect the strengths and weaknesses of churches down through the centuries?

3. What is the significance of John's vision of the Lamb on the throne for understanding Christian history? For understanding the end of the age?

4. Why do martyrs play such a prominent role in the prophecies of Revelation?

5. Distinguish between the "wrath of the devil" against God's people (great tribulation) and the "wrath of God" against evil people (Day of the Lord).

6. How can God's people today be aware of the many antichrists that are already present? What is the "spirit" of antichrist?

7. What do you think the trumpet judgments portray (Rev. 8—9)? How would people react if a third of all humans were killed in just a few days?

8. Have you come to any personal conclusions about whether Christians will be present during the great tribulation? What Bible texts support your perspective?

9. What is the wrath of God? Do you believe God has the right to express His anger against sinners? Why or why not?

10. Summarize what the "Day of the LORD" is. If this refers to a future terrible time of judgment, why should Christians look forward to it?

11. How do you picture the second coming of Christ to reward the righteous? What Bible texts do you use?

12. How do you picture the second coming of Christ to punish the wicked? What Bible texts do you use?

13. Why is Babylon a good name for the evil kingdom at the end of the age?

14. Have you come to any personal conclusions about whether the martyrs that will be raised and rewarded for 1,000 years can also include other saints? What Bible texts support your perspective?

15. What is important about Christ's judgment of mankind in the Bible?

16. How does God's redemption of His people work itself out in Chapter Five of the Kingdom Story?

17. What evidences of God's glory are evident in Chapter Six of the Kingdom Story?

18. What evidences of joy in the lives of God's redeemed people do you see in Chapter Six of the Kingdom Story?

[1] Taken from my earlier work, Holman New Testament Commentary: Revelation (Broadman & Holman, 1998).

Epilogue

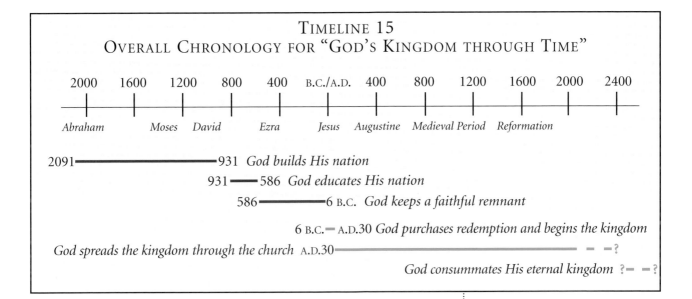

TIMELINE 15
OVERALL CHRONOLOGY FOR "GOD'S KINGDOM THROUGH TIME"

2000	1600	1200	800	400	B.C./A.D.	400	800	1200	1600	2000	2400

Abraham   Moses David   Ezra   Jesus Augustine Medieval Period Reformation

2091————————931 *God builds His nation*

931———586 *God educates His nation*

586————6 B.C. *God keeps a faithful remnant*

6 B.C.—A.D.30 *God purchases redemption and begins the kingdom*

God spreads the kingdom through the church A.D.30————————— ━ ━?

God consummates His eternal kingdom ?━ ━?

T he kingdom of God will last forever. God's people will be filled with everlasting joy. God's glory will be magnified as His redeemed people fully enjoy Him forever, without any taint of evil. This is visualized in the last two chapters of Revelation that describe a new heaven and new earth. The people of God are compared to a great and glorious city, as well as to a wonderful bride. God's servants will reign with Him forever and ever, and they will serve Him gladly, fully beholding His face. The epilogue to the Kingdom Story shows in a brief glimpse the glory that will be. The end of the story in time is only the beginning of the story in eternity, for *the Lord God through His Christ has graciously built a kingdom of redeemed people for their joy and for His own glory.*

THE BRIDE CITY, NEW JERUSALEM

When God created mankind, He made them to live on the earth. The final state of redeemed mankind is heaven come to earth. After the horrors of the Day of the Lord and the last judgment, a new heaven and a new earth will come into being (Rev. 21:1). The depiction lies beyond space and time as we can possibly understand it. What could a renewed earth, yet with no sea, no sun, or no moon look like?

New Heaven and New Earth (Revelation 21—22)

Throughout the Old Testament the city of Jerusalem was crowned with glory as the place where the Davidic king ruled and where the temple to Yahweh was established. Although some prophecies spoke of a coming glorious day for earthly Jerusalem, the Epistle to the Hebrews explained that the true and great hope of Abraham and the other saints of old was the city with everlasting foundations, whose builder was God Himself (Heb. 11:10,16; 12:22).

This city, New Jerusalem, is described in Revelation 21—22 in symbolic terms as a glorious bride, in contrast to Babylon, the horrible harlot city. The language goes beyond imagination to suggest the wonders of eternity.

- Walls and twelve (apostolic) foundations: perfect security
- Golden street and twelve (patriarchal) pearl gates: perfect splendor
- Enormous cube-like shape: room for all the redeemed in a new "holy of holies"
- River of life and tree of life: moral and spiritual perfection forever

The Lord as the Light of All Nations

During the time of Solomon, Jerusalem had been a shining beacon, and such worthies as the Queen of Sheba came to acknowledge the splendor of the king and of the Lord's temple (2 Chron. 9:1-12). The ancient prophets held out the hope that one day this would happen again (Isa. 66:10-14). At last it will happen.

- The Lamb will replace the sun and moon as the source of light
- The temple will not be needed, for the entire place is God's dwelling
- Kings and nations of the earth will bring their splendor to it
- Sinners are excluded from participating in the city's glory

Jesus among His People Forever

One of the great Bible promises God made to His covenant people, those He redeemed, was that He would be their God, they would be His people, and He would dwell among them (Lev. 26:12; Jer. 24:7; 31:33; Ezek. 11:20; Zech. 8:8; 2 Cor. 6:16; Heb. 8:10). Revelation 22:1-5 shows that all eternity is about God's fulfillment of this promise.

- The Lord will be present forever with His people, showing them His "face"
- The Lord will write His name on the foreheads of His people
- The Lord will be perfectly served by His people
- The Lord's people will reign with Him forever

FINAL SUMMARY

The Kingdom Story has been described in full. Now the narrative can be reviewed in an even more compact form.

PROLOGUE: THE NEED FOR REDEMPTION

Scripture begins by explaining why the story must be told. God is building a kingdom of redeemed people because human beings are rebels who cannot save themselves. Other religions begin by assuming that people can do enough good works or perform enough religious deeds to earn a place in heaven. The Bible starts by telling the opposite story. Genesis 1—11 belongs to real human history, but the events are almost impossible to date. The prologue describes events involving the entire human race and shows that mankind has rebelled against God since the beginning.

CREATION AND FALL

God made everything, including the first man and woman, created as a special divine act in His image. Yet the man and woman—the whole race—deliberately disobeyed God and fell under His curse.

FLOOD AND BABEL

Two more events show universal human sin. God destroyed the entire rebellious race with a flood, except for Noah and his family. Then later at the tower of Babel, God cursed the race for its religious arrogance by multiplying the languages and scattering the nations. (Ultimately God will undo the curse of Babel when people from all the languages and nations gather before His throne praising Him forever.)

(see p.7)

GOD BUILDS HIS NATION:
ISRAEL CHOSEN AS THE PEOPLE OF PROMISE

Chapter One in God's plan to build an everlasting kingdom was to build an earthly nation in a particular time and place. This chapter carries the plot from the first family He called to His covenant (Abraham and Sarah) to the full splendor of that nation at its grandest expression (under David and Solomon).

THE FOUNDATION:
FROM ABRAHAM'S CALL TO JACOB'S MIGRATION TO EGYPT

Genesis 12 begins with God's call to Abraham. He received God's unconditional promise to become the ancestor of a great nation and to be a worldwide blessing. This covenant promise extended down the generations

(see p.15)

to Isaac, Jacob, and Jacob's children. God then moved the covenant people into Egypt where they multiplied into numbers worthy of the name nation.

(see p.25)

THE REDEMPTION:
FROM EGYPTIAN SLAVERY TO WILDERNESS FREEDOM

God called a leader for the nation, Moses, through whom He sent ten plagues to redeem the Israelite nation from slavery in Egypt. He revealed the full significance of His glorious covenant name, the Lord (YHWH or Yahweh in Hebrew). Israel's exodus became the most powerful Old Testament portrayal of salvation. Traditionally Bible scholars have dated the exodus around 1446 B.C.

THE LAWS AND THE LAND:
FROM MOUNT SINAI TO THE CONQUEST OF CANAAN AND JOSHUA'S DEATH

National identity requires not only people but laws and a land. Through Moses God gave the Israelites His laws, both moral, ceremonial, and civil. (According to Hebrews, these Mosaic regulations had a built-in obsolescence.) The Israelite rebellion in the wilderness led to a forty-year delay in possessing the land. Under Joshua, a new leader for a new generation, the Israelites entered and conquered their promised land, around 1406 B.C.

(see p.30)

THE MONARCHY AND THE TEMPLE:
FROM JOSHUA'S DEATH TO SOLOMON'S DEATH

After Joshua's death the nation drifted through the dreadful period of the judges, which ended with the leadership of Samuel. The first king, Saul, failed. David, the next king, received God's unconditional covenant promise that His dynasty would endure forever. The promise included both an eternal kingdom and an eternal King. David wanted to honor Yahweh by building a temple for His name in Jerusalem, but that privilege went to Solomon his son. The temple was dedicated around 959 B.C., and with that the nation of Israel reached its most glorious earthly expression.

(see p.51)

GOD EDUCATES HIS NATION: DISOBEDIENT ISRAEL DISCIPLINED

Chapter Two in the Kingdom Story was to educate Israel about the consequences of sin. The Israelites compromised by worshiping other gods during the entire time they were in their land. God raised His spokesmen the prophets to urge people to repent of idolatry and injustice, to warn of the coming day of the Lord in judgment. They also predicted the coming of Messiah. Their message was largely ignored. This chapter carries the plot from the division of the nation (because of sin) to its destruction (because of sin).

(see p.84)

NATION DIVIDED:
NINETY YEARS OF FIGHTING BETWEEN ISRAEL AND JUDAH

With the death of Solomon around 931 B.C., the nation Israel began to decline. The first step was God's division of the people into a Northern Kingdom (called Israel or Samaria, ruled by several dynasties of kings, all wicked) and a Southern Kingdom (called Judah, ruled by kings of the Davidic dynasty, some good and some wicked). The great prophets Elijah and Elisha were God's messengers to call the people back to true worship. The two Davidic kings that led religious revivals during this period were Asa and Joash. The worst king of all was Ahab of Israel.

(see p.85)

THE ASSYRIAN MENACE:
ONE HUNDRED TWENTY YEARS OF DECLINE AND DEFEAT

The second step in God's discipline of His people was the captivity of the Northern Kingdom. Prophets such as Amos and Hosea warned Israelites in the Northern Kingdom of God's wrath against their sins. In Judah, Isaiah and Micah spoke equally powerfully. Finally the Lord sent the Assyrians, the world superpower of that era. Samaria fell and the Northern tribes were expelled from the land. They were absorbed into the places of their exile, losing their Israelite identity entirely. Israel fell to Assyria about 722 B.C.

(see p.98)

The third step in God's discipline of His people was the captivity of Judah. After the fall of the Northern Kingdom, there were two religious revivals in Judah, the first led by Hezekiah and then almost a century later one led by Josiah. The people, however, reverted to idolatry and injustice. The harsh rejection of the Prophet Jeremiah shows how low the people had fallen spiritually. God called into being a new world super-

(see p.102)

power, the Chaldeans or Babylonians. They invaded Judah three times, destroying Jerusalem, ending kingship in Judah (with Zedekiah as the last of the Davidic dynasty to rule in Jerusalem). The Babylonians destroyed the temple and forced thousands of people from Judah into exile in 586 B.C. With this, God's educational program of His people was complete. They learned their lesson well. Never again did the people of Israel worship idols.

GOD KEEPS A FAITHFUL REMNANT: MESSIAH'S SPACE AND TIME PREPARED

Chapter Three in the Kingdom Story is the quiet chapter. Outwardly, it appeared that God was doing little for more than five centuries. For those who read the story carefully, however, He was doing two important things. On one hand, God was keeping a minority of His people—now called the Jews—together as a nation. They had their own land, laws, and temple, even though the kingship and national independence had disappeared. God was preparing to send His Son in the fullness of time. On the other hand, God scattered most Jews throughout the nations to be

testimonies to His name. By building synagogues to preserve their religious and ethnic identity, these Jews were often the starting point for proclaiming the message that the promised Messiah had come. This chapter carries the plot from the Babylonian captivity until the birth of the Messiah.

(see p.129)

BABYLONIAN DOMINATION:
THE "HEAD OF GOLD"—ISRAELITES BECOME JEWS

The Babylonians fell to the Persians. Under the Persians' enlightened policies, exiles were allowed to return to their homeland. King Cyrus of Persia became God's agent, and under Sheshbazzar's leadership, thousands of Jews migrated back to Jerusalem, beginning about 537 B.C. This was nearly seventy years after the first deportation of Jews from Jerusalem, the one in which Daniel and many others were first taken to Babylon (about 605 B.C.).

RESTORATION FROM CAPTIVITY:
LAND, TEMPLE, AND GOD'S LAW UNDER EZRA AND NEHEMIAH

The Jews who returned from exile were truly committed to the Lord, yet there was some delay in rebuilding the temple. God raised up the Prophet Haggai to kindle their commitment to complete the temple. The Jewish governor that led the people in this project was Zerubbabel. This temple was dedicated in 516 B.C., exactly seventy years after Solomon's temple was destroyed. Later on it was expanded and made more splendid, but the sec-

(see p.135)

ond temple endured until the Romans destroyed it in A.D. 70.

God called Ezra to teach a new generation of Jews how to live in the land according to God's law. The land was made more secure by building Jerusalem's walls, led by Nehemiah. With the dedication of the city walls in 445 B.C., everything—people, temple, law, and land—was in place for the coming of the Messiah. There was a fundamental continuity in Judea and in Judaism during the four centuries between Nehemiah and Jesus.

PERSIA, GREECE, AND ROME RISE AS WORLD EMPIRES

The beautiful story of Esther shows God's providential working outside the land of Israel during this chapter of the Kingdom Story. Daniel prophesied God's continuing providential work, showing four successive evil world empires: Babylon, Persia, Greece, and Rome. A number of his prophecies were fulfilled during the Greek period (especially during the Maccabean period in the second century B.C.). By the time this chapter in the Kingdom Story ended, however, the Romans had defeated the Greeks and risen to the place of world dominion.

(see p.145)

(see p.167)

GOD PURCHASES REDEMPTION AND BEGINS THE KINGDOM: JESUS THE MESSIAH

Chapter Four in God's plan to build an everlasting kingdom of redeemed people is the most important one of all, told by the four Gospels. It shows how God's unconditional covenant promises—first to Abraham, then to David—were fulfilled by the new covenant of Jesus. This chapter carries the plot from the birth of the Messiah to His resurrection and exaltation.

"IMMANUEL," GOD WITH US:
THE VIRGIN BIRTH AND GROWTH OF JESUS

The fourth Gospel opens with the declaration that the Word became flesh. God incarnated Himself as a human being, Jesus Christ. Matthew and Luke describe the coming of Jesus into human history in terms of His virgin birth to Mary. Jesus was born about 6 B.C.

(see p.182)

THE SON OF MAN:
MINISTRY, TEACHINGS, AND MIGHTY WORKS OF JESUS

All four Gospels tell about Jesus' central message: the good news of the kingdom of God. His miracles were signs that God's kingdom had arrived in His person. Jesus was baptized about the fall of A.D. 26 and ministered for more than three years, until the spring of A.D. 30.

SUFFERING SERVANT AND SON OF DAVID:
CRUCIFIXION, RESURRECTION, AND EXALTATION OF JESUS

Jesus' crucifixion redeemed His people to God for eternity, just as the exodus had redeemed the people of Israel for time. According to His own words, Jesus' death secured the new covenant relationship of God with His people, the one Jeremiah had prophesied. Jesus' bodily resurrection and exaltation by His Father demonstrated that His sacrifice was satisfactory. The dates of Jesus' crucifixion and resurrection, using modern calendar notation, were almost certainly Friday, April 7, and Sunday, April 9, of A.D. 30.

(see p.189)

290 *The Illustrated Guide to Biblical History*

God Spreads the Kingdom through the Church: The Current Age

With Chapter Five in the Kingdom Story, we come to our own part of the story. This is the period of the Great Commission, when God's plan has changed from focusing on persons of one ethnic group in one place (Israel) to redeeming persons out of every ethnic group in every place. Wherever and whenever God's people are, they meet as churches, worshiping communities of the new covenant. From Pentecost until the end-time scenario unfolds, God is about the business of spreading the message of the kingdom through the church.

(see p.217)

The First Christians in Jerusalem:
The Church as a Jewish Sect

With the experience of Pentecost, the church of Jesus was fully thrust into existence (Acts 2). A new era began, the age of the Spirit, when all redeemed persons have the gift of the Spirit. Although Christianity soon moved beyond its nest in Jerusalem, the congregation there was a critical first step.

Ministry of the Apostle Paul:
The Church Reaching More Gentiles than Jews

The unique calling and contribution of Paul was to serve as Jesus' apostle to Gentiles. Through his ministry of traveling evangelism and extensive letter writing, the church expanded greatly, both quantitatively and qualitatively. In numbers the church grew to include congregations all over the Roman Empire. Further, the church's identity grew to embrace both Jew and Gentile as one body in Christ.

(see p.247)

Solidarity of the Christian movement:
The Church as Separate from the Synagogue

The general epistles suggest, among other things, that the church began separating from the synagogue at an early date. Letters written after the destruction of Jerusalem in A.D. 70 show the permanence of the division. The final biblical portrait of the spread of God's kingdom through churches is Revelation 1—6. The risen Lord is pictured both on earth walking among His churches and in heaven worshiped by the heavenly host. The seven churches of Asia show the strengths and weaknesses that have been exhibited by churches down through the ages.

The details of the Kingdom Story for nineteen centuries (second through the twentieth centuries) are told not by Scripture but by church historians. In God's kingdom purposes for the current age, both the Jewish temple and Israel as a nation are obsolete. Thus the destruction of the temple and Jerusalem in A.D. 70 by the Romans serves as important historical evidence that the former way of (national, ethnic) Israel has been supplanted by the new way of (international, multiethnic) Christianity.

(see p.256)

GOD CONSUMMATES HIS ETERNAL KINGDOM: REDEMPTION COMPLETED

In Chapter Six God's plan to build an everlasting kingdom of redeemed people through His Christ for their joy and for His own glory is fully realized at last. Although students often disagree in interpreting the details of this chapter, the main points are clear. There will be violent hostility against God's people in the end times. Yet God will prevail through the personal, bodily, glorious return of Jesus. When He returns, the world's kingdoms will become the kingdom of Christ forever under His visible rule. This chapter carries the plot from church history to the final judgment.

(see p.272)

SATANIC WRATH AGAINST GOD AND GOD'S PEOPLE

Revelation depicts one final evil kingdom to oppose God's people. So far in previous chapters of God's story, six kingdoms tried without success to eliminate God's people (Egypt, Assyria, Babylon, Persia, Greece, and Rome). In the end times the seventh and worst will arise. The beast from the sea and the beast from the land are agents of the devil. They try one more time to destroy God's people from the earth. These three form a vile "unholy trinity."

(see p.268)

GOD'S VENGEANCE AGAINST SATAN AND ALL EVIL: THE DAY OF THE LORD

Just as the Israelites in Egypt experienced the wrath of pharaoh but did not experience the plagues, so it will be on the Day of the Lord. The peo-

(see p.275)

ple of God will experience the wrath of the "unholy trinity" but will be spared God's wrath. The people of Christ will be harvested like good grain, but the people of antichrist will be thrown into the winepress of God's wrath (Revelation 14:14-20). This is the final exodus, with the glorified saints praising God beside the heavenly sea while the last plagues of divine wrath demolish the wicked inhabitants of the earth (Revelation 15—16).

CHRIST'S COMING IN GLORY: FULFILLMENT OF THE BLESSED HOPE

Revelation 19 portrays the second coming of Christ like a conquering general riding a white horse with His armies behind Him. With Christ's return, little remains to bring God's kingdom to its final glorious form. The explicit biblical material that deals with this, Revelation 20, does so in terms of God's great reward for the martyrs and the last judgment, when the wicked are ruined forever in the lake of fire.

(see p.279)

EPILOGUE: NEW HEAVEN AND NEW EARTH

The kingdom of God will endure eternally. God's people will be filled with everlasting joy. God's glory will be magnified as His redeemed people fully enjoy Him forever, without any taint of evil. This is visualized in the last two chapters of Revelation that describe a new heaven and new earth. The people of God are compared to a great and glorious city, as well as to a wonderful bride. God's servants will reign with Him forever and ever, and they will serve Him gladly, fully beholding His face. The epilogue to God's story shows in a brief glimpse the glory that will be. The end of the story in time is only the beginning of the story in eternity, for *the Lord God through His Christ has graciously built a kingdom of redeemed people for their joy and for His own glory.*

Even so, come Lord Jesus. Amen.

REFLECTIVE QUESTIONS

1. What is the meaning of the symbol of God's people as a beautiful bride?

2. What is the meaning of the symbol of God's people as a huge, holy city?

3. What descriptions of the New Jerusalem do you find the most encouraging?

4. Compare the old Jerusalem (with Solomon reigning in a splendid city) with the new Jerusalem (with Christ reigning in a splendid city). How are they alike? How are they different?

5. Compare the prologue (need for redemption, Gen. 1—11) with the epilogue (new heaven and new earth, Rev. 21—22). How is mankind's beginning and end alike? How is it different?

6. Throughout this book the Kingdom Story has been summarized with the words, *The Lord God through His Christ is graciously building a kingdom of redeemed people for their joy and for His own glory.* Explain this in your own words. How would you change the wording of this summary?

List of Maps

List of Timelines

Topical Index

Mary, 163, 164, 165, 166, 167
Mary Magdalen, 207
Mary of Bethany, 195,198
Masada, 33, 251, 252, 253
Mattaniah, 120
Mattathias, 149, 152
Matthew, 163, 165, 183, 198, 289
Maydum, 24
Medes, 139
Medieval Period, 283
Mediterranean Sea, 240, 242, 278
Meggido, 64, 67, 68, 114
Melchizedek, 18
Menahem, 96, 98, 103, 251
Menorah, 31
Mephibosheth, 59
Mercy, 12, 16
Meschach, 128
Mesopotamia, 9, 15, 145
Messiah, 72, 103, 104, 126, 135, 139, 143, 160,
162, 165, 168, 171, 173, 176, 188, 189, 191, 200,
218, 222, 223, 228, 229, 240, 255, 270, 287
Micah, 50, 91, 96, 104, 105, 121, 287
Micaiah, 83
Michael, 268
Michal, 57, 59
Midianites, 46
Mikveh, 33
Miracle, 163, 168, 217, 289
Miraculous catch of fish, 181
Miriam, 164
Mizpah, 51, 131
Moab, 38, 46, 85, 89
Modein, 149
Mohammed, 270
Monarchy, 286
Moral, 33
Mordecai, 142
Moresheth-Gath, 104
Moses, 23, 25, 28, 29, 29, 30, 32, 35, 36, 38, 39,
40, 41, 45, 52, 69, 85, 110, 172, 186, 275, 283,
286
Mount Ararat, 7
Mount Carmel, 82, 84, 86
Mount Gilboah, 54
Mount Hermon
Mount Moriah, 19, 65
Mount Nebo, 39, 40
Mount of Olives, 199, 200, 201, 204, 208
Mount of Temptation, 172
Mount of Transfiguration, 85
Mount Sinai, 8, 25, 29, 31, 34, 39, 86, 286
Mount Tabor, 46
Murder, 7, 31
Naaman, 88
Nabal, 57
Nabonidus, 127, 140
Naboth, 82, 86
Nadab, 80
Nadah, 78
Nahum, 97, 111, 121
Naomi, 50
Naphtali, 20
Nathan, 59, 85
Nathaniel, 174, 183
Nazareth, 164, 166, 167, 169, 179, 185
Nebapolassar, 116

Nebuchadnezzar, 116, 118, 119, 120, 127, 128,
129, 131, 134, 139, 144, 154
Nehemiah, 125, 127, 131, 135, 136, 137, 138,
139, 141, 157, 162, 168, 289
Nero Caesar, 188, 213, 242, 244, 249, 251, 270
Nerva, 213
New covenant, 31, 118, 121, 122, 203, 204, 249
New earth, 293
New heaven, 293
New Jerusalem, 139, 265, 284
Nicodemus, 169, 175, 176, 177
Nile Delta, 23
Nineveh, 72, 95, 110, 111, 114, 115, 117, 129
Nisan, 27
Noah, 7, 7, 8, 9, 10, 12, 30
Nole Valley, 24
Northern Kingdom, 75, 77, 79, 80, 82, 85, 86,
88, 90, 91, 92, 93, 95, 98, 101, 102, 104, 106,
108, 121, 179, 275, 287
Numbers, 34
Obadiah, 97, 119, 121
Obedience, 7
Octavian, 125, 154
Old Testament, 250
Olivet Discourse, 201
Omri, 78, 80, 81, 82, 90
Onesimus, 243
Paddan-aram, 21
Palestine, 40, 145, 146, 166, 222, 223, 252
Panium, 146
Parables, 176, 188, 195, 200
Parents, 31
Passover, 27, 112, 114, 166, 167, 174, 184, 192,
197, 199, 200, 202, 203, 207, 211, 214, 223
Patmos, 256, 262, 263
Patriarchs, 19
Paul, 6, 52, 161, 208, 213, 225, 228, 229, 230,
231, 232, 233, 234, 235, 236, 238, 239, 240, 241,
243, 244, 246, 247, 272, 291
Paul's arrest and imprisonment, 241
Paul's conversion, 225
Paul's missionary ourneys, first, 227; second,
230; third, 233; voyage to Rome, 247
Peace sacrifice, 32
Peace, 32
Pekah, 96, 98, 104
Pekahiah, 96, 98
Peniel, 20, 79
Pentateuch, 29, 39
Pentecost, 212, 213, 214, 215, 218, 219, 265,
291
Perea, 168, 170, 195, 196
Pergamum, 265, 267
Persecution, 217, 249, 264
Persepolis, 141
Persia, Persians, 117, 126, 129, 135, 136, 139,
140, 144, 146, 157, 275, 289, 292
Peter, 161, 174, 179,182, 188, 189, 191, 202,
204, 207, 213, 217, 218, 219, 220, 222, 223, 224,
228, 229, 249
Pharaoh, 25, 110, 277, 291
Pharaoh Neco, 114, 117
Pharisees, 135, 151, 157, 173, 184, 187, 200,
229, 251
Philadelphia, 265, 266, 273
Philemon, 235, 243
Philip, 174, 183, 218

Philip II of Macedon, 144, 145
Philippi, 146, 231, 244
Philistia, 90, 97
Philistines, 40, 48, 51, 54, 57, 61
Phoenicia, 82, 145, 222, 223
Pigs, 148
Pilate, 206, 218
Plagues, 25
Plains of Moab, 36
Polygamy, 7
Pompey, 132, 154, 158
Pontius Pilate, 161, 177, 205, 211
Pontus, 231
Pool of Siloam, 107, 110
Popes, 270
Porcius Festus, 241
Post-resurrection catch of 153 fish, 181
Premillennialists, 280
Priesthood, 31, 43, 253
Priestly garments, 31
Priests, 32
Priscilla, 213, 231, 233
Procession Street, 127, 270
Promillennialists, 280
Promised land, 36, 72
Prophecies, 222
Prophet, 51, 215
Ptolomy, Ptolemies, 146,158, 269
Pul, 98
Purim, feast of, 142
Pyramid of Khafre, 25
Quail, 29
Queen of Sheba, 67, 68, 284
Qumran, 158, 280
Rachel, 20, 20
Rahab, 41
Rainbow, 8, 30
Raising Jairus's daughter from the dead, 185
Ramah, 51, 77
Rameses II, 24
Ramoth Gilead, 82, 89
Rapture of the church, 272, 277
Rebekah, 19
Red Sea, 28, 41
Redemption, 8, 21, 28, 163, 286
Reformation, 283
Rehoboam, 75, 78
Religious syncretism, 104
Repentance, 169
Resurrection, 162, 175, 189, 198, 207, 208, 215,
290
Return of Christ, 272
Reuben, 20, 43
Revelation, 275
Rezin, 104
Righteousness, 7, 16
River of life, 284
Roman army, 254
Roman centurion's servant, 185
Roman empire, 125, 165, 222, 225, 256, 291
Roman governor, 199, 205
Roman legion, 251
Roman senate, 154
Roman soldiers, 204
Roman trial, 205
Rome, Romans, 117, 126, 129, 132, 154, 205,
213, 222, 240, 242, 244, 247, 249, 251, 252, 263,

Scripture Index

Old Testament

Photo Credits

(All Rights Reserved)

Biblical Illustrator: 8; 75; 132; 135; 141, lower; 275.

Biblical Illustrator/ Bill Latta: 102; 142.

Biblical Illustrator/ James McLemore: 5; 10; 18; 31; 38, upper; 39; 41; 74, lower right; 79; 120; 152; 189; 191; 192; 195; 196, upper; 204; 218; 222; 228; 278.

Biblical Illustrator/ Richard Nowitz: 215.

Biblical Illustrator/ David Rogers: 6; 9; 19; 62; 68; 80; 84, left, right; 92; 93; 95; 98; 101; 129, lower right (JAC); 133 (JAC); 141, upper left; 143; 216; 256; 257, upper right (JAC); 269.

Biblical Illustrator/ Bob Schatz: 4; 7; 15; 16; 20, upper left, lower; 23; 24; 25; 27, upper right; 28, lower left, lower right; 29; 30; 32 upper, lower; 33; 34; 38, lower; 43; 47; 49; 51; 52; 54; 57; 58; 61; 64; 72; 74, upper left; 77; 82; 83; 84, middle; 85; 86; 88; 89; 103; 105; 106; 107; 110; 111; 114; 119; 124; 126; 127; 129, upper; 144; 145; 149; 151; 154, lower left; 156; 157; 158; 158, inset; 160; 162; 164; 166; 167; 173; 174; 175; 178; 179; 181; 182; 183; 186; 187; 188; 190; 196, lower; 201; 202; 206; 208; 210; 212; 214; 215; 220; 221; 224; 226; 229; 233; 235; 236; 237; 238; 239; 241; 242; 244; 245, lower; 246; 247; 252, upper, lower; 253; 260; 262; 263; 264; 265; 266, upper, lower; 267, upper, lower; 268; 270; 272; 274; 276; 277; 279; 280.

Biblical Illustrator/ Ken Touchton: 97; 147; 154, upper; 172; 207; 217; 248; 251.

Thomas V. Brisco: 12

Corel: 27, lower; 171; 199.

Stephen Smith: 245, upper; 257, lower.

Jerry Vardaman: 138.

JAC = Joseph A. Callaway Archaeological Museum, The Southern Baptist Theological Seminary, Louisville, KY.